ORIGINS AND MEANINGS

OF POPULAR

PHRASES AND NAMES

Origins and Meanings

of

Popular Phrases & Names

Including those which came into use during the great war

BY

BASIL HARGRAVE

LONDON

T. WERNER LAURIE LTD.

COBHAM HOUSE

24 AND 26 WATER LANE, E.C.4

REPUBLISHED BY GALE RESEARCH COMPANY, BOOK TOWER, DETROIT, 1968

NOTE

The Author and Publishers desire to gratefully thank the Editor of that most interesting and fascinating journal " Notes and Queries" for his kindness in permitting them to make use of his lists of terms used in the Great War. (SEE PAGE 351)

First published in this edition 1925

Library of Congress Card Catalog Number: 68–23164

FOREWORD

THIS book is put forward in the belief that a demand
exists for a concise epitome of the origin and meaning of words and phrases which are in everyday use
but which are often not appreciated at their full
significance.

Its size is sufficient to show that it is neither
intended to be an exhaustive philological treatise
nor an academic encyclopædia, but it aims at
throwing an interesting light on many words by
recalling their derivation, and it endeavours to give
useful information in a pleasant and chatty form.

One of the chief difficulties in its compilation has
been the selection of its contents. Some criterion
had to be established, as it was obviously impossible, while confining the book to convenient limits,
to include everything that would be of interest to
all, and yet that which might appear most desirable
to some, might be esteemed valueless by others.
Eventually, as the result of much cogitation, the
compiler decided to cut the Gordian knot by boldly
wielding the sword of his own fancy—only that
which seemed of interest to *him* should be included.

In regard to place-names, especially the names
of London streets, the temptation to enlarge was
almost irresistible, for so much that is deeply interesting is bound up in these names. But a com-
promise has been made by including the principal

prefixes, suffixes and roots which are component in the names of British places and rivers, and it is hoped that by the examples given the origin and meaning of many other names may be made clear.

The encyclopædic character of the book was felt to be of secondary importance, but among the mass of interesting words which the compiler had collected there were many (the word " radium " is a case in point) which denoted subjects of too much interest to be passed over.

For the sins of omission the compiler craves forgiveness: for what is included he begs acceptance.

ORIGINS AND MEANINGS

OF

POPULAR PHRASES & NAMES

A1. An expression derived from Lloyd's "Registry of Shipping," in which letters denote the quality of a ship's hull, and figures that of its equipment. A vessel registered A1 is of the first class in all respects.

Abad. A syllable which is frequently found in Indian place-names, as in Hyder-abad, Allah-abad. It is of Sanscrit origin and means an abode, a dwelling.

Aber. A Celtic word signifying a confluence of two rivers, or of a river and the sea. It is found as a component in many place-names both in Scotland and Wales, and is a sure indication of the presence of Celtic settlements in past times. Sometimes, as a result of the corruption of a particular name, the root may not be readily recognised, as in Barmouth, the original of which was Abermaw.

Absence makes the Heart grow Fonder. However much opinions may differ as to the truth of this dictum there can be no doubt of its being well known. It comes from the song " Isle of Beauty," written by Thomas Haynes Bayly, the author of " We met—'twas in a crowd," " I'd be a Butter-fly," etc., who lived from 1797 to 1839.

Abusing the King's English. How our common phrases persist! Shakespeare, in " The Merry

Wives of Windsor " writes :—" Here will be an old abusing of . . . the king's English.''

Ache. The word comes to us from the Anglo-Saxon *acan* or *acian* (" c " hard), and at one time retained the double syllable to which its derivation entitles it. Isaac D'Israeli, in " Curiosities of Literature,'' states that Swift (1667-1745) in his own edition of " The City Shower " has " old a-ches throb,'' but what the poet and the linguist wished to preserve has been lost by the action of modern printers who, unaware of the old pronunciation, have made " aches " one syllable, and then to complete the metre have foisted in " will ''—" aches will throb.'' Butler (1600-1680) also uses the old form in his " Hudibras "—

" Can by their pains and a-ches find
    All turns and changes of the wind.''

And Shakespeare in " The Tempest,'' when Prospero threatens Caliban, writes :—

" Fill all thy bones with a-ches, make thee roar
    That beasts shall tremble at the din.''

Acre. The word originally meant any field, whatever its size, being derived from the Anglo-Saxon *æcer*, signifying land or anything sown, as did the Latin *ager*. It was not until the time of Edward I. that the word became more definite, and by an Act of George IV. the varying measures of the acre then current in the kingdom were reduced to one uniform standard. But even now the Scottish and Irish acre differ from the English, though the latter is current in the United States.

Adding Insult to Injury. The phrase is from a fable of classical times quoted by the Latin writer, Phædrus, from the more ancient version by Æsop. The fable relates how a bald man who was bitten on the head by a fly, in trying to kill the insect gave himself a sound smack. Whereupon the fly said jeeringly, " You wanted to kill me for a touch —what will you do to yourself, now that you have *added insult to injury?* " In this, as in many other phrases, we quote the classics unknowingly.

Addled. The word is almost exclusively applied to eggs when in a state of decay, putrescent; and in that sense is derived from the Anglo-Saxon *adl*, a disease. But in another sense the word "addle," though obsolete elsewhere, is still used in the North of England and signifies the very opposite of decay, viz. :—to grow, to thrive. In the latter case the word is derived from the Old Norse *odlask*, to get, to grow, coinciding with the Swedish *odla*, to till, to cultivate. The poet Tusser (1523-1580) writes :—
" Where ivye embraseth the tree very sore,
  Kill ivye, ar tree else will addle (grow) no more."

Adelphi. The collective name for several streets and a noble terrace on the south side of the Strand, built by the celebrated architect, Robert Adam (born 1728, died 1792), in conjunction with his brother James, and hence called by the Greek word *adelphi*, which signifies " brothers."

Adieu. An elliptical form of commendation to God— *à Dieu.* Similarly, we have " good-bye," meaning " God be with you," and " Good Friday " is probably but another form of " God's Friday, the day which commemorates the death of Jesus Christ, the God-man. But the French are especially fortunate in having two most appropriate phrases with which to take leave of a friend— *adieu*, as above, and *au revoir*, which is, literally, to (our) meeting again.

Adonis. The beautiful youth of classic mythology, gored to death by a wild bull while hunting, and beloved by both Venus and Proserpina. They petitioned Jupiter to adjudicate upon their claims, and he decided that the boy should spend six months with Venus in the upper world and six with Proserpina in the lower. The myth is generally supposed to be an allegory of the sun and the seasons, symbolising the death of vegetation and its revival. Certainly, festivals in honour of Adonis have been held from a very early date—by the Phœnicians, the Egyptians and the Greeks— and the Hebrews appear to have reverenced such a deity under the name of Thammuz, whose worship is alluded to by the prophet Ezekiel as an abomination (Ch. viii., 14-15).

Æolian Harp. The Æolian harp is an instrument made by stretching strings of catgut over a wooden sound-box, which when exposed to the action of the wind produces pleasing chords of plaintive music, if the strings be properly tuned. The term is derived from the name Æolus, the god of the winds and king of the islands off the coast of Italy, now called the Lipari Islands, in the caverns of which the winds were supposed to be confined.

Agnostic. The word is so familiar to us and its use is now so general that we are apt to forget how recent is its introduction into our language, but there appears to be no doubt that it was first suggested by Professor Huxley, as late as the year 1869. It is formed from the Greek *agnōstos*, unknown, and defines one who disclaims any knowledge beyond that obtained by experience.

Akimbo. The word is interesting because of its uncertain etymology. Some authorities find its origin in the Italian *sghembo*, crooked, awry, asserting that the mediæval English form " agambo " points to the correct derivation. Others believe that it comes from the Celtic *cam*, crooked, with the prefix " a," the superfluous " bow " being a strengthening, by duplication, of the signification of " bent." Skeat, however, suggests that in the Icelandic *kengr*, a crook, and *boginn*, bowed, are to be found the true origin of the word.

Alarum. It seems fairly evident that the spelling of this word has arisen from a strong vocalisation of the " r " in " alarm," and that the two words are

the same. It has been suggested that the word
" alarum " is a corruption of the Norman French
larum, a thief, and although there may be some
justification for this supposition in the fact that the
modern French for thief is *larron*, there seems little
doubt that the true derivation of the word is
all'arme, to the arms, through the Latin *ad arma*.
This etymology has, at any rate, the approval of
Richardson and Wedgwood.

Alderman. The usually accepted signification of this
word is " elder-man," its origin being ascribed to
the Anglo-Saxon *alder*, the comparative of *ald* (or
eald), old; but this derivation is rejected by Dean
Hoare, who interprets the word as meaning " of
all men chief," the first in rank or council. The
Anglo-Saxon *alder*, as a composite with some other
word, was freely used by Chaucer, our first writer
in English; for instance—" For him, alas, she
loved ' alder-best,' " meaning best of all, and there
are many obsolete words in which " alder "
appears in the sense of a superlative of " all," *e.g.*,
" alder-cock, the cock of all, leader of all; " alder
fairest," " alder-first," " alder-last "; while as
late as Shakespeare's time we have the expression " mine ' alder-lievest ' (loved most of all)
sovereign " in the first act of Henry VI. Moreover, the title of Alderman was applied in Saxon
times not only to any one holding an office of rank
and dignity, but also to the first subject of the
realm and even to kings, as in the case of Cerdic,
king of Wessex, so that there appears good reason
for adopting Dean Hoare's derivation.

Aldermanbury. The name is a survival of London in
the Plantagenet days, if not earlier, for it was
here that the ancient Courts of Justice were held
by the Aldermen of the City, and it was not until
the completion of the new Guildhall, in the year
1411, that they were removed.

Aldgate, Aldersgate. These names are reminiscent of
the gates in the wall of old London, which

starting from the Norman fortress on Tower Hill ran northwards to Ald-Gate, the " Old Gate,' the first in that direction. Continuing the circuit in a westerly direction, we come to Bishops'-Gate and then to Alders-Gate, which, as its name signifies (*see* ALDERMAN), was the "Gate of all gates," being the principal way out to all the country lying north of the Thames.

All that Glitters is not Gold. The saying was old in the days of Chaucer (1328-1400), for he says :—

" All thing, which that shineth as the gold
Ne is no gold, as I have herd it told."
(The Chanones Yemannes Tale.)

Allegory. The word is derived from the Greek *allos*, other, and *agoreuo,* to speak publicly, and signifies a story or discourse, describing one thing under the image of another—" Where more is meant than meets the ear " (Milton). John Bunyan is unquestionably the first of allegorists " as Demosthenes is the first of orators or Shakespeare the first of dramatists," says Macaulay, and every reader of " Pilgrim's Progress " will understand what an allegory is and how effectual for the communication of religious knowledge. An allegory and a parable are almost identical, and the difference between a myth and an allegory is explained by Professor Blackie as the one being the unconscious act of the popular mind at an early stage of society; the other the conscious act of the individual mind at any stage of social progress.

Alleviate. " O'er a' the ills o' life victorious," wrote the poet Burns of his hero " Tam O'Shanter," but the ordinary person is generally content if the ills of life be alleviated—their weight reduced, made light. For such is the signification of the word " alleviate," being derived from the Latin *levis*, light, coupled with the preposition *ad.*

Alley. The city streets and its narrow alleys seem to have little in common with the ship ploughing its way through the water, and yet the word "alley," though in its later course derived from the French *aller*, to go (literally a passing or going) comes down to us through the Old French *aner*, which most probably is descended from the Latin *adnare*, to go to by water. A similar association may be traced in the word "arrive," through the Old French *ariver* and the Low Latin *adripare* to the Latin *ad ripa*, to a bank.

Alligator. The crocodile of America. The name was given by the Spaniards, who were unacquainted with the crocodile; but when they saw the creature's resemblance to a huge lizard they called it by the Spanish name for lizard—*el lagarto*, of which word "alligator" is a modification. And in looking at the derivation of the word "crocodile" a remarkable coincidence appears. It was when the Greeks came into Egypt, many centuries before the discovery of America, that they first saw the crocodile, and they also, recognising the resemblance, called it a lizard—*krokodeilos*, from which the English word "crocodile" has been formed.

All Men have their Price. The phrase is commonly attributed to Sir Robert Walpole (1674-1746), and as in his time bribery appears to have been the universal weapon of the politician Walpole is not necessarily to be reprobated for giving concise expression to what was accepted as an axiom of the political life of the period.

Allopathy. The name given by Homeopathists to the general and orthodox practice of medicine, as a contradistinctive term to Homeopathy. The word "homeopathy" (q.v.) being derived from the Greek *homoios*, like, and *pathos*, feeling, is intended to indicate the system which professes to cure by drugs which excite symptoms similar to those of the disease, while the word "allopathy," from the

Greek *allos*, other, and *pathos*, feeling, suggests the reverse of the homeopathic system.

Aloof. Like many of our old words this is derived from nautical phraseology. In full it might be written "on loof," the "a" being the Anglo-Saxon equivalent to "on," as in "fell on sleep" for "fell asleep." The word "loof" is the same as "luff," signifying not only the act of turning a ship towards the wind or sailing her close to the wind, but also the windward side of a ship. From this the inner meaning of the word "aloof" is apparent—it gives the idea of one standing to windward of a person or enterprise so that no taint of anything objectionable should offend his nostrils. It has been pointed out by Trench that the word "aloofness" was in abeyance for some years until revived by Coleridge, who apparently did not know that it had been in use long before.

Alphabet. The word is unique in the English language by reason of it being a mere combination of the two Greek letters *alpha* and *beta*, the first and second in the Greek alphabet. The sources from which our alphabet comes are very ancient, even the order of the letters—as regards the first few, at any rate —can be traced back to the Old Hebrew alphabet, which with the Aramæan and the Greek seems to have come from the Phœnician, itself derived, most likely, from the Egyptian hieroglyphics. The antiquity of the Old Hebrew characters is evidenced by the fact that the original forms of the letters indicate their meaning; thus *Aleph, Beth, Gimel* and *Daleth* (at once suggesting the Greek *Alpha, Beta, Gamma, Delta*) signify respectively an ox, a house, a camel, a door, and each of these objects is roughly represented in the original form of the corresponding letter. There are other groups of alphabets, such as the cuneiform letters of Babylon, Assyria and Persia, the Chinese characters used for representing ideas instead of spelling words, and the Aztec alphabet, the two latter, though independent of each other, having no apparent connection with the other groups.

Alt. A place-name prefix. (*See* OLD.)

Altruism. The word is of modern origin, formed from the Italian *altrui*, others or other person's goods, and from the Latin *alter-uter*, one of two, either. It was M. Comte who framed the word, which was adopted with warm approval by Herbert Spencer to express the power of sympathising with others and appreciating their point of view by general consideration for others, on the principle of doing unto them as you would they should do unto you. Briefly, it is the antithesis of egoism.

Amen. A wealth of significance is stored up in a word of such antiquity as this, especially when bound up, as it is, in the very religion, the highest and best aspirations, of an ancient race who, thousands of years ago, had attained a culture and a civilisation by no means inferior to our own. For Amen (otherwise Amun or Ammon) was one of the oldest deities of the ancient Egyptians, one of their chief gods. His name meant " hidden," " concealed "; his emblem was a man wearing a red crown surmounted by the sun's disc, in token of his dominion over the lower and the upper worlds; one of his titles was *Amen-ka-mut-f*, the husband of his mother, as signifying the oldest and the youngest of created beings. And in the Hebrew language, from which we get the word, Amen signifies " strong," " trustworthy "—in Isaiah lxv. 16, the words rendered " God of truth " are literally " God of Amen "—so that in using the word at the end of our creeds and prayers we do even more than exclaim " so be it "—we asseverate the truth and strength of what has been recited.

Analyse. Antiquarian research shows that the early races were acquainted with gold, silver and copper. The primitive method of gathering gold dust was

to loosen the earth and toss it up in the air, shaking
away the lighter and retaining the heavier matter
—much as one may winnow a handful of grain.
And in searching for all precious stones it was
needful to loosen up the ground to see what was
in it.   Hence our word " analyse "—from the
Greek *ana*, up, and *lyo*, to loosen.   To analyse is
to see what is in a thing.

Anathema. Originally this was not a curse but an
offering to the gods.   The term arose from the
custom among the Greeks and Romans (still
retained in the Roman Catholic Church) of
bringing votive offerings to be *set up* in the
Temple.   The lame man who was healed would
bring his crutch, the sailor returned in safety from
an adventurous voyage would offer a model of his
ship, and so on.   These were *set up* in the Temple
as memorials and thank-offerings—they were
anathema (Greek, *ana*, up, and *tithēmi*, to set).
An offering refused by the priest was *an-anathema*,
not set up (*a* or *an* being the Greek negative prefix).
This became abbreviated to " anathema," an ecclesiastical curse.

Andiron. Generally used in the plural—a pair of and-
irons, or fire dogs.   They consist of two iron rails
or bars, usually terminating in finely ornamented
iron-work pillars, which being placed on the hearth
at some distance from each other were used to
prop up the logs of fire-wood and allow them to
burn more freely.   The origin of the word is
dubious, but Boucher thinks that the " and " in the
word is the Anglo-Saxon preposition implying
opposition (Greek *anti*), and that the name has
arisen from the two irons being placed opposite
each other.

Anecdote. Many anecdotes are now printed in the
public press—little accounts of amusing incidents,
conversation, or events in private life.   But strictly
speaking an anecdote is a story told in confidence,

the word being derived from the Greek *a* (or *an*), not, and *ekdotos*, published, or given out.

Angels could do no more.

" Who does the best his circumstance allows,
Does well, acts nobly; *angels could do no more*."
.YOUNG (1684-1765).

Animated Beings.

Animals are creatures that breathe —Latin *anima*, air, life; Greek *animos*, wind. But the wind was a spirit and the Latin *animus* meant soul or spirit as distinct from *anima*, animal life. The word " spirit " (Latin *spiritus*) also means a breath, from the Latin *spiro*, to breathe. " The wind bloweth where it listeth . . . so is everyone that is born of the Spirit " (John iii. 8)—that is, born to freedom. The ancients were accustomed to bond and free; to be born of the spirit was to inherit the spirit, the breath of life, as a free man; but an animal was a serf who only used the breath of life by tolerance.

Annals.

The annals of a country record the events of the years (Latin *annus*, a year) as a diary records the events of days (Latin *dies*, day).

Annihilate Space and Time.

It was Alexander Pope (1688-1744) who wrote :
" Ye Gods ! annihilate but space and time,
And make two lovers happy."·

Another Yet the Same.

A phrase replete with significance, used by many a poet—by Pope, Johnson, Wordsworth, and Scott among others. We find it, too, in the classic authors—Horace writes " Aliusque et idem."

Ant.

" Go to the ant, thou sluggard : consider her ways and be wise " (Prov. vi. 6). The ant has *literally* acquired a name for industry, as the word " ant " is a contraction of " emmet," the Anglo-Saxon *aemete*, and leads back to a similar significa-tion whether we follow the Teutonic or the Norse language, the German *emsig* meaning diligent, the

Icelandic *amr* work. Ants are of three genders—
male, female, and wingless neuters. The males,
after a short flight with the females, die, the
females lose their wings and are each enthroned in
a colony as its queen. The neuters are the workers
who build the city, make the roads, keep all in
repair, provide the food, watch over the eggs, and
attend to the hatching and feeding of the young.
The community may be said to consist of various
groups—engineers, soldiers, foragers and nurses,
the soldiers having developed extra large biting
jaws—and in each group the members work in
concert and with remarkable discipline, carrying
out the orders of the officers obediently and industriously, and resorting to many manœuvres which
show a high degree of intelligence.

Ante—Anti. These two prefixes are in common use in
the English language, the first (from the Latin)
generally implying " before," and the second (from
the Greek) " in opposition to." Yet they are both
from the same Sanscrit root—*ant*, and *anti* is
essentially the same as *ante*. Hence we find that
" anticipate," being derived from the Latin (*anti-
capio*), does not mean to take " in opposition to "
but to take " before-hand "; and in the words
" antique " and " ancient," also derived from the
Latin, the *anti* at the root of each of these words
means " before " not " opposed to."

Antipodes. This is really a Greek word, first introduced by Plato, who was well aware of the
sphericity of the earth, that doctrine having been
taught by Thales, the Greek astronomer, some 200
years before the time of Plato. It is formed from
anti, opposite to, and *podes*, feet, and denotes those
living on the other side of the globe, whose feet are
thus opposite to ours; or the places on the earth's
surface exactly opposite each other.

Antique. Belonging to an age gone by, before the
memory of the oldest man. From the Latin *ante*,

before. "Ancient" and "antic" both come from the same root, though by a curious process the latter word is now generally used to denote something ludicrous or grotesque. (*See* ANTE—ANTI.)

Apocalypse. The name by which the last book of the New Testament, "Revelation," is often known, from the fact that the contents of that book mainly consist of a revelation or disclosure, the word "apocalypse" being derived from the Greek *apokalupsis*, an uncovering. The apocalyptic number is 666 (Rev. xiii. 18), the mystical number round which many theories have been woven and for which many solutions have been suggested. Perhaps the best answer to the riddle is that which gives "Neron Kesar," the Hebrew form of the Latin Nero Cæsar. The Hebrew letters were used, as in the case of other ancient alphabets, not only as units for the composition of words but also for numerals, each letter having its own numerical value, and as the vowels *e* and *a* are not expressed in the Old Hebrew writing the solution runs thus:

N   R   O   N   K   S   R
50 + 200 + 6 + 50 + 100 + 60 + 200 = 666.

Moreover, Nero was Emperor at the time of St. Paul's visit to Rome—he was the Cæsar to whom Paul appealed—and as a cruel persecutor of the Christians it would most probably be to him that St. John would allude, though he could only do so enigmatically (cryptographically).

Apocrypha. The word is generally applied to the fourteen books of the Old Testament which are referred to in the Thirty-nine Articles of the English Church as "read for example of life and instruction of manners but not to establish any doctrine." Most of these books were written during the last two centuries B.C., and the Jews never accorded them a place in the Old Testament canon, but they were inserted in the Septuagint and thence passed to the

Latin Vulgate. Portions of them are still appointed to be read in Church on days other than Sunday. The word means "things hidden," being derived from the Greek *apo*, from, and *kryptein*, to hide, and is not only applied to these books of the Old Testament but to any fabulous or untrustworthy story, or to writings suitable for the initiated only, or which are spurious. It is curious to note how a derivation may extend to words of quite different significations. For instance, between the apocrypha and the cathedral crypt—the underground chapel with its hallowed associations of religious worship and sepulture of the illustrious dead—a wide gulf seems to intervene; yet the same meaning of "a hidden thing" is appropriate to both words—both take their origin from the Greek *kryptein*.

Apothecary. As long ago as 1606 the Apothecaries of London were incorporated by royal charter, at first, strange to say, with the Grocers, though they soon freed themselves from that association and ultimately grew into an important corporation, obtaining, in 1815, the distinguished privilege of examining and licensing all sellers of drugs. How different was the apothecary of old may be gathered from the description put by Shakespeare into Romeo's mouth (Romeo and Juliet, act v.)—"I do remember an apothecary . . . whom late I noted in tattered weeds, with overwhelming brows, culling of simples; meagre were his looks, sharp misery had worn him to the bones : . . . about his shelves a beggarly account of empty boxes . . . were thinly scattered to make up a show." It is curious to note that the word "apothecary" is derived from the Greek *apothēkē*, signifying a storehouse or what is laid up therein.

Appetite Comes with Eating. It is from Rabelais (1495-1553) that we get this phrase.

Appreciate. The word is often used to express an increase in value—on the Stock Exchange, for instance, when the price of a security is rising it is said to " appreciate," and to " appreciate " a person's conduct is considered to denote approval. But the proper signification of the word is to value justly, as shown by its derivation—the Latin *pretium*, price, with the prefix *ad*, literally to put a price to.

Apricot. At first sight it does not seem probable that there can be any etymological affinity between the words " apricot " and " precocious," though the Old English spelling—" apricock "—gives a hint of the relationship between the two words. In truth they are derived from the same source—the Low Greek *praikokion*, which is simply the Latin *præcoquus* or *præcox*, meaning early ripe, for the tree, in its original habitat of Armenia, flowers very early, and in this precipitation of development may rightly be said to be " precocious."

April Fool. Both in England and on the Continent it is considered legitimate to make " April Fools " on the first day of April—in Scotland the dupe is called a " gowk," in France *poisson d'Avril*, " April-Fish." No reference to the custom has been found in our early literature, and it would seem that both England and Germany derived it from France, but any satisfactory origin has yet to be discovered. One theory traces in it an allusion to Noah sending the dove out of the ark on its first fruitless errand; another refers it to the miracle plays representing the sending of our Lord from Annas to Caiaphas and from Pilate to Herod; another to the change made in France, in 1564, of New Year's day to the 1st January, which left the 1st April bereft of its former festivities. Recently an attempt has been made to identify the custom with the Hindu festival of Huli, celebrated in a similar way on our 31st March, and it is worthy of note that in China the symbolic ploughing by the Emperor takes place in our April, and that in Japan the Feast of Dolls is kept in the same month. The derivation of the

word "April" is generally regarded as a contraction of the Latin *aperilis*, from *aperire* to open,
but it has been pointed out that April was not
always a Spring month. Another etymology connects it with the Greek *aphros*, foam, from which
Venus, to whom the month was sacred, was said
to have sprung.

Ar—Ara. This is a widely diffused root in the nomenclature of rivers, and, as pointed out in Isaac
Taylor's valuable book, "Words and Places," it
has been the cause of much perplexity. Apparently,
it has more than one origin : there is the Welsh
word *araf*, gentle, the Gaelic *ar*, slow, the Celtic
arw, violent, and the Sanscrit *arb*, to ravage, to
destroy. From any of these, according to the
character of the river, its name may be derived.

Arc. A line which is part of a circle, from the Latin
arcus, a bow. But when the "arc" is constructed
we call it an "arch," and when we use "arch"
as an adjective (an arch girl) it is derived from the
German *arg*, mischievous. But "arch" when
applied to a bishop, or as in "architect," is derived
from the Greek *archi*, first, or chief.

Arctic. Most of us associate the Arctic regions with
the great white bear—the polar bear—only because
the pictures and narratives of the explorers so frequently represent and refer to the bear. Yet the
Arctic region means the region of the Bear, so
named from the Greek *arktos*, a bear, after the
constellation of the Great Bear which, as it swings
round the Pole-star, revolves above the northern
cap of the world.

Ard. A Celtic syllable signifying a height, found in
many place-names both in great Britain and on the
Continent, as Ardrossan (Scotland), Ardennes
(Belgium).

Arena. The derivation of the word—the Latin *arena*,
sand—carries us back to the days of old Rome,
when the floor of the Coliseum was strewn with

sand, in order that it might absorb the blood so
wantonly spilt in the combats of the gladiators
between themselves or with wild beasts.

Ark. In an ordinary sense any chest is an ark, for the
word is the Anglo-Saxon *arc*, from the Latin *arca*,
a chest, through *arcēre*, to guard. The Jewish ark
was not merely a chest containing the sacred
things, but was surmounted by a throne or seat—
the Mercy Seat of the English Bible—the Hebrew
name of which signifies the place of meeting, the
trysting-place, between God and man. As long as
the Israelites were wanderers they could have no
fixed local sanctuary, but by carrying the ark with
them they had always at hand a sanctuary and
divine meeting-place. (The Hebrew *Kapporeth*,
the Mercy Seat of the Ark, the Arabic *Kaaba*, the
Meccan Sanctuary, and the Egyptian *Ka*, soul
or worship, seem to be closely connected.) It is
worthy of note that in the Jewish account of the
flood—which is considered by many to have been
borrowed from the Babylonian legends—the word
translated " ark " in our Bible (*see* Gen. vi.) is
literally " chest," and the assumption is that the
word " ship " was recognised by the writer as an
anachronism in the narrative, as in the period
assigned to Noah, mankind, according to the
account given, had not reached the sea and were
ignorant of the possibility of the construction of
ships. The use of the word " chest " is the more
remarkable when we realise that the size of Noah's
ark, according to the dimensions given, would be
about equal to that of the " Great Eastern " steam-
ship.

Arquebuss. (Also spelt *Harquebus*.) A French word
derived from the Dutch *haakbus*, *haak* meaning
hook and *bus* a barrel of a gun. It was larger than
a musket and the marksman supported it upon a
rest by an iron hook attached to the barrel—hence
the name. Henry VII., who established the Yeo-
men of the Guard in 1485, armed half the men with

these firearms and the others with bows and arrows.

Arrowroot. Most of us associate a diet of arrowroot with convalescence from illness, and it is curious that in the derivation of the word we should find a confirmation of such an association of ideas. For the word is an English translation of the native name given to the root by the North American Indians, who had long used it to counteract the poison injected into the blood by means of wounds from poisoned arrows. It is true that other derivations have been suggested, but in this connection it is noteworthy that the German name for the root corresponds exactly with ours, being *pfeil-wurz*, arrow-root.

Artillery Lane. It was here that the Bowyers and the Fletchers pursued their trade of making longbows and cloth-yard shafts, and near at hand, just outside the wall of London (on the great Fen or Moor which Pennant so quaintly calls an " arrant fen," and whence came the names Finsbury, Moorfields, and Moorgate Street) was the Artillery Ground, where the archers used to assemble—on Sundays especially—to practise shooting and display their skill at the mark. For in early days the word " artillery " did not denote big guns and smokeless powder, but bows and arrows, and, indeed, the word retained that meaning right up to the time of James I., as in the Authorised Version of the Bible made in his reign we find Jonathan's bows and arrows referred to as " artillery." (I. Sam. xx. 40.)

Assurance Doubly Sure. " I'll make assurance double sure, and take a bond of Fate," says Macbeth in his interview with the witches, and the phrase seems as fresh and modern as ever.

Assyria. The district took its name from its primitive capital—" the city of Asur," otherwise " al-Asur," the Ellasar of the Bible (Gen. xiv. 1). The city was built in pre-Semitic times by Turanian tribes, in whose language the word meant " water-meadow," or the land between the rivers, which in Greek became " Mesopotamia." The founders of the city of Assur were the Babylonian Accads, as stated in the Bible " out of that land went forth Asshur." (Gen. x. 11.)

At Sixes and Sevens. The phrase is certainly an old one and in its present significance of being at cross purposes or in confusion has been used for at least three hundred years. Shakespeare (Richard II.) makes the Duke of York say that " everything is left at six and seven," and Bacon also uses the phrase. But the origin of the expression has not been satisfactorily traced; in " Notes and Queries " it has been connected with the unlucky number of thirteen, and by Nares with the fall of the dice.

Atom. The researches of Dalton led to the hypothesis that all solids, liquids and gases were alike composed of infinitely small particles more or less closely packed. These were called atoms, because, being the smallest possible particles, they could not be divided (Greek *atomos*, that which cannot be cut). The so-called atoms are invisible units of the various elements, but there is reason to believe that these units are each a collection of still smaller units revolving round a centre, so that an atom may be imagined as in itself an infinitely minute solar system. It is remarkable that Pope, who lived long before Dalton, in his " Essay on Man " says that God sees " with equal eye . . . atoms or systems into ruin hurled."

Average. The first part of the word corresponds to the French *avoir*, to have; or if we put an " h " to it and turn the " v " back to the original " b " we shall see the Latin *habere*, to have. The " havings " or possessions of a farmer were his cattle—oxen, mules and horses—and he was obliged, when called upon to do so, to place them at the disposal of his lord's retainers for carrying their armour and provisions in any warlike expedition. It was incumbent upon him to carry a stipulated quantity—say, 20 or 100 loads—and this was the "average" laid upon his cattle, but the number of cattle he might use was optional. An ox or an ass cannot carry what a horse can—he might have many yoke of oxen and few horses, or the reverse, but the "average" remained the same.

Avoirdupois. This system of weights, like Troy weight, appears at first sight to be a promiscuous table arranged at mere haphazard, but both really embody two primitive and world-wide methods of calculation, viz. :—the numeration by multiples of four and five respectively. The early Babylonian (Shumero-Accad) system—to which we owe the twelve months of the year and our English dozen— was founded on multiples of four, and in the Avoirdupois table we find that four times four (sixteen) drachms make an ounce, sixteen ounces make a pound, and eight pounds make a stone. But the more recent system which takes five and its multiples for a basis of calculation is also found in the table, and we get the 100lbs. of the original hundredweight and the 20cwt. of the ton. For the hundredweight of 112lbs. is an innovation of almost present days; the very name and the sign we still use to express the hundredweight (cwt.) indicate that it consisted of 100 lbs.—c = 100, wt = weight or pound, as the word "weight" is synonymous with "pound," being derived from the Latin *pondus*, a weight. And it may be that the custom of giving 12lbs. extra in each hundredweight was an endeavour, in the absence of an enforced statutory definition of weight, to act up to, and obey in its literal sense, the injunction recorded in Luke vi. 38, viz. :—"Give, and it shall be given unto you ; good measure, pressed down and shaken together and running over . . . For with the same measure that ye mete withal it shall be measured to you again."

Avon. A Celtic word meaning a river. It has become a proper name for many streams in England—the Avon at Stratford (Warwickshire), at Bristol, and at Salisbury may be quoted as examples. The root of the word is found in the Sanscrit *ap*, water, and appears in the name Punj-ab, "the land of five rivers," and Do-ab (Afghanistan), the district between two rivers.

Bab. The Arabic for gate. It appears in Arabic place-names denoting an entrance or a strait, as in Babel-mandeb.

Babylon. This is the Greek form of Babel or Bab-ili, meaning "The Gate of God," taking its name from the great Temple of Il, El, or Bel, afterwards Baal. The temple was a pyramid of brick in eight square stages, the basement stage being over two hundred yards square. A winding stair led to the summit, where stood the shrine with its golden image of Bel, forty feet high; and we now know that the oldest Babylonian sign for a temple is a square with a dot in the middle of it to represent the apex of the pyramid. The native version of the story of the Tower of Babel has recently been discovered among the cuneiform tablets in the British Museum; it is certainly older than 2000 B.C. and is fuller and more complete than the account in the Bible. The tower has been identified with the ruined remains at Borsippa, a suburb of Babylon, and was a pyramid in seven stages, one for each of the seven planets. It was begun by "a former king," who built it to the height of forty-two cubits, but it lay an uncompleted ruin for many centuries and was not finished till the reign of Nebuchadnezzar. There seems evidence that the labourers employed on the building comprised, in the first instance, a mixed multitude of peoples— the Sumirs, the Accads, the Hittites and others—

which would naturally cause much confusion of tongues and may have resulted in the abandonment of the work.

Bachelor. The Latin origin of the word meant a cowherd. *Vacca*, a cow, was, in Low Latin, *bacca*; *baccalia* was a herd of cows, and the youth who tended them was *baccalarius*. This, in Old French, became *bacheler*, a young man, from which our word "bachelor," an unmarried man, is derived.

Backgammon. A game which dates from the tenth century. The men in the game—which, at first, were probably either knuckle-bones or little lumps of clay—are arranged in rows on the board so as to touch one another, like the vertebræ or joints of the back. And this coincides with the origin of the word, which is the Anglo-Saxon *baec*, the back, and *gamen*, a game.

Bacon (To Save One's).

" What frightens you thus, my good son," says the priest,
" You murder'd, are sorry, and have been confest."
" O father, my sorrow will *scarce save my bacon*,
For 'twas not that I murder'd, but that I was taken."

(PRIOR, 1664-1721).

The Old Dutch for "bacon" is *bæc*, and the Anglo-Saxon for "back" is also *bæc*; to save one's bacon seems, therefore, equivalent to saving one's back—from a beating. Moreover it is the back of the pig that was, and still is, chiefly made into bacon—the legs are hams.

Bad. A syllable often found in the names of places, where it means "bath." Bad-en and Carls-bad are examples.

Badge. A sign or mark by which one may be known or distinguished, either in servitude or in honour. The Latin *baga*, a ring, and *bacca*, the link of a chain, show its origin as a mark of servitude, while the Anglo-Saxon *beag* and *beah*, a crown, a brace-

let, point to a sign of honour. The ring on the
finger has been a badge of honour from very ancient
times—" Pharaoh took off his ring from his hand
and put it upon Joseph's (Gen. xli. 42)—but the
ring round the neck (a collar) was the badge of the
serf. It was so in Saxon England, the collar of
the common serf being of iron, though the more
favoured servants wore silver and even gold
badges. In heraldry the badge (technically " cog-
nizance "—that by which one may be known) is a
mark of distinction similar to the crest, though not
worn on the helmet—familiar examples are the
three feathers of the Prince of Wales, the broom-
plant of the Plantagenets, and the red and white
rose of the houses of Lancaster and York. In the
time of Henry IV. the terms " badge " and
" livery " seem to have been synonymous, and
consisted of a device, crest or arms woven on a
separate piece of cloth or engraved on a silver
shield and fastened to the left sleeve. These
badges were worn by servants up to the reign of
Elizabeth, but by the time of James I. had been
generally abandoned, though survivals of the
custom may be found in the shoulder-knots of
footmen and the badges of porters and firemen.

Bag and Baggage. In this, as in many other instances,
two words are found linked together because of
their alliteration, though coming through different
channels and with different meanings. What we
call a bag was formerly a poke, and a small poke
is a pocket. " Bag " is simply the Celtic word
bag, a wallet or bundle, while " baggage " comes
to us through the Old French *bagues*, goods,
articles, belongings. To get rid of a man " bag
and baggage " is, therefore, to send him off with
his bundle and his goods.

Bail (To give bail). Many a burly man who stands
bail for another would be surprised to learn that
in doing so he takes the place of a nurse who
carries a child. Yet the word " bail " comes from

the Old French *bail*, a guardian or tutor; in Low Latin *baila*, a nurse, through the Latin *bajulus*, the bearer of a child. The " bail " of the cricket-wicket is of another derivation—perhaps from the Old French *bailles*, a palisade, or from the Latin *baculus*, a staff.

Bait. The word comes from the Anglo-Saxon *bitan*, to bite, and we can see how all the significations of " bait " are derived from the same root." The " bait " on a hook is a " bite " for a fish, the " bait " in a trap is a " bite " for the animal lured thereby, the " bait " for the horse is a " bite " of hay or corn, and to set dogs on an animal, to worry or " bite " it, is to " bait " it.

Bal, Balla, Bally. In place-names these syllables are indications of Gaelic origin. They signify a village or town, and are equivalent to the Cymric *tre* and the Norse *by*. Bal-moral, Balla-chulish, and Bally-mena are examples.

Balance. In Egyptian mythology the soul is brought into the Hall of Double Truth and weighed in the balance—doubtless the balance was one of the earliest contrivances that man invented. Our word " balance," which is the same in French, comes from the Latin *bilanx*, a double scale, the word being formed from *bis*, double, and *lanx*, *lancis*, a plate or scale. And it is in the word " scale " that we get at the origin of the device of the balance and the wonder of its invention, for we find in the Anglo-Saxon language two similar words—*sceala*, the scale of a fish, and *scala*, a balance, both derived from an ancient Sanscrit root, *skand*, to ascend, whence the Latin *scandere*, to mount, and *scala*, a ladder. This implies that the scale was the thin shell or plate which lifted. Anything might drop—primitive man was well aware of that —but in this device he perceived that the weight in one scale, however little heavier it might be, would lift the weight in the other : here was the original wonder of the balance. But in later—perhaps less imaginative—times, the balance, as shown by the Latin word *libra*, means the level.

Balk. We speak of a "balk" of timber and perhaps do not recognise its connection with the verb "to balk." Yet they are derived from the same Anglo-Saxon word—*balca*, a beam, for the ancient log-hut was protected from within not by a slender bolt to the door, but by a mighty beam which could be thrown across, at any moment, to defend the home from all assailants. Hence "to balk" is to hinder.

Ball (Dancing). When an English word becomes commonplace *élite* society borrows a French equivalent which seems grander. To give a ball is only to give a dance, the word "ball" being the French *bal*, from the Latin *ballare*, to dance, and "ballet" is but the French diminutive of *bal*, thus signifying a little dance.

Ballad. The sentiment that he who makes the ballads of a nation need not care who should make the laws is well known—it appears in a letter to the Marquis of Montrose, in the time of the Commonwealth. Such ballads have exercised a great effect on the heroic spirit of a nation, and before printing was general they served a valuable purpose by presenting a more or less accurate account of important occurrences. Between the 11th and 13th centuries the bard was a welcome guest with persons of rank and culture, for the ballad, though still mainly concerned with heroic exploits, then embraced a wide range of subjects. The word "ballad," under its various spellings of "balad," "balade," "ballet," and "balette" comes to us from the Latin *ballare*, to dance, and the Italian *ballata*, a song in dancing; but in spite of its derivation it was applied to any composition in measured lines, whether serious or religious. Thus in Coverdale's Bible, what we now call "The Song of Solomon" was entitled "Solomon's Balettes," and in Cranmer's Bible and the Bishops' Bible the title becomes "The Ballet of Ballets."

Bank. The first Bankers of modern Europe were the money-changers of Venice, when the great Republic was the resort of merchants from all nations. These money-changers, who were also the chief money-lenders and money-holders (*see* PAWN-BROKER) were mostly long-bearded Lombards, who sat beneath an awning with a bench in front of them on which they displayed piles of money of all countries. It was the bench that gave the name to their business, for the Italian for bench is *banco*, while the word "banker" is the same as "bencher," now applied to a senior barrister. We speak of the Judges or Magistrates as "The Bench" because they originally sat upon a bench while the suitors stood, and the most primitive bench was doubtless merely a grassy bank, for the Anglo-Saxon for bench is *benc*, which means a bank of earth.

Banksia-Rose. A few years ago the banksia-rose was a familiar sight in nearly every village, climbing up the cottage wall and thrusting its clusters of small white or buff flowers into the lattice windows with a seeming riotous enjoyment of the June sunshine. Nowadays it has been displaced, to a great extent, by the ubiquitous "gloire"—not altogether to the enhancement of rural scenery. But in spite of its rural associations the name "banksia" has no connection with the "*bank* whereon the wild thyme grows"—the genus to which the rose belongs was named by Linnæus after Sir Joseph Banks, who sailed from Plymouth with Captain Cook on his exploring expedition in 1768, did valuable work as a naturalist, and became President of the Royal Society in 1778.

Banns. At first sight it is rather startling to find that the word "banns," used in connection with giving notice of an intended marriage, is the same as "ban," to denounce, to condemn; but ecclesiastical phraseology is generally conservative, and it is "ban" which has altered its meaning, not "bann." For both words come from the Anglo-Saxon *ge-bann*, a proclamation, from a root widely diffused in Teutonic languages; and it is only from its secondary meaning of summoning to trial —so often involved in a proclamation—that "ban" has acquired its denunciatory signification.

Barbarian. To the Greeks and the Romans the speech of the foreign races with whom they came in contact appeared but a confused and unintelligible sound of "ba, ba." Hence the Greek *barbaros* and the Latin *barbarus*—both meaning a barbarian —were applied as a generic term to all foreigners. But the practice of calling foreigners "barbarians" was not confined to the Greeks and the Romans; it was in force among the Egyptians and appears, indeed, to have been universal, for the root *barbar* may be traced back to the Sanscrit *varvara*, signifying a foreigner, one who speaks confusedly. A modern instance of a name being given to a race because its speech seemed unintelligible is that of "Hottentot," which is supposed to have been bestowed by the Dutch in imitation of the characteristic "click" of the Hottentot language, a sound resembling a repetition of "hot" and "tot."

Barbican. The name of this street is one of the many survivals of old London and the wall with which the city was encompassed. Starting from Tower Hill, the wall ran to Aldgate, Bishopsgate, Houndsditch and Moorgate to Aldersgate, which, as the principal gate, was guarded by a barbican—an outwork designed to protect the gate and consisting, probably, of two towers, with double walls, built slightly in advance of the line of the wall. The word "barbican" seems to be of Arabic origin, from *bab-khanah*, the usual name in the East for a towered gateway.

c

Bargain. As the word means something cheap it seems
as if it might refer to a price which " bars " or
precludes gain. But the word is more involved;
originally it meant an unusual offer, a rarity of
foreign produce brought from over the water. The
word may be traced through the Old French
bargaigner to the Low Latin *barcaniare*, a thing
imported in a *barca*, a barque, a merchant vessel.

Barley. From the Ancient British *bara*, bread, and
llys, a plant; showing us that the Ancient Britons
made barley loaves. The Anglo-Saxon word for
house is *ern*, and *bara-ern* (bread-house) became
ber-ern, *bern*, and finally " barn." The first syllable of *ber-ern*, prolonged to *beor*, became " beer,"
which also means " barley."

Basalt. This is not a salt, but a hard, dark-coloured
rock of igneous origin, the word being derived
from the Latin *basaltes*, a corruption of an African
word for a marble found in Ethiopia. But " bay-
salt " is salt obtained from sea-water by evaporation.

Basket. The word is but another form of the Ancient
British *bas-ged*, which is derived from *basg*, net-
work, plaiting. The Ancient Britons were renowned
for their manufacture of baskets, which were highly
prized in Rome, and Martial refers to them under
the Latin name *bascauda*—evidently the native
word corrupted by a foreign tongue. In Freeman's
English History for Children it is pointed out that
" basket " is one of the few Welsh (Ancient
British) words which have been retained in English,
and that those words which do exist generally have
reference to women or slaves, showing how completely, except in Wales, the British male population had been extirpated or driven away by the
Saxon invaders.

Baste. Among the poorer classes we often hear the
expression " I'll baste yer ! " and the word
" baste " is good old English, of Norse origin,

from the Icelandic *beysta*, to strike. From the same root we get the word "baton" and "bastinado," and also "baste," a term used in cooking meat. But when we speak of basting the seams of a dress, the verb "baste" is derived from the Old French *bastir*, to build, meaning that we build up the portions of a dress in their proper place till they can be sewn together.

Beacon. The name of many a hill in England, perpetuating the memory of pre-telegraphic days when one watcher "beckoned" to another by kindling a fire on the beacon hill. From the Anglo-Saxon *beacen*, a sign.

Beam. The word has remained unaltered in spelling and signification since Anglo-Saxon times; in the Old Saxon it was *bom*, from which we get the word "boom"—the boom of a ship. We speak of a ship being "broad in the beam" when referring to its width, the term being derived from the great central cross-timbers which stretch across the ship and prevent the sides from falling together; and a vessel is "on her beam ends" when thrown over so far on her sides that her beams, instead of lying horizontally, are more or less in an upright position. In the phrase "to kick the beam"— meaning to be surpassed or out-weighed—the analogy is taken from a pair of scales suspended from a cross-bar, or beam; a weight in one of the scales, with nothing to counterpoise it, would throw the other up to the beam. The essential characteristics of a beam are its length and strength, and probably it is the recognition of these qualities that has gained us the expression of a beam of light, a sun-beam.

Beatitudes. The word comes from the Latin *beatitudo*, through *beatus*, happy, and is applied to the nine sayings of Christ in the Sermon on the Mount, each of which begins with the word "blessed." Trench says that the word *beatitudo* was coined by Cicero, and when scarcely rooted in the Latin was adopted by the Christians. By the incorporation of the idea of happiness, which the derivation of the word warrants, the signification of the beatitudes is much enhanced.

Beauty. The word comes to us, through the French *beau*, from the Latin *bellus*, a contraction of *benulus*, the diminutive of *benus*, which is another form of *bonus*, good !

" And God saw everything that he had made, and, behold, it was very good (beautiful)." (Gen. i. 31.)

Beaver. The word is derived from the old Aryan name meaning " brown water-animal," and comes to us through the Anglo-Saxon *beofer.* The creature undoubtedly had its habitat in this country, and abundant remains of its former presence were discovered, in 1870, when making excavations for the reservoirs of the East London Water Works, not far from the river Lea. It existed in Wales, on the Teify, as late as 1188, and the names of many places in England and Wales bear witness to its having been common in these islands. For instance, Beverley, in Yorkshire, is the Anglo-Saxon " Beofer-leag," Beaver-place; while Beaverstone, in Gloucestershire; Bevercoates, in Nottinghamshire; Llyn yr Afrange and Nant Frangon, in Wales, all have reference to the beaver.

Bedlam. The word is a contraction, or rather a corruption, of " Bethlehem "—the asylum for lunatics called " The Hospital of St. Mary Bethlehem." It was originally a Priory, founded in 1247, by Simon Fitz Mary and situated in Bishopsgate Street, but on the dissolution of the Monasteries the Priory was granted to the Mayor and Citizens of the City of London, and they made it into a Lunatic Asylum. In 1676 it was removed to a site near London Wall, and finally, in 1815, the Asylum was transferred to Lambeth.

Beer. This is a Hebrew word which often appears in place-names mentioned in the Bible. It signifies a well, as in Beer-sheba, the well of the oath. (Gen. xxi. 31.)

Ben. A common prefix in Gaelic and Irish place-names, synonymous with the Welsh *Pen*, and denoting a mountain or a headland, as in Ben Nevis, Pen-zance.

Beth. A Hebrew word meaning a house, often found in Bible place-names; as in Beth-el, the house of God; Beth-lehem, the house of bread.

Better Late than Never. The saying is very old—we find it used by Tusser (1523-1580) in his " Five Hundred Points of Good Husbandry "—and it may have arisen in allusion to the labourers in the Bible parable who were called to work in the vine-yard at the eleventh hour and yet received a full day's pay.

Bevy. We speak of a " bevy " of quails, a " bevy " of pheasants, a " bevy " of ladies; meaning a flock of the birds and a company of the ladies. But what is the original signification of the word and how it comes to be thus applied it is not so easy to determine. Some authorities, among them Wedgwood and Skeat, are of opinion that " bevy " is derived from the Italian *beva*, a drinking, in which case the word would properly denote a drinking party; but Mahn suggests that it comes from the Armorican *beva*, life, thus giving the word the signification of a collection of living beings. Trench has pointed out that " bevy " was included in a list of obsolete words as long ago as the 16th century, but certainly it has since been completely revived, for Milton (1608-1674) in his " Paradise Lost " (Book xi., line 582) writes of " a bevy of fair women, richly clad "; and Macaulay (1800-1859), in his History of England, speaks of " the whole bevy of renegades."

Bible. The word means " books "—from the Ecclesiastical Greek (and Latin) *biblia*, a diminutive of *biblos*, signifying the inner bark of the papyrus.

Thus a bible meant originally any book made of papyrus paper, and we find Chaucer, in his " Canterbury Tales," using the word " bible " in the sense of any book. The English Bi'le, generally called the " Authorised Version," was first published in 1611. It is a revision of " The Bishops' Bible," which was published in 1568 and which was itself a revision made by " able bishops and others," under the auspices of Bishop Parker, of " The Great Bible " of 1539. The previous issues of the printed Bible in English were Matthew's Bible of 1537, Coverdale's of 1535, and Tyndale's of 1526-1530—before these there was no printed English Bible. The " Wickliffe " Bible of 1384 was in manuscript, and copies of Purvey's version of it are still in existence, splendidly illuminated and beautifully bound. But as far back as the English language can be followed there are traces of translations of portions of the Bible, and the earliest relic of such work is an English Psalter translated by St. Aldhelm, Abbot of Malmesbury, who died in 709. It is remarkable how peculiarly satisfying to the English ear is the English of the " Authorised Version." It speaks in a language of its own—a language which is thoroughly English and yet separated by its archaic form from the English of colloquial use and the literary English of most books. Yet this language is not, as is usually assumed, that of Elizabethan and Jacobean times; it can be traced in a direct line through every Biblical revision, and its true ancestor is the " Wickliffe " Bible of the 14th century. That this is no mere theory has been proved (*see* Encycl. Brit.) by placing passages from the " Wickliffe " Bible (in modernised spelling) side by side with the same passages from the " Authorised Version."

Bicker (To). It is distressing to be in the company of those who are addicted to quarrelling and bickering; a constant altercation about trifles jars upon the nerves like a series of blows with a pick upon hard ground. And by its derivation the word "bicker" imports this signification, as it comes from the English *pick*, *picker*; it is akin to *peck*, and is connected with the Welsh *bikra*, to fight.

Bicycle. The word, which has been coined from the Latin *bis*, twice, and the Greek *kylos*, a circle—an unscholarly compound—has no pretensions to antiquity, and it is the newness of the bicycle, as an invention, that is its chief marvel. For thousands of years—for probably the Egyptians and the Assyrians had their chariots as early as 5000 years B.C.—two wheels, with an axle joining them side by side, had been used as a means of conveyance, but though it must have been well known that a wheel (a hoop, for instance) would balance itself in an upright position so long as it retained a rotatory movement, yet, apparently, through all those ages, no one thought of applying that knowledge for the purpose of locomotion. Thus, incredible as it seems, the invention of the bicycle was reserved for the last quarter of the 19th century A.D. !

Bidding-Prayer. The meaning of the word "bidding" in this expression has become confused. There are really two verbs "to bid," one signifying "to pray," "to beseech," the other "to command," "to order." The first is derived from the Anglo-Saxon *biddan*, Old Saxon *biddian*, German *bitten*; the second from the Anglo-Saxon *beodan*, Icelandic *bioda*. In pre-Reformation times the "bidding-prayer" meant "a praying-prayer," the priest reading out, at Mass, a list of subjects for which the prayers of the faithful were requested and which they should remember when "bidding" their beads, *i.e.*, saying (praying) their prayers. In the course of time the meaning of the word "bid" as "pray" was merged into "bid" as "command," and thus the "bidding-prayer" became an exhortation to prayer, as now used before the sermon at visitations, assizes and ordinations.

Biffin. The Norfolk biffin is a commodity common to most households—it is an apple slowly dried in a baker's oven and pressed into a flat cake. The word is sometimes spelt " beaufin," perhaps in the belief that it is of French etymology, but Wright, Mahn and others hold that its derivation is the English *beef*, arising from a supposed resemblance of the pulp of the apple to raw beef.

Big Ben. The name is applied both to the clock in the Houses of Parliament and to the bell upon which it strikes. The clock, which is generally considered to be a masterpiece of time-keeping, was designed, in 1851, by Lord Grimthorpe in conjunction with Sir G. B. Airy, the Astronomer Royal, and Mr. Dent. The bell, which is cracked, was cast by George Mears, in 1858, and seems to have derived its name from Sir Benjamin Hall, who was First Commissioner of Works at the time. It weighs between 13 and 14 tons, and though by day its sonorous boom is drowned in the roar of the street traffic, on calm nights all London is flooded with its solemn tones. Its size, however, is not great in comparison with the second bell of Moscow—the largest in the world in actual use—which weighs no less than 128 tons.

Biscuit. Literally, twice-cooked; from the French-Latin *bis*, twice, and *cuit*, cooked. The origin of this twice-cooked bread was, doubtless, the need of providing ships' crews with bread which would remain eatable during the long time that sailing ships had to be at sea without means of replenishing their stock of fresh food. When designed for very long voyages it was baked four times.

Bishop. The word is derived from the Greek *episkopos* —*epi* signifying upon (over), and *skopos* one who watches. The qualifications of a New Testament bishop are given at length by St. Paul in Tim.

iii. 1-7, and in Titus i. 7-9, and Ruskin, too, has some trenchant thoughts and words on the duties of a bishop. In his " Sesame and Lilies," where he reviews a few lines from Milton's " Lycidas," are these stern passages :—" Nearly all the evils in the Church have arisen from bishops desiring power more than light; they want authority, not outlook. Whereas their office is not to rule : it is the king's office to rule, the bishop's office is to oversee the flock. Down in that back street (are) Bill and Nancy knocking each other's teeth out ! Does the bishop know all about it? Can he circumstantially explain to us how Bill got into the habit of beating Nancy? If he cannot he is no Bishop, though he had a mitre as high as Salisbury steeple; he is no bishop—he has sought to be at the helm instead of the mast-head; he has no sight of things."

Bishop's Apron. A survival of the short cassock which was at one time generally worn by all the clergy and the use of which is enjoined by the 74th canon. The short cassock had no collar or sleeves, and extended only a little below the knees.

Bissextile. The word is formed from the Latin *bis*, twice, and *sextus*, sixth, and is applied to our Leap Year. As shown above it means, literally, twice a sixth, and the term is a survival of the old Roman year, in which, once in every four years, two days in the kalends of March were each called the sixth, thereby effecting the same result as we attain by the introduction of the 29th day in February every fourth year.

Bite the Thumb at. An old custom of showing contempt. Shakespeare makes use of the expression in " Romeo and Juliet " :—" I will bite my thumb at them; which is a disgrace to them, if they bear it." And in an old book (1678) on the " Rules of Civility " it is stated that " 'Tis no less disrespectful to bite the nail of your thumb, by way of scorn

and disdain." Nares maintains that the thumb in
such a case represents a fig, the action of biting
being equivalent to saying " a fig for you ! "

Blackguard. The word is a curious example of
deterioration in meaning, as it originally signified
nothing scurrilous or villainous in its application,
but was used to denote the humble servants who
rode among the pots and pans and other utensils
to guard the impedimenta when a wealthy household was on a journey or a royal progress was
being made from place to place.

Black-Letter. The Old English character derived from
the Old German or Gothic, and conspicuous for its
blackness—hence its name. The word " black-
letter " is sometimes used to denote that which is
old and out of date—Macaulay has applied it in
that sense—as if black-letter writing and printing
were pre-eminently ancient. But such a supposition is not sustained by a review of the facts. It
is true that the Gothic type is a copy of the Gothic
writing prevalent in Europe in the second half of
the 12th century, and that it was used in the
earliest printed books, as shown in the British
Museum copy of the " Speculum Humanæ Salva-
tionis," presumably printed about 1445. But the
Roman type, the characters now in ordinary use,
appeared in printing as early as 1464, and the
British Museum has a copy of a book printed in
that type, another copy of which was bought by
the Basel Library in that year. Roman type is a
copy of that particular handwriting which had
developed into its best towards the close of the
8th century, the individual letters of which were
copies of Roman characters, and thus the letters
which we now use in general printing—the type
called Roman—have come down to us with
scarcely any alteration in form, though reduced
in size, from the Roman hand-writing of the fifth
century. (*See* Uncial.)

Blair. A Gaelic word meaning a plain, a battlefield, as in Blair-athol, Blair-gowrie, Blair-inroan. The last has been identified as the probable site of a battle in which the ninth legion of the Roman army, under Agricola, narrowly escaped destruction.

Blanket. The supposition that the word is derived from the name of the man who first made the article cannot be accepted. There seems to be no doubt that the true origin of the name of the article is to be found in the colour of its material— in the fact of the blanket having been blanched, made white (from the French *blanc*, white). For it must be borne in mind that the natural, un-bleached colour of woollen cloth is not white, and hence the whiteness of the blanket was sufficient to characterise it and become its name. The word "blank" has the same origin—a blank page means a white page.

Bloater. Probably the word has the same derivation as "bloated"—swollen, puffed out—from the Swedish *blöta*, to soak, to steep, derived from *blöt*, soft. It appears that in Sweden it was customary to soak fish in brine preparatory to smoking it, and when first brought to England under the name of *blöt fish* it was thought that the term *blöt* had reference to the smoking rather than the soaking. Certainly the word has the virtue of antiquity, for Ben Jonson (1574-1637) puts into the mouth of one of his characters the remark "Like so many bloat herrings newly taken out of the chimney."

Blood is Thicker than Water. An old English proverb —it may be found in a collection of proverbs (Ray's) published in 1672. Water soon evaporates and leaves no trace of its having been spilt, but a blood-stain long endures. So kinship counts for more than mere acquaintance, yet "one touch of nature (the mother of us all) makes the whole world kin !"

Board (Go aboard). It is interesting to trace the origin of the phrase. The Icelandic *bord* meant the side of a ship; so also, did the word in Celtic, and the Anglo-Saxon *bord* was the side of a ship as well as a plank. The primitive dug-out was a log scooped out by hacking and burning, thus leaving a curved " bord " on each side, and though a vessel is now built of iron we still " go aboard."

Boatswain. Taught by the poets, we generally associate something pastoral and idyllic with the word " swain "—those over-quoted lines beginning " My name is Norval " go on to describe the " frugal swain " whose constant cares were to increase his flocks and keep his only son at home. But the burly seaman whom we picture as the boatswain, hard of feature and bronzed with ocean's sun and wind, whose office it is to call the crew to their duty with his silver whistle, does not seem appropriate as a " swain." Yet that is just what he is—the " swain " of a boat; for " swain " is but the Anglo-Saxon *swan*, a servant, a lad; the word probably coming from the same root as " son."

Bob. To move up and down in a short, jerking manner; anything that moves with a bob or swing. The word is of some interest if only because of its uncertain etymology. By many it is supposed to be an imitative sound, but Skeat puts it as an altered form of the Gaelic *bog*, to wag, to shake, while Mahn connects it with the English *buff* (*buffet*), to strike. It has also the signification of cut or shortened, as in " bob-wig," a short wig, and in " bob-tail," a cut or shortened tail. In bell-ringing we have " bob-minor " (less) rung on six bells; " bob-major " (greater) on eight bells; " bob-royal " on ten bells; and " bob-maximus " (greatest) on twelve bells. It may be that the term " bob " in these instances refers to the swing of the bells as they are rung. " Bob " as the slang term for a shilling is well known; it has been suggested that it took its name from Sir Robert Walpole, as " joey " (a fourpenny-piece) did from Joseph Hume, the M.P.

Boiling. We are so familiar with the figure 212⁰ Farenheit as the boiling-point of water that we are apt to forget that, as it depends on the pressure of the atmosphere, it is not the same in all parts of the globe. It is at sea level that boiling-point is 212⁰F., but on Mount St. Bernard, for instance, which is some 8,600 feet high, it would be less than 200⁰F., it being lowered 1⁰ by an ascent of every 597 feet.

Bonfire. If the opinion of so high an authority as Skeat be accepted, the etymology of this word is more nearly connected with Protestantism than is generally admitted. He considers that it is formed from the English *bone* and *fire*, and that it originally had reference to the burning of ecclesiastical relics in the time of Henry VIII. Certainly the derivations *baun* (as Scandinavian for beacon) and *bon* (French for good) do not appear to be adequately supported.

Bonnet. There seems to be little doubt that this word originally denoted the stuff of which a man's head-dress was made before the introduction of hats, and according to Skeat it may be connected with the Hindustani *banat*, woollen cloth, though it does not seem possible to trace the derivation of the word with any certainty. The " bonnets " mentioned in the Bible (Ex. xxix. 9; Lev. viii. 13, etc.) are the round mitres of the Jewish priest, and the same word (*migbaah*) is translated mitre in Ex. xxviii. 4 & 39.

Book. The word is derived from the Anglo-Saxon *bok*, a beech tree, the smooth, silvery bark of which was a natural roll of parchment easy to write upon. Afterwards, thin pieces of beech-board were used, and in other countries the boards of other trees; but the papyrus so displaced its rivals as to give rise to the word "paper."

Booking-Office. It is extraordinary how a name persists and becomes applied in quite a different sense. This word is an example. It originally denoted an office where a traveller entered his name in a book—perhaps some days in advance—to secure his seat in a coach, and when railways were introduced the name of "booking-office" was retained for the place where tickets were supplied, apparently without any thought of its being quite inapplicable to an office where no "booking" was required. And in the same way we have retained the words "driver" and "guard" for the engineer and conductor of the train, while a railway carriage is still known, technically, as a "coach." Perhaps these verbal anachronisms are but the outcome of the insular conservatism of English-people, for in the United States we find a different nomenclature.

Boomerang. Whilst bows and arrows, spears and slings, are found among the aborigines of widely separated parts of the world, the boomerang is exclusively confined to the blacks of Australia. It is a wonderful weapon, consisting of a piece of hard wood in the curve of a parabola, about two feet long and two-and-a-half inches broad, one side being flat and the other rounded and brought to a blunt edge. It is thrown by one end, the convex being forward and the flat side upward, and after advancing some distance, ascending slowly with a quick rotatory movement, it begins to come back, and finally falls to the ground behind the thrower. It is truly remarkable that a race whose characteristics are an abnormally thick skull, receding forehead and a small cerebral capacity should alone, among all the tribes of the world, have invented so marvellous a weapon, for it may safely be said that we have no proof that any other race ever knew of such an implement. The name is the native word.

Bore. A tidal wave which rushes up the mouths of certain rivers, taking the form of a vast stream of water borne up by the impetus of its own velocity many feet above the surface of the river up which it travels. It occurs on the Ganges and the Indus, and is especially wonderful, according to some accounts, on the Sittang, between Rangoon and Moulmein in the Eastern Peninsula. In England we occasionally have a good example on the Severn: the Spring tides from the Atlantic, coming up the Bristol Channel and being narrowed by the funnel-shaped estuary of the Severn, rise into a bore which sometimes attains a considerable height, and has been known to run up the river as far as Gloucester. It is curious to observe how the idea of being borne up or lifted, which is the peculiar character of the " bore," is signified in the derivation of the word—the Icelandic *bara*, a wave, connected with the Anglo-Saxon *beoran*, to bear or lift.

Borstal. To a lover of the English South Downs there is a wealth of beauty conjured up by this one word —a narrow, winding lane, high-banked from centuries' use, with a profusion of wild flowers topped by untrimmed hedges, and climbing up aslant the foot of the hill until, suddenly, it emerges upon the free and open downs in all their rich untrammelled wildness. Such is a typical borstal of the Sussex downs, where the word is in common use, handed down from the Anglo-Saxon *beorh*, a hill, and *stigel*, a stile, a step; akin to the German *steigen*, to mount.

Bosh. The word is simply Turkish, signifying empty, vain, useless—hence, nonsense. It appears to have come into popularity in England about 1824, through James Morier's " Adventures of Hajji Baba of Ispahan," a Persian romance.

Bottle.   This is a word which is found in Anglo-Saxon place-names, though not of frequent occurrence. It is derived from the Teutonic *botl*, a house, a dwelling, from *bytlian*, to build. New-bottle, the new dwelling, and Wall-bottle, the dwelling near the wall (the wall of Hadrian, which ran from Newcastle to Carlisle) are examples.

Boycott.   An example of a recently coined word, remarkable for its speedy and general acceptance. To " boycott " a person is to refuse to have any transactions with him—nobody may work for him, nobody may buy anything from him, nobody may sell anything to him.   The word arose during the Irish agrarian troubles of 1880-1, from the case of Captain Boycott, Lord Erne's land agent in Mayo, who, for declining to accept rents at the reductions named by the tenants, became the first victim of the system and could obtain no labour to gather in the crops.   In retaliation fifty Orangemen from the North of Ireland organised themselves into a relief band and, under the protection of 900 soldiers, gathered in the crops, bringing Captain Boycott away into a place of safety.

Brahmin.   A member of the sacred caste of the Hindus.   The word is derived from the deity Brahma, the first person of the Hindu Trinity, the others being Vishnu and Siva.   The Brahmins are of the Aryan race, the conquerors of India, and are the first of the four leading castes—Priests, Warriors, Merchants and Labourers.   They are highly intellectual, and having great mental subtlety are admirably adapted for metaphysical speculations and mathematical reasoning, but they care little for natural science.   The Brahmin literature is vast and ancient, and the Rig-Veda, containing 1,017 hymns to the gods, is probably one of the oldest books in the world—Dr. Hang of the Sanscrit College at Poonah, computes it to date from 2,400 to 2,000 B.C.

Brass. The etymology of the word is extremely doubtful—Skeat says that it is from the Icelandic *brassa*, to harden by fire. The metal is an alloy of copper and zinc and is of very ancient discovery—Assyriologists believe it to be mentioned in the cuneiform inscriptions of both Assyria and Chaldea. In the Bible the Hebrew word translated " brass " merely denotes a shining metal, and it is evident from the passages in Deut. viii. 9, and xxxiii. 25, that it was dug out of the hills and molten out of stone, which is impossible with an artificial alloy such as brass. Most probably the metal referred to was copper.

Bread. An Anglo-Saxon word—one of those which have come down to us unaltered, except that it was sometimes spelt *breod*. Its meaning, of course, extends to food in general and to the common necessaries of life—as in " Give us this day our daily bread "—and there are many articles from which bread is made. In England it is almost exclusively made of wheat, but on the Continent rye is largely used, and in India and China millet is a main ingredient, while peas, beans and other seeds are frequently turned to account. The Cassava cake of South America is an unfermented bread made from tapioca, and there are the maize cakes of the United States and the oat cakes of Scotland. The making of bread into loaves, instead of flat cakes, seems to have come to Europe comparatively recently. Even in the beginning of the 19th century loaf-bread was almost unknown in many parts of the Continent, and it is reported that in 1812, when an English captain had ordered loaves to the value of £1 in Gothenburg, the baker stipulated for payment in advance, on the ground that he would be unable to sell the loaves in the city if they were left on his hands.

Buccaneer. Most of us have a sort of admiration for the Buccaneers, and though their acts were sometimes disgraced by atrocities there was really some

D

justification for their piratical methods, for when Pope Alexander VI. ceded to Spain all lands which might be discovered west of the Azores, the Spaniards assumed the ownership of the whole of the New World and endeavoured to seize and put to death all interlopers. England and France naturally objected to this and claimed liberty to push their fortunes within the prohibited regions. Hence a guerilla sea-war was established, which lasted throughout the 16th and 17th centuries. The origin of the word " buccaneer " is curious ; it comes from the Caribbee Indian *boucan*, the name for smoked meat, and as the pirates copied this manner of preserving food they were called " buccaneers."

Buckram. A coarse cloth stiffened with dressing. The name is probably a survival from the time when leather suits were common wear, as the word " buckram " appears to be derived from the Old French *boqueran*, goat-skin, through the Old German *boc*, a goat. Leather suits were worn as late as the 17th century—George Fox, the Quaker, wore one.

Buddha. The name comes from the Pali word *buddho* (or *booddho*) meaning enlightened, wise, and may be used of any great religious teacher—there were many such before the appearance of Gautama, to whom we apply the name. The tradition is that when no Buddha is on earth true religion decays, but is revived when a new Buddha arises. The Buddha who is generally referred to under that name was a distinguished prince of Aryan descent, the son of a king, of the class of the Gautamas, ruling an old Hindu kingdom at the foot of the Nepaulese mountains, some 100 miles north of Benares. As an Aryan the prince was taught to look with contempt upon the Turanian inhabitants and to keep his caste pure, but Buddha, with his wide-reaching human sympathies, broke through this restraint and preached the equality of races.

He is supposed to have been born B.C. 622, to have attained as Buddha in 580, and to have died in 543. Though deified by his admiring followers he himself never claimed divine honours. Buddhism was dominant in India for more than 1,000 years, but when it became corrupt Brahminism prevailed over it and almost extinguished it on the Indian continent, though it continues to hold its own in Ceylon, Burmah and Thibet.

Budget. In former days the budget was literally a sack full of money, the various sums appropriated to specific purposes being sorted into little bags. And the word "budget" is derived from the Latin *bulga*, a bag, coming to us from the French *bouge* and its diminutive *bougette*, a pouch.

Bugle. The word is a contraction of "bugle-horn," the instrument being originally made from the horn of a kind of wild ox called a bugle. "Some call it a bugill and describe it to be like an oxe," writes an old author. The word is derived from the Latin *buculus*, the diminutive of *bos*, an ox.

Bulletin. A short announcement made under authority, as its derivation implies, the word being the diminutive of "bull," an edict issued by the Pope. And the Pope's edict gained its name of "bull" from the Latin *bulla*, a seal—the little round knob of lead attached to the document—which, in its turn, gave rise to our word "bullet."

Bureau. Originally an office in which was a table covered with red cloth, the word coming, through the French, from the Latin *burrus*, dark-red. And, curiously enough, the expression "red tape" has become a synonym for excessive bureaucracy.

Burgh, Bury, Borough. These and similar terminations in place-names are derived from the Anglo-Saxon *burh*, *buruh*, and *byrig*, an earthwork, and hence a fortified town. Sometimes they denote the resting-place—often a funeral mound—where lay the remains of the dead, but more frequently they indicate the embanked enclosure which afforded refuge to the living. *Burgh, brough* and *borough* are Norse forms, while *bury* is distinctively Saxon. Examples are too numerous to quote.

Burn. A suffix of frequent occurrence in place-names, being the northern English and Scotch for a brook (Anglo-Saxon *burna*). Examples may be found in Black-burn, East-bourne, Ty-burn, and Burn-foot.

Bursar. A paymaster, one who keeps the purse, from the Latin *bursa*, a purse; Greek *byrsē*, skin or leather. Hence the French " Bourse " (Stock Exchange). To " disburse " is to take from the purse.

Butler. The man who has charge of the wine; anciently, the cup-bearer. " He restored the chief butler unto his butlership again, and he gave the cup into Pharaoh's hand." (Gen. xl. 21). The word comes to us from the French *bouteille*, a bottle; and from the French *botte*, a leather bottle, we get the " butt " of wine, and also " boot "; hence the familiar sign for an inn—" The Boot "— a corruption of *botte*.

By. A place-name suffix common to both Norwegian and Danish settlements in England and, within a certain region, very numerous. Northward there are some 600 instances—in Lincolnshire alone there are 100—but Southward there is scarcely one. The Scandinavian *by* means an abode or a single farm, and hence it came to denote a village. As a component part of English place-names it is a survival of the Danish conquest, and there is documentary evidence that the Saxon names of some places were changed by the Danish invaders; as, for instance, Derby, which, by the Saxons, was called Northweorthig (or Norworth, as it might now be written), while the Saxon Streoneshalch became the Danish Whitby.

By Hook or by Crook. By one means or another— probably a shepherd's phrase. Rather than lose a stray sheep he will make use of a hook cut from the hedge if he has not his crook with him. Spencer uses the expression in his "Faerie Queene."

By-Law. A by-law is not a law which goes by or beside the law, nor a law which has been allowed inadvertently, as a "bye" in cricket. The prefix is the Danish *by*, a town (as Whit*by*) and a by-law is one which is enacted by a township or corporation. But a bye-election means an extra election, and a bye-path is a side path.

Cab. An abbreviation of the French word *cabriolet*, which is the diminutive of *cabriole*, signifying a caper, a leap, and derived, in its turn, from the Italian *caprio*, a wild goat. The carriage apparently gained its name because of its lightness and easy running. The "cabriolet" was introduced as a public vehicle on 23rd April, 1823, "in honour of His Majesty's birthday," and it is noted as a matter of congratulation that "the fares are one third less than hackney coaches." The name must soon have become shortened into "cab," for we find Macaulay writing to his sister that on leaving the House he "called a cabriolet," and yet, only about two months later, he speaks of having "called a cab."

Cabal. The word is one of those which has degenerated in meaning, as originally it merely denoted a number of persons united for some purpose—the German *cabala* and the French *cabale* may be translated "club" or "society." Its present signification of intrigue and secret machination is accounted for by Macaulay as follows :—" During some years the word ' cabal ' was popularly used as synonymous with ' cabinet,' but it happened . . . that in 1671 the Cabinet consisted of five persons the initial letters of whose names made up the word ' cabal '—Clifford, Arlington, Buckingham, Ashley, and Lauderdale. These ministers were therefore emphatically called the 'Cabal,' and they soon made the appellation so infamous that it has never since their time been used except as a term of reproach.'' Perhaps, however, this reproach may now be wiped away, for in 1910 a representative Conference assembled which, by a curious coincidence, and from the same cause as the above, may be called the '' Cabal.'' The statesmen of whom this Conference was composed number eight, viz. :—Asquith, Balfour, Birrell, Lord Cawdor, Chamberlain, Lord Crewe, Lloyd George, and Lord Lansdowne, but, as may be seen, the initials of their names are four only— c-a-b-l (Cab'l).

Cabinet. Using the word in its political sense, the '' Cabinet '' is one of the many excellent anomalies of the English Constitution, and few things in our history are more curious than its origin and growth. From the earliest times the king was assisted in his government by a Privy Council, whose advice was sought and, more or less, acted upon in the gravest and most delicate affairs of state. But with the gradual increase of the demo-cratic character of Parliament the real government of the nation became more and more vested in the king's Parliamentary Ministers, while coincident with this the rank of Privy Councillor came to be bestowed as an honorary distinction on men to whom nothing was confided. As a result, the Sovereign resorted for advice on the most im-portant questions to his principal Ministers, and hence, although theoretically the Cabinet is still a Committee of the Privy Council it has come to consist, in reality, of the leading Parliamentary Ministers of the party in power. The origin of this signification of the word is obvious. '' Cabinet '' is the French for a little room, the diminutive of *cabane*, a hut—we retain the earlier meaning in our '' cabin ''—and when the king desired to confer with certain of his Ministers apart from the rest of his Council he would naturally take them into his private room, his " cabinet."

Cable. Literally that which ties or holds anything, from the Latin *capere*, to hold, and *caplum*, a halter. A ship's cable must be at least ten inches in circumference—a less thick rope is called a hawser. The word is also used as a nautical measure, viz. :—120 fathoms or 720 feet, by which distances of ships in a fleet are frequently estimated. And from the wire rope or cable used for submarine telegraphs we have made the word " cable " into a verb signifying to transmit by submarine telegraph, and have coined " cablegram " (an unscholarly mixture of English and Greek) to denote a message so sent.

Cadaverous. It is very doubtful whether the full force of this word is popularly recognised. Literally it means " corpse-like," its derivation being the Latin *cadaver*, a corpse.

Caddy. Among the reminiscences of childhood, some fifty years ago, is the highly prized tea-caddy, the contents of which were so jealously guarded and so carefully used—for good tea was then an expensive luxury. For such an esteemed possession to be brought into the category of prosaic weights and measures seem almost sacrilegious, yet the word " caddy " is merely a corruption of the Malay *kati*, a weight equal to about one and one-third of a pound avoirdupois.

Cadet. The word is chiefly applied to a student in a military academy, but formerly it denoted a volunteer in the army who served on the chance of gaining an officer's commission. It comes from the French *cadet*, a younger brother, through the Latin *capitulum*, a little head, and in this sense we apply it to the younger brother or youngest son of a family. The slang term " cad " is usually supposed to be a contraction of " cadet," but the

Slang Dictionary gives it as a shortened form of "cadger," a beggar, a mean fellow, and suggests that "cadger" is derived from the Old Cant "cager" or "gager," a man.

Caer, Cader, Caher. All these syllables are of frequent occurrence in place-names throughout Great Britain. The first two are of Welsh origin, the last Irish, and they are closely related to the Latin *castra*, a castle. They denote a fortified enclosure, and examples are found in Caer-narvon, Car-lisle, Cader-Idris, and Caher (Ireland).

Caitiff. The derivation of this word—the Latin *captivus*, a captive, from *capere*, to take—indicates that its present signification of a mean and cowardly fellow was not always implied, and in Wickliffe's Bible—in the passage of Col. iv. 10, where Paul conveys the salutation of Aristarchus, his fellow-prisoner—the word "prisoner" is rendered "caytyff." But Shakespeare, writing some two hundred years later, calls Cassio, in "Othello," "the pernicious caitiff," showing the extent to which the word, in that time, had degenerated in meaning.

Cajole. To bear in mind the derivation of this word certainly enables us to read a fuller meaning into it. It comes to us from the Old French *cage-oler*, to chatter like a bird in a cage, the Old French *cage* being synonymous with our English "cage."

Cake. Whether the cake be rich or plain, compounded of all luscious dainties or merely the simple flour and water of the girdle-cake, the name is not misapplied, for all have one characteristic in common—they are *cooked!* And the derivation of the word "cake" is the Latin *coquere*, to cook.

Calamity. No doubt our word is a lineal descendant of the Latin *calamitas*, but what may be the origin of the Latin word is very doubtful. By some it is connected with *calamus*, a reed, a stalk, and Bacon writes :—" Another ill accident is drought and the spindling of the corn, which with us is rare but in hotter countries common; insomuch that the word ' calamity ' was first derived from *calamous* when the corn could not get out of the stalk.''

Calceolaria. A plant whose bright blooms, lasting all through the summer, must be a familiar sight to all of us, and the peculiar shape of each blossom must often have been noted as bearing a close resemblance to a little shoe. And that is just what the name means—like a little shoe—from the Latin *calceolus*, the diminutive of *calceus*, a shoe.

Calculation. When we think of the abstruse problems that are solved by means of mathematics, the marvellous discoveries in astronomy, for instance, which mathematical calculations have enabled men to make—such as the simultaneous recognition of Neptune as a planet by Adams and Le Verrier—it is almost inconceivable (though most encouraging for the future progress of mankind) how crude and apparently foolish were the methods of reckoning in barbaric times, which yet were the origin of all arithmetical and mathematical knowledge. And the derivation of the word '' calculation '' enables us to realise this, for the Latin *calculatus* is the past participle of *calculare*, to reckon by means of small stones or pebbles, a method still the use among some uncivilised tribes as an aid in counting. Indeed, in a sense, we are still dependent upon the pebble as a means of calculation, for the integral calculus, invented by Newton, the formula of which enables mathematicians to grasp ideas formerly beyond their reach, has been appropriately called '' the mathematician's pebble.''

Calendar. The word comes to us through the Latin *calendarium*, an account-book kept by money lenders to show the interest which fell due to them, from month to month, on the calends—the first day of each month. The calends gained their name from the Latin *calare*, to call, because the beginning of the month was proclaimed; and in numbering the day of the month the Romans counted backwards—such and such a day in June, for instance, being reckoned as so many days before the calends of July. The expression " the Greek calends "—signifying a time which will never arise—is justified by the fact that the Greeks did not use the term calends. The word " calender," when applied as in Cowper's " John Gilpin "—

> " And my good friend the calender
> Will lend his horse to go "—

and meaning one whose business it is to calender cloth, should be spelt " calendrer," though the verb " calender " is itself a corruption of " cylinder," as it means to roll or smooth out cloth with cylindrical rollers. The " calender " of the " Arabian Nights " has no connection with either " calender " or " calendrer "—the word is taken from the Hindustani *galandar*, and signifies one who belongs to a certain order of dervishes among the Mahommedans.

Callous. As in many cases, the derivation of the word lends facility to a recognition of its full meaning. It comes through the Latin *callosus*, from *callus*, a hard skin; and the appropriateness of the word as indicating insensibility of feeling is obvious when we call to mind how the sense of touch—in the finger-tips, for instance—may be lessened by any thickening or hardening of the skin.

Caller. Although this word is omitted from many English dictionaries as being exclusively Scotch, it is common enough in England by reason of its introduction into songs, novels, etc.—in the " Caller Herrin," for instance, which Antoinette Stirling made so popular by her wonderful singing, and in Sir Walter Scott's " Antiquary." Its meaning is cool, fresh; and we find a similar word in the Icelandic *kaldr*.

Calm. To possess peace and serenity of mind is an inestimable boon, and must tend to health and longevity in these days of stress and struggle, if not to worldly success. But how to obtain a calm frame of mind it is not easy to determine, and it may seem preposterous to look to the derivation of a word for any indication of the point. Yet it is worthy of note that the derivation of the word "calm," which is the Provencal *chaume*, a resting time for flocks, from the Low Latin *cauma*, the heat of the sun, through the Greek *kauma*, noonday heat, suggests that the radical meaning of the word is a rest during the heat of the day !

Calomel. The derivation of this word appears to be the Greek *kalos*, fair, beautiful, and *melas*, black, and the name being originally applied to the black sulphuret of mercury it was quite appropriate. But the "calomel" of the British Pharmacopœia is the chloride of mercury, which is of a dull, white colour, and its claim to the designation "calomel" is inexplicable, unless the following extract from a medical dictionary be accepted as accurate :—" It (the name 'calomel') was applied in joke by Sir Theohore Mayerne to the chloride of mercury in honour of a favourite negro servant whom he employed to prepare it. As calomel is a white powder the name is merely a jocular misnomer."

Calvary. Of the four accounts of the Crucifixion given in the Authorised Version of our Bible it is only in one (Luke xxiii. 33) that we have the word "Calvary"; in the other three (Matt. xxvii. 33, Mark xv. 22, John xix. 17) the word "Golgotha" is used. Both words have the same meaning--the place of a skull; "Golgotha" being the Hebrew (Aramaic) *Gogoltha*, while "Calvary" is the Anglicised form of the Vulgate *Calvaria*, from the Latin *calva*, a bald scalp.

Cam. This word is a component in many names of rivers, as it means crooked. It is of Celtic origin and seems to have been adopted, at one time, into the English language—(*see* A-KIMBO). Examples of its use in river-names may be found in the Cam, the Cam-il or Cam-el (Cornwall), and the Cambeck (Cumberland).

Camellia. This beautiful plant is one of a species of evergreen shrubs which are natives of China and Japan, and its broad, shining, laurel-like leaves, with its glorious white or red blossoms have made it a well-deserved favourite. Its Latinised name, Camellus, was given by Linnæus in honour of George Joseph Kamel, a Moravian Jesuit, who travelled in Asia and the Philippine Islands collecting plants. It is generally believed to have been introduced into our gardens, from China, in 1739, though it has been asserted that Lord Petrie brought it to England previous to that date.

Canary. The canary-bird appears to have been so named because, when first introduced as a singing cage-bird, it was brought from the Canary Islands, and the wine called " Canary "—the Sack upon whose excellent " two-fold operation " Falstaff so feelingly dilates—gained its name for the same reason. But how did the Canary Islands get their name? There is good ground for supposing that the islands were known to the Phœnicians, but the name comes from the Romans, who in the time of Augustus received an account of them which has been preserved to us by the elder Pliny. He mentions " Canaria, so called from the multitude of dogs of great size " which were found there; the word " Canaria " being derived from the Latin *canis*, a dog.

Candid. The word is now seldom used except in its figurative sense of fair, open, ingenuous; but its literal meaning is white and shining, from the Latin *candidus*, white, and *candēre*, to shine. The word " candidate " has the same derivation, from the fact that those who sought office in ancient

Rome vested themselves in white togas—a symbol, presumably, of their immaculate intentions—and our common-place " candle " comes of the same origin—*candēre*, to shine, to glow.

Cannibal. The word appears to have come into use about the close of the fifteenth century and is generally considered to be a corruption of " Caribal," a Carib. Its present spelling has doubtless been influenced by the Latin *canis*, a dog, canine (dog-like) being in some measure descriptive of the revolting practice of cannibalism.

Cancel. The etymological meaning of this word is to obliterate by drawing lines across diagonally in two opposite directions—in lattice form; the derivation being the Latin *cancelli*, lattice-work, *cancellus*, a grating. (*See* CHANCELLOR.)

Canon—Cannon. The meaning of the word when spelt without the double " n " is, in general terms, rule and law, decree and ordinance. There is the " Canon " the Church dignitary, bound by the ordinance of the Chapter to which he belongs; the " canon " of Holy Scripture, those writings which have been included in the Bible by the decree of the Church Councils; the " canon " which is the accepted standard in literature, art, good taste, etc. All such applications of the word are true to its origin—the Greek *kanon*, a straight rod or a rule, by which guidance may be obtained. But it is curious to note that the word " cannon " (spelt *with* the double " n ") has the same derivation, and Skeat offers the opinion that this spelling may have been adopted to create a distinction between the two uses of the word. In confirmation of this view it has been stated that the name Cannon Street, in London, has reference to the Cathedral Chapter of St. Paul's and therefore is an indication of the original identity of the two words " cannon " and " canon," but it is more probable that Cannon Street is a corruption of the old

Candlewick Street, which may be paraphrased as the-Street-where-the-Candle-stands, *wick* being the Anglo-Saxon for station or abode.

Cardinal. We use this word as an adjective to denote that on which a matter hinges or depends, and its application in this sense is fully warranted by its derivation—the Latin *cardo* (*cardinis*), a hinge. But when we use the word as a substantive denoting a dignitary of the Roman Catholic Church its applicability is not so evident. Trench, however, has elucidated the difficulty for us, as the following extract shows :—" A letter professing to have been penned by Pope Anacletus I. in the first century, but in reality forged in the ninth, says—' The Apostolic chair has been constituted by the Lord the hinge and head of all the Churches; and as a door is controlled by its hinge, so all Churches are governed by this Holy Chair.' Pope Leo IX. points out the relation in which the word " cardinal " stood to the idea of a hinge—' The clerics of the supreme Chair are called Cardinals as undoubtedly moving more nearly to that hinge by which all things are moved.' " Cardinals hold the highest rank in the Roman Catholic Church under the Pope; they are seventy in number, in allusion to the seventy disciples sent out by Christ, and they have the right of electing the Pope. Their dress is a red cassock, a rochet, a short purple mantle, and a red hat—to show that they should be ready to shed their blood for the Holy See.

Care will kill a Cat. The phrase is used by George Wither (1588-1667) in his " Poem on Christmas " :
> " Hang sorrow ! care will kill a cat,
> And therefore let's be merry."

Carouse. Some significance may be found in the derivation of this word. It comes to us through the Old French *carous*, from the German *gar-aus*, quite out, empty. The implication of drained glasses and no " heel-taps " is obvious.

Carrick, Carreg. These two words often enter into place-names. The first is Gaelic, the latter Welsh, and both signify a cliff, a crag, a rock. Examples are found in Carrick-fergus and Cerrig-y-Druidion.

Casement. It may be interesting to note that though this word is sometimes used as if it were equivalent to " window," it properly denotes that small portion of an old-fashioned window which opens like a door on hinges attached to one of its upright sides, the rest of the window being fixed. Such " casements " may still be seen in country cottages, and appear to be survivals of a time when the inmates' main endeavour was to keep warm, even to the exclusion of fresh air. The derivation of " casement " gives point to the truth of the word's restricted meaning : it is an abbreviation of " encasement," signifying something framed or cased in.

Cash. The word is one of those which has gradually acquired a change of meaning. Originally " cash " (Old French *casse*) was a case or box in which money was kept, and by its particular use the " case " gave its name to the contents—" cash." It may be well to point out that there is a difference between "cash" and "money"; money is anything which serves as a circulating medium ; cash, in its strict sense, is coin only. All cash is money, but all money is not cash.

Cat's-cradle. (*See* SCRATCH-CRADLE.)

Cauldron (or **Caldron**). An appropriate name—for the word simply means a heater, from the Latin *caldarium*, derived from *calidus*, hot.

Caulk. Of course the practice of caulking—the hammering of oakum, untwisted rope, or some like substance, into the seams of a ship, so as to make it watertight—must be of very early date, and in this connection it is noteworthy that the word itself, in almost its present form, is to be found in the Gaelic *calc*, and in the Old French *cauquer*. Usually, however, the derivation of the word is referred to the Latin *calcare*, to press down, to tread in, from *calx* (*calcis*), the heel.

Ceiling. Although most of us live in houses which have ceilings to their rooms, we are not accustomed to view our apartments as celestial abodes —perhaps it would be better for us if we could— and yet both the words " ceiling " and " celestial " are derived from the same word—the Latin *coelum*, heaven !

Caviare. The use of this word in the figurative sense, as something too fine for the vulgar taste, must be of many years standing. Shakespeare puts it into the mouth of Hamlet (Act ii. sc. 2)—" The play, I remember, pleased not the million; 'twas *caviare* to the general."

Celluloid. (*See* XYLONITE.)

Cemetery. Literally, a sleeping-place, from the Greek *koimeterion*—*koimao*, lull to sleep.

Censure. The derivation in this case is the Latin *censēre*, to value, to judge, and bearing in mind that origin of the word one must endorse the opinion expressed in the following passage :—" It is not creditable to man's candour in judging of others that the word ' censure ' in process of time became limited to the pronouncing of unfavourable judgments, these having from the first been so much more numerous than favourable verdicts that the word ' censure ' ceased to be applied to the latter at all."

Centre. As the dictionaries tell us that the derivation of this word is the Greek *kentron*, a sharp point, we are naturally reminded of that first definition in Euclid—" A point is that which hath no parts and no magnitude." Accepting that definition of a point as applicable to a " centre "—for a point is certainly the " centre " of a circle—we are reduced to the conclusion that there is no explanation of a " centre," as Euclid's definition is, after all, what " The New World " calls "make-believe"—it tells us what a point *is* by telling us what it is *not!*

Chancellor. That even the name of so exalted an official as a Chancellor—The Lord High Chancellor, to give his title in full—should have any connection with so paltry a thing as a lattice-fence seems inconceivable, and yet, as in the case of " cancel " (q.v.) the derivation of the word is the Latin *cancelli*, lattice-work; *cancellus* a grating. The application of the name and the gradual evolution of the office came about thus :—Originally, in the Roman Empire, a " chancellor " was a petty officer stationed at the fence of bars or lattice-work in a law-court, to introduce such functionaries as were entitled to pass inside. The Emperor Carinus, the immediate predecessor of Diocletian, gave great offence by making such a " chancellor " a prefect of Rome. Later, in the Eastern Empire, a " Chancellor " was a secretary who sat *inside* the lattice-work to write, who also became invested with judicial functions and ultimately with a superintendence over the other officers of the Empire. From this high dignity to that of a modern English Lord Chancellor the transition is easy. But it is curious that throughout this process of evolution the appellation gained from the fact that the original station of office was contiguous to the lattice-bars of the court should have persisted to the present day.

Chapel. The word denotes a place of worship subordinate to or lesser than a regular church, or one which is attached to a palace or private dwelling. Probably, however, its most frequent present use is to indicate a place of worship for Dissenters, and in this connection it is interesting to note that the word, at one time, meant a Sanctuary containing Relics! For its derivation is the Latin *capella*,

E

the diminutive of *capa*, a cloak or cope, and Littré's account is that a small cope (Latin, *capella*) was kept in the palaces of kings on which to administer oaths, that the name "capella" was transferred to the Sanctuary where the "capella" was kept, and hence to any Sanctuary containing Relics. Skeat confirms this, and states that the "capella" was originally a Sanctuary in which the cope of St. Martin was preserved, and that the word "capella" thus came to signify any Sanctuary; while our "chapel" is the descendant of the Low Latin *capella*, through the Old French *capele* and the modern French *chapelle*.

Charcoal—Charwoman. By analogy one might imagine that as the word "char-coal" signifies coal made by charred or burnt wood, there must be some implication of burning in the word "charwoman." And however absurd this may appear at first sight we find that, as a matter of fact, the word "char"—according to Skeat—has really the same meaning in each case. Charcoal is so named because, by the process of burning, wood is *turned* into coal; and a charwoman is so called because she does a *turn* of work; the word "char" in Anglo-Saxon and in many Teutonic languages signifying a turn, a turning about, a period.

Chaste as Ice. For this luminous phrase we are indebted, as for many another, to Shakespeare. It appears in Hamlet's conversation with Ophelia (Act iii. sc. 1)—"Be thou as chaste as ice, as pure as snow, thou shalt not escape calumny."

Cheap. The word comes from the Anglo-Saxon *ceapian*, to buy, and *ceap*, price, and to this root may be traced many idiomatic English words and also many place-names which indicate early seats of commercial activity. For instance, a "chapman" is an itinerant seller, and the slang term "chap" was originally an abbreviated form of "chapman," while the sense of bargaining—the old method of making a purchase—is preserved in the word "chaffer." To "chop and change" is to sell and barter, and when we say the wind "chops" from one quarter to another we mean that it changes. In place-names the occurrence of "cheap" and its synonym "chipping" is very frequent. Examples appear in Cheap-side, and East-cheap (which were the old market places of London), Chipping Norton, Chipping Barnet, Chipping Ongar; while Chep-stow and Chip-ping-ham are ancient market towns of much greater importance, relatively, than they are at present. The ultimate root of the word "cheap" is the Sanscrit *kupa*, the beam of a balance.

Chester. The word comes from the Latin *castra*, a camp, and appears under various forms in many place-names. For instance :—Chester, Doncaster, Leicester.

Chess. While there can be no doubt of the great antiquity of the game there is reason to believe that its age has often been much exaggerated. It has been stated that modern chess was played in Hindustan 5,000 years ago, but Van der Linde, in his work published in Berlin in 1874—which is probably the best authority on the origin of the game—inclines to the opinion, after eliminating all that cannot be proved, that the game originated with the Buddhists in India not earlier than the third century of our era. It seems to be agreed that the word "chess" may be traced back to the Hindustani *chaturanga*, *i.e.*, the four *angas*, or members of an army, viz. :—elephants, horses, chariots, and foot-soldiers. This word was corrupted by the Persians into *chatrang*, and by the Arabs into *shatrang*, from which came the still further corruption of the Old French *eschecs* and our "checks," from which latter we have "chess." The names "rook" and "pawn" (two of the six classes of pieces with which modern chess is played) are both of Hindu origin, " rook " being the Hindu *rat'h*, an armed chariot, and " pawn " the Hindu *peon*, an attendant.   The generally accepted derivation of " check-mate "—the final move which decides the victory in the game—is the Persian *shah mat*, which signifies " the king is dead "; but the connection between " shah " and " check " is not very obvious, though it is supposed to be traced through the Arabic to the Old French *eschec*.

Chiltern Hundreds. We are so accustomed to think of the Chiltern Hundreds in connection with Parliamentary procedure that it comes as almost a surprise to find that there really is such a district as Chiltern.   The name belongs to a small range of beech-covered hills in Buckinghamshire, the property of the Crown and formerly the resort of bands of robbers.   To keep these robbers in check a functionary was appointed whose title was Steward of the Chiltern Hundreds, but whose duties have long ceased to be more than nominal. The office, however, has been retained to the present day, in order that a means may be available for a Member of Parliament to retire from his seat. For as no Member is at liberty to resign, it is necessary to provide an expedient whereby he may legally vacate his seat, and in the office of Steward of the Chiltern Hundreds such a method is found, seeing that the tenure of any office of profit under the Crown disqualifies for the privilege of a seat in Parliament.   The Member, therefore, who desires to retire applies for and is given the Stewardship of the Chiltern Hundreds.

Chintz. The derivation of this word carries us back many years, long before the time of Queen Anne, when the material was a favourite in this country. The word comes from the Hindu *chhint*, a spotted cotton cloth, and is derived from the Hindu *chhinta*, a spot, and *chhintna*, to sprinkle.   The chintzes of the Coromandel Coast were celebrated in the time of Marco Polo, in the thirteenth century, and are mentioned as being " admirably painted . . . held in the highest estimation " by Odoardo Barbosa, a Portuguese who visited India in the early part of the sixteenth century.

Chord—Cord. These two words are essentially the same, both being derived from the Greek *chordē*, which signifies an intestine from which musical strings are made. It may be interesting to note that the silent " h " (the relic of the Greek letter " ch ") is retained when the word is applied to music—its primitive sphere—as in the words " common chord," " harmonic chord," etc., but that when the word is used to indicate the material thing—a piece of string—the " h " is dropped, and we write " cord."

Christmas. The festival is so generally observed in England and has such a hold on the imagination of all English-speaking people that it seems strange to find that St. Augustine, one of the four great fathers of the Church, considered it of lesser authority and later origin than Good Friday, Easter, Ascension and Whitsun—these latter, in his opinion, being the only holy-days which had Apostolic origin and the sanction of the General Council. It is certain that the day for keeping Christmas was not fixed without much contention. Among the dates advocated were the 20th or 21st of April and the 20th May, while the Oriental Christians were generally in favour of the 6th January, and it was Julian, Bishop of Rome (337-352 A.D.) who prescribed the 25th December, a date to which the Eastern Church ultimately assented. The festival being ordained for that time of year afforded a convenient opportunity for making it a substitute for the time of rejoicing which various nations had observed on the passing of the shortest day, and coming to the Roman converts in the place of the Saturnalia to which, as heathens, they had been accustomed, it was soon sullied by

revelry and excess; nor can it be doubted that
many of our Christmas customs are but relics of
older faiths.

Christmas comes but Once a Year. A saying of ancient
date; Thomas Tupper (1523-1580) makes use of it
in his " Five Hundred Points of Good Husbandry " :—

" At Christmas play and make good cheer,
For Christmas comes but once a year."

Cider. If the derivation of its name be any guide to
the quality of an article, cider should be denounced
and echewed by total abstainers. The word comes
to us from the Hebrew *shekar*, through the Greek
sikera and the Latin *sicera*, all signifying strong
drink. In Wickliffe's Bible the passage (Luke i.
15) which appears in the Authorised Version as
" He . . . shall drink neither wine nor strong
drink " is rendered " He schal not drynke wyn
and *sydir* "—showing that in old days the alcoholic
strength of cider was fully recognised. It is stated
by Brande that the weakest cider contains over
5% of alcohol, while the strongest is estimated to
have nearly 10%.

Cinnamon. The use of this substance—the aromatic
bark of a laurel indigenous to Ceylon—is very
ancient. Probably it was imported from Ceylon
by the Phœnicians, and by them distributed
through Palestine. It was one of the ingredients
in the holy oil which Moses made for the anointing
of the Tabernacle and its furniture (Ex. xxx. 22-29)
and it was used for the perfume of beds (Prov. vii.
17). The word comes from the Greek *kinnamon*,
through the Hebrew *qinnamon*.

Cipher. The word comes to us from the Arabic *sifr*,
signifying empty, nothing, and the system of the
Arabic numerals o to 1—or, to put it more
properly, 1 to o—is ascribed to the Arabs, being
probably known to them as early as the ninth
century and introduced into Europe in the 12th

century. But it is now generally acknowledged to have been known in India many years previously, and something very like these numerals can be traced in India as far back as the third century. As yet, however, no proof has been found that a system using the cipher and the present method of placing numerals was employed in India before the sixth century, and the real origin of the system is lost in obscurity. Perhaps it is to Egypt, the cradle of so many sciences, that we must look for the first conception of so excellent a method, compared with which those of Greece and Rome were, indeed, cumbersome and ineffective.

Civilisation. The present signification of the word is of modern use, for the only meaning assigned to it in the edition of Johnson's dictionary published in 1773—the last which received his corrections—is the legal definition, viz. :—that by which a criminal process may become a civil one. The derivation of the word is the Latin *civis*, a citizen—he who by his residence in a city, in close contact with his fellows, is presumed to have attained a higher plane of culture than the isolated dweller in the country. "Civil" has the same derivation, and when applied to a person it bears a similar implication of the person referred to having that good behaviour and consideration for others which should be induced by intercourse with our fellows.

Clachan. The word appears very frequently in Scottish place-names. It is of Gaelic origin and signifies a village, often, also, a church. It is derived from the Gaelic *clach*, a stone.

Clandestine. The etymology in this case is very interesting. The word comes to us from the Latin *clandestinus*, which, according to the suggestion of Skeat, is made up of *clam-dies-tinus*, signifying hidden from daylight, *clam* being equivalent to secretly, from the root *kal*, seen also in *celo*, conceal.

Classic. Although the word is in common use—applied to works of art and literature, for instance—it is not easy to define it precisely. Perhaps the explanation by Trench as to its origin may throw some light on its true meaning. His account may be summarised as follows :—The word is derived from the Latin *classicus*, signifying one belonging to a *classis* or division of the Roman people, and especially to the first division. The Roman citizens were divided into several classes, a man of the highest of all being emphatically called *classicus*, that is, of the class pre-eminently so designated—the highest in the scale.

Claret—Clarify—Clarion. At first sight there does not seem much connection between these three words, and yet the root meaning is the same in all. In each case the derivation is the Latin *clarus*, clear, bright—the claret from the bright-red colour of the wine to which the word was at first applied; the clarion from the clear, bright, penetrating sound which the instrument produces; while to clarify signifies to make clear and bright, to free from darkness and obscurity.

Cleanliness next to Godliness. An aphorism beyond contradiction. John Wesley used it in one of his sermons—that on Dress.

Clerestory. This name is given to the " story " which may often be found immediately *over* the arches of the aisles in cathedrals and large churches. It is fitted with windows to admit the light to the nave, and it is to the fact of its thus admitting light that its name (sometimes spelt " clear-story ") is due. Similarly, the term " blind-story " is applied to the triforium of a church, which is usually dark, being the gallery above the nave but *under* the lean-to roof of the aisles.

Cleave. It may be worth while to point out that there are two distinct meanings to this word, or rather, that we have two different words with the same spelling. The one is derived from the Anglo-Saxon *clifian*, connected with our word "clay," and means to stick, to adhere, to hold fast; while the other comes from the Anglo-Saxon *cleofan* (past tense *cleaf*, past participle *clofen*) and means to split asunder, to cut through. Thus the respective signification of the two words is diametrically opposed, and there is no connection whatever between their derivations. It may be thought that "cleave," in its meaning of adhering to, is practically obsolete, but examples of the use of both the words may be found in the Bible :—" If I do not remember thee, let my tongue cleave to the roof of my mouth " (Ps. cxxxvii. 6). "Cleave to that which is good" (Rom. xii. 9). "He that cleaveth wood shall be endangered thereby " (Eccl. x. 9).

Clever. The doubtful etymology of this word makes it interesting. Wedgwood suggests that the notion of seizing was its derivation, and maintains that the Old English words "cliver" a claw, a clutch, and the verb "clever," to climb, to scramble, were the origin of the adjective "clever," in the sense of snatching up, grasping, attaining—a sense which is certainly appropriate to the present signification of the word. Skeat inclines to the opinion that the word is a modification of the Middle English "deliver," which means nimble, active, and he considers it not unlikely that this modification has been aided by the use of "cliver" and "clever" above indicated.

Clergy—Clerk. The root derivation of these words is the Greek *kleros*, a lot, the application of which apparently lies in the Scriptural ordinance that the Lord was the lot or inheritance of the Levites (Deut. xviii. 2), or because the Church may be esteemed the inheritance of the Lord (1 Peter v. 3). The word "clerk" is not only of the same derivation but originally meant a priest, and it still retains its signification of a clergyman in the phrase " Clerk in Holy Orders."

Clove. We are all familiar with this spice and its aromatic flavour in apple-pie; it is the dried un-expanded flower-bud of the clove-tree, a native of the Moluccas. Surely, too, we must have noticed its likeness to a nail—one of those nails used in gardening—but perhaps without giving a thought to the origin of its name. Yet that resemblance to a nail is the explanation—the word comes from the Latin *clavus*, a nail; it has no connection with that other " clove " which is the past tense of " cleave."

Cluan, Clon. A frequent component in Irish place-names, as in Clunie, Clonmel. The word signifies a meadow.

Club. This word—whether used to denote an association of persons, a heavy stick, a suit of cards, or a deformed foot—is one and the same, the root word in all cases being " clump," which comes from the Old German *klimpfen*, to press together, to clamp. It is true, however, that another derivation of " club " cards is to be found in the French *trefle*, a trefoil, and Carlyle has suggested that the origin of the word " club " when applied to a union of persons may be the German *gelubde*, a sacred vow, but the derivation from " clump " has certainly the best authority and is very suggestive in its application to a knot of men combined together for any purpose.

One of the first clubs founded in London was that established early in the seventeenth century, at the Mermaid Tavern, Friday Street, which included among its members Shakespeare, Sir Walter Raleigh, Beaumont, and Fletcher. Ben Johnson's club was that which met at the Devil Tavern, near Temple Bar.

Coach. The coach, as a vehicle, is believed to have been introduced into England by the Earl of

Arundel, in 1580, but it did not become common till the first decade of the following century. Yet notwithstanding the comparatively recent introduction of the article the origin of the word remains doubtful. By some authorities it is referred to the Latin *concha*, a shell, but the latest accepted etymology is the Hungarian *kocsi* (pronounced *kō-chē*), an adjectival word believed to have originally denoted that which belongs to the village of Kocs, a place between Raab and Buda, in Hungary.

Coal. Although this word is now limited to denoting that combustible substance which is dug out of the earth and used for fuel, its original meaning, when wood was the general fuel, was not thus restricted. " Coal " then meant the residue obtained by the process of slowly burning wood under turf—what we now call charcoal—and the name " collier " was applied to charcoal burners as well as coal-miners. The root of the word—*kol*—is common to all Teutonic languages, and is connected with the Swedish *kylla*, to kindle. Thus its true signification may be expressed in the term " kindling "— a word in daily use in provincial England, especially in the Eastern Counties.

Cobble. The various significations of this word have three different roots—(1) the Welsh *cob*, a lump, a tuft; (2) the Welsh *ceubal*, a skiff, something hollowed out, boats being originally made of hollowed trees; and (3) the Old French *coubler*, to join together, to couple. Thus from the first root we have " cobbles " as stones and coals, denoting small rounded lumps; from the second we have the " cobble " of the fisherman, a strong boat admirably constructed for encountering a heavy swell, its stability being secured by its rudder extending beneath its keel; and from the third we have the verb " cobble," to patch or mend clumsily, and " cobbler," the mender of boots and shoes.

Cocoa. It seems curious that we should use the same word for two totally distinct articles—the cocoa which we drink and from which all forms of chocolate are made, and the cocoa-nut the fruit of the palm tree. When used to denote the beverage the word is a corruption of *cacao*, which was adopted from the Mexican *cacautl*, the native name. Prescott, in his "Conquest of Peru," mentions that as the followers of Pizarro sailed along the Pacific coast they saw the lower slopes of the hills covered with blooming plantations of cacao, and referring to the general use of chocolate in Mexico he states that the Emperor Montezuma was exceeding fond of it, no less than *fifty* jars of it being prepared for his daily consumption. The botanical name of the plant—Theobroma—is derived from the Greek and signifies " god-food "; it was bestowed by Linnæus as a mark of his appreciation of the beverage, which he considered to be " fit for the gods." The " cocoa beans " of commerce are the seeds of the fruit, each fruit containing from twenty to forty seeds, arranged in five rows and embedded in a soft acid pulp of delicate pink.

The name " cocoa-nut " seems to be a contraction of the Portuguese *macoco*, a kind of monkey, to the face of which the three marks at the end of the nut bear a grotesque resemblance. The tree is the most prized of all palm trees, and as its congenial habitat is the coast it abounds on the South Sea Islands and along the sea-coast of India, while in the interior it is scarce. The uses both of the tree and the fruit are innumerable : the juice of the fruit may be made into an excellent wine and the spirit called " arrack " is distilled from it; the bud is a delicate article of food; the leaves are used for thatch and fences, or made into baskets and buckets, and as a substitute for writing paper; of the leaves, too, a coarse kind of cloth is manufactured and the midrib serves for oars; the case of the stem is made into drums and the lower part is so hard as to take a polish like agate; while cocoa-nut fibre and cocoa-nut oil are well known in this country.

The words " coca " and " cocaine " must not be confused with " cocoa," with which they have no connection. Coca is an important narcotic stimulant, obtained from the leaves of the coca-plant, a shrub which grows wild in Peru and is cultivated on the Andes at altitudes of 2,000 to 5,000 feet. Cocaine is a valuable local anæsthetic in minor operations, and is obtained from the same shrub.

Code. It is remarkable how many of our words relating to writing or books take us back, in their origin, to the tree or its bark, showing the ancient use of wood and bark as materials for writing upon. The words " book " and " papyrus " may be cited as salient instances, and " code " is another example—it is derived from the Latin *codex* or *caudex*, the trunk of a tree.

Coed. A Celtic word meaning a wood. It is a frequent component in place-names, more especially in Wales. Examples are found in Bettws-y-Coed and the Cotswold Hills. The name Cots-wold is an instance of the duplication of meaning, the second syllable being the Anglo-Saxon *weald*, a wood, a term which is retained in the now treeless " wolds " of Yorkshire and the de-forested " weald " of Sussex.

Coffee. The word is generally considered to be a corruption of the Arabic name *kahwah*, although it has also been traced to Caffa, a province of Abyssinia; where the shrub grows wild. According to some accounts the use of coffee was prevalent among the Abyssinians from the most remote period, and it seems to have been introduced into Arabia about 875 of the Flight, or 1470 A.D. Its use stirred up a fierce opposition on the part of the strictly orthodox Mahommedans, on the ground that it was an intoxicant and. as such, prohibited by the Koran; in connection with which it may be pointed out that *kahwah*, in ancient Arabic, means wine. Coffee reached England in 1652, in which year the first coffee-house was opened in St. Michael's Alley, London, by Pasqua Rossie, a Greek, who had come from Smyrna as a servant to Mr. Edwards, a Turkey merchant, and had prepared coffee daily for his master and his visitors. It is remarkable that the three beverages Cocoa (Chocolate), Coffee and Tea were introduced into England (in the order named) within a few years of each other. The most valuable constituent of coffee is the peculiar brown oil called caffeine, which gives to coffee its characteristic aroma, but which is absent from the coffee-bean in its raw state and is only developed in the process of roasting.

Coffin. This word is but an earlier form of "coffer," chest, a box, coming to us through the Old French *cofin*, from the Latin *cophinus* and the Greek *kophinos*, a basket. Its old signification of a basket may be found in Wickliffe's Bible, where the passage (Matt. xiv. 20) "they took up of the fragments that remained twelve baskets full" is rendered "thei token the relifes of broken gobetis tuelue *cofyns*."

Cohort.

"The Assyrian came down like a wolf on the fold,
    And his cohorts were gleaming in purple and
        gold."

In this vision, which is thus conjured up for us by Byron, of a mighty army panoplied in all the splendour of war, the term "cohort" seems to bear no insignificant part, and yet the word, in its primary root, takes us back to the peaceful garden, the inclosure of security. For it comes to us, through the French, from the Latin *cors*, *cohors*, an inclosure; whence it came to signify a multitude inclosed, and, finally, a company of soldiers. "Cohort," "court," "garden," "yard," are all from the same root, in conjunction with the Anglo-Saxon *geard*, an inclosure.

Coln. A derivative of the Latin *colonia*, a colony, which in its turn is derived from *colonus*, a husbandman, and *colere*, to till. It is found in the names of such places as Lincoln, Cologne (Koln), and perhaps also in Colchester and the two rivers Colne, one of which rises near the site of the Roman colony of Verulam, while the other flows past Colchester. In the immediate vicinity of Colchester a Roman legion was stationed, and the site of its camp is indicated by the remains of extensive earthworks at Lexdon, a name which is a corruption of *Legionis Dunum*.

Comet. Contrary to what we might expect, there is no hint of the dire forebodings with which a comet was associated in old times (and still is, to some extent) in the derivation of the word. It is merely a contraction of the Greek *kometes*, which means long-haired.

Common. It is remarkable what varied meanings have become attached to this word—for instance, belonging to more than one, public, usual, frequent, easy to be had, of little value, vulgar, etc.—so much so that its ethical signification is, unfortunately, greatly obscured. But its derivation shows it to be almost equivalent to what we now call the commonweal, *i.e.*, the public well-being, which can only be fully attained by mutual service and good-will. For the word " common " is but the Latin *com-munis*, a combination of the two words *com*, together, and *munis*, serving, obliging.

Comparisons are Odious. The phrase has been used by Dr. John Donne, the poet and divine (1573-1631), and by George Herbert (1593-1632).

Confute. It is wonderful how much may be conveyed by the mere derivation of a word. In this case, for instance, the heat of an argument, the chilling effect of defeat on the confuted antagonist and its likeness to a douche of cold water—as exemplified in the phrase " throwing cold water on a scheme " —all seem embodied in the word " confute." For it is derived from the Latin *confutare*, which means to cool boiling water by pouring in cold, *con* being the intensive prefix to *futis*, a water vessel, derived, in its turn, from *fundere*, to pour.

Connive. When a man connives at some scandalous transaction he need not be a participator in it— he simply " winks " at it. And the derivation of " connive " bears out this definition—the word comes to us, through the French, from the Latin *connivere*, to wink.

Consider. The derivation here, as in many other instances in our language, takes us back to the days when astrology was an accredited science. The word comes to us from the Latin *considerare*, which is probably a term borrowed from the practise of making auguries by the stars—*con*, together with, and *sidus* (*sideris*) a star. The word " contemplate " (from the Latin *contemplum*) has an analogous derivation : there it is the place of augury, the temple, not the stars themselves, which has given rise to the word.

Constable. Although the term is now most generally used to denote a member of the police, it was formerly applied to a state officer of the highest rank, one who was virtually Commander-in-chief of the army, the office being hereditary and attached to certain manors. It has been held successively by the Bohuns, Earls of Hereford and Essex, with their heirs, the Staffords, and the Dukes of Buckingham. And the derivation of the word " constable " is consonant with this high estate, being the Latin *comes stabuli*, Count of the stable ; nor is the rank of Count to be despised— it means the companion of a prince.

Contemplate. (*See* CONSIDER.)

Copper. The use of this metal dates back to prehistoric times—there may have been a copper age before that of bronze. Certainly it was in use in ancient Assyria, and although the word " copper " only occurs once in our translation of the Old Testament (Ezra viii. 27) the word rendered " brass " may often be taken to indicate the metal we call " copper." Both the Greeks and the Romans were familiar with it, the principal source of their supply being the mines at Tamassus, near Famagusta, in the island of Cyprus, and to this fact we owe our word " copper," which comes from the Latin *cuprum*, a contraction of *Cyprium æs*, literally, Cyprian brass.

Copy. The analogies revealed by even a cursory glance at derivations are very interesting. We find, for instance, that a common-place word like " copy "—the transcription of any document—is a near relation to " copious " and the abundant " cornucopia," the horn of plenty, the emblem of Ceres, goddess of Corn and Tillage. For the derivation of " copy " is the Latin *copia*, plenty; the signification arising because by the making of copies the original was multiplied.

Coward. The accepted derivation of this word is the Old French *couard*, coming from the Latin *cauda*, a tail; the analogy being that of an animal who is afraid and drops its tail between its legs. Moreover, the phrase " to turn tail " is still used to express the action of a coward.

Crescent. The primary meaning of this word is not that of a curve, nor was it originally applied to the new moon because of its shape, but because of its gradual increase in size, as night by night it appeared to grow larger and larger in the heavens. For the word " crescent " is derived from the Latin *crescens*, the present participle of *crescere*, to grow, and therefore means growing, increasing, although by its application to the moon

F

with its bowed outline the term has come to denote a curve. The crescent moon has figured on the national standard of the Turks ever since their conquest of Constantinople in 1453, but they did not bring it with them from Central Asia—they found it at Constantinople and adopted it. The legend of the origin of the symbol is as follows :— In the year 340 B.C. Byzantium, on the site of which Constantinople is built, was besieged by the Macedonians. The general in command, Philip, the father of Alexander the Great, prepared a carefully arranged night assault upon the place, but the inhabitants had their danger revealed to them by the unexpected light of the moon, which " shone suddenly from the north," and in gratitude for so great a deliverance they assumed the crescent as the symbol of their city. Of the fact of the crescent being the emblem of Byzantium there can be no doubt—it is found on various Byzantine coins of an era long previous to the appearance of the Turks in Europe.

Crimson. This word has a remarkable derivation. The similarity of the term may be traced in German, French, Spanish, Portuguese, Italian and Latin, all having their origin in the Arabic *kermez*, which means " pertaining to a worm "—the cochineal insect from which the colour is made. Mahn and Skeat trace the origin still further to the Sanscrit *krimija*, signifying " produced from a worm "—*krimi*, a worm, and *jan*, to generate.

Cubit. In the Bible there are frequent references to the measure called a cubit, but its length appears to have no fixed standard. This, however, is natural when we look at the derivation of the word, which is the Latin *cubitus*, literally a bend, other-wise the elbow, the measure being the length of the arm from the elbow to the tip of the middle finger—about 18 to 22 inches, varying according to the age and sex of the individual. This con-sideration throws a light upon the passage (Rev.

xxi. 17) which occurs in the account of St. John's vision of the New Jerusalem, where an angel is described as measuring the wall and finding it " an hundred and forty and four cubits, according to the measure of a man, that is, of the angel."

Cup that Cheers, &c. The origin of the phrase may be found in Cowper's " The Task," where he writes, describing a winter evening :—

" Let fall the curtains, wheel the sofa round,
   And while the bubbling and loud hissing urn
   Throws up a steamy column, and the cups
   That cheer but not inebriate, wait on each."

Cutlass. The Old Testament prophets (Is. ii. 4 ; Mic. iv. 3) have sung of the glorious time when the " nations . . . shall beat their swords into plough-shares " and not " learn war any more." But, to the regret of all well thinking people, that time has not yet arrived—hitherto the plough-share has more often become the sword. And the derivation of the word " cutlass " gives point to this remark— it comes from the Latin *culter*, a plough-share !

Cwm. The word is of Celtic origin and is frequently found in Welsh place-names. It denotes a cup-shaped depression in the hills, and it often occurs in the Anglo-Saxon form of " combe " in English local names. " In Devonshire," says Isaac Taylor, " we have Ilfracombe, Yarcombe and Combe Martin, and the ' combes ' among the Mendip Hills are very numerous." The Celtic county of Cumberland has been supposed to take its name from the ' combes ' with which it abounds, and Anderson, a Cumberland poet, says of his native country :—

" There's Cum-whitton, Cum-whinton, Cum-ranton,
   Cum-rangan, Cum-rew, and Cum-catch,
   And mony mair ' Cums ' i' the county
   But nin wi' Cum-divock can match."

High Wycombe in Buckinghamshire, Combe in Oxfordshire, Appledurcombe and Gatcomb in the

Isle of Wight, Facomb and Combe in Hampshire, Gomshall and Combe in Surrey, are instances of the wide diffusion of the word.

Cynosure. The word comes from the Greek *kynos-oura*, a dog's tail ! The Dog's Tail is another name for the constellation of the Lesser Bear (Ursa Minor), which contains the North Star, the fixed point round which all the other constellations revolve. Hence the word " cynosure " is applied to one who attracts general attention, the centre towards which all eyes are directed. Milton, in his " L'Allegro " (line 75) writes :—

" Where, perhaps, some Beauty lies,
The cynosure of neighbouring eyes."

Dab—Dub. We speak of a person being a " dab " at something which he does exceptionally well, and although the expression sounds like slang it is really not so. The word " dab " in that sense is probably a corruption of " adept," which comes from the Latin *adeptus*, the past participle of *adipiscor*, and means one who has attained ; the word *adipiscor* being formed of *ad*, to, and *apiscor*, attain, *ap* being Sanscrit for attain. In another sense we use " dab " to denote the act of pressing gently with something soft and moist, and also as the name of a fish. In both these cases the word is derived from a Teutonic root found in the Old Dutch *dabben*, to pinch, and in the Anglo-Saxon *dubben*, to strike, from which latter comes our word " dub," used when we speak of conferring knighthood by the ceremony of gently striking the recipient's shoulder with the flat of the sword.

Dactyl. The word is used to denote a unit of measure in a poetical line ; it consists of one long syllable followed by two short, as in the word " violent." Its derivation is the Greek *daktulos*, and the Latin *dactylus*, meaning a finger ; and yet, curiously enough, when referring to it in general terms as a metrical measure we call it a foot !

Daisy. The literal meaning of the word is "day's eye," from the Anglo-Saxon *daeges ege*, day's eye, *i.e.*, the sun. We can scarcely imagine our country-side without the ubiquitous daisy, and few of our poets have failed to sing its praises. Chaucer, the earliest English poet, seems to have had a special admiration for this familiar little flower, so frequently does he refer to it. He writes :—

" . . . Of all the floures in the mede,
    Than love I most these floures white and rede,
    Soch that men callen daisies in our toun."

And again :—

" That well by reason men it call may
    The daisie, or els the eye of day,
    The emprise, and floure of floures all."

And again :—

" To seen this floure agenst the sunne sprede
    Whan it riseth early by the morrow,
    That blissful sight softeneth all my sorrow."

Dal. A component in Scandinavian place-names, the equivalent of the Anglo-Saxon *del* and the German *thal*, all meaning a valley, a dale. Examples are found in Ken-dal, Arun-del and Lons-dale. When " dal " is a prefix it is usually a corruption of the Celtic *dol*, a field, as in Dal-keith, Dal-rymple.

Damask. Not only by its sound but by its very derivation does the word " damask " carry us back to the old city of Damascus, the most ancient existing town in the world. There it was that those rich silk brocades called damask were made, and from the name of the town is their name derived—a name which has been passed on to that beautiful table linen, with its wonderfully woven designs, now made extensively in Scotland and Ireland. Damascus occupies a site of singular beauty, on a high plain, of vast extent, some 2,000 feet above the sea, stretching far out into Arabia. It is watered by the two rivers Abana and Pharpar, of Bible fame (2 Kings v. 12), and its orchards, gardens, vineyards and fields, covering a circuit of at least sixty miles, owe their unrivalled fertility and luxuriance to the Abana. The origin of the town (its very name is suggestive—Damascus means *activity*) lies far away in the mists of antiquity; it was a noted place in the days of Abraham—his steward was Eliezer of Damascus (Gen. xv. 2)—and centuries later it was the scene of the romantic story of Naaman, the leper (2 Kings v). Soon after Naaman's time it was captured by the Assyrians, and for many centuries it remained a dependency of that empire. In 634 A.D. the city was taken by the Mahommedans, and the reigns of Noureddin and Saladin (the witchery of the " Arabian Nights " stories and the romance of the Crusades are irresistibly recalled by the mere mention of their names) form a happy period in the history of the place. Later, under Sultan Selim, Damascus fell into the hands of the Turks and has ever since acknowledged their supremacy.

Damn. The force and character of this word, if it be gauged by its derivation, has been much exaggerated and seriously altered in recent times. To such an extent, indeed, has this occurred that in the last revision of the English Bible it was deemed necessary to modify the word " damn " to " condemn," as more in accordance with its derivation. (Compare Mark xvi. 16, and Rom. xiv. 23, in the Authorised Version and the Revised Version). For the word " damn " comes from the Latin *damnare*, to condemn, which itself is derived from *damnum*, a loss, a fine; and the signification of " eternal punishment in hell-fire " is an importation entirely unwarranted by its primary meaning.

Dandelion. If we have ever taken the trouble to examine this common wayside plant we must have noticed the jagged, tooth-like edges of its leaves; from this characteristic it gains its name *dent-de-lion*, the French for tooth of the lion. Though little esteemed in general, its sturdy yellow flowers have a charm peculiarly their own in brightening many a dusty country road, and the pretty, delicate, fairy-like "clocks" of the dandelion— floating serenely in the autumn breeze on their adventurous journeys in search of "fresh woods and pastures new" in which to deposit their seeds —are a source of wonder and delight to many a child and many a thoughtful adult, too. Moreover, the plant is not without its practical use; it yields a milky juice from which a valuable medicine (taraxacum) is made—surely, then, the dandelion should not be despised.

Dandy. By merely recognising the derivation of this word, a good idea of its significance may be gained. It probably comes from the same root as "dandle," which means to fondle, to play with, and is cognate with the German *tand*, a toy! Carlyle, in his "Sartor Resartus," gives a trenchant description of a dandy. "Let us consider," he says, "what a dandy specially is. A dandy is a clothes-wearing man, a man whose trade, office and existence consists in the wearing of clothes. Every faculty of soul, spirit, purse and person is heroically consecrated to this one object—the wearing of clothes wisely and well: so that as others dress to live, he lives to dress."

Danger. There are many survivals in our present-day words of the old feudal system, and the word "danger" is a case in point. According to Skeat, it comes to us, through the Old French *dangier*, from the Latin *dominus*, a lord, and originally it implied the absolute power possessed by the feudal lord—hence the power to hurt, which is the underlying meaning of danger.

Daughter. The origin of this word may be traced back to the Sanscrit *duh*, or *dhugh*, which implies the operation of milking, or, perhaps, of giving milk. The same underlying root is present in "dug," the teat, the nipple of the breast, and also in "dairy," a place where milk is stored.

Deacon. The essential duty of a deacon—whether he holds office in the Church of England or the Church of Rome, or in the Presbyterian or Nonconformist Churches—is to serve, either by assisting the priest in his spiritual duties or by ministering to the congregation in temporal matters. And the word is appropriate to the office—it comes from the Greek *diakonos*, a servant.

Dearest. The word means most hateful when derived from the Anglo-Saxon *derian*, to hurt, and the Scotch *dere*, to annoy. In the sense of " beloved " it is derived from the Saxon *deor*, dear or rare.
" Would I had met my ' dearest ' foe in heaven,
    Or ever I had seen that day, Horatio."
                        SHAKESPEARE : Hamlet i, 2.

Death by Burning. Anciently a woman who was convicted of capital offences was burnt to death. The last execution of this kind occurred in 1789. In the following year an Act was passed for discontinuing this judgment against women.

Death-Watch. The Death-watch is the popular name for any species of Anobium; a genus of beetles which bore into dead wood. They make a curious clicking sound, once popularly supposed to presage death.

Debt of Nature. The debt of nature, death. Life is a loan, not a gift.
" The slender debt to Nature's quickly paid,
    Discharged, perchance, with greater ease than
        made."
                        FRANCIS QUARLES (1592-1644).

Debut. This is really a French word, but by frequent use it has become incorporated into English. Its signification of a first appearance—at Court, in Society, on the stage or platform—is illustrated by its literal meaning, viz. :—a first stroke, the word being formed of *de*, from, and *but*, aim, mark.

Decameron. The " Decameron of Boccaccio," a volume of one hundred tales related in ten days.

Hence the title, from the Greek *deca*, ten, and *hemera*, a day.

Decanter. This is a word of interesting origin. The French phrase *de cant* is used of anything set on edge. The English noun "cant" signifies a corner or edge, and the verb "to cant" means to turn an object on its corner or edge. Hence to "decant" is to pour off a liquid by canting the vessel containing it, which was therefore termed a "decanter."

Decide. Probably there are few people who have not found how difficult it is to decide on a measure—the more simple, the more difficult, perhaps. In any complex matter one has to cut away all extraneous issues, and by that means come to a decision. This is exactly what the word implies—it comes from the Latin *decidere*, *de*, away, and *cædere*. to cut.

Decimate. Considering the obvious meaning of the word it is extraordinary how loosely it is often used. Even in the newspapers, and certainly in common talk, it is not infrequently employed to express a great slaughter of a body of men, with a complete indifference to the proportion killed. If the derivation of the word were borne in mind such a mistake could not be made—it comes from the Latin *decem*, ten, and denotes a tenth part, or, even figuratively, some approximation to that proportion.

Decoy Duck. The word "decoy" is derived from the old English verb "to coy," or allure.

> "I'll mountebank their loves,
> Coy their hearts from them, and come home beloved
> Of all the trades in Rome."
>
> SHAKESPEARE : Coriol. iii. 2.

A decoy duck is a duck trained to allure the wild fowl into a net employed for this purpose.

Deer. No wonder the stringent laws enacted by the Normans as to the hunting and killing of deer in

this country excited the fierce resentment of the
common people, for there is every reason to believe
that the creature was looked upon as a wild animal
which anyone might chase and slay for his own
benefit.   Certainly the derivation of the word
" deer " points to this conclusion, as the Greek
ther, the Latin *fera*, the German *thier*, and the Old
Saxon *dier*, all signify a wild beast, and in
mediæval English " dier " denoted any kind of
animal.

Defalcation.   The word is now generally used to
denote a fraudulent default in regard to entrusted
money, but formerly it was employed in a much
wider sense, such as a diminution in quantity, a
curtailment of length.   And perhaps it would not
general measure in value, was the usual method
of trade, for its primary meaning is a cutting
down as with a scythe or a sickle, the derivation
be too fanciful to trace the origin of the word to
the time when barter in kind, with corn as a
being the Latin *difalcare—di (s)*, off, *falcare*, to
cut, from *falx (falcis)*, a sickle.

Defoe.   The original name of the author of " Robinson
Crusoe " was Daniel Foe.   He and his father, being
both active dissenters, the son became generally
known as Mr. D. Foe, to distinguish him from Mr.
Foe senior.   The name became fixed, and ultimately we have the author in a letter to Lord
Halifax, in 1705, signing himself " Daniel De
foe."

Deity.   The word comes to us from the French *déité*,
through the Low Latin *deitas* and the Latin *deus*,
and is cognate with the Anglo-Saxon *Tiw* (the god
whose name is preserved in our word " Tuesday "),
the Welsh *duw*, the Gaelic and Irish *dia*, and the
Sanscrit *deva*, all signifying God.   But the root
of all these, according to Skeat, may be found in
the Sanscrit *div*, a word which, when applied to
the Deity, seems singularly suggestive of the

contemplative mind of the Eastern race and deeply significant of the effulgence of God and His creative power, for it means to shine!

Del. (*See* DAL.)

Deliberate. "The woman that deliberates is lost." So wrote Addison some 200 years ago, while Byron has expressed the same idea in the line "And whispering 'I will ne'er consent'—consented." The maxim is true; for to deliberate—to weigh the consequences in the balance (such is the meaning of the word "deliberate," which is derived from the Latin *libra*, a balance)—when inducement is offered to stray from a course known to be right, is almost certain to end in a fall—as proved in many an instance, from that of Eve, downwards.

Delirious. It is curious to find how many of our words and phrases have their signification bound up in agricultural pursuits. In the word "delirious" we have an example—it is derived from the Latin *de*, from, and *lira*, a furrow, meaning one who goes out of the furrow in ploughing. And in Benjamin Franklin's phrase, urging us to vigilant and energetic labour, we also have an agricultural metaphor—"Plough deep, while sluggards sleep," he says.

Deluge. According to the Hebrew reckoning, the flood described in the Bible (Gen. vi. vii. and viii.) took place in the year 2348 B.C., and by the Septuagint chronology in 3155 B.C. Traditions of such an occurrence are found among many races, but the earliest and most precise document in regard to the event which has yet been discovered is the Babylonian tablet from the library of Assurbanipal, which dates from about 660 B.C., though the Accadian original from which it is probably derived may well have been composed as long ago as 2000 B.C. The story there related bears a remarkable similarity to the account given in the Bible, even to the coating of the ship with bitumen (Gen.

vi. 14), the sending out of a dove which returned (Gen. viii. 8-9), and the release of a raven which did not come back (Gen. viii. 7). The grounding of the ship on a mountain and the offering of a sacrifice (Gen. viii. 4 and 20)—pouring out a libation—the altar is uncertain—are also described, but owing to the mutilated condition of the tablet there is no evidence for what cause the deluge was supposed to have been sent.

Demesne. Skeat says that this spelling is false, due probably to confusion with the Old French *mesnee* or *maisnie*, a household. The word is really equivalent to " domain," which being derived from the Latin *dominus*, a master, a lord, means an estate or a territory which one is master of or lord over. It is not connected with " demean," which comes from the Old French *demener*, to guide, to conduct—to conduct oneself well is to demean oneself properly. And the word *demener* is a derivative of the Latin *minare*, to drive cattle— an instance of how words of even ethical signification are drawn from the analogy of country life and work. There is another sense for " demean," viz. :—to debase, to degrade, but it has been developed from an erroneous compound of the Latin preposition *de*, and the English adjective " mean " used in the sense of worthless, vile.

Demise. It is not an uncommon error to apply this word to the death of a person, the confusion of terms having risen, apparently, from the fact that on the death of a monarch the crown is thereby " demised " to his successors, and hence, euphemistically, his death is called his " demise." The true meaning of " demise " is to transfer, to bequeath—the word is used quite properly in making a will—and this is shown by its derivation, the Latin *dimittere*, to send away, to dismiss. The title of the Prayer Book canticle " Nunc Dimittis " is taken from the same word, as the English version of the first verse shows.

Den. As a suffix in place-names this is of frequent occurrence in the Home Counties. Isaac Taylor gives a table showing that there are no less than fifty-eight local names ending in " den " in Kent and Sussex alone, indicating the existence of large tracts of forest in that district, for " den " is an Anglo-Saxon term denoting a deeply-wooded valley. (*See* LEY.) The " dens " were principally used as pastures for swine, and as late as the seventeenth century there existed a " Court of Dens " to determine disputes arising out of the use in common of forest pasture. An officer was elected annually to see that the swine pasturing in the " dens " were duly provided with nose-rings and were kept within certain bounds. He was called a Hog-warden, and the names Hayward and Howard are corruptions of this. It is noteworthy that the Howard family first comes into prominence in the weald of Sussex, just where their name would lead one to expect it to appear.

Dene-Holes (Dane-holes). These are ancient artificial excavations, and though the name is sometimes spelt " dane-holes " there seems no valid reason for connecting them with the Danes. They are generally made in the chalk, and consist of a round, vertical shaft from two feet to three feet in diameter, ending below in a cavern (a den—hence the name " dene," Old English for " den "). The shafts have foot-holes in the sides, and the chambers in the oldest and the simplest are mere expansions of a bee-hive shape, but in the deeper pits a series of chambers are symmetrically arranged round the shaft, or the walls of the chambers may have disappeared and the roof be supported by pillars of chalk. Of three examples discovered at Hangman's Wood, near Grays, Essex, the greatest length was about 70 feet, the breadth 46 feet, the height 18 feet, and they were all about 80 feet deep. Though often very close together, no communication has hitherto been found between adjacent pits. There is still much to be done in the way of examination, but the few of the older pits which have been explored are found to date back to the Stone Age. It has been conjectured that dene-holes were excavated for the purpose of obtaining chalk or flint, but as they are sometimes concentrated—at Bexley, Kent, for instance—where fifty to sixty feet of gravel overlie the chalk, though there is plenty of bare chalk within a mile, this explanation cannot be accepted. Most probably they were places of occasional refuge and for the secret storage of grain.

Derrick. The old name for a gibbet and now for a high crane. So called after a seventeenth-century hangman at Tyburn.

Devil's Advocate. A phrase which arose from the technical term *Advocātus Diaboli* of the Roman Catholic Church. When a name is suggested for canonisation, some person is appointed to oppose the proposition, before the conclave decides the question.

Diamond Sculls. A challenge sculling race, established in 1844 by the Royal Regatta Committee, and which takes place every year at the Henley Royal Regatta. The challenge prize, held for a year only by the annual winner, is a pair of crossed silver sculls not quite a foot in length, surmounted by an imitation wreath of laurel and having a pendant of diamonds. They are in a velvet-lined box, which also contains the names of all the winners. Each winner receives a cup of silver, which becomes his permanent property.

Dieu et Mon Droit. This was the parôle of Richard Cœur de Lion at the Battle of Gisors, fought with the French in the year 1198. "God and my right," or "To God alone I owe my royalty. I own no fealty to France." The French were defeated, and the cry was adopted as the royal motto of England.

Dilemma. " On the horns of a dilemma." *Dilemma* is a Greek word signifying a double proposition, from *di* or *dis*, twofold, and *lemma*, a thing taken or received; thus, a proposition. A " dilemma," therefore, is a position before which there are two alternatives equally good or equally bad.

Dingo. Although this is the native name of the Australian dog, the animal is, in all probability, not a true native of the continent, but an importation, for it is remarkable as being the only mammal found in Australia which does not belong to the Marsupial group, such as Kangaroos, Wombats, etc. The Dingo seldom barks or growls, but, when irritated, erects the hairs of its whole body like bristles, and becomes furious. Owing to its ravages among sheep, endeavours are being made to exterminate it.

Dished. Dished is contracted from the old English word *disherit* (= disinherit). A person is said to be " dished " when property he is expected to inherit is left to someone else.

"Where's Brummel? Dished ! "

BYRON : Don Juan.

Ditto. From the Italian *detto*, meaning " as aforesaid."

Dog-Watch. A corruption of the word " Dodge-Watch." The crew on board ship are divided into two watches—the starboard watch and the port watch. These two watches go on duty alternately for four hours each. In order, however, to prevent the same watch being on duty during the same hours, week in and week out, the afternoon watch from 4 to 8 o'clock is made into two short watches, one from 4 to 6, and the other from 6 to 8. Thus the number of watches in a day being nine, instead of eight, the same men do not go on duty during the same hours every day.

Doldrums. The " doldrums " is that region of the ocean, near the equator, in which, between the trade winds, calms and light, baffling winds are often met with, greatly delaying the progress of sailing craft. It is no wonder, therefore, that when ships were dependent upon wind alone for the continuance of their voyage the seamen should be depressed and low-spirited at the enforced idleness and irritating delay incurred in this region, and hence the phrase " in the doldrums " came to mean out of spirits, in the dumps. The origin of the word " doldrums " is quite uncertain, but it may be a mere alliteration of " dolt," dull, stupid.

Dollar. This is a variant of the German word *thaler*, a valley. There were silver mines in " Joachim's thal," whence, in the fifteenth century, the counts of Schlick extracted silver, which they coined into ounce pieces. These pieces in time became the standard coins, being originally called " Joachim's thalers," and then simply " thalers." The American sign $ is derived from the figure 8, a dollar being originally a Spanish " piece of eight." The two lines through the $ indicate a contraction.

Dolly Shop. An old name for a rag shop, because it had a black doll over the door for a sign. Dolly shops are in reality no better than unlicenced pawn shops.

Domino. Originally a dress worn by a master or teacher—*domino* Italian, *dominus* Latin. Hence, a hood worn by canons of a cathedral church, a cape worn by priests in winter, a mourning veil for women, a disguise.

Dominos or Dominoes, the plural, is a game played with counters. These are generally made of black wood faced with ivory or bone, from which fact, it is suggested, the name arose. In slang " dominos " is often used to signify the teeth.

Don, Dun. These syllables enter into many Celtic and Teutonic place-names, where their general meaning is a hill-fortress. Lon-dun-um was the fortified hill on which St. Paul's Cathedral now stands—the name has now become London. Dun-stable, Dun-mow, and Dun-dry Hill (Somerset) have the same root, and in Scotland we have Dun-keld (the fort of the Celts), and Dum-barton (the fort of the Britons). In Ireland we have Dun-dalk, Dun-gannon, and many other examples. The term was adopted from the Celts by the Saxons, and was then used as a suffix instead of a prefix, instances of which are Faring-don and Claren-don.

Donkey. The word was originally pronounced so as to rhyme with " monkey," for " donkey " signifies a little " dun " coloured animal, and is applied specifically to an ass because of its " dun " colour.

Don't Care a Jot. A " jot," as in the phrase " a jot or tittle," means anything small, because the letter *Iōta* was the smallest in the Greek alphabet. Moreover it was often, by an abbreviation, written as a dot beneath the line—" Iota subscript." The word " jot " may be from this or from " yod," the smallest Hebrew letter. The Greek *iota* and the Hebrew *yod* are equivalent to the English " i."

Dore, Dour, Duir, Dur. These are widely diffused components in river-names, and are all connected with the Welsh *dwr*, water. Thus we find the Dore in Hereford, the Dour in Fife, the Duir in Lanark, and the Dur-ra in Cornwall. There are many variants of the words, such as the Dairan in Carnarvonshire, the Deargan in Argyleshire, and the Dover or Durbeck in Nottinghamshire. Also we have the Glasdur or (gray water) in Elgin, the Calder (the winding or, it may be, the cold water) in Cumberland and many times in Scotland, the Adur in Sussex, the Cheddar in Somerset, and the lake Windermere. The last is a threefold repetition of what is really one word, for " win," " der," and " mere " all mean water.

Dragons. It must be admitted that no conclusive evidence can be adduced of the existence of dragons

G

within the period of man's habitation of the earth,
and the only creatures known which are in any
way comparable with such monsters are the
Pterodactyls, huge reptiles with wings resembling
those of a bat, whose remains have been found in
the Liassic and Oolitic formations. Yet the
existence of the dragon does not seem to have
been doubted by the old naturalists, and figures
of it appear in the works of Gesner and Aldro-
vandi. Moreover, there are an enormous number
of legends, of circumstantial detail and of wide-
spread extent both in time and locality—from
ancient China to mediæval Europe—which bear
witness to the exploits of men in their encounters
with dragons, and though it is reasonable to
suppose that in many of these the accretions of
time and symbolical myth are responsible for the
wonders they relate, it is almost inconceivable that
they should be devoid of all foundation in reality.
Possibly some monsters of a primeval period,
secure in the fastnesses of their final retreat before
the rise of new conditions of climate and fauna,
may have survived the advent of the human race,
and thus have given origin to the accounts handed
down from age to age.

Dragoons. Cavalry trained to act also on foot. The
name arose from the short-barrelled firearms which
they carried. These were called " dragoons,"
possibly from a fanciful comparison to a dragon
spurting fire. A dragon's head was wrought on
the muzzles of these muskets.

Drat 'em! Corrupted from " 'Od rot them!" or
" God rot them!" Similar phrases are " 'Od's
blood " (God's blood), " 'Od zounds " (God's
wounds). They were once much used colloquially,
and we find them commonly in the old playwrights.
(*See* ODD's.)

Draw It Mild. A metaphor from liquor. In a similar
way we talk of strong language, spicy words,
piquant remarks.

Du. A syllable derived from the Celtic word *dhu*, black, and found in such names as Dublin, the black pool or lyn, and Douglas, the black water. Examples of the latter name are found in Scotland and Lancashire as well as in the Isle of Man.

Duir. (*See* DORE.)

Dun. (*See* DON.)

Dumps. According to etymological fable, this word is derived from Dumops, king of Egypt, who built a pyramid and died of melancholy, as " to be in the dumps " is to be out of spirits. But there is little doubt that the word " dumps " is closely allied to " damp," and to the Dutch *dompig*, which means dull, low, misty.

Dunce. Duns Scotus was a schoolman, called Duns because he came from Dunce in Berwickshire (1265-1305). He was a great supporter of the old theology against the new at that time. He opposed the new learning and the classics. His followers were called " Dunsers," and hence, it is asserted, " Dunce " became the general name for any opponent of progress and learning.

Another derivation of the word is found in the Gaelic *donas*, bad luck, and the Lowland Scotch " donsie," stupid or obstinate.

Dunderhead. " Dunder " is the lees or dregs of wine. Technically, it is the overflow of fermenting liquors. Thus a " dunderhead " has come to denote a stupid fellow without spirit or life.

Dur. (*See* DORE.)

Eager. An old time meaning of this word was sharp, acid or keen.

" It doth posset
And curd, like eager droppings into milk."
HAMLET, i. 5.

Earl—Easel

> " It is a nipping and an eager air."
>
> HAMLET, i. 4.

> " Vex him with eager words."
>
> HENRY VI., ii. 4.

The word is derived through the French *aigre* from the Latin *acer*, sharp, keen.

Earl. From the Anglo-Saxon *eorl*, a warrior, and cognate with the Icelandic *jarl*, *earl*. It is a title of nobility of the third rank—Duke, Marquis, Earl, Viscount, Baron—and is the only one we have derived from the Anglo-Saxons. William the Conqueror attempted to introduce the word " Count " for hereditary Earls, but the name did not remain, though the wife of an Earl is still known as a Countess.

Earn. In this word we have another instance of a term of wide significance which has originated from some agricultural expression or metaphor. It comes from an old Teutonic word for harvest, while it is cognate with the present Dutch *erne*, and the German *ernte*, a harvest. The Bavarian *arnen* signifies both to reap and to earn wages.

Earwig. We have several explanations of the origin of this word. " It is so called," says one, " from a belief that it crept into the ear "; or, according to another, " because the hind wings res mble in shape the human ear." The Anglo-Saxon word is *eor-wicga* (*eor*, an ear, and *wicga*, derived from *wegan*, to carry). Finally, we may quote a further explanation :—" In Old English the word ' ear ' meant an undeveloped flower bud, particularly of corn, and the Anglo-Saxon *wic* (or *wick*) meant a hiding place or dwelling. The favourite hiding place of the insect is in closely shielded bud-ears of plants, hence the name ' earwic,' which was originally so written but has since been corrupted into ' earwig.' "

Easel. The origin of this word is interesting ; it is the Dutch *ezel* and the German *esel*, both meaning, literally, a little ass—evidently in allusion to the burden it bears while the picture is being painted.

Easter Eggs or **Paschal Eggs.** An egg is an age-old symbol of Creation or re-Creation. Thus, in Oriental mythology (Phœnician, Egyptian, Hindu and Japanese) the world is said to have been hatched from an egg, the " mundane egg "; for which, according to Persian legend, Ormuzd and Ahriman, the Angels of light and darkness, were to contend for ever. The custom of presenting eggs is believed to have had its origin in Persia; it was also prevalent among the Jews, and in a slightly altered form was adopted by the Christians at their Easter festivals, as a symbol of the resurrection of Christ, the eggs being coloured red in token of the blood of the redemption.

Eaves-Dropper. One who tries to overhear. The origin of the word is slightly obscure. According to old Saxon Law, no one owning land could cultivate it or build on it within a certain fixed distance of its boundary. The strip thus left was called the " eaves-drip." An " eaves-dripper " or " eaves-dropper " was one who stood in the " eaves-drip " to listen stealthily to a conversation within the house. By law eavesdropping is considered a common nuisance and is punishable by fine.

Eccles. The word appears as the name of a place in Lancashire and is a component in the names of many other places, as in Eccles-all, Eccles-hill, and Eccles-ton. It is a contraction of the Latin *ecclesia*, a church.

Economy. Although the primary meaning of this word is " house-law "—from the Greek *oikos*, a house, and *nomos*, a law—it has acquired a much wider signification, and may mean the disposition, conduct, or arrangement of any system, as in the expressions " Christian Economy," Social Economy," " Political Economy." But it is still used to denote the frugal and judicious expenditure of money, especially in relation to household affairs, and hence we have the common meaning of the verb " economise."

Ecstasy. The derivation of this word gives point to its meaning. It comes from the Greek *ek*, out, and *stasis*, a standing, and in former times it was a very general belief that the soul, on occasions— in a vision, for instance—actually left the body. To be " in the spirit " was equivalent to being " in an ecstasy."

Eden. This is a Hebrew word signifying delight, joy, pleasure. From the account given in the Bible it would appear that Paradise was situated in the south-western part of Asia, and of the four rivers named in Gen. ii. 10, one is thoroughly identified as the Euphrates, while Hiddekel is probably the Tigris. What the Pison and Gihon are, or were, has been much disputed.

Edify. The word in its literal significance, according to derivation, means to build a house, the Latin *aedes* meaning a house, and *facio*, I make or construct. This concrete sense of the word is lost, to some extent, in modern English in the idea of improvement in moral and religious knowledge, but in the Bible the words " edify " and " edification " are employed metaphorically in a sense more strictly in agreement with their derivation.

Effendi. A Turkish title added after the name. It is about equivalent to the English " Esquire."

Egg On or **Edge On.** This is a corruption of the Anglo-Saxon word *eggian*, which means to incite or, more literally, to prick or spur on. The Anglo-Saxon *ecg* signifies a sharp point, and hence *edge-hog* (hedgehog) means a hog with sharp points, a derivation which is corroborated by the French *porc-épic* (*épic*, from Latin *spicula*, spikes), and by the Danish *pin-swin*, a thorny swine.

Eld. A component in place-names. (*See* OLD.)

Eldorado. The word, which has obtained the meaning of a golden illusion, is a Spanish word (*el*, the, and *dorado*, gilt) meaning a land of great wealth, a golden region. It was the term used by Orellana, the lieutenant of Pizarro, who pretended to have found a land of fabulous wealth between the River Orinoco and the Amazon, in South America.

Elgin Marbles. They were brought from Greece by Thomas, Lord Elgin, and consist of fragments of statuary, the work of the renowned Phidias, removed from the Parthenon of Athens, one of the most famous of the Greek temples of antiquity. The marbles were collected in 1802 during the mission of Lord Elgin to the Ottoman Porte, and in 1816 they were purchased from him by the British Government for a sum of £35,000. They are now in the British Museum.

Elia. The pseudonym adopted by Charles Lamb for his " Essays " contributed to *The London Magazine* between 1820 and 1825. *Elia* was the name of a gay, light-hearted foreigner, who fluttered about the South Sea House at the time when Lamb was a clerk there. At the moment of penning his signature to the first essay he bethought himself of that person, and substituted the name of *Elia* for his own.

Emerald Isle. A name by which Ireland is known, the epithet having naturally arisen from the fresh and bright-coloured verdure of the island, produced by the warm, moist winds which sweep across the country from the Atlantic. It would seem that the epithet was first applied to Ireland by Dr. Drennan (1754-1820) in his poem entitled " Erin " :—

" Arm of Erin, prove strong; but be gentle as brave,
And, uplifted to strike, still be ready to save :
Nor one feeling of vengeance presume to defile
The cause or the men of the Emerald Isle."

Ember Days. It is commonly stated that these days gained their name from the practice of penitents sitting in the embers or ashes at these seasons, but there is little doubt that the word " ember " is derived from the Anglo-Saxon *ymbren*, a round course, an anniversary, from *ymb*, about, around, and *rine*, a running or race. The Ember Days are appointed in the English Church to be kept as days of fasting and prayer for those about to be admitted into Holy Orders. They occur four times in the year—on the Wednesday, Friday and Saturday after the First Sunday in Lent, after Whit-Sunday, after 14th September, and after 13th December. There is, however, another suggestion for the origin of the name " Ember " Day, viz. :— that it is a corruption of the Latin *quatuor tempora*, four times, through the Dutch *quatemper* and the German *quatember*.

Empire Day. This anniversary was instituted as a memorial of the solidarity of the British Empire so remarkably evinced in the assistance rendered by the Colonies to the Mother Country in the South African war. May 24th was the day selected in order that the celebration might coincide with that of Queen Victoria's birthday.

Encyclopædia. A book containing general or all-round instruction and information, the word being derived from the Greek *enkylois*, in a circle, and *paideia*, learning. Hence the word means an epitome of the whole circle of learning.

Ennis. A component in place-names. (*See* Innis.)

Enough, Enow. Properly used " enough " refers only to quantity and " enow " to numbers. For example " enough wheat, enow potatoes." But " enough " has entirely taken the place of " enow," except among a few old country-folk.

Epicure. After Epicurus, a Greek philosopher, who taught that pleasure and good living constituted the happiness of mankind. His followers were styled Epicureans. In the light of Christian ethics the words "epicurean" and "epicure" have acquired a debased meaning. An epicure is a man who is merely carnal and sensual.

Epiphany. The word is formed from the Greek *epiphaneia*, an appearance or showing. The season called Epiphany commemorates the appearance of the star which is stated to have heralded the birth of Christ and by which the Wise Men of the East, typical of the Gentile world, were brought to worship Christ and offer him symbolical gifts at Bethlehem.

Epoch. Used as synonymous with "era," but properly the *end* of one era, and so the beginning of the next. It is from the Greek word *epecho*, meaning to rein in, and so to break off suddenly.

Epsom Salts. They were originally obtained by evaporation of the actual spring water, from the mineral springs at Epsom, but are now prepared artificially. The salt is sulphate of magnesia.

Era. It has been suggested that this word, which was formerly spelt "aera" is derived from A. ER. A., the initial abbreviations of *Annus erat Augusti*. These words were employed by the Spaniards to signify the year in which they became subject to Augustus and adopted the Roman Calender. Hence it has been supposed the word "aera" or "era" thus came to signify a series of years after a fixed point or epoch (*see* EPOCH). It seems, however, more probable that "era" is derived from the Latin *aera*, the plural of *aes*, which originally meant copper and was afterwards used to denote counters or items of calculation.

Escurial. The name of the palace of the Spanish sovereigns, more properly spelt *escorial*, and signifying "among the rocks." It is one of the most superb buildings in Europe, and was constructed by King Philip II. of Spain. It lies about fifteen miles north-west of Madrid.

Esk. This is a frequent name for a river—there is an Esk in Devonshire, in Yorkshire, in Cumberland; four in Scotland, and one in Ireland. The word is of Gaelic origin and—like so many words applied as names of lakes, streams, and rivers—simply means water. The Exe, the Isis, the Ouse and the Ux are but other forms of the same word.

Espalier. The English word is taken direct from the French. The French use " espalier " for fruit trees trained against a wall or lattice. In English the word is extended to the support, a sense more in accordance with the original meaning of the word, which probably is derived from the Spanish *espalda*, a shoulder, or *espaldar*, something to lean against. The Italian has *spalliera*, a support for the shoulders.

Esquire. An esquire is a legally recognised title of rank. The primary meaning of the word is " shield-bearer." It is derived from the Latin *scutifer*, a shield-bearer; *scutum*, a shield, and *fero*, I bear. *Scutifer* was used in the middle ages and " esquire " has come to us through the French corruption *escuyer*.

Et Cetera. A Latin phrase, the literal meaning of which is " and the other things." *Cetera* is a neuter plural, and hence the expression cannot correctly be applied to persons. The symbol " &c." is an abbreviation of *et c.*

Etiquette. A French word signifying a ticket, a little note. Formerly a ticket or card of instructions was handed to visitors on ceremonial occasions, instructing them upon the conventional rules to be observed in address and behaviour. Nowadays such rules as pertain to deportment or decorum are supposed to enter into the education of all well-bred persons.

Euphemism. A euphemism is the agreeable statement of an offensive or disagreeable fact. It is from the Greek *eu*, well, and *phemi*, I say. For example, the expression "fell asleep" is used in the place of "died," and thieves are euphemistically called "light-fingered gentry."

Every Man Jack of Them. The old form of "every" was "everich," and "everyone" was often written "everich-on" or "everi-chon." For instance, in Chaucer's Prologue we find :—

"He moste reherse, as neighe as ever he can,
Everich word . . .''

And in the "Shepherd's Calendar" there is the line :—

"I shall soon vanquish every-chone."

Thus, through a series of corruptions,—from "everich" and "every-chon" to "every-John" and "every-Jack"—were evolved the phrases "every man Jack" and "every man Jack of them."

Exception Proves the Rule. This phrase is often thought to imply that a rule is no rule unless it has an exception, or that the fact of an exception in particular only proves the correctness of a rule in general. But the word "prove" anciently meant "to test." "Prove all things," says St. Paul, and in the above expression the meaning is rather that an apparent exception puts a rule to the test —*i.e.*, if the rule is to hold good, the apparent exception will be shown to be no exception on investigation.

Exchequer. A Court which formerly had to do only with the Country's revenue, its primary object being to recover debts due to the King, such as unpaid taxes, etc. It gained its name from the "checkered" cloth which covered the table and on which the accounts were reckoned. The word "checker" is derived from the Old French *eschequier*, a chess-board.

Ey, Ea. These are suffixes which appear in many Anglo-Saxon place-names, where they denote an island. They enter into the names of many places

by the side of the Thames which are now joined
to the mainland. Bermondsey, Battersea, Chelsea,
Moulsey and Iffley are examples. The word
" Chelsea " is a contraction of *chesel-ea*, meaning
shingle island, and the natural features of the place
must once have resembled the eyots found in the
Thames. It may be mentioned that " eyot " is but
the diminutive of " ey," and thus signifies a little
island.

Fairy Ring. The belief in fairies or some such
ethereal beings is naturally of pre-historic age, and
the " fairy ring " is the circle of grass, greener
than the surrounding turf, on which it was supposed the fairies danced around, hand in hand,
during their joyous midnight revels, thus causing
the grass to assume a brighter hue. In these
unromantic days the explanation is much more
prosaic. The circle begins at the centre with
a single fungus, and the next season another
patch is produced outside the original spot, thus
forming a small ring which increases in size from
year to year. The decay of the fungus year by
year renders the soil unfit for a new crop of
fungus, but increases the fertility of the ground
for the growth of the grass, and hence there
appears a gradually enlarged circle of grass
brighter and greener than the surrounding turf.
On the beautiful close turf of the Sussex Downs
the process may be witnessed to perfection.

Fake. This word, in common parlance, means to do
something with a view to cheat or deceive. It is
often also used in the sense of to patch up, to make
serviceable for a time, and in thieves' slang the
term is employed to denote something to be done
—" Fake away, there's no down," meaning " Go
on, there's nobody looking." Mayhew states that
the word comes from the Latin *facimentum*, and
there seems little doubt that it is derived in some
way from *facere*, to make. The Gaelic *faigh* is to
get, to acquire, to reach.

Fare. Although this word is now used in the sense of food and provisions, ill or well happenings, etc., its original meaning was restricted more closely to its derivation—the Anglo-Saxon *faran*, to go, to travel. We retain this sense when we use the word " fare " to denote the money paid for a journey—the going somewhere—by land or by water, and also in describing a person conveyed by cab, etc., as a " fare "; while in the expression " fare-well " the same idea is prominent, as it means " may you go well," be fortunate on your journey. (*See* FORD.)

Farm. There are two sources from which the application of this word to the land may have originated. The one is the Low Latin *firma*, a feast, a tribute, and also a contract, an oath, and connected with the Latin *firmus*, firm, durable; from which it would appear that " farm " is a doublet of " firm," meaning that the land is held on a firm and durable contract. The other explanation — the more probable of the two—is that given by Wedgwood, who ascribes the derivation of the word " farm " to the Anglo-Saxon *feorm*, a feast, and shows how the modern sense of the word arose by degrees. In the first place lands were let on condition of supplying the lord with so many nights' entertainment for his household. Thus the Saxon Chronicle, A.D. 775, mentions land let by the Abbot of Peterborough on condition that the tenant should pay annually £50 and " anes nihtes feorme " (one night's entertainment), and this mode of reckoning constantly appears in the Doomsday Book. But the inconvenience of payment in kind soon produced the substitution of money payment, which was called *firma alba* or *blanche ferme*, from being paid in silver (white money) instead of victuals. Thus the rent came to be called simply " firma," and the same word, under the form " farm," became the name of the land from which the rent accrued.

Farrago. This word is generally used in its figurative sense of a confused jumble and muddle. It is really a Latin word denoting a mixed corn or fodder for cattle.

Farthing. The word means literally a fourth part, being derived from the Anglo-Saxon *feorth*, fourth (*feor*, four), and the diminutive *ing* or *ling*. It was not always used to denote the fourth part of a penny—a " farthing " was once the fourth part of a noble, a gold coin of the value of 6/8 sterling, and also indicated a division of land : " Thirty acres make a farthing-land; nine " farthings " make a Cornish acre; and four Cornish acres a Knight's fee."—(Carew's Survey of Cornwall.) In old days a penny was nicked right across with two transverse lines, so that it could be divided into two or four parts.

Farthingale. A corruption of the Old French *verdu-galle*, meaning, literally, provided with hoops, from *verdugo*, a young shoot or rod (Latin *viridis*, green). The farthingale was a circle of hoops made of whalebone used to extend the wide gown and petticoat of the sixteenth century. It survived in a more or less modified form as long as the reign of George III., and the crinoline of the Victorian period was but a revival of the farthingale.

Fathom. This is a nautical measure now fixed at six feet, but originally it was the distance between a man's finger-tips when both arms were extended. The word comes from the Anglo-Saxon *faethm*, denoting a grasp, an embrace. Lineal measures were, of old, generally taken from a man's body, as in the foot, the yard, and the cubit (q.v.).

Fat in the Fire. The allusion in this phrase is to the process of frying, and it refers to the catastrophe (the turning over, as the word means) which occurs when the frying-pan is tilted and the grease runs into the fire, causing such a flame and smoke that the food which is being cooked is spoilt,

Feather. It is curious to observe the frequent use which is made of this word, in a symbolical sense, in our common phrases. For instance :—" Birds of a feather," meaning persons of similar tastes and habits; " In full feather," " In grand feather," " In high feather," meaning, respectively, flush of money, in grand attire, in exuberant spirits, in allusion to the way in which birds, after moulting, regain their health and spirits with their plumage. Also we have " Broken in feather," crippled either in means or in reputation; " An oiled feather," applied to one who is kind in speech and manner and endeavours to ease the asperities of life, as an oiled feather will smooth the movements of a stubborn lock. In the phrase " Feather his own nest " there is usually an implication of over-reaching and undue aggrandisement, while " A feather in your cap " betokens that you have gained some well-deserved honour. This last phrase is an allusion, according to Dr. Brewer, to the general custom among the American Indians of adding a new feather to their headgear for every enemy slain, as did the ancient Lycians and many other races; and with the Chinese, that people of carefully preserved custom and procedure, the " yellow jacket and peacock's feather " is still a mark of great distinction—it was an honour accorded to General Gordon in recognition of his success in quelling the Taiping rebellion in China.

Fee. This is one of those words—there are many of them—which derives its significance from the pastoral and agricultural pursuits with which all commerce was bound up in old days. It comes from the Anglo-Saxon *feoh*, cattle, which, of course, was formerly one of the principal means of making payments—fees—such as those to physicians, lawyers, etc.

Feeble. The full significance of this word is brought to light through its derivation. It comes from the Latin *flēre*, to weep.

Fee-Simple. A tenant in " fee-simple " is one who holds lands or tenements for himself and his heirs for ever, generally absolutely and simply, without mentioning what heirs. Yet, as showing the strict control the Crown maintained over land in feudal days, the property is not absolutely (in the fullest sense) the tenant's own, since it is held of a superior lord, in whom the ultimate ownership resides.

Fell. This is the usual name in the north-west of England for a hill. It is a Norse word and means a place where the ground is on the fall, a hill-side, a mountain. Examples are found in Goat-fell, Carter-fell, and Snae-fell, the snow mountain.

Fellow. In common parlance this word has gained an implication of contempt. We speak of one whom we despise as a " worthless fellow," " a mean fellow," though the word is still used in an honourable or affectionate sense, as in the case of a " fellow " of a University or a scientific Society, or when addressing one's friend as " my dear fellow." In mediæval times the word was written " felawe," which more nearly approaches its derivation, viz. :—" fee-law," which may be construed as " property laying together," " fee " meaning cattle (property) and " law " that which is laid down, from the Anglo-Saxon *lah*, to lay.

Fenchurch Street. From an ancient church in the fens or marshy ground through which ran the Lang Bourne from Beach Lane to the Wall brook behind the Stocks Market, where the Mansion House now stands in London.

Fenian. A name assumed by an association formed for the purpose of overthrowing the British government in Ireland. It is probably derived from the Irish Fion or Fian, a race of heroes celebrated in Irish mythical history, whose achievements formed the theme of ancient romances and songs. Their leader was Fiona MacCumhal, claimed also by the

Scottish Celts under the name of Fingal, as in Fingal's Cave. His date has been fixed hypothetically at 213 to 253 A.D., but it is probable that he belonged to an earlier race than that which now inhabits Ireland.

Fetish. The word comes to us, through the French and Portuguese languages, from the Latin *factitius*, something made. It may be described as any material object which is supposed to be the vehicle or instrument of a supernatural being, the possession of which gives power over that being. Thus a fetish differs from a talisman in that personal power or consciousness is attributed to it, and from an idol because a fetish is not necessarily worshipped. Lubbock, in his " Origin of Civilisation," tells us that " an idol is indeed an object of worship, while, on the contrary, a fetish is intended to bring the deity within the control of man."

Fetter Lane. Considered by some to be a corruption of " Fewters Lane," from the Norman-French *faitour*, an evil-doer, on account of the idle vagabonds who infested it in days when this lane led to some pleasure gardens. More probably, however, the name comes from the word " feuterer," a keeper of dogs, as the lane (which runs between Fleet Street and Holborn, London) has always been famous for dog fanciers.

Feudal. Although the corresponding substantive of this word is " feud " it has no connection with the " feud " denoting enmity and hatred, this last being derived from the Anglo-Saxon *fah*, hostile; while " feudal " comes from the Low Latin *feudalis*, a vassal, and means that which pertains to feuds or fiefs. Traces of feudalism are to be found among the Anglo-Saxons, but the full force of the system came in with William the Conqueror. He would not permit any land to be held in absolute possession; all belonged to him as paramount lord. Some result of this remains to the present

H

day, as in the distinction, in law, between property
" real " and " personal "—the first being land
and the latter any other possession. Feudalism
was in many ways well adapted to the needs of
mediæval times, especially in its policy of land
tenure, but when towns began to gain importance
through commerce the inhabitants became restive
under the domination of the feudal lord, and the
decline of feudalism was commensurate with the
increase of commercial activity.

Feuilleton. This is a French word, the literal meaning
of which is a little leaf, from *feuille* a leaf, *feuiller*,
to come into leaf. It was first applied to that part
of the French newspapers devoted to a tale or
some other light literature, and has been adopted
in England to denote a serial story appearing in a
newspaper.

Fiacre. The name given to the French cab or hackney-
coach, introduced into Paris by Sauvage in 1640.
It was so called because the office for these cabs
was in a wine-seller's shop frequented by gardeners
and dedicated to St. Fiacre. Fiacre, according to
Alban Butler, was the son of an Irish king, born
in 600 A.D., to whose tomb pilgrimages were made
in the month of August. His commemoration day
is August 30th.

Fiasco. The word is the Italian for flask or bottle,
and, according to Edwards, gained its meaning of
failure or breakdown from the fact that in making
the beautiful old Venetian glass it was the custom,
when any flaw occurred in that delicate work, to
turn the article into a common flask—a *fiasco*. In
the Italian opera-house the cry " Ola, Ola, fiasco,"
is used to express the disapprobation of the
audience when a singer makes a false note or
otherwise fails to please.

Fib. " Ask me no questions and I'll tell you no fibs,"
writes Goldsmith in " She Stoops to Conquer,"
but he was probably using what was already an

old and well known phrase. The word " fib " is generally considered to be a mild term for a lie, and, on the authority of Skeat, is a weakened and abbreviated form of " fable," which comes from the Latin *fari*, I speak.

Fiddle. At first sight there seems little in common between the two words " fiddle " and " violin," although they denote the same instrument. But the root from which the two words are derived is the same, viz. :—the Latin *vidula*, from *vitulari*, skip like a calf, make merry, from *vitula*, a calf. It is curious that, while the word " violin " retains a certain stately significance, a contemptuous tinge should have been imported into the word " fiddle," of which the phrases " fiddle-faddle " and " fiddle-sticks " are an evident expression.

Field. The word comes to us from the Anglo-Saxon *feld*, and signifies a place where the trees have been " felled "—equivalent to the American term " clearing." It is of frequent occurrence in place-names in the English Home Counties, especially in Sussex, where alone there are as many as twenty-five to thirty examples, indicating the extent to which the land in that county was once covered with forest. (*See* DEN, HURST, LEY.) The prevalence of local names terminating in " field " testifies to the great amount of unfelled timber which still remained when these settlements were made, and in old writers the terms " wood " and " field " are continually used as contrasts, though with the progress of cultivation the antithesis of the two words has lost its force. It is interesting to notice that the word " veldt," so extensively used in South Africa, is but the Dutch equivalent for " field," brought into South Africa by the early Dutch settlers.

Fiend. The derivation in this case gives point to the significance of the word. It is the Anglo-Saxon *feond*, or *fiond*, a hater, properly the present participle of *feogan*, to hate, and cognate with the Danish and Swedish *fiende*, an enemy. The special characteristic of the archfiend, Satan, is, as Milton puts it, the " study of revenge, immortal hate."

Fiery-Cross. In a note appended to Sir Walter Scott's " Lady of the Lake " we have a vivid description of the method employed in sending out this call to arms, of which the following is an extract :— " When a chieftain designed to summon his clan upon any sudden or important emergency, he slew a goat and, making a cross of any light wood, seared the extremities in the fire, and extinguished them in the blood of the animal. This was called the ' Fiery Cross ' or the ' Cross of Shame ' (*Creau Tarigh*), because disobedience to what the symbol implied inferred infamy. It was delivered to a swift and trusty messenger, who ran at full speed with it to the next hamlet, where he presented it to the principal person with a single word giving the place of rendezvous. He who received the symbol was bound to send it forward with equal despatch, and thus it passed with incredible celerity through all the district which owned allegiance to the chief. At the sight of the ' Fiery Cross ' every man, from sixteen years old to sixty, capable of bearing arms, was obliged instantly to repair, in his best arms and accoutrements, to the place of rendezvous, and he who failed to appear suffered the extremities of fire and sword, emblematically denounced to the disobedient by the burnt and bloody marks upon the signal."

Fig. The fig-tree is reputed to have been first brought into England by Cardinal Pole, in 1525, but there is little doubt that the fig itself—the fruit—was imported here by the Romans during their occupation of this country, for it is stated on good authority that the Anglo-Saxon *fic*, a fig, is derived directly from the Latin *ficus*.

Filbert. A word of doubtful origin. Skeat is of the opinion that it is named after St· Philibert, whose feast was on August 22nd (O.S.), but according to Wedgwood the word is " fill-beard," because the nut just fills the cup made by the beards of the calyx. In German the name is *Lambert's nuss* (Lambert's nut), St. Lambert's day being on September 17th. The nut is the fruit of the cultivated hazel.

Firkin. A measure equal to the fourth part of a barrel, as the derivation of the word implies, viz. :—*vier*, the Old Dutch for four, and " kin " the diminutive suffix.

Flag. In spite of the inspiration which every patriot feels at the sight of his country's flag—the flag which, as Campbell sings, " has braved a thousand years, the battle and the breeze "—the derivation of the word " flag " is quite prosaic. " Flag " is but the weakened form of " flack," to flap, to flutter in the wind.

Flannel. This is a corruption of the word " flannen," from the Welsh *gwlanen*, meaning woollen, from *gwlan*, wool. In the time of Charles II. an endeavour was made to promote the woollen trade by ordering that all coffins should be lined with flannel.

Flea. This is an Anglo-Saxon word cognate with the Icelandic *flo*, the German *floh*, and the Dutch *vloo*, all from the root *plu*, to fly or jump. There is also the Sanscrit word *plu*, to swim, fly, or jump, of which the word *pulex*, the generic name for the insect, seems to be a modification, and the Old Hebrew name *parash*, signifies to leap. Certainly the allusion to leaping and jumping which appears in all these words is justified by the capability of the insect, for it can leap thirty times its own height and draw eighty times its own weight.

Fleet. The word comes from the Anglo-Saxon *fleotan*, to float or swim, and as a suffix in place-names it indicates a channel where water " fleets " or runs, a small stream. We find it in the names Ebb-fleet,

North-fleet, South-fleet and Pur-fleet.   Fleet Street,
in London, also gained its name from the river
Fleet, a small stream which flowed along the outside of the city walls.   And this stream also gave
its name to the street which crossed it at right
angles and led out of the city by the Fleet-gate,
otherwise Flood-gate, and now corrupted into
Lud-gate.

Flint Implements.   A generic term denoting spear-
heads and such like relics of early man found in
the Pleistocene or more recent deposits.   The
discoveries made in a cave at Brixham (Devon)
carry back the antiquity of man to a period when
the Hyena, the Elephant and the Rhinoceros
inhabited Great Britain, but the relics of the river-
drift man found in the valleys of the Somme and
the Thames are considered to be still older, and
have led to the belief in the existence of man, or a
man-like creature, in the Miocene period.   (NOTE :
Pleistocene = most recent, Miocene = less recent.)

Florin.   So called because the original Florentine coin
was stamped with a lily, the national badge of
Florence, the word being derived from the Latin
flos, *floris*, a flower.   In the time of Edward III.
there was an English gold coin called a " florin,"
a pound weight (old standard) of gold being coined
into fifty florins, which were current at six shillings
each.

Flute.   One of the most widely used of ancient musical
instruments and to this day an important item in
an orchestra. The derivation of the word brings us
back to the earliest method for the production of
musical sounds, for it shows that the meaning of
" flute " is simply something to be blown through.
(Latin *flo*, *flatum*.)

Fool.   In the Bible the term " fool " is sometimes used
in such a way as to be almost equivalent to
" wicked," as in Proverbs xiv. 9, " Fools make a
mock of sin," and in Psalm liii. 1, " The fool hath

said in his heart, there is no God." But in the present day acceptance of the word there is an implication of jocose contempt, with which, indeed, its derivation has much in common; for " fool " comes from the Latin *follis*, a wind-bag, plural *folles*, puffed out cheeks—the typical grimace of the buffoon.

Force. The word is the ordinary name for a waterfall in the Lake district. It is exclusively Norwegian, and corresponds to the Norwegian and Icelandic *foss*. High-force, Wilber-force, and Fos-ton may be quoted as examples.

Ford, Fiord. These two words have a close connection in place-names although they now bear a meaning directly opposed to each other, the first denoting a place where water may be crossed on foot and the latter a long, narrow, rock-bound inlet of the sea. The following extract from Isaac Taylor's "Words and Places" gives an interesting explanation of the way in which this apparent discrepancy arose. " The word ' ford ' is a derivative of *faran* or *fara*, to go. A cabman's or a waterman's ' fare ' is the person who ' goes ' with him, and ' fare-well ' is an imperative, meaning ' journey-well,' while the field-' fare ' is so called from its characteristic habit of moving across the fields. (*See* FARE.) From *faran*, to go, to pass, we get ' ford,' a passage, and the suffix ' ford ' occurs both in Anglo-Saxon and in Norse place-names, but with a characteristic difference of meaning. The ' fords ' of the Anglo-Saxon husbandman which are scattered so abundantly over the South of England are passages across rivers for men and cattle (Bland-ford, Dart-ford, and Walling-ford are examples), but the ' fords ' of the Scandinavian sea-rovers are passages for ships, up the arms of the sea, like the fjords of Norway and the firths of Scotland—these Norse ' fords ' are found on the coasts which were frequented for the purposes of trade or plunder. We have instances in the names

Wex-ford and Water-ford in Ireland, Haver-ford
in Wales, Or-ford in Suffolk, and in the Firth of
Forth in Scotland."

Fop. The word is of uncertain origin, but it probably
comes from the Dutch *foppen*, to cheat, to mock
—*foppen*, a wag. Certainly it is not of recent
origin in English, for as long ago as 1697
Vanbrugh, in his comedy of "The Relapse,"
introduced a character of the name of Lord
Foppington, as an empty-headed coxcomb, intent
only on dress.

Fops'-Alley was the gangway between the last
row of the stalls and the first row of the pit in
Her Majesty's Theatre, and we learn from Sala
that in its palmiest days it was always graced
by the presence of a subaltern of the Guards, in
full uniform, daintily swinging his bearskin.

Forks. As an implement of general use at table the
fork did not appear until the seventeenth century,
though as early as the thirteenth century gold and
silver forks were made. Queen Elizabeth is
reputed to have been the first English Sovereign
who used a fork at table, but her example was so
scantily followed that an audacious divine of those
days preached a sermon in which he asserted that
"it was an insult to the Almighty not to touch one's
meat with one's fingers." Even so late as the
reign of George I. forks were so little customary
that few inns provided them, and yet in 1611,
according to an old book of travels of that date,
the Italians always used "a little forke when they
cut their meate."

Fresco. This is an Italian word signifying cool, fresh,
and signifies the painting in water colours on
fresh plaster, or on a wall covered with mortar
not quite dry. In such a case the plaster is only
laid on as the painting proceeds, no more being
done at once than the painter can despatch in a
day, and thus the colours, being prepared with

water and applied over plaster quite fresh, become incorporated with the plaster ar l retain their beauty for a great length of time. It is not uncommon to use the term " frescoes " for ancient paintings found on church walls, etc., but they are generally merely distemper paintings on plaster, and quite distinct in their durability and mode of manipulation from the true " fresco," which was well understood by the ancients and was brought to a pitch of real importance by the Italians in the sixteenth century.

Frigate. The name was originally applied to a Mediterranean vessel propelled by oars as well as sails, and afterwards came to denote a ship of war of a grade between the sloop and the ship of the line employed as a cruiser or scout. The word " frigate " is derived from the Spanish *fragata*, probably corrupted from *fargata*, a contracted form of the Latin *fabricata*, the feminine singular past participle of *fabricare*, to build,—in itself an indication of the antiquity of the name.

Fuchsia. So named after Leonard Fuchs, a German botanist, who lived from 1501 to 1566. The plant is a native of South America, and was introduced into England in 1837.

Fudge. An exclamation of contempt of common occurrence in old writers but perhaps not much used now. Goldsmith, in his " Vicar of Wakefield," puts it into the mouth of Mr. Burchell, and it appears in Thackeray's and Lord Lytton's books. Curiously enough, though it sounds like a word of no meaning its derivation has a precise signification—it comes from the Low German *futsch*, begone !

Gab. The " gift of the gab "—if used with discretion —is a faculty not to be despised. The word " gab " is connected with the Irish " cob " or " gob," the mouth, and is found in some similar form in the Danish, Swedish, Icelandic, Portuguese and Italian languages. The Old French *gob* means a mouthful.

Gaffer. The word is now generally used as a term of contempt for an old labourer, but formerly denoted respect, being a contraction or corruption of " grandfather," and there is some implication of its primitive meaning when the word is applied to the foreman of a gang of men. (*See* GANGER.)

Gainsay. The word is frequently used in the Bible in the sense of contradiction, opposition or denial. (*See* Luke xxi. 15; Acts x. 29; Rom. x. 21; Jude 11; Titus i. 9). As a prefix, " gain " was largely used in the sense of " back," " against," in direct opposition to the signification of acquiring or profiting by, but of these compounds only " gainsay " now remains in use.

Galaxy. We use the term " galaxy " to denote any assemblage of splendid persons or things, but in the strict sense of its derivation it is applicable only to that wonderful congregation of innumerable stars called the milky-way. For the word " galaxy " comes to us, through the French and the Latin, from the Greek *galaxias*—*gala, galaktos*, akin to the Latin *lac, lactis*, milk.

Galley. The origin of the word seems to be quite unknown, but the vessel it denotes is certainly of great antiquity. It is said to have been invented by the Corinthians 700 years before the Christian era, and it developed into huge crafts of 100 to 200 feet long, with one to five banks (rows) of oars and as many as fifty oars in a single tier, each worked by two or more men, generally slaves. The horrible sufferings sometimes endured by these slaves are too terrible to recount. Galleys, manned by criminals, were introduced into France in the reign of Charles VI.—he kept forty in his service—but were abolished by Louis XV. in 1748.

Gallipot. This is simply a corruption of the Old Dutch word *gleypot*, a glazed pot, from the Dutch *gleis*, meaning glazed.

Gambler. This is comparatively a modern word, substituted for "gamester," and described by Johnson as "a cant word."

Gammon. This word, in its signification of a hoax or nonsense, has no connection with a "gammon" of bacon, etc., but is derived from the Anglo-Saxon *gamen*, a game, a sport. We retain its full sense in the word "backgammon," a game which has gained its name from the fact that, under certain circumstances, the pieces are obliged to go back and come on the board again.

Ganger. The word is formed from the verb to "gang," which is derived from the Anglo-Saxon *gangan*, to go, to travel together, and in "gang" we retain the meaning of a number of persons going together for a certain purpose. In "ganger" we have an extension of the word "gang," thus meaning one who leads, directs or controls a gang, the fore-man or overseer of a number of men engaged on some particular work.

Gaol. This word (now often spelt Jail) must not be confounded with the "goal" of the football field or the racecourse, which is derived from the French *gaule*, a pole. The word "gaol," denoting a prison, is derived from the Latin *cavea*, a cage, *cavus*, hollow. It is said to be the only English word in which the diphthong "ao" occurs.

Gargoyle. Undoubtedly a wealth of imagination and skill must have been expended on many of the gargoyles which we see adorning the walls of old churches and other ancient buildings, and yet they served the humble purpose of a spout to convey the rainwater from the roof. All sorts of quaint and hideous figures of man, beast, and bird are chiselled out of the solid stone, but the most common is that of a dragon, the emblem of Satan, cast out from the holy precincts of the church and condemned to perform a menial office. In this connection it is worth remembering that Gargouille

was the name of the great dragon that lived in
the Seine and ravaged Rouen, and was slain by
Romanus, Bishop of Rouen, in the seventh
century. Possibly there is some allusion to this
dragon in the name " gargoyle," but the general
explanation of the origin of the word is its derivation from the French *gargouille*, meaning the
windpipe, the throat, and applied to these figures
because they were made to convey the water
through their throats.

Garlic. The word conjures up a vision of the Italian or
Portuguese peasant eating bread and slices of
garlic, and yet it is essentially an English word,
direct from the Anglo-Saxon *gar*, a spear, and
leac, a leek, a plant, the name having reference
to the spear-like shape of the leaves of the plant.
The word *leac*, as meaning a plant, is also retained
in " char-lock " and " hem-lock."

Garnet. This is a precious stone of the crystallised
mineral type and is of various colours, red, brown,
yellow, white, or even black with a white streak.
The red is that most usually seen, and to this
colour the name of the stone has been ascribed,
the cochineal insect from which the red dye is
obtained being called *granata* in Low Latin, the
insect having been supposed to be a berry or seed.
But a more generally accepted explanation is that
the name came from the resemblance of the stone
to the seeds of the pomegranate, the Latin for
pomegranate being *pomum-granatum*, an apple
having many seeds.

Garret. The old meaning attached to this word was
that of a watch-tower, a look-out, and in the
romance of Sir Tryamour we find it used in that
sense :—

> " Then was that lady sett
> Hye up in a garett
> To behold that play."

We now restrict the word to denoting a room

next the roof of a house, but the old signification is quite in accordance with the derivation, which is the Old French *garite*, a place of safety, connected with the Anglo-Saxon *warian*, to defend, from which we get the English "wary" and "warn." The words "garrison" (a supply of soldiers for a *fortified* place) and "garnish" (to *surround* with ornaments) are from the same root. So also is "garnishee," a legal term indicating a person *warned* to refrain from paying money owed to another, because the latter is indebted to the person who gives the *warning* and who is called the "garnisher."

Garth. This is the Norse equivalent for the Anglo-Saxon "yard" (*see* COHORT) and in places-names bears nearly the same signification as "ton," denoting some place "guarded" or "girded" around. Fish-guard in Pembrokeshire, and Applegarth in Yorkshire may be quoted as examples.

Gas. This is one of the few words which may claim to have been invented, as distinct from being derived or deliberately formed from some older language. Nevertheless, the inventor—Van Helmont, a Flemish chemist (1577-1644)—is considered by Dr. Murray to have been influenced by the Greek word *chaos*, and it is also asserted that the word was probably suggested by the Flemish *geest* and the German *geist*, spirit.

Gate. As applied to place-names the word is commonly used, in districts of England where the Scandinavian language has left its mark, to denote a road or a street, as in the case of Harro-gate. In many northern towns the older streets bear this suffix; in Leeds we have Brig-gate (Bridge Street), and Kirk-gate (Church Street), while in York there are no less than twenty streets with names ending in "gate." In the South the word usually takes the sense of a passage through a town wall, as in the case of New-gate, Bishops-gate, and the other gates of London, but in High-gate we again have the sense of a road. Passages through a line of hills or through a cliff to the sea are frequently denoted by the word "gate." Rei-gate, for instance, is a contraction of Ridge-gate, the passage through the North Downs, and Gat-ton, near by, is the town at the passage; Pole-gate and Hassocks-gate are passages through the South Downs; while Rams-gate, Mar-gate, Kings-gate, and Sand-gate are all names denoting passages to the shore through the cliffs. The difference between the northern and southern use of "gate" —the first as a street or a road and the latter as a passage—arises from the fact that in the one case the word is derived from the Scandinavian *gata* and in the other from the Anglo-Saxon *geat*. The distinction between them is analogous to that in the words "fjord" and "ford" (*see* FORD), the one being a passage *along* and the other a passage *through*.

Gaudy. The signification which we now attach to this word—that of ostentatious, showy, tastelessly fine —is of long duration, for Shakespeare (Hamlet i. 3) makes Polonius say :—

" Costly thy habit, as thy purse can buy,
　But not expressed in fancy—rich, not gaudy;
　For the apparel oft proclaims the man."

Yet with many old writers the word "gauds" is used to denote beautiful gems, as in Sir Walter Scott's line :—

"Gauds have no glitter, gems no shine;"

and the derivation of the word is the Latin *gaudium*, joy, delight.

Gavotte. The name originally denoted the dance of the Gavotes, a people of Gap, in the Upper Alps, but it was soon identified with an instrumental piece and became a favourite movement in suites and sonatas in the latter part of the seventeenth century.

Gawk, Gawky. These words have a curious origin; they are direct descendants of the Anglo-Saxon *geac*, which, in more or less similar form, is found in the German, Swedish, Danish, and Icelandic languages, and means a cuckoo. In the "Morte d'Arthur" we find the word "gawk" used in the sense of "cuckoo":—

"Thare galede (sings) the gowke fulle lawde."

Gazette. According to Wedgwood it is a mistake to suppose that the original newspaper was named from the small Venetian coin called *gazetta*, as the value of the coin was so small—less than an English farthing—that it could not have been the price either of a written or printed sheet, and that the word "gazette" is derived from *gazza*, a magpie, meaning all sorts of idle chattering. But in Brewer's dictionary the name is connected with the issue of a manuscript newspaper, once a month, by the Venetian Government during the war with the Turks in 1563, when the news was read publicly in certain places and the fee for *hearing* it read was one gazetta. The supposition that the coin was the origin of the name "gazette" does not necessarily exclude a concomitant derivation from the magpie.

Gehenna. The literal meaning of the word is Valley of Hinnom, from the Hebrew *ge*, valley, and Hinnom, the name of the original owner. (*See* Josh. xviii. 16.) The place lies a short distance south of Jerusalem, and it was there, during the later period of the Jewish kings, that the people made their sons and daughters pass through the fire to Moloch, the Ammonite fire-god (2 Kings, xxiii. 10), or actually burnt them in the fire (2 Chron. xxviii. 3). The furnace in which these human sacrifices were offered was called Tophet, and derived its name from the tabrets (Hebrew *tophet*), musical instruments of the tambourine type, used with cymbals to drown the cries of the victims. Later, when King Josiah had put an end to these practices, the Valley of Hinnom became a defiled place where refuse of all sorts was cast, for the consumption of which fires were kept continually burning. Hence Gehenna became an apt simile for the final place of punishment, of eternal torment.

Gem. The beauty of the gem has been extolled by poets from time immemorial, and Moore writes of woman as

" First flower of the earth and first gem of the sea,"

a particularly appropriate simile; for the word " gem " may be described as meaning that which has come to the full and budded, being derived from the Latin *gemma*, a bud, and allied to the Greek *gemo*, to be full.

Gentiles. In the Old Testament the word translated " Gentiles " is the Hebrew *goim*, meaning peoples, nations. The Jews seem to have used this word, at first, in a purely ethnological sense and quite respectfully, but as they grew in importance and became more thoroughly imbued with the belief of their superiority as a God-chosen people, they used it more and more scornfully of other nations. To such an extent had this developed that —as shown in Acts x., and specially in verse 28 of that chapter—it was deemed beneath the dignity of a Jew to consort with one of another nation, and it is recorded that a direct vision was vouchsafed to the Apostle Peter before he could bring himself to visit and preach to a gentile—the centurion Cornelius, good and honourable man though he was.

Genus. It is interesting to observe how numerous are the words we have derived from the Latin *genus*, which means birth, descent, origin. For instance : we speak of a generous disposition, a gentle nature, a man of genius, the gentleman and the gentry, a genteel demeanour, the genesis of a thing (its beginning, as the first chapter of the Bible, containing an account of the Creation). All these words which begin with " gen " have their origin in *genus*, cognate with the English " kin," " kith," and " kindred," and with the Sanscrit *jan*, to beget.

Geometry. The science of geometry extends over a wide field, and even Euclid's " Elements," with its definitions, axioms and postulates, is difficult for many of us to grasp. Euclid is reputed to have founded a school of mathematics at Alexandria some time between the years 323 and 284 B.C., but who first invented—or even cultivated—geometry as a science it is impossible to say. It has been ascribed to the Hindoos because they have a system of apparently indigenous growth, and to the Egyptians because a knowledge of it was necessary for the building of the Pyramids, but it has been rightly said that " the first geometrician was the ploughman pacing out his field." And the derivation of the word " geometry " implies as much— it is the Greek *geometria*, land measure, from *ge*, the earth, and *metron*, a measure.

Georgic. The term must not be confused with " Georgian," that which relates to the period of the four King Georges of Great Britain (1714-1830). The word " georgic " is derived from the Greek *ge*, the earth, and *ergon*, a work, and denotes something which pertains to agriculture or rural affairs. " The Georgics " is the title of four books on husbandry written by Virgil.

Geranium. It is said that the first red geranium grown in England was raised by a florist in the King's Road, Chelsea, in the year 1822. According to an Islam legend the geranium was a common mallow, which was changed by the touch of Mahomet's garment. The word " geranium " is derived from the Greek *geranos*, a crane, in allusion to the likeness of the seed-vessels of the plant to a crane's bill, and the common name for the English wild geranium is "crane's-bill."

German. In the term "cousins-german" the word "german" is equivalent to "germane," and means closely allied, being derived from the Latin *germanus*, akin, having the same ancestors, from the root *germen*, *germinis*, a bud, origin. The English word "germ" has the same derivation.

Get. The following extract from Eliezer Edwards' Dictionary is a good example of the manifold and rightful uses of the verb "to get":—"I *got* on horseback within ten minutes after I *got* your letter. When I *got* to Canterbury, I *got* a chaise for town; but I *got* wet through before I *got* to Canterbury, and I have *got* such a cold as I shall not be able to *get* rid of in a hurry. I *got* to the Treasury about noon, but first of all I *got* shaved and dressed. I soon *got* into the secret of *getting* a memorial before the Board, but I could not *get* an answer then; however, I *got* intelligence from the messenger that I should, most likely, *get* one the next morning. As soon as I *got* back to my inn, I *got* my supper and *got* to bed. When I *got* up in the morning, I *got* my breakfast, and then *got* myself dressed that I might *get* out in time to *get* an answer to my memorial. As soon as I *got* it, I *got* into the chaise, and *got* to Canterbury by three, and about tea-time I *got* home. I have *got* nothing for you, and so adieu."

Gewgaw ("g" hard). In the opinion of Skeat the word is a duplication of "give," being a corruption of the Old English "giuegoue," "give-gove," but it has now lost its meaning of a gift and is used to denote any showy trifle.

Ghastly. According to some authorities this word is derived from the Anglo-Saxon *gaestlic*, terrible, from the root *gais*, which is found in the words "aghast" and "gaze," the idea implied being that of a fixed look of terrified attention; while others connect "ghastly" with the Anglo-Saxon *gast*, a ghost, a spirit. It seems possible, however, that the two words *gais* and *gast* may themselves have a common origin.

Gherkin. It seems curious that we should have two distinct names for what is essentially the same article, for a gherkin is, of course, a cucumber of the small variety used for pickling. The explanation is that in the one case ("gherkin") we borrow the word, through the Dutch *agurkje*, from the Arabic *khirgar* and the Hindu *khivar*, all of which denote a cucumber; while in the other case ("cucumber") we take the name from the Latin *cucumis* (acc. *cucumerem*). The cucumber must have been known and used from very ancient times, for we learn from the Bible (Numb. xi. 5) that it was enjoyed in Egypt before the exodus of the Israelites, and it is said to have been common in England during the reign of Edward III., but that in the Wars of the Roses it was allowed to go out of cultivation and was re-introduced from the Netherlands about 1538.

Gibberish. The opinion has been advanced that this word is derived from Geber, the name of an Arabian alchemist of the eleventh century, because of the mystical jargon in which he wrote in order to avoid the penalty—most probably death—which he would have incurred from the ecclesiastics of the day had he written openly. It is more likely, however, that the word has been formed from the verb "to gibber," a variant of "jabber," which is a weakened form of "gabber," "gabble," derived from the old word "gab" (q.v.).

Gig. The word, by which we now denote a light, two-wheeled, one-horse vehicle, has a curious origin. It used to denote a fiddle, and Chaucer has it in that sense, but in that meaning it is now obsolete. Yet the etymology of the word makes it more applicable to a fiddle than a vehicle, for there is little doubt that "gig" is cognate with the Icelandic *geiga*, to vibrate. The French *gigue* means a lively dance, and the gig may have obtained its name in allusion to this, as a vehicle that moves lightly.

Gill. A Scandinavian word meaning a ravine and very prevalent as a suffix to place-names in the Lake district. Butter-gill, Dungeon-gill, Orms-gill, and Ay-gill may be cited as examples.

Gin. The name is derived from the Dutch *giniva*, which comes from the French *genievere*, meaning juniper, and the application of the name arose from the fact of the spirit being flavoured with juniper-berries. The spirit is also called "Geneva" and "Hollands," the first being merely a corruption of *genievere* and the latter a name for gin made in Holland.

Gingham. A common nickname for an umbrella, the stuff called "gingham" being used as a covering for an umbrella instead of the more expensive silk. Gingham is a fabric of cotton coloured in the thread, and is supposed to have gained its name from the town of Guing-amp, in Brittany, where the material was made.

Gipsy. The word is a corruption of the Middle English "Gyptian," a contraction of "Egyptian," applied to the gipsies because they were supposed to have come from Egypt. There is little doubt, however, that India was their original home, and though it is impossible to say when the exodus occurred they are now scattered all over Europe. Each nation seems to have given them a different name, but by themselves they are called *Rom*, a man, and hence we get the name Romani, by which they are often called.

Glade. It is doubtless true that an appreciation of the beauties of the natural prospect—especially of such scenery as we call "grand"—is of very modern growth, and our poets seem silent on the subject

until the beginning of the nineteenth century. But
in the etymology of many words we find an indication that our forefathers had a deep sympathy with
and an overflowing delight in its peaceful aspects.
The glade in which their swine pastured was to
them a joyous sight, which found expression in the
very word "glade"; for "glade" is almost
synonymous with "glad," so closely are the two
words connected. And the Hebrew poets seem to
have been suffused with the same idea—"The
valleys stand so thick with corn that they shall
laugh and sing." (Ps. lxv. 14, Prayer-Book
version.)

Gladiator. The literal meaning of the word is swords-
man, from the Latin *gladius*, a sword. Gladiators
were men whose profession was to fight in public
for the entertainment of the people. They usually
fought in pairs, and were principally recruited from
prisoners of war or refractory slaves sold by their
masters to the trainer for the purpose. Male-
factors also were occasionally condemned to fight
as gladiators, and under the more worthless and
dissolute Emperors, citizens, senators and priests
contended in the arena in order to attract the
attention and favour of the Cæsar, while even
high-born women consented to pander to the
vicious propensities of the period by fighting with
each other or with dwarfs.

Glamour. The derivation of the word seems peculiarly corroborative of its general meaning, for
"glamour" comes from the Icelandic *glam*, dim-
ness of sight, and *glamr*, a mythical ghost or
spirit.

Glass. The word is from the Anglo-Saxon *glæs*,
derived from the root *gal*, widely diffused in
Teutonic languages and seen in "glare,"
"gleam," and "glow." Pliny reports that glass
first became known through some seamen with a
cargo of "nitrum" (soda, or some such salt)
having used some blocks of their cargo as a grate

for the fire they had lighted on landing near the mouth of a small stream at the base of Mount Carmel, when the heat fused together the sand and the salt and produced glass. Such an occurrence may have happened, but glass was certainly known in Egypt as early as 1740 B.C., and remains of it have been found in the ruins of Assyrian cities. Gregory of Tours reports that churches had coloured glass windows in the fourth century, but glass was not manufactured in England until 1557.

Glen, Glyn. These two words are respectively the Gaelic and the Welsh names meaning a narrow valley, as in Glen-coe and Glyn-neath.

Gloaming. There are few people who have not felt the subdued melancholy of the fall of the evening—the gloaming—when the days begin to shorten with the passing of summer. And the word is evidence of the natural inherence of such a feeling, for it comes to us from the Anglo-Saxon *glomung*, which is derived from *glom*, gloom.

Glove. The glove appears to have been of ancient use, even in this country, for the word has come to us direct from the Anglo-Saxon *glof*, equivalent to *ge-lof*, which is probably the Gothic *lofa*, the palm of the hand, combined with the common Anglo-Saxon prefix *ge*, a prefix which often becomes " a " in English, as in " a-ware."

Glyn. A component in place-names. (*See* GLEN.)

God. In Anglo-Saxon the word is *God*, in Dutch *God*, in German *Gott*, in Gothic *Guth*, and in all Teutonic languages the root of the word is *Gutha*, which means God, and is quite distinct from " good." It is probably connected with the Persian *khoda*, lord, and with the Sanscrit *gudha*, secret. Professor Max Muller says :—" Though it is impossible to give a satisfactory etymology of either ' God ' or ' good,' it is clear that two words which thus run parallel in all the dialects without ever meeting cannot be traced back to one central point. ' God ' was most likely an old heathen name of the Deity, and for such a name the supposed etymological meaning of ' good ' would be far too modern, too abstract, too Christian."

Gold. This is a word which we retain from the Anglo-Saxon, and in most Aryan languages the word is very similar, as the German *gold*, the Swedish and Danish *guld*, and the Dutch *goud*. It is believed that they all arise from a primary root, viz. :— *ghar*, which means to be yellow. Thus the slang term " yellow-boy " (a sovereign) and the expression " the yellow metal " are but reversions to the original type. But in Hebrew the most usual word for " gold " is *zahab*, meaning to shine, and from this fact it has been deduced that gold may not have been discovered until after the separation of the Aryan and Semitic races.

Gooseberry. In this word the first syllable—" goose " —has lost an " r "; it was originally " grose " or " groise," from the Old French *groisele, groselle,* or *groiselle*; the Irish being *groisaid* and the Gaelic *groiseid*; all meaning a gooseberry. The root of the word seems to be the Old German *krus*, crisp, curled, in allusion to the hairs with which some varieties of the gooseberry are covered. In the term " gooseberry-fool " the suffix is a corruption of the French *foulé*, pressed or mashed. We have two phrases connected with the word " gooseberry " :—" To play gooseberry " and " To play old gooseberry." The first means to play propriety to two lovers, to be present with them but to hear, see, and say nothing; the second means to play the deuce, to throw everything into confusion. It seems impossible to trace how such expressions arose.

Gordian Knot. The term is used to denote an inextricable difficulty, and " to cut the gordian-knot " is to get out of it in a bold and summary manner.

Gordius was the peasant-king of Phrygia; he dedicated his waggon to Jupiter and fastened the yoke to a beam with a rope so ingeniously knotted that no one could untie it. Alexander the Great was told that whoever undid the knot would reign over the whole empire of Asia, and to inspire his army with confidence and his enemies with the belief that he was born to conquer, he cut the knot with his sword, thus claiming that the prophecy was fulfilled in himself.

Gospel. The word is commonly stated to be derived from the Anglo-Saxon god-spell, meaning good news, and thus a translation of the Greek *eu-anggelion* (*eu*, well, and *anggelion*, a message). But more probably " gospel " is the Anglo-Saxon *God-spell*, meaning God-story, a narrative of God, and so not connected in any way with the word " good." (*See* GOD.)

Gossip. This is a word the significance of which has materially altered. Its early form was " god-sib," denoting one who was related to another in the service of God, *i.e.*, a sponsor in baptism. *Sib* or *gesib* is the Anglo-Saxon for kinsman, and " sib " is still used in Scotland to indicate a cousin or near relation. Dean Hoare attributes the present meaning of the word " gossip " to the custom of god-parents meeting together to have a chat.

Gothic. The term, as applied to architecture, was originally bestowed in contempt, at the time of the Renaissance, to buildings which did not conform in their style to the classical Italian architecture, and which were considered, therefore, to belong to a barbarous and uncivilised age, like the Goths of old.

Grail. The Holy Grail (*San Greal*, from the Old French *graal* or *greal*, a dish) must not be confounded with the *Sans Real*, or Holy Blood. The Holy Grail, according to various legendary accounts, is the dish in which our Lord instituted the sacrament of the Last Supper. Having been stolen by a servant, it passed into the possession of Pilate and was used by him to wash his hands in at the condemnation of Christ. It was afterwards given by Pilate, as a memorial of Christ, to Joseph of Arimathea, and was used by him to collect the blood which flowed from our Lord while he hung upon the cross. Joseph is supposed to have brought it to England, where it disappeared, and the quest for its recovery is the source of many of the adventures of the Knights of the Round Table. Sir Galahad, the chaste and righteous knight, saw it and died, and each of the one-hundred-and-fifty knights of King Arthur caught some glimpse of it, but it could remain with no one who was not absolutely pure in heart and holy in conduct.

Grange. The word is now frequently used to denote a house and premises of some importance, but the original meaning was simply a barn, a granary, a place in which to store corn. It comes from the Latin *granum*, a grain, corn.

Granite. So named because the stone has a coarse, granular structure, the word being derived from the Latin *granum*, a grain.

Grape. The word is used with us to denote a single berry of the fruit of the grape-vine, but the Old French *grappe*, from which it is derived, meant a bunch of grapes, and *grappe* comes from the Old High German *chrapho*, which originally denoted a hook, and then came to mean a cluster of fruit hooked on or attached to a stem. The phrase " sour grapes," meaning something unattainable and therefore condemned as worthless, is derived from one of Æsop's fables, in which the fox decides to believe the grapes he tried to get were sour because he could not reach them. The " wild grapes " of which we read in the Bible (Isaiah v. 2-4) are the black and shining fruit of the deadly nightshade, a common plant in the vineyards of Palestine.

Gravitation. There is little doubt that some faint idea of this force was entertained nearly five hundred years before the Christian era; it seems to have been present in the minds of Democritus and Epicurus in ancient times, and, perhaps, was more clearly discerned by Bacon, Galileo, and Kepler at the dawn of modern science. But the decisive discovery of the universality of gravitation and the law of its operation was reserved for that wonderful man—Isaac Newton.

Greengage. The name, in part descriptive of its colour, was given in honour of the Rev. M. Gage, who first brought the fruit to England.

Grenadier. The grenadiers were originally foot-soldiers armed with grenades; they were necessarily men of approved courage, and only a few were attached to each regiment. After the disuse of grenades, the grenadiers retained their name as a regiment— the Grenadier Guards.

Greyhound. The name has no reference to the colour of the animal, but is derived from the Icelandic *greyhundr*, *grey* meaning a dog, and *hundr*, a hound. It must be a very early variety of the canine tribe, for the figure of a dog, apparently of this type, is found on Egyptian monuments.

Groat. Although this was but a small silver coin, formerly current at the value of four-pence, and its name used proverbially for any trifling sum, the word " groat " means great, derived from the Old Dutch *groote*. It is supposed to have gained its name from the fact that it was larger than the small copper coins formerly in use.

Grocer. Though this word is now used to denote a dealer in tea, coffee, sugar, dried fruits, etc., its derivation gives it a much wider application. " Grocer " comes to us from the Old French *grossier*, derived from *gros*, great, and may properly define one who sells by the gross or wholesale.

Grotesque. This word comes to us from the Italian *grottesca*, derived from *grotta*, which means a grotto, a cave, a crypt. In Italy the term *grottesca* was applied to the monumental paintings —many of them of strange and curious design— which were discovered in the subterraneous chambers decorated in the time of the ancient Romans, and hence our word " grotesque " came to denote all subjects of a quaint or anomalous character.

Grove. The sacred character of a grove is of unknown antiquity, and while closely connected with Tree and Serpent worship, is probably older than either. One can imagine how the solitude and mystery of the primeval forest must have affected uncultured races and led them to hold such places in reverence, as the abodes of mighty unknown forces. Both in ancient Greece and Rome—as shown in the writings of Catullus and Ovid—groves were held sacred to the worship of the gods, and among Teutonic nations (as we learn from Grimm) altars and sacred vessels stood in the forest, and there worship was performed and sacrifice offered. We know, too, how important in the rites of the ancient Druids were the groves of oak-trees, and in remote places there still lingers a belief in the sacredness of groves. Lord Avebury has stated that " even recently an oak copse in the Isle of Skye was held to be so sacred that no one would venture to cut the smallest branch from it." In the English translation of the Old Testament the word " grove " is frequently used in connection with idolatrous worship, but it seems almost certain that the Hebrew *Asherah* so rendered is an idol, and not a plantation of trees. *Asherah* probably denotes the idol which was made to represent Ashtoreth, the Phœnician goddess, and clearly there was a relation between Baal and Asherah, for when, at Elijah's demand, there assembled at

Mount Carmel 450 prophets of Baal, there were with them 400 " prophets of the groves "—*i.e.*, of Asherah (1 Kings xviii. 19). The worship of Asherah seems to have been connected with phallic rites, from which the Jewish nation was certainly not free.

Guillotine. The apparatus was in use in the Middle Ages, under the name of The Maiden (q.v.) but it was improved and re-introduced at the French Revolution by Dr. Guillotin, after whom it received its present name. It is an error to suppose that Dr. Guillotin perished by the machine—he lived till 1814, and founded the Academy of Medicine.

Guilt. The old idea—so ingrained in human nature that it still persists—that wrong-doing can be expiated by the payment of money, or its equivalent, is strangely exemplified in the word " guilt." It comes from the Anglo-Saxon *gylt*, which means a fine.

Gwent. This was the name of an ancient kingdom comprising the counties of Monmouth and Glamorgan, and its Latinised form may still be traced in many place-names, as in Win-chester, Da-vent-ry, and Caer-went. The word means an open plain.

H. Although much difference is often produced in the meaning of a word by the omission of the aspirate, there is sometimes a curious analogy between two words with and without the " h." For instance, with the " ear " one " hears," with an " axe " one hacks," at the " edge " of a field there is a " hedge," the " hall " of the castle was for " all." On the other hand, " hair " is distinct from " air," " harrow " from " arrow," " helm " from " elm." " H " should still have its value in such words as " whither " and " where," which are the descendants of the Old English *hwidir* and *hwoer*; but the letter has been entirely dropped in " loaf " from *hlaf*, in " neck " from *hnecca*, and in " ring " from *hring*.

Habeas Corpus. A writ commanding the production of the body of one detained in prison, in order that a properly constituted court may judge of the reasons of such detention. The Habeas Corpus Act was passed on 27th May, 1679, and its enactment is referred to by Macaulay as " a great era in our history. The law respecting personal liberty had been inefficacious for want of a stringent system of procedure, and such a remedy the Habeas Corpus Act supplied."

Hackney. The whole of this district originally belonged to a Danish Chief named Hacon. The suffix *ey* expresses an island—*i.e.*, land intersected by rivulets (in this case of the Lea)—or low, marshy ground.

Hackney Coach. The name is derived from the French *coche-à-haquenée*, a vehicle drawn by a *haquenée*, a hired horse. In " Stafford's Letters and Despatches " there appears a letter dated 1st April, 1634, which says :—" Here (London) one Captain Bailey hath erected some four hackney coaches, put his men in a livery and appointed them to stand at the Maypole in the Strand, giving them instructions at what rates to carry men into several parts of the town. Everybody is much pleased, for whereas, before, coaches could not be had but at great rates, now a man may have one much cheaper."

Haigh. (*See* HAY.)

Hail. An exclamation of greeting derived from the Anglo-Saxon *hæl*, " health." The Scandinavian *heill* expressed the same sentiment.

Halberd (Halbert). The derivation of this word has been assumed to be from the German *helm*, a helmet, and *barte*, a broad axe, but the real meaning, according to Skeat, is a long-handled axe, from the Middle High German *halm*, a handle, and *barte*, a broad axe. It consisted of a pole, about five feet long, surmounted by a head of steel, generally crescent-shaped, but it took a variety of fanciful forms and was sometimes gilded. Ultimately it became a mere decorative weapon for display in public ceremonials.

Halcyon Days. The term is applied to indicate days of peace and tranquility, and arose from the once popular belief that kingfishers (the Latin for which is *halcyon*) "lay and sit about mid-winter, when daies be shortest; and the time whiles they are broodie is called the *halcyon daies*, for during that season the sea is calm and navigable," it being supposed that these birds nested and laid their eggs in floating seaweed, knowing by instinct when the weather would be calm.

Hall. As a suffix to place-names in England this is indicative of Anglo-Saxon origin. It is synonymous with "sall," and denotes a stone house. Coggles-hall, Eccles-hall, Ken-sall, and Wal-sal are examples.

Hallelujah. The word is the Hebrew *hâllelû-Yâh*, praise ye Jehovah. It is an ascription of praise occurring in many of the Psalms and became a doxology in the Jewish synagogues. It was introduced into the Christian worship by St. Jerome about the fourth century, and he tells us that, in those days, anyone walking in the fields might hear the ploughman at his hallelujahs. "Hallelujah-lass" is a name given to a woman of the Salvation Army, who takes an active part in leading, and accompanying on the tambourine, the singing at the services of that body.

Hall-mark. The mark stamped by the Goldsmiths' Company on articles of gold and silver as a guarantee of their standard value. The assay mark on gold designates its quality; thus 18 indicates that 18 carats out of one pennyweight are pure gold. Two qualities of silver are hall-marked; one which has 11 oz. 10 dwts. of pure silver to 1 lb. Troy, and the other 11 oz., 2 dwts., the standard of the English coin. The finest silver is marked with a figure of Britannia and the standard with a lion passant.

Hallow. Derived from the Anglo-Saxon *hálig*, holy, and connected with "Hale," "Heal," "Holy," "Whole." Dean Trench has pointed out that more than two hundred years ago this word was said to have almost fallen into disuse, yet in the present day it is still commonly employed. It was formerly used in the place of "Saint," *e.g.* :— All Hallows (All Saints), Hallowe'en (All Saints Eve), Hallowmas, Hallowfair. The connection between the words "Holy," "Hale," and "Whole" is worthy of note.

Halo. The word is a transfer into English of the Latin *halos* (gen. and acc. *halo*) and the Greek *halōs*, a round threshing-floor. Haloes round the sun and moon are due to the refraction of light when passing through surrounding mist. The halo as a sacred emblem round the head of a god or a saint is of unknown antiquity, and doubtless it was originally associated with sun-worship, but though thus used as an emblem of holiness the word "halo" has no connection with "hallow."

Ham. An Anglo-Saxon word very prevalent in place-names. It has a double signification, the importance of which is sometimes overlooked. When, in old documents, we find it with a short "a" (since modified, in many cases, into "hen"), it denotes merely an enclosure, that which hems in, analogous to "ton" or "worth." But with the long "a" (hame) it involves a finer and more sacred meaning—it becomes the "home," the place consecrated by the family bond. In Anglo-Saxon charters this suffix may frequently be found united with names of families, as in Billingham, Wolsingham, etc.

Hammer and Tongs. A phrase denoting reiterated force, probably derived from the work of the blacksmith when he brings down the hammer on the glowing iron which he holds by the tongs.

High-Falutin'. Bombastic, pompous, affected. Probably a corruption of " high-flighting." The French *Haute-Volée*, literally high-flight, signifies " Upper Ten."

Hammer-cloth. The covering hanging below the " box " seat of a coach or old-fashioned carriage, and draping the box on which the seat is placed, and in which were carried the hammer, bolts, nails, etc., used in case of emergency. It is generally assumed that the term arose from the contents of this box, but, according to Skeat, " hammer " is here derived from the Dutch *hemel*, signifying, broadly, a covering above, a tester, heaven, and cognate with the German *himmel*. The hypothesis that " hammer " in this connection is a corruption of " hammock," because the driver's seat was slung, seems devoid of any substantial authority.

Hammock. A word which comes through the Spanish *hamaca*, of West Indian or Brazilian origin. Columbus, in the account of his first voyage, relates that many Indians came for the purpose of bartering their cotton and *hamacas*, or nets in which they sleep; and in Hawkins' " Voyage to the South Sea " it is stated that the Brazilians call their beds *hamacas*. The ship hammock is a hanging bed formed of canvas, about six feet by four, suspended by short ropes from rings in the beams supporting the deck.

Hampstead. From " Homestead," signifying the enclosed property—*i.e.*, farm buildings—of a rural mansion. Until the beginning of the eighteenth century the Parliamentary elections for the county of Middlesex were held on Hampstead Heath.

Hampton. From the Anglo-Saxon *hâm*, home, and *tun*, an inclosure, a village. In *Hampton-Wick* the suffix is derived from the Anglo-Saxon *vîc*, a marsh.

Hampton Court. A palace on the Thames (Middx.), built by Cardinal Wolsey and presented by him to Henry VIII. in 1525. It was a royal residence for more than 200 years and remains the property of the Crown.

Handicap. A corruption of "hand in cap," from the drawing of lots out of a hat or cap. The purpose of a "handicap" is to bring competitors in any contest as nearly as possible on an equality, either by allowing some advantage to the inferior competitor or by imposing some disadvantage to the superior.

Hand-kerchief. The word "kerchief" is derived from the French *couvrir*, to cover and *chef*, head, signifying head-cover; and the prefix "hand" was added as the kerchief came to be carried in the hand for use on the face. The kerchief is still the common head-dress of factory-girls and fisherwomen in the northern counties of England.

Hang. There are two verbs "to hang," one intransitive, the other transitive. The first has the past tense and past participle "hung," the second "hanged." It is correct to speak of a gate or a curtain being "hung," and of a criminal being "hanged." Formerly, execution by hanging was made by the criminal standing in a cart under the gallows with a rope round his neck, the cart being drawn away at a given signal. The first to be executed by the drop was Earl Ferrers, in 1760.

Hanged, Drawn, and Quartered. Formerly the capital sentence for treason. The criminal was drawn to the place of execution upon a hurdle, hanged, and his body was hewn into four quarters, each being spiked in a public place as an example to the multitude.

Hank, Hanker. Both these words are connected with the word "hang," the first signifying a skein of thread, or two or more skeins of yarn, silk, wool or cotton tied together, or a rope or a withy hoop.

K

To "hanker" after is to desire that which is set out of reach—the simile is that of something hung from a loop beyond one's grasp. To "hanker" after is not the same as to desire or long for; "we desire that which is near at hand and long for that within view, but we hanker after pleasures which are denied, which have been once enjoyed."

Hansard. The name given to the authorised publication of the Parliamentary Debates. It is so-called because it was printed by Luke Hansard (born 1752), who for many years worked as a compositor to the Printer of the House of Commons. In 1800 Hansard succeeded to the business, which has since been carried on in his name.

Hansom Cab. The "Safety Cab" patented in 1833 by Joseph Aloysius Hansom. It was apparently a a horse-drawn adaptation of the Sedan chair on wheels, introduced at Brighton at the commencement of the century.

Harem. The women's apartments, and also their occupants in a Mahommedan household. The word comes from the Arabic *haram*, sacred, which is derived from *harama*, prohibited.

Harlequinade. In the early days of the Pantomime the Harlequinade was the longer portion, the principal character being Harlequin, the lover of Columbine. To his ingenuity in evading the clown and pantaloon, confusing them by wondrous tricks brought about by his magic wand, the success of the old English pantomime was due. Speaking clowns did not come into existence before the days of Grimaldi, and in 1814 the "Gentleman's Magazine" refers to the novelty of dialogue being introduced.

Harpsichord. A stringed instrument similar in form to a small grand pianoforte. It is practically a harp, encased longitudinally, played upon by means of quill or leathern plectra operated from a key-board. The quantity of tone produced bears no reference to the pressure on the keys, and the method of

percussion on the strings introduced by the pianoforte, producing soft or loud tones, as its name
implies, was a great advance.

Harum-scarum. A word used both as an adjective and
a substantive denoting a rash and careless person.
Probably it originated from a combination of the
two verbs " hare," to excite, to worry, and
" scare," to frighten. An example of the use of
" hare " as a verb is found in Locke's essay " On
Education " :—" To ' hare ' and rate them is not
to teach but vex them."

Hatch. This is not an uncommon word in the names
of places and generally indicates the boundaries of
forests, " hatch," according to Skeat, being anything made of cross-bars of wood, and originally
applied to a gate—the hitch-gate which kept cattle
from straying out of the forest. Thus Colney-
hatch marks the southern extremity of Enfield
Chase. It seems probable, also—again following
Skeat—that the word " hatch," used in the sense
of producing young from eggs, is derived from
the bird sitting in a hatch or coop.

Hatchment. As applied in heraldry, this word is a
corruption of " achievement " (atchievement, atch-
ment), and signifies an escutcheon or armorial
shield granted in memory of some achievement—
usually an escutcheon over a tomb. It has no
connection with the word " hatch," in the sense
of cutting or hacking.

Hauled over the Coals. An expression dating back to
the Ordeal by Fire, where persons accused of a
crime were made to walk barefooted over red-hot
iron shares or glowing embers. If they did so
unharmed it was considered a proof of their
innocence.

Hautboy. From the French *hautbois*, literally high
wood, being a high-toned reed instrument, taking
the highest register in the reed orchestra. It was
introduced into England in 1720. Called also
" oboe."

Havelock. The white cloth forming part of the military cap as a protection against the scorching rays of the sun, introduced by General Havelock during the Indian Mutiny.

Haversack. Properly, an oat-sack, from the German *hafer*, oats, and *sack*, a sack, but now applied to the strong linen bag used by the soldier for carrying his rations. "Haver" is the common term for oats in Westmoreland, *e.g.*, "havercake" means oatcake.

Hawker. One who hawks goods about for sale, a pedlar, a huckster. The word is interesting because of its disputed origin, it being assumed by some to be derived from the German *hoken*, to carry, while the accepted authorities refer it to the Old Dutch *hucken*, to stoop, and consider it to be cognate with "huckster" and "huckle," huckle-shouldered meaning round-shouldered, bow-backed.

Hawthorn. The May-tree, called also "Quick-set," because quick (or living) sprigs set in rows quickly form excellent hedges. The word "haw" is equivalent to hedge.

Hay, Haigh. The meaning of these words as components of place-names is that of a place surrounded by a hedge, usually an enclosure for the purposes of the chase. Examples are found in Haye Park, at Knaresborough, Horsehay, near Colebrookdale, and Rothwell Haigh, near Leeds. The Hague (in full, Graven-hage, meaning the Count's hedge) was originally a hunting seat of the Counts of Holland.

Hearse. The word is derived from the Old French *herse*, a harrow, a triangular frame. Such a frame was used at funerals for setting candles at the head of the coffin, and a frame with fittings for candles was used to carry a corpse from the house to the church. The application of the term to the modern hearse was an easy transition.

Heathen. Literally a dweller on the heath, in the open country. The term was applied by the dwellers in towns to those who were cut off from urban civilisation, and it acquired its modern theological sense when the towns were Christian and the country chiefly of the older faith. The Hebrew *gōim*, signifying heathens, may also be rendered nations, peoples, gentiles, and is so translated in the Authorised Version of the Bible.

Heaven. Derived from the Anglo-Saxon *heofon*, and connected, according to some authorities, with the word " heave," meaning lifted up. Among the Greeks and Latins heaven was looked upon as the home of the greater gods, not for men after death, but in most religious beliefs heaven is the realisation of highest bliss by man. The place where such happiness is to be found is represented by some Hindu writers to be vast mountains to the north of India; in the *Æneid* it is described as below the earth, and many of the lower races still hold that idea; while an opinion of much poetic beauty is that which locates it in the extreme west, as the land where the sun descends to his home and where there is no night. With the Jews, and more definitely in the Christian belief, the locality of heaven was upward from the earth, and it is recorded of Christ (Luke xxiv. 51) that he *ascended* from earth in order to return to heaven.

Hebrews. A race supposed to be descended from Eber, the great-grandson of Shem (Gen. x. 21-24), an ancestor of Abraham. The name is more probably however, derived from the *country* called Eber (Hebrew *hébhĕr*), signifying " the region beyond " the Euphrates (Gen. x. 21).

Hector. To " hector " is to bully, to treat insolently, to swagger, and the usually accepted derivation is that of Hector, the brave and celebrated Trojan warrior killed by Achilles. To the ordinary reader of the Iliad this derivation seems incredible; more

probably " hector " is a corruption of " heckler,"
one who harasses and annoys.

Hedge-Priest. A poor, illiterate cleric, admitted to
Holy Orders direct from a Hedge-School, without
having attended any theological college. In
Ireland, before the establishment of Maynooth, it
was a common practice thus to admit men, in
order that they might gain a stipend by saying
mass.

Hedge-School. An open-air school, at one time common in the poor rural districts of Ireland, con-
ducted under the shelter of a hedge.

Hedonist. One who accepts the philosophy of
Hedonism (a word derived from the Greek
hēdonē, delight), which teaches that pleasure is
the true aim of life and that it is the duty of a
wise man to delight in every pleasure without being
controlled by it, and that such control can be
acquired by knowledge and culture. The school
was founded by Aristippus, a disciple of Socrates,
and later gave way to Epicureanism.

Heir-apparent. " Heirs-apparent are such whose right
of inheritance is indefeasible provided they outlive
the ancestor ; as the eldest son, who must be heir
to the father whenever he happens to die."—
(Blackstone's Commentary).

Heir-presumptive. " Heirs-presumptive are such who,
if the ancestor should die immediately would in the
present circumstances of things be his heirs; but
whose right of inheritance may be defeated by the
contingency of some nearer heir being born."—
—(Blackstone's Commentary).

Heliograph. The word is coined from the Greek *hēlios*,
sun, and *graphō*, I write. The instrument was
invented by H. C. Mance, for signalling by means
of the sun's rays, and consists of a circular mirror
revolving on a horizontal axis and adjustable to any
required angle, so that the sun's rays can be
directed to any point with the utmost precision.

The Morse system of dots and dashes is used, and in fair weather the signals can be read, without field-glasses, at as much as fifty miles' distance.

Heel of Achilles. The phrase is used to denote a vulnerable spot in an otherwise invulnerable body or position. (Carlyle speaks of the " Heel of Achilles " to invulnerable England.) The metaphor is drawn from the story that when Thetis, the mother of Achilles, dipped her son in the river Styx, to make him invulnerable, she held him by the heel, which, being thus untouched by the Stygian water, remained liable to a wound.

Hell. From the Anglo-Saxon *hel*, the Teutonic goddess of death being *Hella*, from the same root as the Anglo-Saxon *helan*, to hide, and cognate with the Latin *cel-āre*, to hide. " Hell," as a place of punishment, is common to nearly all forms of religion. Among the Greeks, under the name of Tartaros, it was a deep and sunless abyss, as far below earth as earth is below heaven, where the wicked received their due punishment. It has been stated that three definite stages may be traced in the conception of " hell " :—a vague notion of a future to be spent in misery, but with little of moral retribution ; a place of torment for those offending the gods, but with limited duration ; and an important factor in the moral government of the universe, a place where all evil-doers are punished as they deserve. In the Old Testament, and to some extent in the New, the word " hell " is used generally to denote " hades," the resting-place of the departed awaiting judgment, not necessarily a place of torment, and in this sense it appears in the Apostles' Creed, in the article " He descended into hell." Yet in the New Testament the word " hades " is used to denote a place of torment— at least, in part—as in the Revised Version the passage appearing in Luke xvi. 23, is rendered " And in ' Hades ' he lifted up his eyes, being in torments."

Henchman. A word of doubtful origin, by some attributed to a corruption of "haunchman," the servant in attendance at the "haunch" of his master's horse. According to Skeat, however, it is derived from the Anglo-Saxon *hengest*, a horse, and "man."

Heptarchy. From the Greek *hepta*, seven, and *archē*, rule—a country under seven rulers, the Anglo-Saxon kingdoms of Kent, Sussex, Wessex, Essex, East Anglia, Mercia and Northumbria, which are commonly stated to have existed concurrently and independently, but for the truth of which there is no evidence.

Heraldry. The office of a herald, the science of recording genealogies and blazoning coats of arms. The word "herald" is derived from the Old High German *hari*, an army, and *wald*, *walt*, strength, and the duty of a herald was, originally, to challenge to battle and to proclaim peace or war, and later, to settle all the etiquette of chivalry and keep a register of genealogies and armorial bearings. Heraldry has been brought to a complex science; the Heralds' College, or College of Arms, is a royal corporation, founded by Richard III. in 1483, and consists of the Earl Marshal, the Heralds and a Secretary.

Hibernia. The ancient name of Ireland, from the Irish *Eire* (Erin).

Hieroglyphics. From the Greek *hieros*, sacred, and *gluphō*, I carve. The term is applied to the most ancient language of Egypt and other lands, being that used in various monumental inscriptions in which picture-writing by figures of objects is employed instead of the conventional signs of an alphabet. Hieroglyphics are of two kinds—phonetic and ideographic; in the former the signs represent sounds, in the latter ideas. They abound on Egyptian temples, obelisks, sarcophagi, etc., but all attempts to read them had for centuries been given up, when, in August 1799, there was found among the ruins of Fort St. Julien, near the Rosetta branch of the Nile, a stone—since called the Rosetta Stone (q.v.)—on which there is an inscription not only in hieroglyphics but also in the hierotic character of Egypt and in Greek, affording a key to the hieroglyphics, though one very difficult to apply. Silvestre de Sacy, in 1801, Dr. T. Young, the most successful of any, in 1819, and many others, made advances in solving the problem, so that hieroglyphics are now continually translated from the monuments. Hieroglyphics are not confined to Egypt; they exist in Mexico, where they emanated from the Aztecs, and in the Hamathite inscriptions they are probably of Hittite origin, the invention of an early population of Northern Syria. Hieroglyphics are supposed to be a modification of the more ancient and shorter form of picture-writing called hieroglyphs, and became, in their turn, modified into alphabetic writing.

High. The word is often applied in the sense of being high above all private rights, *e.g.* :—High-road, High-seas, High-street, High-way.

Highbury. From the *bury* or enclosed land belonging to the Knights of St. John of Jerusalem in Clerkenwell. In 1271 they built a priory here, of which the barn remained standing until modern days. Compared with the low-lying district round about, this was elevated ground.

Highgate. By some supposed to be named from the ancient toll gate on the road from London to Barnet. The tolls levied here were for the benefit of the Bishop of London.

Hilary Term. One of the four terms of the English Law Courts, deriving its name from St. Hilary, Bishop of Poitiers (died 367), whose festival is 13th January. The Term extends from 11th to 31st January.

Hithe. An Anglo-Saxon word frequent in place-names and signifying a wharf, a landing place, a haven. We have examples, in London, in Green-hithe, Rother-hithe, and Lambeth (the latter being a corruption of Loam-hithe, meaning the muddy landing-place), and in Hythe and Erith, Kent.

Hob-nob. The word is now used in the sense of being familiar or intimate with, but its derivation is the Anglo-Saxon *hab* and *nab*, have and not have, and it certainly was formerly used in this sense. Shakespeare gives us an example in his " Twelfth Night " of such a use of the word :—

> " Hob-nob is his word :
> Give 't or take't."

Hobson's Choice. In the seventeenth century Tobias Hobson kept a livery stable at Cambridge, and would only let out his horses in strict rotation, saying :—" This or none." So Hobson's choice settled the question.

Hock-day. An old English festival held on the second Monday and Tuesday after Easter, popularly supposed to be in commemoration of the expulsion of the Danes in 1074. It has been stated that the name it derived from the " houghing," or " hocking," to which the Danes were subjected to prevent them reaching their boats, but more probably it is merely a corruption of " high " day. The English landlords levied what was called " Hock Money " on this day f.om their tenants, in return for which they treated them to a good supper. In modern times people stopped pedestrians in the streets with ropes, and declined to release them until they had parted with hock money.

Hockey. The word is the diminutive of *hook*, the club used in this game being slightly hooked at the end.

Hodge. The generic name for a farm labourer; a corruption of " Roger." There is no authority for its being a corruption of " Hedger."

Hoist with his own Petard. Caught in his own trap, blown up with his own engine of destruction. The petard was an ancient infernal engine filled with gunpowder; he who fired it stood in great danger of sacrificing his own life. Shakespeare makes use of the expression in Hamlet, Act iii. Sc. 4, where he says :—

" For 'tis the sport to have the engineer
Hoist with his own petar."

Hoity-toity. An exclamation of mingled astonishment and disapproval, probably an imitative duplication of the Old English verb *hoit*, to be riotous. (" Hoyts and revels among his drunken companions."—*Knight of the Burning Pestle.*)

Holborn. The name is derived from the Anglo-Saxon *hole*, a hollow, a ravine, and *burn*, a stream, a brook, and signifies, therefore, " the stream in the hollow." This stream (Holeburn) rose near Holborn Bars, the western limit of the City of London, and gave its name to the street down which it flowed.

Holm. A word found in place-names of Scandinavian origin, and denoting an island situated in a lake or in a river. Stock-holm, for instance, stands on such an island, and we have Flat-holm in the Severn, and Ling-holme in Lake Windermere.

Holocaust. From the Greek *holos*, whole, and *kaiō*, I burn. The word is often loosely applied to any great and general sacrifice of life, but its strict meaning, as its derivation indicates, is a sacrifice completely consumed by fire. The Mosaic " burnt-offering " was a sacrifice of this character. (Lev. i. 1-9, and vi. 8-13.)

Holt. This is an Anglo-Saxon word denoting a wood; it is a frequent component in English place-names where every vestige of a wood has disappeared. Bags-hot and Alders-hot are examples, while we have Chittleham-holt in Devonshire, and numerous places of the name of Holt.

Holy Cross. It is alleged that, about the year 326, Helena, the mother of Constantine, discovered the three crosses which were used at the crucifixion of Christ, and that the question which of the three was that of Christ was set at rest when, at the suggestion of Macarius, Bishop of Jerusalem, it was found, by trial, that only one could work miracles. Under the title " Invention of the Cross " ("invention," in this instance, retaining its original meaning of " finding "), this supposed discovery is commemorated in the Calendar of the Church of England on 3rd May.

Holyrood Palace. This residence of the ancient kings of Scotland grew out of the Abbey of the Holy Rood (Holy Cross), built by David I. (1128) as the permanent abode of the Black Rood, brought to Scotland by St. Margaret in 1070. This precious relic was a piece of the true cross set in gold and ebony. It fell into the hands of the English at the battle of Neville's Cross in 1344, after which all trace of it was lost. James II. was born at Holyrood; here, too, he was buried. The foundations of the new palace were laid by James IV. in 1500.

Homage. The word is derived from the Latin *homo*, a man, and signifies the service made by a vassal to his lord. (" The vassal did ' homage ' to his lord, professing he did become his ' man ' from that day forth."—BLACKSTONE.)

Homer. A Hebrew measure. (*See* OMER.)

Homœpathy. From the Greek *homoios*, like, and *pathos*, suffering. The name indicates a system of medicine which enunciates the Latin dictum " Similia similibus curantur " (Like things are cured by like). Its founder was Samuel Hahnemann, who, in 1790, while investigating the properties of Peruvian bark, found that a dose of the bark produced symptoms like those of the fever it was designed to combat. Believing he had discovered a general law, he pursued his experiments, and in 1810 published a treatise in which he explained his system, calling it Homœopathy. Upholders of the system maintain that its truth has been experimentally ascertained, and though it is rejected by the majority of medical men it has many adherents both in England and abroad.

Honeymoon. The term is derived from the custom, common to most of the Northern nations of Europe, of drinking mead, a fermented liquor made from honey, for thirty days after a marriage feast.

Honi soit qui mal y pense. The motto of the Order of the Garter, the illustrious order of British Knighthood, instituted at Windsor by Edward III., in 1348, as a revival of the Round Table of King Arthur. The commonly accepted translation —"Evil be to him who evil thinks"—is inaccurate; it is more properly "Dishonour be to him who thinks evil of it."

Horn Book. A primitive text-book for children. It was really no book at all, but a piece of paper containing the alphabet, the nine digits, and at times the Lord's Prayer, mounted on a small flat board, over which was stretched a transparent sheet of horn; below was a handle to hold it by.

Hornpipe. An old wind instrument, so called from the bell or open end being sometimes made of horn. It is also the name of an English dance which was usually danced to the music of the hornpipe and was as varied as any country dance. Nowadays it is relegated to a single performer and to a tune in common time.

Horoscope. From the Greek *hōra*, an hour, a season, and *skōpeo*, I observe. A term in astrology applied to an observation of the sky and the position of the stars at a certain time, such as that of a person's birth, from which it was claimed, the character and future of that person could be foretold.

Horse-Power (H.P.). The measure of a steam-engine's power as originally settled by James Watt, being 33,000 lbs. raised 1 ft. per minute. Engines are frequently said to be of so many h.p. nominal, but the real power often exceeds the nominal by three to one.

Horse-shoe. The horse-shoe has long been accepted as a token of good luck, and is frequently to be seen in the country nailed to a gate or a barn or stable door. Probably the superstition comes through the Saxon race, but it has been asserted that the early Christians used to hang a horse-shoe on the door of a house as a secret sign of their faith, the horse-shoe, when placed in a certain position, being taken to represent the first letter of Christus.

Houndsditch. The name of this street had its origin in the open ditch, 200 feet broad, which protected the wall of the City of London between Aldgate and Bishopsgate.

House of Keys. The Representative Council of the Isle of Man, so called from the Manx *Kiare-as-feed*, four and twenty, this being the number appointed by statute to form the "Court of Tynwald." Tynwald is an artificial mound in the centre of the island whence every new law has from time immemorial been promulgated.

Hoy. A small, one-masted vessel, usually rigged as a sloop, which conveyed passengers from place to place along the coast. Charles Lamb, in one of the "Essays of Elia," refers, with delightful reminiscent touches, to the Margate Hoy.

Humble-bee. Called also, and more accurately, Bumble-bee, the Latin name for the genus being *Bombus*. Darwin has shown how large a part the Bumble-bee takes in the fertilisation of plants.

Humble-pie. A pie made of the "umbles" or "numbles" (the entrails) of the deer. Humble retainers and poor dependants must be content to be served from such a pie, while the lord and his guests eat venison joints and pasties. Hence the phrase "to eat humble-pie" means to submit to humiliation or insult.

Humbug. Controversy as to its origin has raged around this word and many different derivations have been suggested—"Notes and Queries" are reputed to have had nearly a dozen during the early fifties. Dr. Johnson did not acknowledge the existence of the word, but there is little doubt that it dates back as far as the seventeenth century or, at any rate, to the beginning of the eighteenth. The explanation which has the acceptance of most authorities is that given by Dr. Brewer in the "Dictionary of Phrase and Fable," to the effect that the word is a compound of "hum," signifying to hoax, to cheat, and "bug" from "bugbear," a false alarm, a sham. "He threatened, but, behold, it was all a *hum*," wrote "Peter Pindar" long ago. Another suggestion is that the word arose from the spurious coin common in Ireland in the reign of James II., which was called *uim bog*, the Irish for base copper, so that such a phrase as "Don't pass off your *uim-bog* upon me" became general, and resulted in giving its present significance to "humbug."

Hundred. A Saxon subdivision of the English shires said to have been introduced by Alfred the Great. Each hundred comprised a colony of "ten times ten" families—that is to say, ten divisions of ten freeholders and their dependants in each. In all then there were one hundred champions to defend the common cause. In legal and ecclesiastical documents relative to lands such property is still said to be situate in a particular "hundred" as well as parish.

Hurly-burly. This expression, according to Trench, is derived, as to its first half, from the Old French *hurler*, to howl, its second being merely a rhyming addition. In "hurdy-gurdy," where the first part of the word comes from *hur*, to snarl, we have a similar re-duplication.

Hurrah. This exclamation is said to be derived from the Scandinavian *Hurra*, and to have been originally *Thor-aie*, an invocation to the god Thor for aid in battle, just as the battle cry of the Normans was *Ha-Rou*, in honour of Rollo.

Hurricane. A corruption of the Caribbean word *huracan*, which is probably an imitative sound of rushing wind. The word was introduced into Europe through the Spanish *hurracan*, and has become incorporated in various languages.

Hurst. The word comes to us from the Anglo-Saxon *hyrst*, a thick wood, and is found in the names of many places which are still well wooded—Lyndhurst, in the New Forest, is a typical instance. But its most frequent occurrence is in Sussex, the weald of which was once an extensive forest which for many years supplied the fuel for the Sussex Iron-works. Isaac Taylor tells us that in Northern Sussex alone no fewer than forty local names terminate in " hurst." (*See* LEY.)

Hussar. This word is supposed by some to be derived from *huszar*, the Hungarian for twentieth, the story being that in 1458 when Matthias Corvinus ascended the throne of the Magyars he decreed that, in order to provide a regular cavalry, each twenty families must enrol and equip one mounted soldier free of all cost to the State. An interesting point in connection with this is that the Hussar regiments always allowed the right sleeve of the upper jacket to hang loose on their backs, in keeping with the general custom of the Magyar peasantry, who had the right arm free on all occasions. But the real derivation of the word is probably from the Slavonic *hussar*, gooseherd, the sobriquet of a tribe of wild horsemen, organised into Cavalry Regiments by Matthias Corvinus, much in the same way as the Cossocks came to be enrolled under the Russian Czars.

Hyde Park. The name has its origin in the " Hyde Manor " belonging to the Abbey of Westminster, which became Crown property on the dissolution of the monasteries (1539). It contains about 400 acres. The old English measure called a " hide " is variously estimated at 60 to 120 acres, but this wide difference in extent is explained by the fact that the word " hide " is derived from the Anglo-Saxon *hid*, a contraction of *higid*, which, according to Beda, signified land sufficient to support one family. It is evident, therefore, that the measurement of a " hide " of land must vary in proportion to its productiveness.

Hydra. A celebrated monster in Greek mythology, having one hundred heads. It was one of the labours of Hercules to destroy this monster, but for each of its heads cut off two grew up if the wound were not stopped by fire. He effected this task with the help of Iolaus, who applied a red-hot iron as each head was cut off. The word is derived from the Greek *hudra*, water-snake (*hudōr*, water), and is used figuratively in the sense of evil arising from many sources.

Hydro. A contraction often used to designate a hydropathic establishment, to which patients resort for the water-cure. The cure of disease by means of hot and cold baths and the drinking of water is of very ancient date. Hippocrates, in the fourth century B.C., advocated it, and in mediæval times it had many followers, but it was reserved to Vincent Preissnitz to systematise hydropathy and to make it popular. In 1825 he set up a hydropathic establishment at Graffenberg, and within twenty years some 10,000 persons had been treated by him, while his system had been more or less adopted in all civilised countries. The water-cure in hydropathic establishments has valuable auxiliaries in the open-air exercise, early hours and cheerful society, which are adopted as part - the treatment.

L

Hygeia. In Greek mythology the daughter of Esculapius and the goddess of health. From this is derived the word " hygiene," signifying the study of health by the prevention of disease. Already by sanitary precautions the death-rate in our towns has been reduced and disease robbed of some of its worst features, and it is to be hoped that every effort may be continued for the improvement of the national health, to which end the appointment of a Minister of Hygiene might be very valuable.

Hymns. The correct definition of a hymn, though the word is so familiar, is not easily attained. A hymn is not a metrical rendering of the Psalms, such as were composed by Tate and Brady and were printed at the end of the Book of Common Prayer as late as the third quarter of the nineteenth century—they were called Psalms. Nor may it be taken directly from any other part of the Bible, for then it becomes a Paraphrase. It is, or should be, poetry, in metrical verse, composed with the object of giving praise to the Deity, either by extolling His attributes or by recalling man's duty to and dependence on Him. The first hymn for Christian worship is said to have been composed by Hilary, Bishop of Arles, about A.D. 431, but as early as the time of Pliny the Younger Christians are reported to have habitually sung a hymn to Christ as God. Luther did much to extend the use of hymns, and in England Isaac Watts, Charles Wesley, John Wesley and Cowper were prolific in hymnology.

I am escaped with the skin of my teeth. We frequently hear the expression " by the skin of his teeth," but few persons recognise how ancient it is. It appears in that epic poem called " Job " (Job xix. 20), one of the books of the Old Testament, perhaps the oldest of the books comprised in the Bible.

Iceberg. A word signifying ice-mountain, *beorh, berg,* being the Anglo-Saxon for a hill, a mountain. An iceberg begins its existence as a glacier, but when, in its progress down the mountain side, it reaches the cliffs and glides down into the ocean, it takes the name of iceberg. Some icebergs are of enormous size—Sir John Ross saw several in Baffin's Bay which, though in water of 1,500 feet deep, were aground, and off the Cape of Good Hope one has been seen of two miles in circumference and 150 feet high. They often tower as high as 250 to 300 feet above the sea, and for each cubit foot above there must be eight below. From the North Polar regions they drift partly westward and seldom reach Britain, but many encounter the eastern coast of Iceland, or, escaping that, drift towards the eastern shores of America. They carry with them earth and rocks obtained in their glacier state, and sometimes transport seeds, and even animals, to great distances.

Ich Dien. The German for "I serve," the motto of the Prince of Wales, originally adopted by the Black Prince after the battle of Cressy, and continued to the present day. But the popular belief that the motto was that of the King of Bohemia, slain by the Black Prince at Cressy, is not confirmed by any good authority, and Verstegan contends that its origin is Anglo-Saxon, from *Ich thian, theyn* signifying a free servant, from which is derived *thian*, serve. In connection with this theory it is well to bear in mind Grimm's law of the interchange of "*d*" and "*th*."

Idea. The word comes to us through the Latin *idea*, from the Greek *idein*, to see, and is allied to the Anglo-Saxon *wit*. To trace the signification of the word as applied by the philosophers of the world —from Plato to Hegel—would be an entire history of philosophy, and yet in popular language the word is now generally used as expressing a belief or an opinion, an intention or a purpose. To quote from Trench, "in no other instance.

perhaps, is a word so seldom used with any
tolerable correctness; in none is the distance so
immense between the sublimity of the word in its
proper, and the triviality of its common and
popular use. How infinite the fall of the word
when this person has an ' idea ' that the train
has started, and the other no ' idea ' that the
dinner would be so bad." In English philosophical
writings of the present day the word is used as an
equivalent of concept or mental representation of
anything.

Identity. From the Latin *idem*, the same. Yet
though to be identical may sometimes mean to be
the same, as in the identity of stolen goods, it does
not always have that meaning, as in the case of a
sound now heard being identical with that heard
previously—the two sounds were identical but not
the same. Similarly, there is the identity of the
individual, though the atoms of which the body is
composed are being continually reproduced, and
the habits, dispositions, modes of thought and
general character are incessantly changing.

Ideograph. The word is derived from the Greek *idea*,
a semblance, and *graphō*, I write, and denotes a
symbol which conveys an idea without expressing
its name. In the Chinese written language there
are an immense number of ideographs, many of
them of most interesting and significant origin.
It is related of Confucius that he used one of these
ideographs to enunciate his " golden rule "—" do
not to others what you would not they should do
to you." The ideograph he used for this purpose
is composed of two other characters, one denoting
" heart " and the other—itself a composite character—" as," thus indicating, in one small
character, the great doctrine of sympathy with
others—" my heart as yours." Two other
examples may be given, that of the character
meaning " brightness," which is composed of a
combination of the sun and the moon; and that

denoting "emperor," composed of the characters meaning "oneself" and "ruler," for, said the ancient sages, to rule others a man must first be master of himself.

Idiot. The word is derived from the Greek *idios*, private, one's own; the Greek *idiotes* signifying a man in private life as distinguished from one holding an official position, on the assumption that the latter would be of higher intelligence and better education. In this sense it was used by old English writers, but as the knowledge of letters permeated the masses more generally, the application of the word became more and more restricted, until, in the present day, it denotes a person who is weak in intellect or deficient in common understanding.

Idle as a Painted Ship upon a Painted Ocean. The quotation is from "The Ancient Mariner," by Samuel Taylor Coleridge (1772-1832). According to Skeat, the word "idle" has come through many changes of significance; he maintains that the original sense was probably clear; then pure, mere, sheer; then vain, unimportant. But the Anglo-Saxon *idel* meant vain, empty, useless, and Coleridge has evidently used the word in that sense—useless, inactive, motionless.

Idol. The word is derived from the Latin *idolum*, through the Greek *eidolon*, signifying that which is seen—in other words the visible representation of an idea. The words "idol" and "idea" are closely connected, for the word "idea" comes from the Greek *idein*, to see, and may be defined as an image formed by the mind. We can imagine how strenuous must have been the endeavour of early man to give expression to his mental conceptions, and language being then inadequate for that purpose the idol became the outward and visible sign of his inward and spiritual conception. The more worthy his conception the higher were the attributes with which he invested his idol, but when he ceased to attribute to it the highest perfection he could conceive, his service to it ceased to be spiritual worship and became idolatry.

If the Salt have Lost its Savour. (Matt. v. 13; Luke xiv. 34). This illustration, like many another in the Bible, lacks its full force in Western people's ears. Our salt has not the typical value given to it in the East; it is an unimportant item in our grocer's bill and, as far as our experience goes, it does not "lose its savour." But the following extract from a description by a traveller in Palestine gives point to the aptness of the Bible simile. "Along one side of the Valley of Salt there is a small precipice occasioned by the taking away of the salt. I broke off a piece that was exposed to the sun and the air, and though it had the sparks and particles of salt it had entirely *lost its savour.* Yet the inner part, which was connected with the rock, retained its savour, as I found by proof."

I. H. S. These letters are commonly used as the initials of the Latin words *Jesus Hominum Salvator*, Jesus Saviour of Men, but originally they were the contraction of the Greek word *Ihsous*, Jesus, the " *h* " representing the long " *e.*" As a contraction the letters were *I H C* (the Greek *c* being equivalent to *s*), with a line over the " h " to signify abbreviation, but the Latin " s " being substituted for the Greek " c," they became " I H S," and were taken to indicate the above Latin motto. St. Bernardine of Sienne (1347) is reputed to have been the first to attribute to the letters this signification.

I Know a Trick Worth Two of That! The phrase sounds quite common-place and modern, yet it occurs in one of Shakespeare's plays—King Henry IV. (Part I.), Act. ii., Sc. 1.

Iliad. The word is derived from the Greek *Ilios*, the city of Ilus or Troy, named after Ilos, the grand-father of Priam and son of Tros. The Iliad is a grand epic poem in the Greek language, consisting of twenty-four books, and ascribed to Homer, of whose parentage and life, however, nothing is known. Briefly stated, the argument of the poem is that Paris, a son of Priam, king of Troy, is received as an honoured guest by Menelaos, King of Sparta, and elopes with Helen, his host's wife. To avenge such perfidy the Greeks lay siege to Troy, which, after seven years, is taken and burnt to the ground. The authorship of the poem has been, and is likely to remain, much in dispute, some contending that it is a collection of ballads united into a continuous whole by some person after Homer's time, and it is suggested that Pisistratus, the tyrant of Athens, arranged them in the present form.

Illusion. The word is derived from the Latin *illudo*, to play upon; *il* (equivalent to *in*), upon, and *ludo*, I play. It is often confounded with " delusion," but while " illusion " refers to a deception of the senses, such as an optical deception by sleight of hand, " delusion " refers to a deception by one's own mind, such as that of one who is insane. In the first example the person viewing the deception knows that he is being deceived, but in the second case the deception is taken for reality.

Immaculate. The word is derived from the Latin *macula*, a spot, with the prefix *im* (equivalent to *in*), not, and signifies spotless, pure, unstained. The dogma of the Immaculate Conception, defined by Pope Pius IX. (1854), is to the effect that the immaculate conception of the Virgin Mary is an article of divine faith, in that she had no taint of original sin. As long ago as the twelfth century, a day was given to the commemoration of the conception of Mary, and it was included in the calendar in the fourteenth century. The word "maculate," in the sense of defiled, impure, is seldom now used, but it appears in more than one passage of Shakespeare, *e.g.*, "Most *maculate* thoughts, master, are masked under such colours." —(Love's Labour Lost).

Imp. The word is derived from the Greek *emphuō*, to graft—literally to produce in—and is now usually taken to denote a little devil or wicked spirit. But formerly it retained the significance of its origin and denoted a scion of nobility, an offspring, a child. In Stow's Annals (1592) we have—"The King preferred there eighty noble 'imps' to the order of knighthood"; and in an old devotional book we have—"Let us pray for the King's most excellent majesty and for his beloved son, Edward our Prince, that most angelic 'imp'"; while Thomson, the poet, wrote "Arise, and sing that generous 'imp' of fame." It is a good example of a word—and there are many—which has had a malignant meaning, not due to its origin, imported into it.

In a Crack. A common expression denoting an action done quickly, instantly; probably derived from the analogy of the instantaneous crack of a whip.

Inch. A component in place-names. (*See* INNIS.)

Indian Ink. A black pigment which might more properly be called Chinese ink, since it is manufactured in China, and is still used there and in Japan for writing with small brushes, instead of with pens. It consists of very fine lamp-black, baked up with a glutinous substance, the finer Oriental kinds being delicately perfumed. There is a great difference, both in price and quality, in the various kinds, the finest article being quite costly. Presumably the name "Indian" Ink arose from its being imported by the East India merchants.

India Paper. A name given to a thin, yellowish printing-paper, imported by the East India

merchants, and made in China and Japan from
vegetable fibre. It is used for taking the finest
proofs from engraved plates, and hence these
impressions are called " India proofs."

India-rubber. The first record we have of this substance is that given by Herrera, about five hundred years ago, he having observed, in the second
voyage of Columbus, that the natives of Hayti
played a game with balls made " of the gum of a
tree," and that they bounced better than the wind-
balls of Castile. Torquemada, however seems to
be the first (1615) to mention the tree by name,
and even at that early date the Spaniards used the
juice to waterproof their cloaks. Yet no rubber
seems to have reached Europe till long afterwards,
and Dr. Priestley, in his book on perspective
(1770), writes :—" Since this work was printed off,
I have seen a substance excellently adapted to the
purpose of wiping from paper the marks of a
black-lead pencil. Mr. Nairne, opposite the Royal
Exchange, sells a cubical piece of about half-an-
inch for 3/-, and he says it will last several years."

Indigo. The word is derived from the Latin *Indicus*,
Indian, and when the substance first came to
England it was called " indico." It has long
occupied an important place among the commercial productions of India, being a valuable dyestuff
extracted from various plants of the species
Indigofera. Yet in England at one time it was
believed to be a mineral, and was described as
" a blue stone brought out of India, used for
dyeing, painting, etc." And now we find that the
dyeing property of the plant does not consist of
any " colouring matter," but in the chemical
compound $C_{16} H_{10} N_2 O_2$

Infantry. Although other derivations have been suggested for this word, there can be little doubt
that its real origin is the Latin *infans*, an infant,
a youth. In the days of chivalry, youths of good
family marched on foot, with the ancestral depen-

dants and servants, in rear of the knights, and from such a body has gradually developed the Infantry of the Army. The weapons of the Infantry have varied, with years, from slings and javelins, bows and spears, to the magazine rifle and smokeless powder of the present day, and their number—on paper—is enormous, Europe alone claiming nearly three millions on a peace establishment, with the ability to provide fifteen millions and upwards in time of war.

Ing. This is an important syllable in Anglo-Saxon place-names, for it occurs in more than one-tenth of the whole number of English villages. Often it appears as a suffix, but more frequently as a mid-syllable. Bark-ing, Dork-ing, Ketter-ing, and Wok-ing are examples of the suffix, while Buck-ing-ham, Kens-ing-ton, and Isl-ing-ton are examples of the mid-syllable. " Ing " was the usual Anglo-Saxon suffix to denote " son," having the same significance as the prefix " Mac " in Scotland, " O " in Ireland, and " Ap " in Wales; and it seems probable that places with names ending in " ing " were called after the individual person, while those with " ing " as a mid-syllable took their names from the family or clan.

In his good books. Probably an amplification of the phrase " in your books," which we find in Shakespeare—" The gentleman is not *in your books*."—(" Much Ado About Nothing," Act i. Sc. 1.)

Inn. From the Anglo-Saxon *in*, *inn*, meaning within, indoors. The Inns of Chancery were colleges in which law students began their studies. The Inns of Court—viz. : The Inner Temple, The Middle Temple, Gray's Inn, and Lincoln's Inn—are voluntary corporate societies which have the exclusive right of calling persons to the English Bar, and in the buildings belonging to these societies the members of the " Inn " dine together and barristers have their chambers. It has been stated—though the ground for such a belief is not very evident—that our first inns for entertainment of travellers were the houses of the aristocracy temporarily given up to the purpose during the absence of the owners at the wars at home or the Crusades abroad, and that the escutcheon of such a house is the origin of such inn-signs as the " Blue Boar," the " Red Lion," the " Bull's Mouth," etc. That these signs are of heraldic origin is doubtless true, but they were probably only given to the inns in honour of the landed gentry of the neighbourhood.

Innis, Inch. These two words—the first Celtic, the latter Gaelic—both signify an island, and may be found in many place-names in Wales, Scotland, and Ireland. In Wales the spelling generally takes the form of " Ynys," in Ireland that of " Ennis," and in Scotland " Inch." For example, in Scotland, there is Inch-colm (meaning the island of St. Columba); in Ireland there is Ennis-killen (the island cell or church); while in North Wales, in the Tremadoc district, there is Ynys-Gwertheryn, now a mile inland, but once a port from which Madoc is said to have sailed in quest of unknown lands.

In the nick of time. The word " nick " in this phrase is a modified form of " nock," which is the older form of " notch." Doubtless the phrase arose from the old practice of keeping reckoning of both time and money by notches on a stick (*see* TALLY), and thus came to indicate the critical moment, the exact time required by necessity or convenience. " God delivered them in the very ' nick ' of time," says an old divine.

Inver. This is found in many place-names in Scotland and is believed to be the Gaelic form of " Aber " (q.v.). It is remarkable that in Wales there are about fifty names in which " Aber " appears, but not a solitary one in which " Inver " is found. In Ireland, however, where " Aber " is unknown,

"Inver" is common; while in Scotland (as pointed out by Isaac Taylor) if a line be drawn across the map, from a point a little south of Inverary to one a little north of Aberdeen, we shall find that, with a few exceptions, the "invers" lie to the north-west of the line and the "abers" to the south-east of it.

Is there no balm in Gilead? The phrase "balm in Gilead" is quite common in present day literature, and the above extract from the book of the prophet Jeremiah (viii. 22) shows that it was in use as long as some 600 years B.C. In the story of Joseph being sold to the Ishmaelites (Gen. xxxvii.) we find that even then—some seventeen centuries B.C.—Gilead was noted for its balm, for the traders to whom Joseph was sold "came from Gilead, with their camels bearing spicery and balm and myrrh, going to carry it down to Egypt." Balm is the gum of a fragrant tree, for which Gilead is famous.

It's an ill wind that blows nobody good! A proverb of everyday use and of general application. Who can tell when it was first formulated? Thomas Tusser, the poet, who lived from 1523 to 1580 seems to have had it in mind when he wrote :
" Except wind stands as never it stood,
        It is an ill wind turns none to good."

In quad (quod). The word "quad" is manifestly a contraction of quadrangle. Boys at our public schools say they are "in quad" when they are confined to their own quadrangle. The phrase became popular in connection with a prison when debtors were confined in the Fleet, the Marshalsea, and Whitecross Street, because they were free to receive visitors in the exercise court or quadrangle.

Jack. Though used as a substitute for " John," the derivation of this word is the French *Jacques*, through the Latin *Jacobus*, from the Hebrew *Yáăgōb*, equivalent to "James." In English, the name—as are its equivalents in most modern languages—is used with some contemptuous familiarity, as in Jack-fool, Jack-an-apes, Jack-in-the-box, Jack-in-office, and, perhaps, in Jack-ass. In a similar way it is applied—still with some tinge of contempt—to implements, etc., as in boot-jack, bottle-jack (for turning a roasting joint), black-jack (a pitcher), jack-boot (the long boot worn by the soldier), jack, or knave (servant) in cards; these are all more or less the result of the word "Jack" being a soubriquet for a humble servitor. The phrase "Jack of all trades but master of none" is an illustration of this.

Jacket. From the French *jacquette*, a diminutive of *jaque*, a jack or coat, the defensive body armour worn by soldiers from the 14th to the 17th century. It was a leathern sleeveless coat, sometimes quilted, worn over the hauberk, a coat of mail of interwoven steel rings.

Jack Ketch. A name for the hangman, the executioner; said to be derived from Richard Jaquette, the lord of the manor of Tyburn, where felons were executed up to 1783.

Jack Tar. The familar name for a sailor. "Tar" is probably a contraction of the word tarpaulins, the waterproof suits which sailors wear in stormy weather. For derivation of "Jack," see above.

Jacobite. The name "Jacob," of which this word is a compound, is synonymous with "James," and thus the word "Jacobite" was applied to the adherents of James, generally known as the Pretender, the son of James II. On the death of his father he was proclaimed as King James III. of England by Louis XIV. of France, and an attempt was made to perform a similar ceremony in London. A rebellion in his favour was raised in the Highlands in 1715, but was practically extinguished at the battle of Preston.

Jade. The word when applied to the stone is supposed
to be derived from the Spanish term *pietra di
hijda*, kidney-stone, and the scientific term
nepprite refers to the reputed value of the mineral
in renal disease. True jade is a compact or crypto-
crystalline variety of hornblende, and may be
divided into two varieties—Oriental Jade and
Oceanic Jade, both being white, greenish-gray and
many shades of green. Oceanic Jade possesses a
peculiar silky lustre due to its exceedingly delicate
fibres. Jade has been known to the Chinese for
more than 2,000 years, and has always been
highly prized and often elaborately carved. It was
much used by ancient peoples, having been found
as implements and ornaments in the remains of
pre-historic lake-dwellings and on the site of Troy.
It appears *in situ* in Central Asia, China, and New
Zealand, but not—so far as is known—in Europe,
though it is a suggestive fact that the relics of jade
implements have been found in the pile dwellings
of the Swiss Lakes.

Jalap. Named from the city of Xalapa, or Jalapa, in
Mexico, whence the drug was first brought to
Europe in 1610.

Janissaries. The word comes to us from the French
Janissaire, which is derived from the Turkish
yeni, new, and *'askari*, soldier. The Janissaries
form an interesting and apparently unique example
of the treatment of a subjugated race. On the
taking of Constantinople the Turks ordained that
every fifth Christian boy was to be surrendered to
the service of the Sultan. All connection with his
parents was cut off and he was carefully trained
for war. In this way was formed the corps of the
Janissaries. History speaks in the highest terms
of the discipline and courage of this body of
troops; they were devoted to the Sultan and
equally savage both to Turk and Christian. They
occupied the best positions open to Mahometans,
and the honour of serving in the corps was so

much coveted that Turks bargained with the Christians to take their children and give them for Janissaries.

Jehovah. The most sacred of the names given in the Old Testament to the Supreme Being. The word is generally derived from the Hebrew *havah*, an old form of *háyáh*, He Is, and the import of this name is explained in Exod. iii. 14, " I am that I am," thus implying self-existence in a sense inapplicable to any created being. So holy was the name deemed by the Jews that they intentionally mispronounced it, by altering the vowel points to those of Adonai or of Elohim, less sacred names for God. It has been suggested that the word Jehovah is of Phœnician origin, connected with the Phœnician *Iao*, the Sun-god, and with the Chaldean *Iao*, the Intelligent Light.

Jehu. A cabman or coach-driver, in allusion to the furious driving of Jehu, the son of Nimshi. (2 Kings ix. 20.)

Jerry Builder. A speculative builder who uses materials of the cheapest kind without any care for their durability. Probably the word " Jerry " is a contemptuous abbreviation of Jeremiah, in the same sense as " jeremiad," jerry-building being fore-doomed to speedy decay and ruin such as the prophets foretold.

Jerusalem. The meaning of the name is obscure, and the current interpretation of " abode of vision of peace " is not now accepted by the best authorities as free from difficulties. The old Hebrew pronunciation seems to have been *Yerushalem*, whence we have the English form. But the mere mention of the name is sufficient to conjure up a vision of its wonderful history. A natural fortress, standing on spurs of hills surrounded on three sides by valleys 300 to 400 feet deep, it was considered impregnable until David wrested it from the Canaanitish inhabitants, the Jebusites, in one of his first exploits on becoming King. At his behest, the temple—" exceeding magnifical "— was built by Solomon in the zenith of the people's glory, but after the Babylonian Conquest fell into decay, as did the city itself, during the subsequent captivity. Under the prophet Nehemiah, both city and temple were re-built, while later, under Herod, arose a third temple, grand and huge, covering some five acres of ground. Then follow the advent of Christ, the hallowed association of its narrow streets with Him, with His crucifixion and sepulture; the horrors of the Roman siege and the ultimate occupation of the city by the Turks; the fierce and prolonged wars of the Crusade to rescue the Holy Sepulchre from the Mohammedans. All this, its ancient history, combined with the present-day mixture of nationalities to be seen there at Easter— the European tourist, the Turkish nizam, the hooded Armenian, the long haired Greek monk, the native peasants in yellow turbans and striped mantles, Jews in oriental costume, Russians in knee boots and padded robes—presents a picture that we gaze upon with amazement and awe, as evidence of Jerusalem having been a holy city for more than twenty centuries !

Jesuit. The mere name seems to have struck terror into the hearts of English people in the days of Queen Elizabeth, as connected with the horrors of the Spanish Inquisition, and a Jesuit had a reputation for diabolical cunning and deceit. (The idea remains to the present day in the significance of the word Jesuitical.) The Society of Jesus, the most celebrated ecclesiastical order of modern times, was founded in 1534 by Don Inigo Lopez de Recalde, commonly known, from the place of his birth, as Içnatius Loyala. He was an officer in the army, was severely wounded, and during the long process of recovery formed the resolution to devote himself to the religious life. He conceived the idea of founding a religious society which should have strict military discipline for its guiding principle, with a general in command and none above him but the Pope. Paul III. sanctioned the order; it spread with great rapidity, and on the death of Loyala in 1556 it consisted of more than 1,000 persons with 100 houses. The Jesuits became the most adventurous missionaries, penetrating into the unknown wilds of the New World and into the forbidden cities of the Old. They were the first Europeans to establish themselves in China.

Jetty. From the Old French *jettée*, the past participle of *jetter*, to throw; the signification being something which is thrown forward, juts out—into the sea when the word is used to denote a wharf or landing-pier, or beyond the general line when applied to part of a building which juts over the ground plan. In the name Jutland, the peninsula stretching out into the sea, northward from the kingdom of Denmark, we appear, at first sight, to have the same root signification as that of Jetty, but in reality it means the land of the Jutes or Goths.

Jewels. The word has a significant origin, being derived from the French *joyau*, joy, pleasure. Personal ornaments appear to have been among the very first objects upon which the ingenuity of man was exercised, and jewels took an early place in this direction. A remarkable collection of Egyptian jewellery has been discovered in the coffin of Queen Aah-hotep, now preserved in the British Museum, and in these examples we find a perfect mastery of handicraft and material, complete in every respect, far surpassing the incongruous effects of the 18th and early 19th centuries of the Christian era.

Jews' Harp. A simple musical instrument, common enough in the streets some thirty or forty years ago, consisting of a harp-shaped metal frame, across which, longitudinally, is set a steel spring.

M

The frame is held between the lips and the spring twitched with the fingers, the sound produced being altered in pitch and intensity by means of the mouth and tongue. By some the name is supposed to be derived from the French *jeu*, play, by others it is believed to be a corruption of " jaw," the harp being held between the jaws, but in all probability it is merely a derisive allusion to the Jewish harp of old.

Jig. The word has more than one signification and may be ascribed to two sources at least—the Old French *gigue*, a wind instrument, and the German *geige*, a fiddle. It used to be applied to a comic rhyming ballad, and it denotes a handy tool—in many trades small machines are called *jigs*—or a trick, a prank. But its usual meaning at the present day is that of a quick lively dance and the tune suited to such a dance. It is popular in many nations and varies, accordingly, from a sober, jog-trot dance to a wild exercise displaying all the agility of the performer. " Jig " music is found in many works produced in the latter part of the 17th century and onwards to the time of Haydn, and in the course of time it was lengthened and elaborated for the use of harpsichord, becoming the origin of the last movement of the sonata.

Jilt. The word appears to be a contraction of the old English " Jillett," which itself is the affectionate diminutive of " Jill," and " Jill " being a very common girl's name it came to denote *any* girl, in the same way as " Jack " came to mean any boy. The old nursery rhyme is an example :—

> " Jack and Jill went up the hill
> To fetch a pail of water."

The name " Jill " is probably a contraction of " Gillian " or " Juliana," the feminine of the Latin *Julius*.

Joe Miller. A term often used to denote a stale jest, because a compilation called " Joe Miller's Jests," the work of John Motley (1692-1750), contained many jokes manufactured long after Joseph Miller's death. Joseph Miller was a witty actor who lived from 1684 to 1738, and was a great favourite at the time when Congreve's plays were fashionable.

John Bull. This national nickname for the typical Englishman, bluff and open-hearted, is derived from the political allegory entitled "The History of John Bull," written by Dr. John Arbuthnot and published in 1712. It was an admirable piece of satire, throwing ridicule on the Duke of Marlborough and voicing the disgust then felt at the protracted war against France. The nations at war are represented as tradesmen involved in a law-suit, and their characteristics are skilfully pourtrayed, together with the devices of Marlborough, as the principal attorney, to prolong the contest. At the time of the appearance of the skit it was attributed to Swift, but it has since been made quite clear that Arbuthnot was the author.

John Doe and Richard Roe. Doubtless most persons are aware that these are fictitious names formerly given to the plaintiff and defendant respectively in actions of ejectment, but probably few know why so ludicrous a fiction was deemed necessary. The explanation is this :—a writ of ejectment was formulated in the reign of Edward III. as a remedy to a Lessee who had been ousted of his term; but it was only a Lessee who could recover, and when the title to a Freehold was at issue, the actual entry thereon, with the names of the persons to whom it was leased and the Ouster therefrom, were all necessary to found an action. This procedure was attended with so much difficulty that Lord Chief Justice Rolle, during the Protectorate, substituted for the assumed Lessee and Ouster the fictitious names of John Doe and Richard Roe. All this was swept away by the Common Law Procedure Act of 1852, and now, by the Judicature Act, 1875, an action for the recovery of land may proceed in the same manner as any other.

John O'Groat's House. The name still appears in our maps at the Northernmost point of Scotland, and the phrase " from Land's End to John O'Groat's " is frequently used to indicate from one end of Britain to the other, but no such house has been in existence for many years past. According to tradition the house was built towards the close of the 15th century, by a man who came from Groot, in Holland, for the use of travellers crossing to the Orkneys; and a small green knoll is still shown on the shores of the Pentland Firth as the site of the house.

Jot. From the name of the Greek letter *iōta*, which was frequently indicated by a dot under other letters, and from the Hebrew *yod*, the smallest letter in the Hebrew alphabet, thus denoting the smallest particle. The " tittle," with which the word *jot* is so closely associated by Bible readers (Matt. v. 18.), is stated by commentators to be a very little mark by which one Hebrew letter was known from another.

Journeyman. The double signification of the origin of this word is often overlooked. The French *journée* indicates not only a day's work but also a day's travel, as shown by the English word " journey " ; and the journeyman originally denoted one who travelled from place to place offering his services where his craft was needed, either to work from day to day or until the job he agreed to do was finished. To this day we have a survival of the custom among sheep-shearers, who along the line of the South Downs go from place to place and do all the sheep-shearing of the district, while in mediæval times the masons and workers on the great Cathedrals of the Continent and in this country adopted the same method.

Jovial. A survival of the belief in astrology, the word denoting one who was born under the influence of the planet Jupiter, supposed to be the most joyful of all the planets, so that a " jovial " person has come to mean one of gay and cheerful disposition. Why such a characteristic should be ascribed to the planet named after the great god Jupiter is not apparent, as he was the supreme Roman deity, king and father of men, but from whom mankind received miseries as well as blessings, for the Fates were not subservient even to his will.

Juggernaut. The word in the Sanscrit language means " Lord of the world," and is one of the 1,000 names of Vishnoo, the second god of the Hindoo trinity. The great seat of the worship of Juggernaut is at Pûri, in Orissa, where he is associated with Balbhadra and his sister Sabhadra. Juggernaut's car is forty-three feet high, and has sixteen wheels, each six and a half feet in diameter. The brother and sister also have cars, and at the Car Festival, when the three idols are brought out in their cars, dragged by multitudes of devotees, fanatics used to throw themselves beneath the wheels, a practice which is now prohibited.

Jury. The word is derived from the French *juré*, past participle of *jurer*, to swear. In the English courts the jury consists of twelve men, whose verdict, in the cases of misdemeanour, felony and high treason, must be unanimous, though in civil and revenue cases it need not be so. In Scotland the number of the jury is fifteen, and the verdict is given by the majority. It is a disputed point whether the germ of our present jury system was of Anglo-Saxon or Norman origin; by many it is attributed to King Alfred, and that it was well established in the time of King John is evident from the fact that it is insisted upon in Magna Charta.

Justice is Blind. An expression derived from the allegorical representation of Justice, who, holding the scales, is blindfolded so that she may not see bribes. It was the custom of the ancient Egyptians to conduct their trials in a darkened chamber, in order that the prisoner, the pleader, and the witnesses being alike unseen, the judges should be impartial in their judgment and not be moved to misplaced sympathy.

Kaaba. The small cubical oratory in the Mahomedan temple at Mecca, within which is the famous Black Stone said to have been given to Abraham, by an angel, for an altar. It is the most holy spot on earth to the Moslem, towards which he ever turns to pray. Sir Richard F. Burton, disguised as an Arab, obtained access to the Kaaba, and describes it as an oblong massive structure, 18 paces in length, 14 in breadth, and some 35 to 40 feet in height, having no windows and with the only entrance 7 feet above the ground. Though rebuilt again and again, the last time in 1627, it appears to have preserved the outline and dimensions of the pagan shrine which it certainly originally was; for the black stone, probably an aerolite, had been an object of adoration long before it was given a place in Mahomedanism. The word *Ka* is of extreme antiquity as denoting a sacred place, and in Egypt it signified both the act of worship and the soul, or worshipping part, of a man. It is represented in Egyptian hieroglyphics by the two outspread arms in the act of adoration. The Chaldean *Ka-bel*, the worship of Bel, became the verb *Kabbel*, to receive (from the gods), from which is derived the *Kabalah* of the Jews, the secret science of the Rabbis for the interpretation of the hidden sense of the Scriptures, and whence we have the word *cabalistic* in its present sense of having a hidden meaning, or being of magical virtue. The last syllable of *Kaaba* (*ba*) means the house, or gate, as in *Ba-bel*, the house of Bel, and although the word *Kaaba* has come—because it is a square building—to signify, in Arabic, the square house, originally it meant the Sacred House.

Kaiser. This title of the German Emperor is synonymous with the Latin word *Cæsar*. By Diocletian's arrangement certain Roman provinces near to the

Danube were assigned to a Cæsar, and in 1438 these provinces came into the possession of Austria. The titles Cæsar, Czar, Kaisar, Shah, are doubtless all forms of the Babylonian *Shar*, King. The name of Sargon, the great Semitic king, whose reign is placed at about 3,800 B.C., may be written *Shar-gina*, and the name Belshazzar, familiar in Bible history, may be spelt *Bel-Shar-Usur*, God-the-King-save.

Kaleidoscope. The word is composed of the Greek *Kalos*, beautiful, *eidos*, appearance, and *skopeō*, I behold. It is an instrument which, by means of reflection from two mirrors fixed at a suitable angle, presents an endless variety of beautiful forms of perfect symmetry. It was invented as long ago as the 16th century, by Baptista Porta, and was perfected by Sir David Brewster in 1817, when it at once became a favourite toy, 200,000 (it is said) having been sold in London and Paris during the first two months after it was put upon the market. It is useful as a scientific apparatus for illustrating the optical problem of the multiplication of images by reflection, and is of service to designers of patterns for dress materials, wall-papers, etc.

Keel. The word denotes the longitudinal beam at the bottom of a vessel, supporting the whole structure of the ship. But there was no keel to the boats of early man, to the skin-and-wickerwork boats of the ancient Britons, or to the Indians' bark canoe; while to the present day the kayaks of the Esquimaux are keel-less. The addition of the keel makes all the difference; the rolling log at once becomes a ship, able to support masts and sails, and curiously enough the derivation of the word carries this import, for the Anglo-Saxon *ceol*, from which our word "keel" comes, means a ship.

Keen. The word has come to mean "sharp"—we speak of a razor being brought to a "keen" edge, and even in the phrase "a keen man of business" there is an implication of sharpness. But the

Anglo-Saxon word *cene* meant " bold," while the Icelandic *kaenn* meant " wise," and is connected with *can*, able. We may gather, therefore, that a " keen " man ought to be not only sharp but also bold, wise and able.

Keep. The word comes from the Anglo-Saxon *cépan*, to traffic, to sell, to store up. Like the word *make* it is used in many senses in the English language, of which a few are illustrated in the following examples :—

" O Lord, keep (guard) the door of my lips." (Ps. cxli. 3.)

" Keep (retain) this for ever in the imagination of the thoughts of Thy people." (1 Chron. xxix. 18.)

" Keep (restrain) me from presumptuous sins." (Ps. xix. 3.)

" God put him into the garden of Eden to keep (tend) it." (Gen. ii. 15.)

" Ye shall keep (observe) it a feast to the Lord." (Ex. xii. 14.)

" A fool cannot keep (preserve secret) his counsel." (Eccles. viii. 17.)

To keep one's bed, to keep things for sale, to keep accounts, to keep house, to keep company, to keep a term or chapels (at college), to keep in touch, to keep the peace, to keep wicket—these are examples which by no means exhaust the list of the varied significations of the word " keep." There is one example, however, of especial interest—that of " shop-keeper." Why does he " keep " a shop? The usual answer is because the shop keeps him. But, as shown above, the Anglo-Saxon for " keep " is *cépan* (*keepan*), meaning to traffic, and " shop " in the Anglo-Saxon is *sceoppa*, a treasure store, so that a " shop-keeper " is literally a treasure trafficker, one who traffics in, buys and sells, all manner of treasure.

Keep the Pot Boiling. The phrase implies that there must be no rest, no cessation of effort, and is obviously in allusion to the bubbling and throbbing, the stir and movement, which the boiling causes not only to the contents of the pot but to the cauldron itself, especially when, as in former days, it was swinging over the fire by pot-hook and chain.

Ken, Kin. Both these words denote a head, a promontory. "Kin" or "Cin" (the older form being "Cind") is a survival of the old dative or locative of the Gaelic "cenn," equivalent to the Welsh "penn." In Scotland they may be found in such place-names as Ken-more, meaning the great head ("more" being the same as the Welsh "mawr") and in Kin-ross, which is a duplication of terms, "ross" also signifying promontory in the Celtic tongue. In Ireland we have Kin-sale and Ken-mare, and in England Ken-ton (Middlx.), Ken-cot (Oxon), and the county of Kent, with its bold headland jutting out to the sea.

Kendal-green. To lovers of Shakespeare the words at once conjure up the burly form of Falstaff with his braggadocio about "three misbegotten knaves in Kendal-green," but probably it may not occur to every one that Falstaff is referring to the green cloth made at Kendal, in Westmoreland, for which the town was long famous and where the manufacture of cloth is still an important industry. Robin Hood and his merry men are reputed to have worn a livery of Kendal-green.

Kernel. No country can afford to neglect agriculture; it lies at the innermost heart, the very core, of a nation's welfare, and it may truly be said that a single grain of corn represents the turning point between barbarism and civilisation. The man of pre-historic times who first noticed that by sowing a grain of corn he could reap ten, twenty or a hundred-fold, was the pioneer of all progress, for it is this use of natural forces for the production of increase which is at the root, the very "kernel" of civilisation. And the derivation of the word "kernel" emphasises this point—it is the Anglo-Saxon *corn-el*, a grain of corn; German *kern*.

Kil. A Gaelic word originally denoting a hermit's cell, though afterwards used to denote a church—of which the hermit's cell was so often the precursor. It is a frequent component of place-names in Scotland and Ireland; as, for instance, in Kil-marnock, Kil-donan, Kil-mallock, and Kil-meadan. I-colm-kill, meaning the island-of-Columba-of-the-church, is another example. There is a peculiar interest attached to the prefix " kil," for by its means may often be traced the spot where the first hermits had each his lonely cell, which became the vigorous local centres whence Christianity was successfully promulgated to the half-savage Celts. It is stated that no less than 1,400 names containing this root exist in Ireland alone.

Kin. (*See* KEN.)

' Kindly Fruits of the Earth.' A phrase familiar to all Church-goers from childhood upwards, but the meaning of which—perhaps because of its familiarity—long remains buried in obscurity. That the fruits of the earth should be apostrophised as " kindly " seems incomprehensible, until it is recognised that the word is here used as the adjective of " kind," in its meaning of nature, sort, variety.

Kine. " The seven good kine . . . the seven thin and ill-favoured kine." (Gen. xli. 26, 27.) This short word of one syllable is a curious example of a double plural. The Anglo-Saxon for " cow " is *cu* (coo), the plural of which is *cy* (ky, the Scotch " kye "). This being again plural-ed, by adding *en*, became *kyen*, which is our word " kine."

King. The word signifies a man among his own " kin," being a contraction of the Anglo-Saxon *cyning*, son of a tribe. From which it may be inferred that a king was elected by his own people, as one who represented their own race; they were his men because they were of his blood—because he was of their " kin " he was their " king."

King-at-arms. This title, which is of great antiquity in chivalry, is held by three officers, named respectively Garter, Norroy and Clarencieux. The first of these is the principal king-at-arms, the other two being provincial kings-at-arms, officiating north and south of the Trent respectively. From an early period the name of king-at-arms has been borne by the principal heralds, especially by those attached to the Sovereign, and in the time of Edward I. an official called Norroy was placed in charge of heraldries north of the Tweed. The present offices were constituted in the reign of Richard III., when the existing College of Arms was instituted.

King's Bench. Literally the bench or seat of the king, the name given to one of three chief courts of English law, because the king used to sit there (called Queen's Bench when a queen is reigning). It grew up in early Norman times, when the judicial business of the nation was transacted in the king's palace. It gradually separated into three—the Courts of King's Bench, of Common Pleas, and of Exchequer—and exercised control over other courts, taking special cognisance of trespasses against the king's peace. Its separate existence was abolished by the Judicature Act of 1873, and it is now the King's Bench Division of the High Court.

King's Evil. The practice of invoking the king's touch as a cure for the " king's evil " (the old name for scrofula) was in force as long ago as the time of Edward the Confessor (1042-1066) in England, and can be traced back to a much earlier period in France. Samuel Johnson was " touched " by Queen Anne in 1712, and Prince Charles Edward " touched " a child at Holyrood in 1745. Louis XVI. is alleged to have " touched," as a cure for disease, no less than 2,400 persons in one year (1775). We are told that great benefit ensued to the afflicted, and in view of the known effects of Mesmerism it is scarcely wise to be too incredulous of this assertion.

Kissing goes by Favour. The phrase is commonly
used to imply that the choice of a person for this
or that office or emolument is a matter of favour-
itism, and the usually accepted interpretation is
the analogy between a kiss and a choice, from the
fact that both are often gained by favour rather
than by merit.   But it is interesting to note, also,
the close alliance in the derivation of the two words
" kiss " and " choose."   To kiss, in Anglo-Saxon,
is *cyssan* (*kissan*), and in German *küssan*, while to
choose, in Anglo-Saxon, is *coesan* (*koesan*), and in
Dutch *kiesan*.

Kitchen-middens.   The word means " refuse-heaps,"
and " middens " is current in the North of England
to denote a " dung-heap."   Although there may
be nothing interesting in the derivation of the word,
the particular " refuse-heaps " to which it is
applied have proved of vast importance to scientific
discovery, for they have supplied us with evidence
of the ways of life and the configuration of continents in the early Neolithic age, when man had
only just begun to make flint implements.
" Kitchen-middens " were first observed along the
coasts of Denmark, where they were generally
believed to be nothing more than raised beaches,
and it was not until it was discovered that they
contained the shells of species which do not live
together nor require the same conditions of life that
it became apparent that they were the refuse-heaps
of villages of vast antiquity, the population of which
lived chiefly on shell-fish, but partly on the produce
of the chase.   " Kitchen-middens " are not limited
to Denmark; they exist on the shores of the Moray
Frith, in Cornwall and Devonshire, in the Malay
Peninsula, and in Australia.

Kith and Kin.   This is a good example of the preservation of a phrase chiefly by reason of its alliteration
and assonance, for the two words " kith " and
" kin " have little difference in meaning.   But from
their derivation a distinction can, however, be

drawn, the root of " kith " being the Anglo-Saxon *cunnan*, to know, thus signifying an acquaintance, a friend; whereas the root of " kin " is the Anglo-Saxon *cynn* (in its turn derived from *gan*, to beget) meaning a race, a tribe, offspring; thus bringing in the meaning of relationship and kindred.

Knapsack. The word, in its origin, is bound up with the idea of something to eat, although now used to denote a case for a soldier's kit or a tourist's clothes. It is derived from the Danish *knappen*, to eat, and *sak*, a bag, and apparently was originally restricted to a sack or scrip in which provisions were carried.

Knave. The word is derived from the Anglo-Saxon *cnafa*, a boy, cognate with the Dutch *knaap*, a lad, a servant, and with the Swedish *knäfvel*, a rogue. In English it was originally used to denote a boy— in Wycliffe's Bible (Ex. i. 16.) we have " If it is a ' knave ' child, sle ye him." In " Piers Plowman," which, though its author died in 1400, was not published till 1550, we have an example of the use of the word in the sense of servant—" and bit (bid) his " knave " knele, that shall his coppe (cup) holde." Later the word is used to denote a false or dishonest fellow, as in Macaulay's " History of England "—"Of these a large proportion were " knaves ' and libertines."

Knell. The very word has a doleful sound—to toll (or knoll) the knell! " It is the knell of my departed hours," says Young in his " Night Thoughts." All three words—" knell," " knoll," " toll "—are probably derived from the Low Latin *nola*. But the " passing bell " was appropriated, not initiated, by the Church, for long previous to Christianity it was customary to make a great clamouring, a noisy clanging (Mark v. 38, 39.) with the object (as supposed) of frightening away evil spirits, lest they should bar the way to the passing of the soul. The Anglo-Saxon word for " knell " is *cnyllän*, to beat noisily, the Swedish and German is *knall*, a loud noise; the Icelandic is *gnella*, to scream.

Christianity took the knell and changed its scream into a prayer !

Knock. This is a word often found as a component of place-names in Scotland, and Sir Herbert Maxwell states that there are as many as two-hundred-and-twenty " Knocks " in Galloway alone.   It is a Gaelic word, signifying a knoll, a hill.   The name Knock-toe, near Galway, is a corruption of Knock-na-tuadh, meaning battle-axe-hill, the place being the site of a great battle between the Earl of Kildare and the Earl of Clanricarde, in the year 1504.

Knowledge is Power. A phrase which is on everyone's lips and which, in its essence, has been stated by more than one writer of old.   In the Bible (Prov. xxiv. 5.) we find " A wise man is strong ; yea, a man of knowledge increased strength " ; but it was Francis Bacon (1561-1626) who wrote " *Scientia potestas est*," the Latin counterpart of the phrase. The true meaning of " knowledge " seems often misunderstood, being accepted as the equivalent of learning acquired by reading, but the word, in its old form of " know-leche " was in common use long before books were accessible.   Learning is properly a scholastic acquirement, a means of gaining knowledge, but " know-leche " implies a grace received, the gift of knowing.   For the second syllable, " leche," is a form of the Anglo-Saxon *lac*, a gift, also exemplified in the word " wed-lock," (q.v.) by some interpreted to mean " pledge-gift " or " security-gift "—the woman giving herself in exchange for the man's protection.

Knuckle under. The full applicability of this phrase, in the commonly accepted sense of " knuckling under " being an act of submission, is made more evident when it is borne in mind that the word " knuckle " originally meant not only a finger-joint but also a knee-joint, or any joint.   To " knuckle under " is, therefore, equivalent to kneeling, an

attitude which has always betokened submission.
The meaning of a knee-joint is retained in the term
" knuckle of veal."

Koran. The word is the Arabic *kurān*, which, with
the article *al*, the, signifies that which is read, from
kará, to read. It denotes the Moslem Bible,
believed to consist of revelations made by Allah
(God) to Mahomet, by the mouth of the angel
Gabriel. Mahomet, like Christ, wrote nothing
himself, but his followers noted down his utterances
on leather, palm-leaves, stones, and shoulder-
blades of sheep. On the death of the prophet his
successor collected these, but many disputes and
discrepancies emerged, to settle which the Caliph
Othman caused an edition to be prepared which
was to be considered canonical, while to prevent
further disputes all the earlier codices were burnt—
an irreparable loss to criticism. One of the earliest
pieces of the Koran, generally esteemed the gem
of the whole, is the Lord's Prayer, as follows :—
" In the name of God, the compassionate Compassioner. Praise is to God, the Lord of the worlds,
the compassionate Compassioner, the Sovereign of
the day of judgment. Thee do we worship and of
Thee do we beg assistance. Direct us in the right
way, in the way of those to whom Thou hast been
gracious, on whom there is no wrath and who do
not go astray."

Kraal. The name given to the Hottentot villages in
South Africa, generally a mere collection of huts
arranged in a circle. The word is believed by some
to have its origin in the Dutch *Koraal*, coral, on
the supposition that the early Dutch settlers
traced a resemblance to the coral-reef in such a
circular assemblage of huts. But other authorities
connect the word with " corral," (from the Spanish
corro, a circle) which denotes a pen for cattle, or
the space enclosed by the trekkers' wagons when
they are ranged up for the night in defensive order.

La Belle Sauvage Yard. This was originally the yard of a well-known coaching inn in London, and the history of its name is interesting. As proved by a legal document dated 5th February, 1453, the sign of the inn was at first " The Bell in the Hoop," indicated by a bell which clanged within an iron hoop at the top of a pole, but as the house was, at one time, kept by a certain Isabelle Savage, it became known as " The Belle Savage," and as such is referred to in a deed of reversion to the Cutlers' Company in 1586. In the year 1616, Pocahontas, the Indian princess who had married John Rolfe on the supposed death of her first husband, John Smith, (whom she had rescued from the hands of her tribe at the risk of her life) came to England and lodged at " The Belle Savage." Her romantic story having preceded her arrival, she was already known as "La Belle Sauvage," and when there occurred the coincidence of " La Belle Sauvage " having stayed at " The Belle Savage " it naturally became irresistible to call the place " La Belle Sauvage."

Laboratory. We are so accustomed to consider this word as merely denoting a place to work in, a workshop, that we are apt to lose sight of the deeper meaning which its derivation discovers to us. For the word is formed by a contraction of the Latin *elaboratorium*, which, in its turn, comes from *elaborāre*, to work out fully and completely, to elaborate. There is a delightful significance in this suggestion of elaboration when we bear in mind the valuable work and the wonderful research which is carried on in our pathological and chemical laboratories.

Lackadaisical. A curious word—how has it originated? Perhaps as the designation of one who was continually crying " A-lack-a-day ! " which means " a lack (a loss) to-day ! " Or it may be connected with " alas-the-day " (French *hèlas*, Latin *lassus*, wearied). There seems no possibility of arriving at any certainty as to the derivation.

Lad. A youth is sometimes called a fine young " sprig " of a fellow, and in doing so we go back unwittingly to the origin of the word " lad "—the German *latte*, which signifies a shoot. We find the same thought in the mind of Thompson, the poet, when, in " The Seasons," he says, " to teach the young idea to ' shoot ! ' "

Lady. The term is not easily defined, for allied with the common illusion that a " real lady " would demean herself by doing any menial work there is the instinctive feeling in every woman that she is entitled to be called a " lady "—so much so, that among the poorer classes it is often the final word of abuse for an angry woman to tell another that she is " no lady." And the derivation of the word shows that the working woman, as head of her household, has not only an ancient right to the title of " lady " but that the " real lady " has gained the title by virtue of her being a working house-wife, for the word comes to us from the Anglo-Saxon *hlaef-dige* ("*lae-dige*") the literal meaning of which is bread-kneader. The importance formerly attached to household duties is shown by the fact that in old days the girls were literally " spinsters," while the word " daughter " can be traced back to Chaldean origin in two words mean-ing cow-girl or milk-maid, the sons being those duty it was to protect and perpetuate the family, as shown by the Sanscrit *sunu*, derived from *su*, to beget.

Lager Beer. A kind of light beer much used in Germany. It derives its name from the fact of it being kept in a *lager*, the German store-house or cellar, until it is sufficiently natured for consump-tion.

Laid on the Shelf. Like a book read and laid aside as of no further use.

Laid on with a Trowel. Quite a familiar phrase—a little vulgar, perhaps—but see how long it has lasted ! Shakespeare makes use of it in " As you

N

like it " (Act i, Sc. 2) and may-be it was old in his day.

Laid up in Lavender. Carefully preserved, as linen strewn with lavender is kept sweet and fresh.

Lake Dwellings. The smooth, inviting surface of the lake with its level bed, its inexhaustible supply of food and water ready to hand without the labour of clearing the forest or tilling the ground, its comparative security in contrast with the hazardous plight of living in perpetual dread of wild beasts and fierce foes—all these conditions combined became a powerful inducement to primitive man to fix his habitation on the water and to make those villages which we call Lake-dwellings. To this day the natives in Borneo, Central Africa and New Guinea live on the water in wooden huts supported on piles—a primitive Venice. The remains of a lake-dwelling were discovered in Moorfields, London, and large numbers are found in the Swiss lakes. From the implements they contain they are shown to date from Neolithic times and extend through the Copper, Bronze and Iron ages up to the beginning of the Christian era. The huts were made of woven twigs plastered with clay, a gangway was built to the shore and the cattle lived with the villagers. The remains include arrow-heads, stone axes, rude nets, dug-outs, heaps of animal and fish-bones, pottery, seeds of corn, etc.

Lamb. The expression " I'll lamb you," used as a threat, is often heard among the poorer classes, and one might well imagine that, like so many phrases, it was merely a corruption of something else—the lamb being an innocent creature with nothing threatening about it. But the verb to *lamb* (*lamm, lam*) is good old English : " A fellow whom he lambed most horribly " says Misson in his " Travels." The Icelandic is *lama*, to bruise; the Anglo-Saxon is *laeman*, to thrash.

Lambeth. The word is of Anglo-Saxon origin, a corruption of *lam-hithe*, signifying the *loam-hithe* or muddy landing-place, and marking one of the chief *hithes* or landing-places on the banks of the Thames in Anglo-Saxon times. Queenhithe and Rotherhithe are examples of names of other landing-places near London.

Lamb's Conduit Street. The names of several streets in London bear witness to the general use of conduits as a means of water supply, and we have here a well known example. William Lambe was a wealthy clothworker, who, in 1577, built here, at his own cost, "a faire conduit and standard," (a standing pipe, with a tap) probably conveying water from the little stream after which Holborn is named—the Holeburn, the Burn in the Hollow, as the Anglo-Saxon word signified.

Lame Duck. The name given to a member of the Stock Exchange who, because he cannot meet his liabilities on settling day, has been black-boarded and struck off the list of members. Wild ducks, when in flight, marshal themselves into battalions of triangular form, each individual with legs and head in a horizontal attitude. A duck which is lamed or disabled in any way cannot keep its place —it must fall out.

Lammas Day. An ecclesiastical festival observed on the first day of August. Shakespeare refers to it in "Romeo and Juliet"—"How long is it now to Lammastide?" (Act i, Sc. 3). The derivation of the word is generally ascribed to the Anglo-Saxon *hláf-mæsse*, loaf-feast, at which it was the custom to offer loaves of bread as representing the first fruits of the earth. Another theory put forward is that "Lammas" is an abridgment of *Vincula-mass*, the feast to commemorate the deliverance of St. Peter from chains, which is also celebrated on 1st August.

Lan, Llan. A Celtic word denoting an enclosure, and hence, in later times, the sacred enclosure—a church. It is a common component of Welsh place-names, and Isaac Taylor states that it occurs no less than ninety-seven times in Wales. It is also found, but less frequently, in place-names in Cornwall, Shropshire, Herefordshire, Gloucestershire and Devonshire, and we have some examples of it in Scotland, as in Lanark and Lanrick. It has been pointed out that the original meaning of " llan " was probably not an enclosure but a level plain, and that, as in a mountainous country like Wales, such level places would be the first to be enclosed, the transition of meaning was an easy process.

Lane. Probably we often use the phrase " a lonely lane " and fail to recognise that in so doing we are guilty of tautology. Yet when we look at the derivation of " lane " it seems to point indubitably to the word being synonymous with " lone," for it comes to us from the Anglo-Saxon *làne* or *lone*, and the Scotch word " lane " still retains the significance of " lone " (alone). In Sir Walter Scott's " Old Mortality " a character says :—" Sae dizzy that I canna stand my *lane* " (alone).

Language. The word is derived from the Latin *lingua*—the tongue, akin to the Latin *lingere*, the Greek *leichein*, the Sanscrit *lib*; all meaning to lick, showing how close its original significance was to the tongue and its action. And yet we use " language " as the most general term of that which conveys thoughts, whether by writing, or by speech, or by gesticulation, or by painting and drawing; while, in that sense, we restrict the word " tongue " to words written or spoken, and " speech " to articulate words.

Laocoon (La-o-kò-on). A notable antique sculpture in marble, now in the Vatican. Laocoon had been a priest of Apollo, but having married against the will of the god he and the two sons of this marriage were attacked by serpents while preparing to sacrifice at the altar of Poseidon, whose priest Laocoon had become. The group was found in 1506, near the baths of Titus, and there is no question of its being the same which Pliny speaks of as in the palace of Titus, and as the work of three Rhodian sculptors.

Laudanum. The name is an example of how the significance of a word may be transferred and assume another meaning. There grows in Candia and Syria a shrub which exudes a odorous resin much valued by the ancients for its healing properties, and called by the Persians *ladan*, in Latin *ladanum*. It seems that when opium was first brought from the East it was believed to be this Persian gum, and was given that name— " laudanum."

Laugh in your Sleeve. Anciently the sleeves of all outer garments were very wide, and when a person covered his face with his hand there might be a suspicion that he was hiding a laugh.

Laugh on the wrong side of your Face. The point of the phrase is the play on the word " laugh," which was formerly—and is still in country places in the North of England—clipped of the " f " sound, just as " trough " is called " trow." " La ! "—an expression almost obsolete—was formerly the common exclamation on every possible occasion; good examples may be found in the prattle of some of Jane Austen's characters. You might exclaim " la " with a smile and an accent of pleasure, or, on the other hand, you might again say " la," with a face drawn with annoyance or grief, to express your disappointment or sorrow.

Laureate. The title of the court poet, from the Latin *laurus*, the bay-tree. In classical times a poet who became famous by reciting his heroic verse was publicly crowned with a wreath of leaves from an ever-green tree—the bay or laurel—in token that his song and his fame deserved to remain " evergreen," to be remembered for all time. The heads of Homer and Virgil, Plutarch and Tasso are represented as crowned with laurel—" to wear the

laurel " was to the poet what " to bear the palm "
was to the victor.

Lavender. In London streets, not so long ago, there
might often be heard in the early autumn the cry
of " Sweet Lavender," shrilly voiced by little girls
selling tiny brooms made up of the stalks of the
fragrant plant. Those poor dirty children would
seem to have little connection with cleanliness
except their need of a good wash, and yet their
small brooms were survivals of the careful washing
of fine linen, too delicate to be beaten on the stones
in the stream in the usual way of washing clothes.
So it was rinsed in soap and water, spread on a
line, and gently beaten with soft brooms of
lavender. And the derivation of the word
" lavender " recalls this, for the name comes to us
from the Low Latin *lavendula*, the root of which
is the Latin *lavāre*, to wash, and in which also our
word " laundress " and the French " lavandiere "
(washer-woman) both originate.

Law. The law of the land is that which is *laid upon*
everyone. Various duties, burdens and trials are
laid upon different individuals, but the *law* is *laid
upon* all. This is plainly adduced from the derivation of the word " law "—the Anglo-Saxon *lah*,
from *lecgan*, to lay. So also we get " legislate "
through the Latin *lex*, *legis*, the law, from the
Greek *lego*, lay. And the word " ledger " denotes
the principal book of accounts in which entries
from other books are *laid up* or entered.

Lawn. We of to-day can scarcely conceive that at one
time this land of ours was virtually all morass and
forest. Although it was called land (Angle-land)
in distinction to the sea over which the roving
pirates came, the interior was found to be another
sea—a sea of waving woodlands—through which
the adventurers had to force their way, and when
they came to an open grassy spot they called it
" land " (the word is found in all Teutonic lan-

guages) as the only place where land—as ground—was visible. In Chaucer it becomes " laund " and with us it has become our garden " lawn."

Lazar-House. On many of the great roads of England, as you approach some old town, you may often see a small, square, over-grown, disused building; and if your curiosity leads you to examine it you may find a half-defaced inscription on a stone in the wall, and may perhaps still be able to decipher the words " Lazar-House." It was built, most likely, some seven hundred years ago, when leprosy dogged the footsteps of the returning Crusader, and used later, perhaps, as a " Pest-House," when the sacred citizens of London, flying from that dreadful pestilence, the Plague, were stricken with it on their way. The word " lazar " means leper, or one infected with a loathsome disease, and is a contraction of the Latin *Lazarus*, the name of the beggar in the parable (Luke xvi. 20.), while the word " Lazarus " is itself a contraction of the Hebrew *E-leazar*, signifying " he whom God aids."

Leader (Leading Article). The name originated in the printing-shop, newspaper articles being called " leaders " when the lines of print of which they were composed were separated by a thin plate of lead, so as to give them more importance and space in the paper.

Lead Pencils. The use of the mineral lead, as a substance with which to make a more or less black mark, must be very old, and probably it was from the fact of a pencil being put to a similar purpose that the name " lead " pencil arose—certainly the plumbago (otherwise graphite) of which a pencil is made has no lead in its composition. Plumbago is a mineral found in many parts of the world, a celebrated mine being at Borrowdale, Cumberland, where, however, the supply has become scarce, so that a method has been invented of using the dust by consolidating it under great pressure.

Least said Soonest Mended. Like so many of these phrases it is impossible to say when and where it took its origin, but this is certain—that some three hundred years ago George Wither wrote :—

"I oft have heard defended
Little said is soonest mended."

Leave no Stone Unturned. The phrase may be traced as far back as Euripides, an Athenian poet born 480 years B.C.

Lee. The "lee" side is the sheltered side, the quarter of a ship opposite to that from which the wind blows. Hence the word is used to denote any kind of shelter, and in its older form of "lew," the descendant of the Anglo-Saxon *hleow*, it is used in rural England to denote a cattle-shed, or the side of the hedge or stack where the labourer eats his meal and smokes his pipe, or the side of the hill where the shepherd and his flock find some shelter from the force of the winter's wind on the bare South Downs.

Left-Hand. Although the word "left," as expressing opposite to right, cannot be traced in the Anglo-Saxon, it is probably of English origin, and we find *leefter-hond* for "left-hand" in North Friesland. Its suggested relation to "leave," in the sense of being left, is now considered extremely doubtful, although approved by Trench, but its origin may, perhaps, be safely ascribed to the Anglo-Saxon *lefan*, to weaken, *lef*, weak. And this interpretation of the word at once appeals to our sense of probability, for throughout historic times in all civilised nations, from the Assyrian and Egyptian onward, the right hand has been given the pre-eminence and the left has become emphatically the weak hand.

Left him Alone with his Glory. The quotation is from Charles Wolfe's poem on the burial of Sir John Moore, and this one poem has made the writer famous. He was not present on the battle-field, but wrote the verses from an account given him; they appeared in an Irish newspaper in the year 1817. Wolfe was an Irish Clergyman, and died at the age of 32.

Left in the Lurch. The phrase signifies to be deserted, to be left at a disadvantage, and is said to take its origin from the card table, being used in the game of cribbage when one party gains every point before the other makes one. But probably the phrase had an older significance, for to "lurch" is to "lurk." A poacher "lurches" when he lurks about laying traps for game, and robbers and highwaymen lurking in ambush may be said to be "in the lurch." If one man found himself deserted by the rest of the gang having crept silently away, he would complain of being "left in the lurch"—left at a disadvantage, in a difficult position, without the help on which he had relied.

Legacy. That which is left to a person by will, a bequest of personal property, is a "legacy," but although it is by the will of the testator that the property comes to the legatee it is only by the law of the land that the Will is put into force, the origin of the word "legacy" making this evident, being derived from the Latin *lex*, (*legis*) law (of the law).

Legend. What we now understand by a legend, or legendary lore, is a story largely fabulous, handed down from ancient times. The Legenda (from the Latin *legendus*, to be read) was, however, the name for a book of the lives of the saints, read in the refectory of religious houses and at matins. It is because of the marvellous stories in some of these biographies that we come by the meaning now attached to the word "legend."

Legion. "My name is legion, for we are many," said the man with the unclean spirit (Mark v. 9). The word came to mean *many* because in ancient Rome a body of soldiers numbering as many as six thousand was called a legion, but originally it meant the troops on whom the duty of serving was laid, from the Latin *legere*, to levy. (*See* LAW.)

Leigh. A component in place-names. (*See* LEY.)

Let. The word has two significations—(1) to allow, to permit, to grant use of, to leave alone; and (2) to hinder, to prevent. It has also two derivations, both from the Anglo-Saxon; the first from *lètan*, and the second from *lettan*. The latter word means "to make late," formed from *laet*, slow, (like "hinder" from "be-hind") and its root is found in most Scandinavian languages, though practically obsolete in English.

Letter. Many a letter we receive is almost illegible— nothing but a scrawl and a smear. Perhaps we ought not to expect more, for the word is derived from the Latin *litera*, through *linere*, (*litum*) to smear. It was an appropriate appellation because the characters—now called letters—were smeared or scrawled on parchment instead of being cut into a tablet. Literature has the same derivation.

Letters-Patent. The "letters" are the letters of the writing, and "patent" means open. The document gets its name from being written on open sheets of parchment, bearing a seal but not folded. Derived from the Latin *patere*, to lie open.

Leopard. The name originated from a misconception of the genus of the animal, which was long supposed to be a cross between the "pard" (panther) and the lioness. The belief in the hybrid nature of animals which was generally accepted in old days is astonishing, especially when, as in the case of the "jumar," it was held in regard to domesticated animals. The "jumar" was supposed to be a cross between the bovine and equine species, the offspring of a bull and a mare or a bull and an ass. John Leger, in 1669, gives an engraving of one, and reports that he rode on a "jumar" for eighteen miles in the mountains, much more comfortably than he could have done on a horse. But in later times dissection has established the fact that these pretended "jumars" were mules, and that there is no probability of the hybrid called the "jumar" having ever existed.

Lever. A bar for lifting by forcing it against its fulcrum or prop. Literally, that which lifts, from the Latin *levare*, to raise. The lever was certainly a very early discovery in mechanics and of it Archimedes is reported to have said: "Give me a fulcrum on which to rest and I will move the earth."

Lewd. This is an example of a word where the signification has become debased, the Anglo-Saxon *lœwed* being equivalent to lay, belonging to the people generally, to the unlearned, in distinction to the cleric who alone was able to read and write. In "A Short Catechism" (1553) the sentence "as necessary for the 'lewd' as the learned" is an instance of the old meaning of the word, while less than a century later, the Authorised Version of the English Bible uses the word in the debased sense— "But the Jews which believed not . . . took unto them certain 'lewd' (in the Vulgate *malos*, bad) fellows of the baser sort" (Acts xvii. 5.)—and in the present day the word has become still further debased, signifying unchaste and lascivious.

Ley, Leigh. These are suffixes frequently met with in place-names in the English southern counties. They are of Anglo-Saxon origin, from the word *leah*, the root of which is the verb to "lie," and "leys" were open forest glades where cattle would browse and lie. It is not surprising, therefore, that in the weald of Sussex, which was formerly densely wooded, many local names terminate in "ley," 'hurst,' "den," or "field." While the "leys" indicate the open glades, the "hursts" denote the denser parts of the forest, the "dens" the well-wooded valleys, and the "fields" the patches of "felled" or cleared land. (*See* DEN.)

Librarian. The word differs but little from the Latin designation—*Librarius*, but the duties differ considerably. The modern Librarian has a responsible post in taking charge of the library, but he is not called upon to add to its contents by writing new volumes. It was the duty of his Latin prototype to transcribe the few treasured manuscripts of which he was in charge.

Libretto—Libel. The name " libretto "—the book containing the words of an opera—is the diminutive of the Italian *libro*, a little book. Although " libel " has a very different meaning the derivation is similar—from the Latin *libellus*, the diminutive of *liber*, a book—and the application of the word arose from the rancorous pamphlets, often of a libellous character, which were issued broadcast before newspapers were in general use, especially during the civil and religious upheaval of the Puritan period.

License. It is curious to observe how from this word (derived from the Latin *licet*, to be allowed) there have been formed two words of opposite signification. The " licentiate " is one who honourably holds a license to practice his profession; the " licentious " man is one who permits himself a license in the practice of debauchery.

Lich. The word—used by us as a prefix to several names—is the Anglo-Saxon *lic*, a corpse, and is found, in one form or another, in all the Scandinavian and Teutonic languages. The most familiar example of our use of the word is in " Lichgate," the covered gate at the entrance to a Church yard, under which the bier may be rested preparatory to forming the funeral procession to the church, headed by the clergyman. " Lich-owl," also called " Screech-owl," is the white owl that often screams horribly as it flies along at night—there is a famous colony in the church-belfry at Ditchling, Sussex—and probably from this screaming arose the belief in an imaginary screech-owl which is supposed to be in waiting for dying persons. It is no new superstition that connects the owl with misfortune and death; Pliny, Ovid and Virgil all refer to it as announcing impending disaster, and Shakespeare has frequently availed himself of the common belief in the owl being a bird of evil omen.

Lick into Shape. The phrase means the act of giving method or system; the metaphor being taken from the once popular notion that the young of the bear are born shapeless and are licked into their proper form by their dam.

(The) Light that never was on Sea or Land (Wordsworth). The poet is referring to the visionary world of imagination. Looking at one of Turner's pictures—a wonderful sunset—a visitor remarked to the painter : " I never saw anything quite so wonderful as that in nature." " No," said the master, " but don't you wish you could ! "

Like Angels' Visits. The phrase is that of the poet Campbell, but various renderings of the idea were afloat long before his time. No doubt the allusion originated in the New Testament reference made to the angel visits received by Abraham—" Some have entertained angels unawares." (Heb. xiii. 2.) A hundred years before Campbell, John Morris writes :—

" Like angels' visits short and bright."

A little later comes Robert Blair, and sings of visits

" Like those of angels short and far between."

At last comes Campbell, and settles it, apparently, for all time by saying :—

" Like angels' visits few and far between."

But it had taken a hundred years, we see, to perfect that line !

Lilac. Not only in cottage gardens all over the country, but even in the London smoke, it thrives and blossoms, giving us delightful pyramids of bloom in May. We take it as part of the English scenery, one of the joys of an English Spring. Yet it is a native of Persia and was only introduced here at the end of the 16th century. The Persian name is *lilaj*.

Line. Every line we draw, every line we read, every line we follow, are, as it were, the threads of a piece of linen, for the word " line " is the lineal descendant of the Latin *linum*, flax.

Ling. As a suffix " ling " is frequently used as a diminutive or to express affection, as duckling, darling (dearling). Sometimes it implies depreciation, as in underling, worldling.

Linn, Lynn. Celtic words, derived from *lleyn*, smooth, and signifying a deep, still pool. From them we get such place-names as Lin-coln, Lin-lithgow, Dub-lin, King's Lynn, and many others; while from the same source are the river-names Leven, (found in Scotland and many English counties), the Loin, the Leane, the Line, the Lane, and the Lain.

Llan. (*See* LAN.)

Lode-Star. The ancients had no compass to help them in their wanderings over land and sea, but they had the stars to guide them—the wise men of the East, as we read in the Bible, were guided by a star in their long journey to Bethlehem—and a " lode-star " is a leading-star, by which a direction may be taken and followed. For though the word is sometimes spelt " load-star " it has no connection with a burden, a weight; it is derived from the Icelandic *leidh*, which signifies a leading, a course, a way, and we retain that meaning when we speak of the " lode " of a mine to denote the course taken by the mineral for which the mine is being developed.

London Stone. As in the Forum of old Rome, so in Roman London this stone marked the centre of the town from which all the great roads of the country radiated and from which they were measured—

such is the usually accepted theory. But the fact of the stone having been preserved with such reverential care for so many ages is suggestive of it having had originally a more important purpose and intent. It was fixed deep in the ground (within a few feet of the wall of St. Swithin's Church, Cannon Street, against which it is now preserved) and is mentioned as early as the times of Athelstan, king of the West Saxons, without any reference to its being considered a Roman military stone. Moreover, the fact of Jack Cade striking it and exclaiming " Now is Mortimer lord of London " indicates that the mob who followed him attached some meaning to his action, and it is highly probable that London Stone marked the place where legislation for the government of the City was made and suitors causes adjudicated. In many of our old towns—at Kendal, for instance—there exists a similar stone, from which are still made, as they have been from time immemorial, all important proclamations—such as the accession of the king—and the general consensus of tradition throughout the country tends to corroborate the supposition that London Stone is a momument of pre-historic times.

Look a Gift Horse in the Mouth. Obviously the metaphor is taken from the practice of examining a horse's mouth to discover its age and value. The phrase is of unknown antiquity—it is quoted by St. Jerome, the compiler of the Latin Vulgate. (A.D. 340-420).

Look before you Leap. The germ of this phrase, if not the phrase itself, can be traced back some hundreds of years, for Thomas Tusser (1523-1580) wrote " Look 'ere you leap, see 'ere you go "; and in Samuel Butler's " Hudibras " (1600-1680) we find " Look before you 'ere you leap."

Loom. Although the common use of this word is to denote the machine in which yarn is woven into a fabric, the Anglo-Saxon *gèloma*, from which the

word is derived, had a much more general signification—that of a tool, an implement, or any utensil
or personal chattel of the household. Hence it is
that we have " heir-loom," which Blackstone
defines as an " implement of furniture which by
custom descends together with an house, neither
land nor tenement, but a mere moveable; yet being
inheritable is comprised under the general word
hereditament."

Loose Fish. A " loose fish," a " queer fish," " fishy,"
are all terms used to denote a dissipated man, a
doubtful or suspected character. Why the nature
of a fish should be applied to indicate some matter
or person of suspicious or unsound character it is
difficult to decide; perhaps the corruption which
so rapidly sets in when a fish is dead may have
something to do with it.

Love me little, Love me long. This is another phrase
of considerable age. It is found in Christopher
Marlowe's works (1565-1593) and also in Robert
Herrick's verse (1591-1674).

Low. As a suffix in place-names, this word is derived
from the Anglo-Saxon *hlaw*, meaning a rising
ground. Examples may be quoted in Houns-low,
Lud-low, and Mar-low, and in the numerous
" laws " in Scotland.

Lozenge. A small cake of flavoured or medicated
sugar, so called because originally—and still very
generally—cut in the shape of a lozenge, *i.e.*, a
parallelogram with the corners cut off. Epitaphs
—which, as we all know, so often give an exaggerated estimate of the virtues of the deceased
whom they are designed to commemorate—are
usually of a lozenge shape, and it is worthy of
notice that the word " lozenge " is derived from
the Old French *losange*, which means flattery.

Lucid Interval. A common-place expression, not of
sufficient importance to be inserted, one might say;
yet it has been used by men as celebrated as Bacon,
Fuller, South, Dryden, Johnson, and Burke.

Lucre. The word means, not merely money or riches, but gain, for it is derived from the Latin *lucrum*, gain, and is akin to the Greek *leia*, booty, the Hindu *lut*, loot, and the Sanscrit *lotra*, stolen goods. The epithet " filthy " so often applied to " lucre " is, therefore, by no means inappropriate, especially when used to designate gain which is dirtily come by.

Lug. The word, when used as a verb, means to pull, to drag along ; as a noun it means the projecting part of anything by which it may be lugged or lifted. Its origin is the Scandinavian root found in the Swedish *lugga*, to pull by the hair, and in the Norwegian *lugg*, the hair. Hence we get our word " luggage," signifying something which is dragged about; and the words " lugger " and " lug-sail " come from the same root.

Lumber-Room. A room which generally contains a strange assortment of rubbish, where things broken, unsightly and useless, are stowed away. But, oddly enough, it derives its name from the rich treasure-room of those bankers of old, the merchants and pawnbrokers of mediæval times, the Lombards, whose memory is enshrined in the name of Lombard Street, not only in London but in other old towns of England. When, however, we come to the " lumber " of the Canadian woods we have quite a different meaning and derivation; to the early French settlers the shady depths of the Forest were *l'ombrage*, easily corrupted to the English " lumber."

Luncheon. The word, though itself old, is evidently a prolongation of the older word " lunch," possibly a corruption of " lunching," while " lunch," strange as it may at first appear, is the equivalent of " lump," of Scandinavian origin. We still use " lump " as synonymous with " hump " and " hunch "—the " hump " on a camel is the " lump " on its back, a " hunch " of bread is a " lump " of bread—and by an easy transition a " hunch " (of

o

bread) became " lunch " (a piece of bread).   In Sussex and Hampshire, and may be elsewhere, the word " nuncheon " is commonly used among the poorer classes, a corruption, most likely, of " luncheon," with some reference to the time of day at which it is eaten—noon.

Lute.   Although the lute is a stringed instrument the sweetness of its music depends upon the wood of which it is made :—

" It is the little rift within the lute
    That bye and bye will make the music mute,
    And, ever widening, slowly silence all.
                                        TENNYSON.

A lute must be made of specially chosen wood, well seasoned, without a flaw, lest it develop the smallest crack.   And the origin of the word indicates this, being derived from the Arabic *al-ud*, the wood.

Luxury.   How impossible to define the word !   To be arrayed in purple and fine linen, to fare sumptuously every day, was considered luxury, yet what was then luxury is now ordinary, for the standard of luxury advances continually.   But the word itself contains a definition and a warning—it is derived from the Latin *luxus*, excess !

M. A.   The common abbreviation for the Latin words *magister artium*, the university degree, meaning literally, Master of Arts.   The term " arts " is now generally applied to drawing, painting, modelling, etc., and it would seem incongruous that a scholar who may have no knowledge of these arts should receive the degree of " Master of Arts." But the earliest letters were pictures drawn by prehistoric artists, and we still speak of a writing or deed being " drawn," while up to comparatively recent times the scribe or the clerk who had learnt to draw letters was considered to have acquired an " art."

Ma adamised Road.   A system of road-making introduced by John Loudon Macadam, Surveyor of public roads in 1827. The process consists of breaking up granite, or other hard stone, into small, angular pieces—an iron ring was originally used to regulate the size—and the stone then consolidated and levelled by means of heavy rollers.

Maccabees. Five brothers of a patriotic Jewish family, who revolted against the Romans, B.C. 168. Three years later the Maccabees took Jerusalem and purified the Temple, an act commemorated by the Feast of Dedication (St. John x. 22). After this success a Maccabean dynasty reigned for about a century, Herod the Great, slaughterer of the infants of Bethlehem, putting to death the last scion of the house, who was also the High Priest. There are five Books of the Maccabees, four of which are included in our Apocrypha.

Macaroni. The word comes from the Italian *maccheroni*, a mixture, and hence denotes a medley, an idle fancy. Towards the close of the 18th century the leaders of fashion went by the name "macaroni" because they affected a fanciful costume. They wore an immense knot of artificial hair, a very small cocked hat, and very tight small clothes, and they carried a long walking-stick ornamented with tassels. In Garrick's "Bon Ton" we find: "This fellow would turn rake and "macaroni" if he was to stay here a week longer."

Macassar Oil. So called because first exported from Macassar, the capital of the Celebes. It was, at one time, much used for the hair, and hence the need of Anti-Macassars.

Mace. This well-known spice is really one of the coats of the nutmeg. In former days the nutmeg, which was scarce, was so highly esteemed and so greatly valued that we find it handed down by will. As great wealth could be amassed by importing it from the east, the rivalry between the Dutch and the English merchants led to war between the two countries. The Greek word for spice, *maker*, is connected with the Sanscrit, *makar-anda*, the nectar of a flower; the cup-shaped or globular blossoms being those that hold the dew—the flower's nectar. It may be that the bulb-like shape of the nutmeg or mace, gave the name to the weapon called the " mace "—a rod headed with a heavy ball of iron, like a tulip on its stalk. The weapon has come to be merely an ornamental staff, borne by high officials of the crown as an emblem of their authority. " He was followed by the maces (mace bearers) of the two houses, and by the two Speakers." Macaulay, Hist. Eng. ch. xi.

Machiavelian. Cunning, perfidious, destitute of politi cal morality, after the manner of Machiavelli, who taught that right should be systematically subordinated to expediency. He was born at Florence in 1469, and becoming a politican was employed in matters of State. It is said of him, " He was colour-blind to commonplace morality."

Mad as a Hatter. A corruption of " Mad as an atter," where " atter " signifies adder, viper. " Mad " was formerly used in the sense of hurtful, venemous; hence " mad as a hatter " really meant " venemous as a viper."

Madonna, Madona. Literally, in Italian, my lady, from the Latin *mea domina*. Applied to the Virgin Mary, in same manner as " Our Lady." Hence pictures of the Virgin are called " Madonnas."

Madrigal. The word is probably derived from the Italian *madre*, mother, the early madrigals—songs, or hymns without music—being addressed to the Virgin Mother.

Magazine. From the Arabic *makhzan*, a store house, and still so applied; but also a periodical containing miscellaneous articles or a *store* of reading. The first publication of this kind in England was the " Gentleman's Magazine," brought out in 1731.

Magh. A frequent component in Irish place-names, in which it has the signification of a plain, a field.

Ar-magh, Magh-era, and May-nooth may be cited as examples.

Magi. The term is used to denote the " wise men " who (as recorded in the New Testament) came from the East to worship Christ at His nativity, and is a Latinised rendering of the Greek *magoi*, which is the word employed in the original Greek version of the Bible. The chief of the " Magi " is referred to in Jer. xxxix. 3. 13. under the name Rab-Mag, and Herodotus mentions the " Magi " as one of the six Madian tribes. They were a sacred caste in Persia, but ultimately sank into mere magicians.

Magnet. From the Greek *magnes*, signifying stone from Magnesia, in Lydia or Thessaly. The natural magnet is the Lodestone, or Loadstone, a mineral (magnetic oxide of iron) common in many places, and which has the property, when hung so as to move freely, of pointing to the earth's poles and of attracting iron and other metals. The word Lodestone is derived from the Anglo-Saxon *lad*, a way, a course, indicating its ability to lead or guide, as in " Lodestar," the Pole star, " Lodesman," a pilot, and " Lode," a course or vein of ore.

In connection with the Magnet the following extract from a letter by Brunetti Latini (1258) is of interest :—" At Oxford I did not fail to see Friar Bacon. He showed me a black, ugly stone called a Magnet, which has the surprising property of drawing iron to it; and if a needle be rubbed upon it and afterwards fastened to a straw, so that it should swim upon water, the needle will instantly turn towards the Pole Star. Therefore be the night ever so dark, so that neither moon nor stars be visible, yet shall the Mariner by means of this needle be able to steer his vessel aright. But no Master Mariner dare use it, lest he should fall under the imputation of being a magician; nor would sailors venture themselves out to the sea under his command if he took with him an instrument which carries so great an appearance of being constructed under the influence of some Infernal Spirit.''—Yet before the end of the 13th century the Mariner's Needle was in general use, while the Chinese assert that they were acquainted with its properties 2500 years B.C., and they certainly used it at sea A.D. 300.

Magpie. The name is indicative of the bird's parti-coloured plumage, which looks as if a black-feathered bird had been painted with white patches. The word is a compound of " Madge," the diminu-tive of " Margaret," and the Latin *pica*, from *pingere*, to paint. There are many instances of this combination of pet names in English nomencla-ture of birds, *e.g.*, Jack-daw, Jenny-wren, Robin-redbreast, Tom-tit, etc.

Mahatma. From a Sanscrit word meaning "high-souled," and applied to one who is an adept in Theosophy, skilled in religious mysteries and gifted with spiritual powers, as the result of deep psycho-logical study and high intellectual development.

Mahdi. The word is of Arabic origin, having the meaning of leader, and denotes the Mahomedan Messiah who is to appear in the last days. A person claiming to be this divinely-promised Mahdi arose in the Soudan, defeating the Egyptian army under Hicks Pasha and Baker Pasha respectively, in 1883 and 1884, and killing General Gordon at Khartoum in 1885. The Mahdi died in that year at Omdurman, from small-pox, and eventually, in 1898, the Soudanese were completely defeated by the British and Egyptian forces.

Mahomet. The word means " praised," and is the name of the great prophet of Arabia, who, in the year 613 A.D., began to proclaim his views, and ultimately established the Mahomedan faith. At Medina, while at the head of only 300 followers, he defeated 950 of the Meccans, and in a short time became virtual sovereign of Arabia. During the Caliphates of his immediate successors (632-646) the Arabs conquered Syria, Persia and Egypt, and established the new faith. In 710, under the leadership of Tarik, they landed in Spain, the Straits and Rock being thereafter named Gibraltar (from the Arab *Gibel-Tarik*). About the middle of the 8th century the Arab empire began to be broken down by the Turks, then a savage Tartar tribe, who embraced Mahomedanism, and afterwards took Constantinople.

Maiden. The name given to a machine for beheading, a kind of Guillotine, (q.v.) introduced from Italy into Scotland by the Regent Morton, who was executed by it in 1581. The word is a corruption of the Italian *mannaia*. In Devon and Lancashire, and perhaps elsewhere, the word " maiden " is used to denote a clothes-horse. (*See* " Notes and Queries," 17/12/59, 21/1/60.)

Mail-Coach. The first mail-coach left London at 8 o'clock in the morning on 8th August, 1784, and arrived at Bristol at 11 at night. Till then the Post Office had sent the mails by passenger coaches which, with the view of picking up fares, ran at any time which suited the owner or the driver, the guard or the ostler, the squire or my lady. It was John Palmer, of Bath, who conceived the idea of running coaches with the special object of carrying the mails. He went to Mr. Pitt and succeeded in convincing him that the scheme would not only be of great advantage to letter-writers but also remunerative to the Government, and from that time forward mail-coaches continued to run until they were superseded by railway trains. Recently, the conveyance of the mails (parcels especially) by road, in coach and motor, has been revived by the Post Office.

Make. The word comes to us from the Anglo-Saxon *macian*, and is cognate with the German *machen* and the Gothic *magan*, all derived from the root *mag*, seen in the Latin *mag-nus* and the Greek *meg-as*, great. It is remarkable that " make " is frequently used in the English language to express some other verb, by a process of uniting it with a noun or by employing it as a kind of prefix. For example :—

Make comparison = to compare
,,   complaint   = ,, complain
,,   confession = ,, confess
,,   haste   = ,, hasten
Make amends
,,   away with, off with
,,   free with
,,   believe
,,   default
,,   good
,,   little of, much of
,,   out
,,   over
,,   peace
,,   sail
,,   shift
,,   sure, certain
,,   up, up to, up with, up for
,,   weight
,,   a charge
,,   a demand
,,   a loss
,,   a mark
,,   a price
,,   a score
,,   an abode
,,   an affidavit
,,   an obeisance
       etc., etc., etc.

Make a Bed. As late as the fourteenth century a bed was actually " made " by throwing down a heap of straw in any room of the house.

Make Bricks without Straw. This phrase, suggested by the practice, common in the East, of making bricks of straw and mud dried in the sun, is an allusion to the command laid upon the Israelites in Egypt as related in Exodus v. 18 : "Go therefore now, and work; for there shall no straw be given you, yet shall ye deliver the tale of bricks."

It is remarkable, in confirmation of the account given in the Bible, that an examination under the microscope reveals the fact that some of the Egyptian bricks were mixed with papyrus instead of straw.

Make Things Hum. To use extraordinary energy; from the analogy of making machinery hum by setting it working at full speed.

Make Tracks. An Americanism meaning to vanish, to quit. When a settler deserted the colony and set out to seek his fortune as a pioneer he left nothing but the track of his waggon across the prairie to show what had become of him.

Mall. A place for playing in with mallets (malls) and balls. Hence the name *Pall Mall*, from the Italian *palla*, a ball, and *maglio*, a mace or mallet.

Mameluke. The word is a form of the Arabian Mamluk, which means a slave, and is the name of a tribe of fierce horsemen of Tartar race, enslaved by the Arabs and employed by the great Saladin as his mounted guard. Originally serfs, they were so greatly feared that at the close of the Saladin dynasty in Egypt they became Sultans at Cairo and reigned in barbaric splendour and luxury for nearly 300 years. When the main body of the Tartar (or Turkoman) race possessed themselves of the country, now called Turkey, the Mamelukes were brought under the allegiance of the Turkish Sultans, but, as Beys, they continued to be the virtual rulers in Egypt, until 1811, when they were treacherously massacred by the Viceroy of Egypt at Cairo.

Mammon. The Syrian word for riches is *mamona*, and it has been thought that an idol was worshipped under that name, but probably the word is merely a personification of earthly desires—wealth, honours, sensuality. ("Ye cannot serve God and Mammon."—Math. xi. 24.)

Man. The word is derived from a root common to many languages—Anglo-Saxon, Dutch, Icelandic, Danish, Gothic, German, Latin, Sanscrit—the signification of which is "thinking animal." It may be noted that in compounds the English plural of " man " is not necessarily " men " but " mans,' as in " Nor-mans," " Ger-mans."

Man in the Moon. There are many traditions to account for this appearance, *e.g.* :—that it is the man who picked up a bundle of sticks on the sabbath day (Numb. xv. 32-36); that it is Cain, and the " bush of thorns," an emblem of the curse upon the earth (Gen. iii. 18); that it is Endymion taken there by Diana; that it is a hare, as recounted in the Sanscrit fable of " The Story of the hare and the Elephant." These and other traditions all originate from the spots in the moon, which are really shadows thrown by the lofty summits of the mountains, mostly craters of extinct volcanoes. In proportion to its size the mountains of the moon are far higher than those of the earth.

Man in the Street. A metaphorical expression for the average man, with no more than an average knowledge of matters in general. Since everybody makes use of the street, the man in the street is the average man.

Man of Destiny. A name given to Napoleon I., who is generally considered to have looked upon himself as an instrument of destiny in all his acts. Sir Walter Scott wrote :—" The man of Destiny had power for a time to bind kings with chains and nobles with fetters of iron."

Man of Ross. The name given to John Kyrle of Ross, Herefordshire, because of the improvements he effected in his native town, though he had but little money at his disposal. Of him Pope wrote :— " Richer than miser, nobler than king or king-polluted lord."

Man of Straw. One who has nothing to lose. The term is derived from the men who hung about the Law Courts with a straw in their shoe, to denote that they were ready to swear to anything for a bribe.

Mandarin. Although this name for the Chinese official, whether civil or military, is the usual term adopted in European languages, the word is of Malayan origin, being a Portuguese rendering of the Malayan *mantri*, a counsellor, derived from the Sanscrit *mantra*, counsel, and cognate with our word " man." It was applied by the early settlers of Macao to the Chinese officials of that colony, and has ever since remained a European designation for a Chinaman of rank.

Manito (or Manitou). The " Great Spirit " of the North American Indians, who acknowledge two supreme Spirits—of good and of evil—the good symbolised by an egg, the evil by a serpent. (*See* Longfellow's " Hiawatha " xiv.) The Indian's sacred name for the Great Spirit is enshrined in the name of the Canadian province of Manitoba

Manna. The description of this substance, as given in the Bible (Ex. xvi.), may be summarised as follows :—A small round thing, as small as hoar-frost, which lay on the ground around the camp of the Israeltes every morning, except on the sabbath-day, throughout their forty years' wandering in the wilderness; which melted when the sun became hot, and which bred worms and stank if kept till the next day. Attempts have been made to identify various substances now called " manna " with this description, but they have not proved successful, nor does the origin of the word help us in any way. " Manna " is but a corruption of the Hebrew *man-hu*, which signifies, literally, " what is this? "—an expression used by the Israelites when first they saw this wonderful food and (as in Ex. xvi. 15) " wist not what it was "—could give it no name.

Mansard-roof. A form of roof designed by the French architect, Francois Mansart, to give more space in attics, as, by the Municipal law of the 17th century, front walls in Paris were limited in height. The restriction was evaded by the mansard method of lifting up parts of the roof.

Mansion House. The title applied to the official residences of the Lord Mayors of London and Dublin. It is a redundancy in terms which is not easily accounted for, and the suggestion that it means a " house of houses " can hardly be accepted, as Bacon, in his " Use of the Law," writes :—" This party, purposing in this place to make a dwelling, or—as the old word is—his *mansion-house* or manor-house, did devise . . . "—evidently accepting the word " Mansion-house " as equivalent to manor-house or dwelling-place.

Mantel-piece. Originally a shelf, with pegs attached to it, above the fire-place, on which wet *mantles* or other clothes were hung to dry.

Manure. A contracted form of the French *manœuvrer* —to work with the hand, to till the soil ; and hence to use material to improve the soil.

Marabout. A member of the priestly order of the Mahomedan Arabs in North Africa ; whose duty it is to attend the mosques and call the people to prayers. The name is derived from the Arabic *Marabath*, sacred or devoted to God.

Marconigram. A wireless telegram, named after William Marconi, the Italian pioneer in wireless telegraphy. The invention soon made great progress, and it is reported from Berlin that wireless communication between Germany and her Colonies in East and South-West Africa is about to be established. From New York comes the announcement that the system is to be installed at the Metropolitan Opera House, so that any subscriber within a radius of seventy-five miles—whether at home, in an hotel, or at sea—may hear the performance. It is estimated that with antennal wires, such as are on the roof of the Metropolitan Life Office, New York, Caruso's voice could be heard within a radius of 200 miles.

Marigold. A golden-coloured cup-flower growing on marsh land, and at one time dedicated to the Virgin Mary—hence its name. Windows having these flowers represented on them often appear in "Lady" Chapels, and are called Marigold Windows. The flowers are also called King-cups from their size—the King of golden cup-flowers.

Marine Store Dealer. Though the name is often used for any rag and bone dealer it is strictly only applicable to one who is licensed to buy old ships material—canvas, rope, iron, etc.—and who must have his name, with the words "Dealer in Marine Stores," painted in letters not less than six inches long over his door.

Mark Lane. A corruption of "Mart Lane," in which an ancient annual fair or mart of Flemish merchants was held.

Marlborough House. The residence of H.R.H. the Prince of Wales, built by Sir Christopher Wren for John Churchill, Duke of Marlborough, in 1709, at a total cost of a million of money.

Maroon. The word is derived from the French *marron*, a shortened form of the Spanish *cimarron*, which means wild, unruly. To be marooned is a sailor's term for being cast ashore on a wild desolate place where it is only possible to sustain life as a wild man, and the name was also applied to the Negro slaves who had escaped from their masters in the West Indies and who became a formidable danger to the Colonists. When Jamaica was taken by the English in 1655 about 1500 slaves defended themselves in the mountains and continued to harass the island for a century.

Marquis. The word is derived through the Old French *marchis*, from the root *march*, a boundary, and was the title of the officer who guarded the marches or borderland of a country. It is now a title of English nobility, ranking next below a duke, and is often held by the eldest son of a duke during his father's lifetime.

Marry. An old expletive derived from the practice of swearing by the Virgin Mary. In Foxe's "Book of Martyrs" the term appears in original form— "Yea, *Mary!* you say truth."

Marsala. A town in Sicily which received its name— *Marsa Alla*, Port of God—from the Arabs, who seized on the place as a suitable base for spreading their faith into Europe. The wine called Marsala takes its name from the town.

Marseillaise. It was so called because of the wild enthusiasm with which it was sung by the men of Marseilles when taken up by the whole populace as they marched into Paris at the breaking out of the French Revolution. Its composition was the work of Rouget de Lisle, an artillery officer stationed with the French garrison at Strasburg. He fell asleep at the harpsicord, and, on awakening, recalled the song as a dream and wrote down the words and music.

Marshal. From the Teutonic *marah*, horse, and *schalk*, servant, originally signifying (through the French *maréchal*) groom of the horse. The office of the Earl Marshal of England, an hereditary one held by the Duke of Norfolk, is to regulate rank and order at an assembly and to arrange processions, etc.

Marshalsea. The old Debtors' Prison in Southwark, deriving its name from the words "Marshal" and "See," meaning a place in the jurisdiction of the Marshal, and so called because the court of the Knight Marshal, for the settlement of disputes between members of the Royal Household, was held within its walls. The prison was demolished in 1842.

Martello-towers. Circular, isolated towers of masonry erected at short distances from each other on the coasts of the south of England, Ireland and Jersey, as a defence against invasion in the time of Napoleon I. The origin of the name is doubtful; it may be derived from the practice of striking a bell with a " martel " (hammer) on the approach of an enemy, or from Mortello Bay, Corsica, where such a tower was captured by the English in 1794. The name was also applied to towers on the coast of Sicily erected against pirates in the 16th century.

Marylebone. A corruption of " St. Mary at the Bourne," the church of the parish, dedicated to St. Mary, being situated on the brook of Tybourne (Tyborne, or Tyburn) which ran from Hampstead to the Thames. The seal of the parish depicts a figure of St. Mary with a stream beneath her feet.

Masher. A slang term for a fop, a dandy, a would-be fascinator of the ladies. The origin of the word is uncertain. Some assert it to be derived from the Romany *masha*, a fascinator; others believe it to come from *maçhinaw*, a blanket worn by the North American Indian, who, thus arrayed in extravagant colours, became the type of a showily-dressed young man.

Mass. The derivation of the word is doubtful. It may be the Greek *maza*, a barley-cake, but it is commonly attributed to the Low Latin *missa*, dismissal, in allusion to the " *ite, missa est* " with which a congregation at the Office of the Mass (the Lord's Supper) was dismissed. It is still retained in our nomenclature of certain days, *e.g.* :—Christmas, Michaelmas, Candlemas, Martinmas, etc.

Masterly Inactivity. The phrase seems to have been first used by Sir James Mackintosh, in " Vendiciœ Galliciœ,"—" The Commons, faithful to their system, remained in a wise and masterly inactivity . . . "

Maudlin. Probably a corruption of *Magdalen* (*i.e.*, Mary Magdalene) who was usually represented as

shedding tears—the result of her penitence. The
pronunciation of Magdalen as *maudlen* is still
retained in Magdalen College, Oxford.

Maundy Thursday. The day next before Good Friday,
when the royal almoner distributes to as many poor
men and women as the Sovereign is years old certain
silver coins called Maundy Money, consisting of a
four-penny piece, a three-penny piece, a two-penny
piece, and a penny piece. The ceremony is a survival of the old custom of the Royal washing of
poor persons' feet, in imitation of Our Lord. The
word " Maundy " is derived from the Latin
mandatum novum, which are the first words of the
Latin anthem, appointed to be sung at the function,
and which, in the English equivalent " A new com-
mandment " (John xiii. 34) is still used on the
occasion.

Mausoleum. The word is derived from *Mausolus*, the
name of the king of Caria, to whom a magnificent
tomb was erected by his widow Artemisia in the
year 353 B.C.   The site has recently been excavated,
and many fragments of sculpture, including some
of the statue of Mausolus, have been received at
the British Museum.

Maydew Cherries. A corruption of Medoc cherries,
from the district in France where they are cultivated.

Mayfair. On the site of this fashionable London district
Edward III. established a six days' fair in the
month of May for the benefit of the leper hospital
of St. James the Less, where St. James's Palace
now stands.

Mazarin Bible. A very rare edition of the Scriptures,
being one of the earliest printed by Gutenberg with
separate metal types, between 1450 and 1455.   It
received this name from the fact that a copy was
discovered in the library of Cardinal Mazarin.

Mecca. The sacred city to which pilgrimages are
made by devout Mahomedans, as the birthplace of

Mahomet and from which he had to flee on 16th July, 622 A.D. The Moslem era of the Hegira (Arabic for flight) begins from this date.

Medina. To this city Mahomet came when driven out of Mecca, and here his tomb has been erected on the very spot where he died in the lap of his favourite wife, Ayishah, 8th June, 632. His coffin is reported to be suspended in mid-air, some say by means of magnets, but according to Moslem belief by four angels.

Mediterranean Sea. The sea " in the middle of the earth " between the three great continents, Europe, Africa, and Asia.

Meerschaum. Expresses the German for " sea foam," the fine white clay out of which pipes are made being at one time thought to be the petrified scum or foam of the sea.

Mercenaries. From the Latin *mercenarius*, a hireling, applied to foreign soldiers who enlist only for the sake of getting a living.

Mercer. The old name for a dealer in silks and woollen fabrics, so called from the Latin *merx (mercis)*, wares, mechandise. Nowadays such a one styles himself a Draper.

Mere, Moor, More. Anglo-Saxon words which are components of many place-names. They signify a lake, a marsh; as in Key-mer, Sussex (formerly spelt Kye-mere, meaning the kine (cattle, marsh), Black-more, Devon, and More-ton, Dorset.

Merino. A woollen fabric made from the fleece of the merino-sheep. The name expresses the Spanish for an inspector of sheep walks.

Merry Andrew. A buffoon or clown, said to have been so called after Andrew Borde, a noted physician of the time of Henry VIII., whose witticisms were on a par with his medical skill. His saying were widely repeated, and since it happened that Andrew was then the most common name for a man-servant,

P

facetious fellows came to be dubbed Merry
Andrews.

Mesmerism. A system of curative effects named after
Franz Anton Mesmer (1733-1815) a Swiss physician. His treatment, under the name of Animal
Magnetism, was to stroke his patients with magnets, but he afterwards abandoned the use of
magnets, being persuaded that a mysterious force
within himself was the means by which his cures
were effected. Mr. Braid, a surgeon of Man-
chester, investigated the subject, and within the
last few years much scientific attention has been
directed to the closely allied phenomena of Animal
Magnetism, Hypnotism, Mesmerism, and Odylic
Force. The principal characteristic is the production of a trance-like state in the patient, rendering
him insensible to pain and making him more or
less subservient to the will and the suggestions of
the operator.

Merry as a Grigg. A grigg is a grasshopper, a
cricket, and also a small, lively sand-eel. The
appositeness of the phrase is apparent, whichever
signification be taken of the word " grigg," and
all the more so when it is borne in mind that the
old English meaning of the word " merry " is
happy, cheerful. The true punctuation of the old
Christmas Carol, " God rest you, merry Gentlemen," is with the comma after " merry " and not
after " you," equivalent to " God keep you happy
and cheerful, Gentlemen."

Mesopotamia. The word signifies " between the
rivers," from the Greek *mesos*, middle, and
potamos, river. It is the region lying between the
Tigris and the Euphrates, the Land of Shinar,
whose earliest known inhabitants were a mixed race
called Shumero-Accads.

Mess. The word comes to us through the Old French
mes, a dish, a course, from the Latin *missere*,
missum, to send, to place (on table). Originally
it signified a dish or portion of food—" Uriah de-

parted, and there followed him a mess from the king " (2 Sam. xi. 8)—but it is now applied to a number of persons sitting down together, or to the food provided for them, as a regimental or ship's mess.

Metals. The " precious metals "—gold and silver— were known to nations of great antiquity, and also the more common metals, copper and tin. At a far distant date it was discovered that by smelting copper and tin together a new substance was pro- duced, much harder than either—bronze. With the acquirement of this art mankind rose from the " Stone Age " of flint and bone implements, to the " Bronze Age " of war-chariots, armour, spears and battle-axes. There is evidence of considerable knowledge of metals in Chaldea before the advent of the Semitic people, and probably not only iron, but steel was known to some of the craftsmen of antiquity—the blades of Damascus (the most ancient of cities, coeval with Abraham) were famous in distant ages.

To the *transmutation of metals* an enormous amount of time and labour has been devoted by many great and learned men—alchemists they are called, and we laugh at them as fantastic dreamers, groping after the impossible. For many years modern science declared natural metals to be *elements*, original and unchangeable; but Mons. and Madame Curie bring to light a speck or two of radium, and the theory of the original and un- changeable character of metals is at an end. Both lead and silver are now believed to have been evolved from radium, and all three perhaps, from uranium. The word " metal " is derived from the Greek *metallan*, to search after, and we are still searching !

Maid of Athens. There are but few persons who are unacquainted with the couplet by Byron :—

" Maid of Athens, ere we part,
    Give, oh give me back my heart."

The Athenian maid to whom this was addressed was Theresa Macri, and twenty-four years after the song was written she was sought out by an Englishman, who found her married and with a large family, without a vestige of beauty and in abject penury.

Meteors. So named from the Greek words *meta*, among and, *eōra*, suspended, and commonly called shooting stars. The most brilliant displays occur about Nov. 13-14, one of the most notable, which was seen all over Europe, and at the Cape of Good Hope and elsewhere, having occurred on 13th Nov., 1866. It is held that a ring of meteors revolves round the sun, through which the earth's orbit cuts every year, and at intervals through that part of the ring where the meteors are most crowded. Meteors are composed of iron (perhaps magnetised), and striking the earth's atmosphere with immense velocity they ignite, and are usually —but not always—burnt to dust before reaching the earth's surface. In this connection the following recently received report may be of interest :—"About 8 o'clock this morning, when 10 miles south-west of the Wolf Rock, we heard a loud, sharp report, like the firing of a cannon, and our vessel, trembling violently, seemed a mass of flame. We saw a large, fiery body, with a huge tail of light, strike the sea about twenty feet from us, and the interior of our ship glowed with a brilliant light, faintly violet, from which millions of sparks emanated. Looking at our compasses we found them all demagnetised and awry, and it was with difficulty, following the coasting vessels, that we got into Falmouth."

Methodists. A name given (or rather revived) at Oxford University to the members of a religious society which existed there in 1727, and among whom were John and Charles Wesley and George Whitefield, then studying for Holy Orders. The word was used in derision of the methodical manner with which the members of this society performed their religious duties, but it is not of modern origin, as it was applied, in very early times, to a certain school of philosophers and to a body of physicians, and in the seventeenth century it was used in religious controversy between Roman Catholics and Protestants.

Mews. The word originally denoted a place where hawks were " mewed " or confined, and it came to be used as a designation of stables because the Royal Stables retained the name of the mews, being built on the site where, from time immemorial, the king's falcons had been kept.

Mile. Derived from the Latin *mille passuum*, a thousand paces, equal to 1614 English yards. The present statute mile of 1760 yards was instituted in the time of Elizabeth.

Mile End. The name arose from a toll gate which formerly stood on the high road, distant *one mile* east from the city boundary at Aldgate.

Millbank. From an old mill that stood on the Thames bank, on the site of which the Grosvenors built a mansion, subsequently displaced for the prison.

Milliner. A corruption of *Milaner*, after the city of Milan, which at one time set the fashion throughout Europe for elegance and taste in matters of dress. In the present day the word is applied to a dealer in hats, feathers and ribbons, now usually a woman, but originally a man. Shakespeare in the " Winter's Tale " (Act iv, Sc. 3) writes :—"No milliner can so fit *his* customers with gloves."

Mincing Lane. A corruption of Mynchen Lane, referring to the property of the *Mynchery*, the Anglo-Saxon for Nunnery—that of St. Helen's, Bishopsgate Street, London.

Mind your P's and Q's. The origin of this phrase is uncertain, but one explanation is that " P " and " Q " denoted pints and quarts in the old ale-

house score, and that the phrase was an injunction
not to allow the score to run too long.

Miniature. Though applied to small paintings, or
anything on a reduced scale, this word takes its
origin from *minium*, the Latin for red-lead, because
of the practice of illuminating manuscripts with
pictures beautifully coloured with minium and
vermilion. Thus its derivation has no connection
with minute, small.

Minim. From the Latin *minimus*, very small, and
thus applied to anything small—a dwarf, a pigmy.
Milton, in " Paradise Lost," writes " Minims of
nature."

In medicine it is the smallest liquid measure, or
a drop (60 minims = 1 drachm).

In music it is now the longest time character,
but in old music notation it was the shortest, the
notes being then named " long," " brief," " semi-
brief," and " minim." The first two are now
obsolete, though " brief " (under the name
" breve ") is still met with in Church music.

Minories. This thoroughfare was laid out across the
lands belonging to the Minoresses or Nuns of St.
Clare (" Poor Clares ") after their priory had been
demolished at the Reformation. The order is the
second of St. Francis of Assisi, founded about
1212, and has now houses in England and Ireland.

Minster. A word applied to churches and to places
originally connected with a monastery—as York
Minster and Beverley Minster, Bedminster and
Leominster.

Minuet. From the Latin *minutus*, small, probably on
account of the short, graceful steps which distinguish the dance of that name. The dance is said
to have been invented in Poitou early in the seventeenth century, and it continued to be fashionable
as late as the reign of George III.

Minute. It is worth noting that this word retains its
signification of small, trifling, of little consequence,

in whatever way applied; *e.g.* :—a minute is a small portion of an hour; the minutes of a meeting or of an agreement are brief notes of what has occurred or is intended, which may afterwards be set out at large (en-grossed).

Miser. Though this word is now restricted to the mean and avaricious person hoarding money, its true signification is "wretched," from the Latin *miser*, implying that to be avaricious is to be miserable.

Miserere. A hinged folding bracket in a church choir-stall, enabling a person, while apparently standing, to support the body by leaning against it. It was used by the monks in repeating their "Office," which comprised the daily recitation of the whole of the Psalter.

Mistletoe. From the Anglo-Saxon *mistel*, mist or dirt, and *tan*, twig; probably referring to the propogation of the plant, as a parasite on apple and other trees, by means of bird-droppings. It was held sacred by the Druids, of which the present custom of kissing under the mistletoe may be a survival. There is a Scandinavian legend to the effect that Balder, the favourite of the gods, was killed by an arrow made of mistletoe, and being, through the love of the gods, restored to life, the mistletoe became the emblem of love, and everyone passing under it was to receive a kiss.

Mitre. The word comes to us from the Greek *mitra*, a fillet, and is akin to *mitos*, a thread. As a religious head-dress the mitre is of great antiquity. It was worn by the Jewish High Priest as divinely appointed, and bore, on a golden plate, the inscription "Holiness to the Lord." (Ex. xxxix. 28-30.) The Bishop's mitre, which was probably worn as early as the seventh century, was doubtless derived from that of the Jewish High Priest, but is taken to symbolise the "cloven tongues like as of fire" (Acts ii. 3) which appeared to the Apostles. The mitre was worn by Cardinals until the Council of Lyons, in 1245, ordered the use of the Cardinal's Hat.

Mob. As applied to the people the word is a contraction of the Latin *mobile vulgus*, the fickle common people, and came into use during the reign of Charles II. North, writing at that time, refers to the " rabble " having changed its title to " mob " by a natural contraction of *mobile vulgus*. " Mob," in the word " mob-cap," has a different derivation, viz. :—the Dutch *mop*, a woman's coif.

Mohair. From the Arabic *Mukhayyar*, " goatskin hair," through the French *moire*, the fine silken hair of the Angora goat.

Mohawks. The name, which is that of a tribe of North American Indians, signifies " man-eater," and was applied to the night revellers who infested London streets in the early part of the eighteenth century. There have been various previous names for street-bullies of this sort, such as "Muns," " Hectors," " Scourers," " Nickers," and " Hawcubites."

Monastery. It is curious to observe that the two words " Monastery " and " Convent," both of which denote a house in which live persons devoted to a religious life, are derived from words of opposite meaning, the first from the Greek *monos*, alone, and the second from the Latin *convenire* (*conventum*), to come together. By Roman Catholic writers the word monastery is usually restricted to Benedictine Houses, *e.g* :—A Carthusian monastery, a Franciscan convent. The monastic life was practised long before the Christian era, the Buddhist and Jain monasteries existing five, or even six, centuries B.C.

Money. The word has the same origin as " mint," *i.e.*, *Moneta*, the surname of Juno, in whose temple at Rome money was coined.

As an example of the alteration in the value of money it may be stated that in the reign of Edward VI. a marriage dowry of £5, given by a yeoman to his daughter, was considered to be evidence of his prosperity.

Money makes Money. An adage of ancient date, still accepted as a truism. Though the Mosaic Law forbade the taking of usury or increase (Lev. xxv. 36) the principle of giving interest must have been accepted by the Jews in later times, or the climax of the parable recounted in Matt. xxv. 27, would have had no point. Although Ruskin, in his endeavour to reform our social economy, discountenanced the payment of interest, the principle is bound up in modern commerce, as witness, especially, Banks and Insurance Offices.

Monger. The word is derived from the Anglo-Saxon *mang*, a mixture, and was formerly applied to one who sold a mixture of things. In the present day it is generally used in conjunction with a word denoting some specific article of trade, as in Cheesemonger, Fishmonger, Ironmonger, etc. The word Costermonger appears to be an exception, but originally it denoted a seller of costards (otherwise apples), though it is now applied to the itinerant seller of fruit and vegetables of all sorts.

Monkey. Probably the origin of the name may rightly be traced to the creature's resemblance to a little old woman clad in furs, for the word "monkey" is derived from *monicchio*, the diminutive of the old Italian *monna*, a nickname for an old woman, and a contraction of *madonna*. In the phrase "to get one's monkey up" (meaning to be angry) the word monkey is probably a corruption of the Welsh *mwn*. Icelandic *mön*, signifying an animal's neck or mane, which, as is well known, bristles up when the creature is excited.

Moor. (*See* MERE.)

Mor. This is a word of Celtic origin, which often appears as a suffix or prefix under the spelling "more," or in the Welsh form of "mawr." It signifies great, and must not be confused with the Anglo-Saxon "more." (*See* MERE.) As examples there may be cited Ben-more and Penmaen-mawr, both meaning the great mountain; Kil-more, the great church; and Glen-more, the great glen. But "mor" has another signification in place-names, viz. :—that of the sea; as in Gla-mor-gan ("mor," the sea, and "gant," the side), and in Mor-ay, or Murray.

More. (*See* MERE.)

Morgue. Though applied to a mortuary, this word really means the inner wicket of a prison, where the indentification marks of new arrivals are taken before they have their cells and tasks assigned to them. It has, therefore, come to denote the place of public examination and identification of the unknown dead.

Mormons. A sect named after a mythic person, Mormon, who, according to Joseph Smith, the founder of the sect, led an immigration of Jews into America in ancient days. Joseph Smith asserted that, in 1823, as he was praying, he received from an angel certain revelations engraved on gold plates which he made known by publishing, in 1830, the "Book of Mormon." In 1844 Smith was arrested on a charge of sedition and was shot dead by a mob which broke into the jail. Brigham Young, who then became the prophet of the sect, took his followers, in 1847, to Salt Lake valley (then Mexican territory, but now ceded to U.S.) where they settled and, mightily prospering, built a city. Formerly the sect practised polygamy, but that is now renounced.

Morris-Dance. The word "morris" is probably a corruption of "Moorish," as the dance is believed to have been brought from Spain in the time of Edward III. The characters were dressed partly in Spanish costume, but represented the various grades of English society—the king and queen, the knight, the friar, and the franklin.

Morrow. Equivalent to the salutation " Good morrow," found so often in Shakespeare and the early play-writers, and to our familiar " Good-morning." " To-morrow " is the morn that is the next morn. " Good morwen " (Middle English) is still heard in some parts of the country. " Morrow," " morn," "morning," all represent the same Anglo-Saxon word, *morgen*.

Morse-code. A system of telegraphic signalling (now applied to other methods of signalling) invented by Professor Sam. F. B. Morse, born in 1791 at Charlestown, Massachusetts, a painter and sculptor of considerable repute. It consists of dots and dashes in various combinations, indicating the different letters of the alphabet, and thus language may be rendered by two simple symbols—the dot and the dash. It seems fitting that, as the alphabet probably originated with some unknown picture-makers of the Old World, its latest extension, with its wonderful simplicity, should come from a picture-maker of the New World.

Mortar. The word comes from the Anglo-Saxon *mortere*, through the Latin *mortarium*, from the widely diffused Aryan root *mar*, signifying to crush or bruise. The application of the derivation may be seen in the mortar in which substances are bruised and pounded, and in the crushed up material made into mortar for building purposes. It may be of interest to note that the durability of old buildings is largely due to the excellence of the mortar used in their construction, and it would appear that *eggs* were an ingredient of mortar in former days. In a statement of charges for repairing the spire of Newark church in 1571 it is mentioned that 350 eggs were supplied with which to temper the lime.

Mother Shipton. There seems no reason to believe that there was a person named " Mother Shipton."

According to Dr. Brewer she was the heroine of an ancient tale entitled " The Strange and Wonderful History and Prophecies of Mother Shipton," written by T. Evan Preece, of South Wales, and these predictions, generally in rhyme, were widely current throughout England, especially in Glamorganshire. Among the predictions fulfilled was the well known prophecy that ships should go without sails and vehicles without horses.

Mosaic. This word, when used to describe work inlaid with small pieces of coloured stone, glass, etc., has no reference to Moses, but is derived from the Greek *mouseois*, pertaining to the Muses, who were the divinities of painting, poetry and music.

Muff. The dandy at one time, like the ladies, carried a muff to keep his hands warm in winter, and it may be that as this incapacitated him from defending himself with his sword, a "muff" came to denote a silly, spiritless fellow.

Mull. A Gaelic word, denoting a headland, and found in the place-names Mull of Cantyre, Mull of Galloway, etc.

Mum. A word of imitative origin, denoting silence by a compression of the lips. The phrase " Mum's the word" enjoins secrecy. " Mumchance " is a silent game with cards or dice.

My Eye and Betty Martin. The origin of this phrase is a very vexed question. The assumption that it is derived from the Latin " O mihe, Beate Martine " can scarcely be correct when the pronunciation of Latin in mediæval times is taken into consideration. In " Notes and Queries " (17/12/59) it is stated—though perhaps, not intended to be taken as sober fact—that the phrase is to be found in an old blackletter volume, showing that it has been in use for some three hundred years, but throwing no light on its origin.

Muslin. Called by the French *Mousseline*, from Mosul in Mesopotamia, whence, during the Middle Ages, this fabric was sent to supply all the markets of Europe.

My Stars and Garters. It has been suggested that the origin of this old phrase is an adjuration by the star and garter of knighthood, but such a derivation is very doubtful Far more probably the phrase is merely an enlargement on the old invocation of the stars which, under the teaching of astrologers, governed the destiny of each individual. ("The stars in their courses fought against Sisera."—Judges v. 20.)

Myddleton Square. After Sir Hugh Myddleton, who brought the water supply to London by constructing the New River from Chadwell, in Hertfordshire, nearly forty miles distant. One of the reservoirs occupies the enclosed portion of this square.

Nabob. A word much used during the first half of the nineteenth century to denote—generally with a touch of contempt—the English merchant who had made his fortune in India and had returned to his country more or less imperious in manner and degenerate in habits from long association with a servile race. It is a Hindu word—*nawwab*, the plural of *naib*, meaning a vicegerent, a deputy governor.

Nant. This is a Celtic word common in Welsh place-names, and signifies a valley. Nant-frangon, in Carnarvon, means the beavers' valley, Nan-bield, in Westmorland, is the name of a steep pass, and there is Nant-wich standing in a valley in Cheshire. In Cornwall we find Nan-cemellin, the valley of the mill, Pen-nant, the head of the valley, and Trenance, the town in the Valley.

Nap. The derivation of this word as signifying a little sleep is curiously expressive of the nodding head and bent attitude of one dozing in a chair, for "nap" comes to us from two Anglo-Saxon words meaning respectively to nod and to bend oneself.

Nation of Shopkeepers. This phrase is found in Adam Smith's "Wealth of Nations," and is believed to have been used by Samuel Adams in a speech given at the State House in Philadelphia on 1st August, 1776.

Nature's Chief Masterpiece. This is an expression which is not infrequently used to describe a man of noble parts and high integrity, but it was not employed by its author in such a connection. It appears in an " Essay on Poetry " by Sheffield, Duke of Buckingham (1649-1720), the context being :—

" Of all those arts in which the wise excel,
Nature's chief masterpiece is writing well. "

Naughty. This is a word which has undergone more than one change in meaning. It is an extension of the English " naught," which is derived from the Anglo-Saxon *naht*, meaning nothing (*na*, no, and *wiht*, thing) and the primary meaning of " naughty " is good for nothing, worthless. In the Bible we find it used in that sense—" The other basket had very naughty figs." (Jer. xxiv. 2.)— Gradually the meaning of worthless became strengthened to that of evil, corrupt, and we find Shakespeare writing of " a good deed in a naughty world.". (" Merchant of Venice," act v.) Now the word is applied to describe mischievous and disobedient behaviour in children, and is even used in a kind of mock censure.

Nave. One of the most primitive of structures is the gipsy tent, made by sticking two rows of wands in the ground and tying the tops together to a horizontal rod, over which is thrown the covering of the tent. Early English cottages may still be seen built on the same pattern, the timbers arching upwards from the ground to support the roof, like the ribs of a ship turned keel upwards. And, as the central portion of a Church—the Nave—presents the same appearance, with curved beams supporting the roof and springing from the columns on either side, it has been conjectured that it gained its name from this likeness to a ship, for the derivation of the word is the Latin *navis*, a ship.

Navvy. The term used to denote a general labourer in digging and excavating the ground. It reminds us of the enormous labour expended, before the invention of the locomotive, on making long canals throughout the country. These canals, as Spencer tells us in his " Principles of Sociology," were looked upon as lines of inland navigation, and hence it happened that the men employed in excavating them were called navigators, a word which was afterwards shortened into " navvies."

Naze. A component in place-names. (*See* NESS.)

Neat. French *net*, from the Latin *nitēre*, to shine. The neat house-wife unconsciously connects the word with its true origin—before her house is really neat in her eyes all the surfaces must be polished until they shine.

Necessity the Mother of Invention. This phrase appears in a play called " The Twin Rivals," by George Farquhar (1678-1707), the author of " The Beaux' Strategem," but there is every reason to believe that it was in common use before that time.

Neck and Crop. To come down " neck and crop " is to topple over completely, entirely, suddenly. It is not easy, however, to throw any light on the origin of the phrase; the dictionaries are generally content to give its meaning without any attempt to explain its allusion. But probably the solution of the difficulty is to be found in the fact that one of the old significations of the word " crop " is the top or highest part of a thing. Thus an old writer describes man as " a tre of whilk the crop (the top)es turned donward," and the expressions "crop of corn," " crop of fruit," " crop and root," " crop of the causeway," all seem to point to " crop " being almost synonymous with topmost, for the ears of corn are its uppermost extremity and the antithesis of " root " is " top." If this surmise be correct the phrase "neck and crop" is simply a strengthening of the idea of "top" by a duplication of terms—a very common usage in the English language—for "neck" is closely allied to "top" through the Norwegian *nakk*, a knoll, the top of a hill.

The Needful. It is curious that although this expression is considered to be slang—it is included in the "Slang Dictionary"—it is accounted quite correct to speak of "the poor and needy." Yet the poor are, of course, those who are in need; in need of the needful—ready money.

Needle in a Bottle of Hay. There is little doubt that the word "bottle" in this phrase is derived from the French or Breton *botel*, a diminutive of *botte*, a bunch, a bundle. With this meaning for the word "bottle" the appositeness of the phrase is apparent, for the task of finding a needle in a bundle of hay is almost an impossible one.

Ness. A syllable in place-names which denotes a nose of land, a headland, a promontory. It is of Scandinavian origin and a doublet of "naze." Examples are found in Sheer-ness, Shoebury-ness, Bow-ness, Fur-ness, and in the Naze, near Harwich.

Nettle—"Grasp it like a man of mettle." The line is to be found in some verses which were written on a window in Scotland and are ascribed to Aaron Hill (1685-1750). They are as follows :—

> " Tender-handed stroke a nettle,
>   And it stings you for your pains ;
> Grasp it like a man of mettle,
>   And it soft as silk remains.
> 'Tis the same with common natures :
>   Use 'em kindly, they rebel ;
> But be rough as nutmeg-graters,
>   And the rogues obey you well. "

New. A component in place-names. (*See* OLD.)

New Worlds. When, towards the close of the fifteenth century, Columbus landed (as he supposed) upon one of the outlying islands of that strange land vaguely called " The Indies," the dream of his life was realised. He had made a new and unheard of voyage and had found a new route to all the riches of India and Cathay. But he died with no idea that he had discovered a " New World "—a world so vast that it reaches from the Arctic almost to the Antarctic circle—and the very name it now bears (America) commemorates not him but Amerigo Vespucci, who landed some years after the discovery by Columbus.

Another " New World " of the fifteenth century was that discovered by Guttenberg, when, having hit upon the idea of printing with moveable type, he thus opened the gates—not of a hemisphere only, but—of the whole sphere of ancient and modern knowledge.

And yet another " New World " was evolved during this century when John Huss was burnt at the stake and Martin Luther was born, for the Reformation may be said to have given us a New Spiritual World into which all may enter without money and without price.

Again, a " New World " came to view, in this same century, when Copernicus enunciated his great doctrine—lost sight of for nearly two thousand years—that the sun, and not the earth, was the centre of our planetary system; whereby we have gained a New Heaven as well as a " New World," so that we might imagine the voice of an archangel ringing through the length and breadth of the land at that time, crying, " Behold I make all things New."

Nib. A nib is not a pen—not even a steel pen— though the word is often used in that sense; it is the point of a pen. Nevertheless, the word " nib " takes us back to the very beginning of writing, the invention of which was ascribed by the ancient

Egyptians to the god Thoth. He was the scribe of the gods and was typified on earth by the sacred Ibis, the bird which stood on the river flats writing mystic signs on the smooth mud with his long, pointed beak. And this beak may rightly be called a " nib," for the word " nib " is the same as " neb," which means a beak.

Nice. When we speak of people being " nice " we mean that they are agreeable, delightful. Yet the derivation of the word " nice " is the Latin *nescius*, ignorant, from *ne-scire*, not to know, and the Old French *nice* meant foolish, simple.

Niche. From the Italian *nicchio*, a shell. " Everyone has his niche "—his appointed place in the architecture of the universe, just as a statue of a Saint has its niche, or shell-like recess, in a Cathedral. There the Saint, not its niche, is important, but with the tiny creatures of the ocean—also each in its own niche, or shell—it is the covering, and not the creature, that counts, since out of myriads of such delicate niches, deposited during pre-historic ages, have arisen our " white cliffs of Albion."

Nicotine. In the year 1560 Jean Nicot first sent tobacco seeds to France. Nicotine is the poisonous extract of tobacco named after him.

Nigger—Lazy Nigger, Nigger-driver, etc. The word " nigger " is, of course, a corruption of " negro," the Spanish name for the African black man, and it is curious that it should revert so nearly to the Latin *niger* from which the Spanish word is derived. The original home of the negro race was probably all that part of Africa south of the Sahara, the greater part of Southern India, and a large part of Australasia.

Nightingale. The name " night-in-gale " seems peculiarly inappropriate to the bird that sings in the calmest of midsummer nights. The stormy petrel may be blown upon the gale and the cry of the screeching owl may be heard above the noise of the wind, but this bird, the sweetest singer of the woodland, loves profound peace.

" Already with thee ! Tender is the night,
And haply the Queen-Moon is on her throne,
Clustered round by all her starry Fays."

KEATS.

But when we find that the termination " gale " is from the Anglo-Saxon *galan*, to sing, we can understand that this is the bird who passes the *night-in-song*.

Niminy-Piminy. An expression which one might suppose to be merely imitative and nonsensical, but which, when traced to its source, has much meaning. For the Anglo-Saxon word *nim*, is to steal, to pilfer, and the French *pim-per* is a nasalised form of piper, to pipe, to decoy, to cheat. Hence arises the contempt implied in speaking of affectedly delicate ways as " niminy-piminy."

Nine Days' Wonder. The phrase appears to have originated from the religious festivals called " Novena " which last nine days. Throughout this time the image of the saint in whose honour the festival is held is paraded with relics and votive offerings, and a recital is made of the special virtue, miracle or wonder ascribed to the saint. H. W. Bates, the naturalist, in his book " On the Amazon," says :—" The grandest of all these festivals is that held in honour of Our Lady of Nazareth. It lasts, like the others, nine days." The word " Novena " is derived from the Latin *novenus*, nine each; it is also connected (or confused) with *novus*, new, wonderful.

Nines (Up to the.) In former days, and until quite recently, the continual use of classical allusions stamped the scholar, and to the influence of this custom we probably owe the phrase " up to the nines." For the " nines " alluded to are doubtless the nine Muses of Greek and Roman mythology, three of whom were supposed to inspire the various passions of Poetry, while the remaining six presided over History, Comedy, Tragedy, Music, Dancing,

and Astronomy. Thus to be " up to the nines "
was to reach as nearly as possible to perfection.

The Nine Worthies. " For it is notoriously known
through the universal world that there be nine
worthy and best that ever were. That is, to wit,
three Paynims, three Jews, and three Christian
men." (Caxton's original preface to " Morte
D'Arthur.")

The *Nine Worthies* are :—Hector, Alexander the
Great, Julius Cæsar, Joshua, David, Judas Macca-
bæus, Arthur, Charlemagne, and Godfrey of
Bouillon.

The game of Ninepins and the Old English game
called nine-men's-Morris appear to have some
allusion to the Nine Worthies.

Nob. A word which has gone through several phases,
for it is but a shortened form of " knob," while
" knob " is, again, but a later form of " knop."
It denotes the top of anything, as the summit of a
hill, or any kind of protuberance, such as a bud
or a button. Thus the slang phrase " one of the
nobs " is correct in so far as it means one of the
upper members of society, and the expression " one
for his nob " means, rightly enough as regards
" nob," a blow on the head.

Nocent. It is curious that while retaining the word
" in-nocent " we have discarded " nocent," the
first meaning guiltless, and the second guilty.
" Nocent " is derived from the Latin *nocens*, the
present participle of *noceo*, I hurt, and we find it
used as lately as Foxe's "Book of Martyrs" and in
the account of the State Trials which took place in
reference to the Gunpowder Plot.

A Nod is as Good as a Wink. The full phrase runs
" A nod is as good as a wink to a blind horse,"
implying that to one who will not see no indications
are of any avail. But the phrase is now more commonly used without the words " to a blind horse,"
and is generally meant to convey the idea that

there is a secret understanding which need not be expressed in words.

Noise. Two suggestions are put forward for the origin of this word—the one referring it to the Latin *nausea*, from which we have our word " nauseous," and the other to *noxia*, from which is derived " noxious." In either of these derivations there is a sympathetic reminder, irresistible to the literary and contemplative man, of the distress and annoyance caused by noise.

For the Nonce. The older phrase was written " for then anes " or " for then ones," the word " then " being formerly used as the dative case of " the." In process of time the " final " n " in " then " was attached to " anes " and " ones," and thus the phrase became " for the nonce," meaning for the one time, for this occasion only. We have other instances of this transfer of the final " n " to a word following; thus " an ewt," " an eke-name," have become respectively " a newt," " a nickname "; while, on the other hand, the initial " n " has in many cases become attached to the preceding article, as in " an adder," " an apron," " an orange," for " a nadder," " a napron," " a norange."

None but the Brave, etc. It is wonderful how long a good phrase will persist. " None but the brave deserves the fair " is a line written by John Dryden in 1694 in " Alexander's Feast," an ode composed in honour of St. Cecilia's Day (November 22nd).

Noon to Dewy Eve. This phrase comes from Milton's " Paradise Lost," and is often misquoted as " From *morn* to dewy eve." The stanza is :—
" From morn
To noon he fell, from noon to dewy eve,
A summer's day ; and with the setting sun
Dropt from the zenith like a falling star."

Not worth his Salt. This may seem a drastic expression, but it should be borne in mind that salt, though now so lightly esteemed, was formerly a valuable and highly prized commodity—as, indeed, it still is in the East. "The labourer is worthy of his hire," the Bible tells us, but if he "be not worth his salt" he is not worth his "pay." For the words "salt" and "pay" are closely connected; the clerk's salary is his pay, and the word "salary" is derived from the Latin *salarium* (*sal*, salt), the allowance made to the Roman soldier in order that he might provide himself with salt. Moreover, the ceremonial importance of salt is shown in the salt-stand of the Saxon table, where its position marked out the upper and the lower board, separating the lord and those who shared his salt as honoured guests from those who earned it. The Normans, too, had the same custom, but their word for the salt-stand was *saliere*, which we have corrupted into "cellar," making the term "salt-cellar" a duplication equivalent to "salt-salt-stand." And even in such a common word as "salad" we have evidence of the value originally put upon salt : it denotes, of course, the green food we eat raw, and because we season it with salt it is called "salad," the literal meaning of which is "salted."

Numbers (Book of). The fourth book in the Old Testament, and so named because it tells of the numbering of the twelve tribes at the beginning and end of their sojourn in the wilderness (chs. i-iv. and xxvi). The Hebrew custom was to name a Book of the Law from its opening words, but as the first six words are the same both in Leviticus and Numbers the Jewish title for the latter book is "In the Wilderness"—words which follow immediately after the first six words.

Nut. We speak of a difficult problem as "a hard nut to crack." Like monkeys, birds and squirrels the primitive man was glad to get nuts to crack. But in many cases the hard shells were too much even for the strong teeth of the savage, and he had to invent some method of cracking the nut, if only by hammering at it with a stone. And we, civilised as we may be, with all our modern inventions, must still, metaphorically, keep " hammering away " at " hard nuts to crack " in the solving of many a difficult problem for the advancement of our race.

Oak-Apple Day. The 29th May—but not the day on which Charles II. climbed the oak to hide himself from Cromwell's troopers after the battle of Worcester. This episode occurred on 3rd September, 1651, and although the 29th May commemorates that escapade it is the anniversary of the king's entry into London at his Restoration in 1660. The oak-apple is not the fruit of the tree, but an excrescence caused by insects. The fruit is, of course, the acorn, a word which, at first sight, seems to have nothing to do with "oak." But in Saxon days the words "oak," "oath," "oar," "oats," etc., were spelt without the "o"; the oak was *ac*, and the nut it produced was a *kern*, and thus, it is thought by some, came the word *ac-kern*, acorn. But Skeat is of the opinion that "acorn" more probably comes from the Anglo-Saxon *aker* (acre), a field, and meant primarily "the fruit of the field." There can be no doubt that acorns were looked upon as a valuable crop for feeding the large herds of swine possessed by the Saxons.

Obey. "To hear is to obey" is the recognised phrase in the East to signify the acceptance of a command, while we in the West enforce an order by the exclamation "Do you hear what I say?" The idea in each case is embodied in the word "obey," which is derived from the Latin *obedire*, a union of the preposition *ob* with *audire*, to hear.

Oblige. The common phrase " I am much *obliged* to you " is really equivalent to " I am *bound* to your service," while a legal *obligation* is a *bond* under which a penalty is incurred in case of failure. Such expressions take their origin from the actual binding of a hostage—we read that Joseph took Simeon from his brethren "and bound him before their eyes." (Gen. xlii. 24.) The binding of the one was to oblige (or bind) the others to keep their agreement—they were bound to return if they would claim the release of the hostage. All which is implied in the derivation of the word "oblige," which comes from the Latin *obligare*—*ob*, before (in face of), and *ligare*, to bind.

Obviate. It is often said "Don't meet trouble half way," but the very meaning of "obviate" is the reverse of this injunction—the difficulty must be met in the way. "While the other is yet a great way off, he sendeth an ambassage, and desireth conditions of peace." (Luke xiv. 32.) For the word comes from the Latin *ob-viare*, to take the road against (*ob*, against, *via*, a way).

Ochil. A component in place-names. (*See* UCHEL.)

Odd. In the Anglo-Saxon language the word means a point, and it may be that the expression "at odds," applied to persons who are at variance among themselves, has some reference to this meaning, seeing that, figuratively, such persons are bristling all over with points. The phrases "by long odds" and "that makes no odds" are both derived from betting parlance. From the time of Pythagoras onwards, and probably much earlier, good luck has been ascribed to odd numbers, and in China they are considered to belong to Heaven. It is said that "the gods delight in odd numbers."

Odd's or **Od's.** These expressions frequently appear in old-fashioned oaths, and are perversions of the word "God's." Thus "Odd's bodikins!" means "God's body" in reference to the sacrament of the Mass, and "Odd's fish!" meaning "God's flesh"—a favourite exclamation of Charles II.— has the same allusion. Then we have "Odzounds" for God's wounds," "Od's heart" for "God's heart" and "Od's pittikins" for "God's pity." (*See* DRAT 'EM!)

Odours. The use of odours, not only in the form of incense as a symbolical offering to the Diety, but in the simple capacity of pleasant perfumes, must be very ancient. We find frequent mention of them in the Bible, and their association with the idea of holiness and chastity is well exemplified in the account of the anointing of the feet of Christ with costly ointment, the odour of which, we are told, filled the house (John xii. 1-3). The same idea is retained in our phrase " in the odour of sanctity," while, on the other hand, an evil reputation is indicated by the expression " in bad odour."

Og. The frequent mention in the Bible of Og, the king of Bashan, shows how important a personage he appeared in the minds of the Children of Israel, and according to the account given of him in Deut. iii. 11, he must have been a giant of no mean stature, his bedstead being made of iron, more than fifteen feet long and nearly 7 feet broad. But the mythological traditions of the Rabbis give him a vast bulk—a height of more than 23,000 cubits, or nearly six miles. His drink was from the water of the clouds and his food was cooked by toasting it before the sun, and he was able to survive the Flood because, at its deepest, it reached only to his knees. He lived 3,000 years and was slain by the hand of Moses.

Ogre. A malignant giant, of fairy-tale celebrity, said to live upon human flesh. The word seems to be of Eastern origin and is supposed by some to be derived from a savage race called Agurs, inhabitants of Asia, who overran part of Europe in the fifth century. By others it is derived from the Latin *Orcus*, the god of the infernal regions.

Oil. From the earliest ages the olive has been grown for its oil, and so closely was the olive associated with oil that the two words " olive " and " oil " were originally synonymous. Our word " oil " comes to us from the Old French *oile*, through the Latin *oleum* and the Greek *elaion*, which latter is derived from *elaia*, meaning the olive. Thus in speaking of " olive oil " we are really using a duplication of terms.

Old, Eld, Alt. There are many English place-names in which one of these syllables appears as indicative of age, such as Old-bury, El-bottle, Elt-ham, Ald-bury and Al-ton. On the other hand, there are in England no less than 120 places called Newton, besides some eighty names in which the term " new " is found, and it should be borne in mind that the terms " new " and " old " denote only relative, and not absolute age. Thus New-castle, built by the Normans on the Tyne, is more than 800 years old, and New College is one of the oldest colleges in Oxford, having been founded in 1386, while New Palace Yard, Westminster, is a memorial of the palace built by Rufus.

Old Bailey. The site on which this prison was built must have been close to the wall of old London, for the word " bailey " is derived from the Latin *ballium*, an open space between the line of the outer wall and the advanced gate of the city, the gate in this instance being Lud-gate, which stood at the Southern extremity of the street now called Old Bailey. A similar site with respect to the city wall is found in the Old Bayle at York, and in the church of St. Peter in the Bailey at Oxford. From this word *ballium* is derived the title " bailiff," the officer in charge of the " ballium," the name " bailiff " being originally " bayle-reeve," in the same way as " sheriff " was " shire-reeve."

Old Lady of Threadneedle Street. A colloquial name for the Bank of England, situated in Threadneedle Street. According to Dr. Brewer the nickname arose from a caricature by Gilray, dated 22nd May, 1797, entitled " The Old Lady in Threadneedle Street in Danger," referring to the temporary stoppage of cash payments on 26th February, 1797.

Old Nick. The familiar name for the Devil. The word "Nick" comes to us from the Anglo-Saxon *Nicor*, the water spirit, a name which is found in similar form in German, Swedish, Danish and Icelandic. Its prevalence shows the extent to which the cult of a water-deity was carried—seas, rivers and lakes were alike worshipped among all Aryan nations. Our respect for the devil seems to have waned of late, but formerly, and especially in ancient times, the powers of evil were treated with considerable reverence. Thus the Greek Furies, the avenging deities, were named Eumenides, meaning the Well-wishing Ones, and in the Bible (Jude 9) we read that "Michael the archangel, when contending with the devil he disputed about the body of Moses, durst not bring against him a railing accusation, but said, The Lord rebuke thee." A homely instance of the desire to stand well with the devil is given in Conway's "Demonology," in the story of a Hampshire lady who asked a friend if she made her children bow when they mentioned the Devil's name, adding solemnly, "I do, I think it's safer!"

Old Things Best. "No man having drunk old wine straightway desireth new; for he saith, The old is better." (Luke v. 39.) And it is reported of Alonso of Aragon that he was wont to say there were four things that were best when old, viz :—Old wine to drink, old friends to trust, old authors to read, old wood to burn.

Olive Branch. As a type of peace and security the olive branch is said to date from the Flood, when the dove returned to the ark with an olive leaf. "So Noah knew that the waters were abated" (Gen. viii. 11) and that the retributive vengeance of the Flood was at end. Children are called "olive branches" from that simile being used in Psalm cxxviii. 4. (Prayer-Book Version.)

Olla Podrida. The term is used figuratively to denote an incongruous mixture, a miscellaneous collection.

It is of Spanish origin, and in the literal sense means a putrid pot, but the accepted sense in Spain is that of a pot in which every sort of eatable is thrown and stewed together, like the French *pot au feu.*

Omer. This was a Hebrew measure of capacity, containing the 1/100th part of a homer, while a homer was equivalent to about ten bushels and three gallons. The word translated " homer " in the Bible is the Hebrew *khomer*, a heap, derived from *khamar*, to swell up.

On Tick. The expression is not of modern growth— it was certainly in use more than two hundred years ago. There seems little doubt that it is an abbreviation of " on ticket," meaning to buy or take goods which are to be set down on a ticket or bill—hence on credit.

Open. In all Teutonic languages the verb " to open " or " to ope " is from an older verb—" to up," reminding us of the time when doors were merely skins, to open which was " to up " them. And we have not quite lost the word " up " in connection with " open," for we speak of a railway " opening up " a country and of a discussion " opening up " a matter.

Opportune. The derivation of the word brings to mind the richly laden merchant-vessel safely back in port, bringing wealth and profit for her owner, for " opportune " comes from the Latin *ob*, before, and *portus*, the harbour. Moreover, there is the same association of ideas in the phrase " When my ship comes home," as expressive of a fortunate time to come.

Oracle. The oracle of the temple at Delphi, a town of ancient Greece, was world-famous, and on all important occasions was consulted by the devout and listened to as the voice of the god. But the answer was not shouted in the street or proclaimed from the temple steps ; it was given in a low, soft whisper in the ear of the inquirer. And the inner meaning of God's admonition to Elijah (1 Kings, xix. 11-12) was not contained in the mighty wind or the terrible earthquake or the raging fire, but in " a still, small voice." It is not surprising, therefore, to find that the Latin *ora-culum*, from which " oracle " is derived, is the *double diminutive* of *orare*, to speak.

Oratorio. A sacred drama in which the music and voices of the opera are retained while the acting and scenery are dispensed with. So called because first performed in the Oratory of the Church of Santa Maria Maggiore, near Rome, under the care of St. Philip Neri (1571-1594.)

Orchestra. Although we are prepared to find a close connection between music and dancing it is curious that the word " orchestra," which now denotes the musicians or that part of the building where they are placed, should originally have meant the place where the chorus danced, being derived from the Greek *orchesthai*, dance.

Order. It was Alexander Pope (1688-1744) who gave us, in his " Essay on Man," the pointed phrase " Order is Heaven's first law."

Oriel Window. A projecting window generally divided by mullions into different bays, and in most cases supported on brackets or corbels. Its name has no significance in relation to its form or aspect, for the word " oriel " comes from the Old French *oriol*, a porch, a chamber or recess, and such apartments were so named because they were usually highly ornamented with gilding, the word being derived from the Latin *aureolus*, gilded.

Orrery. An astronomical arrangement by means of which the relative motions of the planets are illustrated. In 1715 such a machine was constructed by Rowley, the instrument maker, after a pattern devised by George Graham, a clockmaker. It was made at the expense of the Earl of Orrery, and in compliment to him received his name.

Orthodoxy. " I have heard frequent use," said the late Lord Sandwich, in a debate on the Test Laws, " of the words ' orthodoxy ' and ' heterodoxy '; but I confess myself at a loss to know precisely what they mean." " Orthodoxy, my Lord," said Bishop Warburton, in a whisper, " Orthodoxy is my doxy; heterodoxy is another man's doxy."— (Priestley's Memoirs.")

Ostrich. As the largest of all living birds, the ostrich naturally appeals to our imagination and interest. It stands from six to eight feet in height, and has been known from remote antiquity. It is mentioned twice in the book of Job (supposed by many to be one of the oldest of the books of the Bible), and Xenophon speaks of it as frequenting the plains of Artemisia, while there are many references to it in later Roman literature. Heliogabalus is said to have had a dish served up composed of the brains of 600 ostriches, and modern hunters report that the flesh is palatable. The ostrich is now largely bred in South Africa for the sake of the quill feathers of the wings and tail; it is a vegetable feeder, though it swallows stones and other hard substances to aid the gizzard in its functions, and newly-hatched birds have been observed to pick up little stones before taking any food. The wings of the bird are useless for flight, but are of so much help in running that it is said the ostrich can outstrip the fleetest horse. The hens lay their eggs in a common nest—a hole scratched in the sand—and the cock-bird relieves the hens in the task of hatching.

Ottoman Empire. The empire gains its name from Othman (or Osman) who founded it in 1299. He was the first Sultan of the East, a great conqueror, and a man of magnanimous and noble mind.

Oubliette. A dungeon the very name of which was sufficient to strike terror to the condemn.d, for the word comes from the French *oublier*, to forget. The inmate of such a place could only hope for perpetual imprisonment and might be left to slow starvation and death, forgotten of his captors, lost to his friends. The remains of such dungeons may still be traced in some old castles; they were entered by steps reaching to the top of a chamber, where was an opening into the dungeon through which the prisoner was lowered, and which served also for the admission of light and air.

Ought. What we *ought* to do is what we *owe* to do, for the word "ought" comes to us from the Anglo-Saxon *ahte*, the past tense of *agan*, to owe.

Out of Sight, Out of Mind. As long ago as the time of Thomas a Kempis (1380-1471) this phrase was in force, for in the "Imitation of Christ" we find the line "And when he is out of sight, quickly also is he out of mind."

Over the Left. A phrase expressive of disbelief or negation, and therefore of contempt. It is often set down as a modern colloquialism, but it can, at least, claim the respectability of age. For the left side, from time immemorial, has been considered sinister and unlucky, and in the augury of the ancient Greeks all signs seen over the left shoulder were taken to forebode misfortune. Doubtless our phrase is a survival of this universal belief in the evil augury of all that was done or seen "over the left."

Oxen. There are a few places in England where one may still see ploughing done by oxen, and from Iceland to India the patient ox has been the servant of man for unknown ages. The abundance of corn in Egypt was obtained by the use of oxen, and in the papyrus of Ani may be seen, in one place, oxen treading out the corn, and, in another, Ani following them at the plough. We gather from the Bible (Gen. xii. 16) that even in Abraham's time the ox had long been a domesticated animal, and the prophet Isaiah (chap. i. 3), denouncing the Jews' rebellion against God, complains that "the ox knoweth his owner and the

ass his master's crib; but Israel doth not know,
my people doth not consider." Moreover, the
antiquity of the domestication of the ox may be
inferred from the fact that the ox is known by
almost the same name throughout the whole range
of Indo-European languages. (Icelandic, *uxi*;
Sanscrit, *ukshan*). " Oxen " is one of the few
words in which the Anglo-Saxon suffix " en " (or
" on ") has been retained as a plural.

Oz. This is the usual contraction to denote the word
" ounce," but the " z " has intruded itself in the
place of the old terminal mark of a contraction, a
figure like a " z " with a tail. The expression
" viz." (q.v.), a contraction of the Latin *videlicet*
(namely), is another instance of the misuse of " z."

Pad. The word has two distinct meanings and derivations. It may mean a cushion, or anything stuffed
with soft material; in which case it is related to
" pod " and " pudding," and is derived from a
common root meaning a bag. Or it may mean a
path, cognate with the Dutch *pad*, a path, from
which we have the expression " to pad along,"
meaning to trudge along a path. A similar
reference to " path " is found in the term " foot-
pad," meaning one who loiters about to rob
passers-by on the foot-path, in distinction to the
highway-man, the horseman who robs on the high-
road. And the same word " pad " is used, half
contemptuously, to describe a horse suitable for
ambling along bridle-paths and country lanes, but
neither a carriage horse nor a hunter.

Pageant. A " pageant " is a " page " of history.
From the Latin *pangĕre*, to fix (or arrange in its
place), came the word *pagina*, a slab, on which
written characters or numerals were arranged in
fixed order; hence the leaf of a book becomes a
" page " when the order of the type has been
arranged and fixed upon it. When living characters were used to tell the story (instead of
written ones) the *pagina* was called in Old English

" pagin "; Middle English " pagent "; and now
" pageant."

Pagoda. The word is so familiar to us in connection
with the Chinese that it comes as a surprise to find
it is a corruption of the Persian *but-kadah*, meaning an idol-temple, transmitted through the
Portuguese merchants who made their voyages
round the Cape.

Pain. The ingrained belief that pain is a punishment
for evil which has been committed is implied in
the very word " pain," which is derived from the
Latin *pœna*, penalty, punishment. And even
death—" dear beauteous death, the jewel of the
just," as Henry Vaughan (1621-1695) has written
—may be accounted a punishment, for Milton, in
" Paradise Lost," speaks of death as " the
penalty imposed," and reminds us
" Of man's first disobedience and the fruit
Of that forbidden tree, whose mortal taste
Brought death into the world and all our woe."
Yet we now know that, through countless ages,
innumerable creatures were alive upon this earth
and became extinct through death long before
man appeared in the world.

Palm. Though there are many varieties of the palm-
tree, all are alike in one characteristic—the leaves
which form their plume bear a strong resemblance
to the palm of the hand with the fingers open.
The ancient nations, who gloried in the strong
right hand of the victorious leader, perceived this
and called the tree the palm, making it also the
emblem of victory. Thus by the Greeks it was
named *palamē*, and by the Romans *palma*. But
there is a further significance in this little word
" palm." It typifies not only strength and victory
but also the renewal of life and the resurrection
from the dead. When in the early spring the
willow begins to bud the people of the English
southern countries call it " palm," and bring it
into Church on Palm-Sunday or lay it on the

R

graves of their dead. They know, of course, that it is willow and that it has no likeness to the Eastern palm, but at this time of the year it is called "palm" because it is budding, and has come to life again after its winter death. And not only throughout the length and breadth of this country, but from the Baltic in the north to the Mediterranean in the south this word "palm" is instinct with the signification of revival from the dead; whenever there is a budding and breaking forth into new life, the growth—whatever it may be—is called palm.

Palimpsest. The word is formed from the Greek *palimpsestos*, meaning scraped again, and many an old document has thus been used for a subsequent record. The original writing can sometimes be restored by treating the parchment with an infusion of gall and dilute hydrochloric acid, by which means traces of the ink—more or less visible—which have become ingrained in the skin, are revealed.

Pamphlet. A word of doubtful origin, for which various etymologies have been suggested. Thus it has been thought to have come from the Old French *paume*, the palm of the hand, and *feuillet*, a leaf of a book; while Wedgwood favours a Spanish origin, from *papeleta*, which means a written slip of paper, a written newspaper. Skeat, however, is of opinion that the derivation is *Pamphila*, the name of a female historian of the first century, a Greek lady, who wrote a book of anecdotes and numerous epitomes.

Panic. The word was originally used as an adjective, panic-fright being ascribed to the sudden appearance of Pan, the god of the country as opposed to the town. He presided over the flocks and herds, and is represented with the head and breast of an elderly man, but with his lower parts like the hind quarters of a goat and with a goat's horns on his forehead. The sudden fright or causeless dread which sometimes overtakes the lonely shepherd or the lost wanderer in the woods was ascribed to the unseen presence of Pan, and music was esteemed the most effectual means of preventing this panic fright. The Pan-pipe was a simple musical instrument, the earliest form of a compound wind instrument, made by fixing together seven, eight or nine short hollow reeds, cut in graduated lengths so as to produce a musical scale. It was used by the Greeks, by the Romans, and, probably, by the Hebrews, and is undoubtedly the precursor of the organ.

Pannier. The word is generally used to denote a basket, usually in pairs, slung over the back of an animal to carry a load, and the ancient Egyptian paintings show that panniers, slung over the back of an ass, were used in those days to carry children in. Nevertheless, the derivation of our word " pannier " is the Latin *panarius*, pertaining to bread, from *panis*, bread; and the word " pannier " seems to have been originally restricted to a basket in which bread was carried.

Pan Out. An undertaking may or may not prove remunerative—we say we don't know how it will " pan out." The phrase comes from the gold-diggings, where the old custom was to shake the auriferous earth with water in a *pan*, the heavier part (the gold) sinking in the pan while the twirling caused the lighter part to fly off.

Pansy. The French call the flower *pensée*, from *penser*, to think; and Ophelia says " There is pansies, that's for thoughts." (Hamlet iv. 5.) Yet it seems probable that this meaning of " thought " was suggested merely by the similarity of sound between " pansy " and " pensée." The " daisy " was certainly the " Day's eye " (the sun), and it seems not unlikely that " pansy " was " Pan's-eye "; while the eye of the flower, shaped like a heart, probably gave rise to its other name —" heart's-eyes," now become " heart's-ease."

Pantheon. This famous Roman temple was built by Agrippa, the son-in-law of Augustus, about the year 27 B.C., in memory of the victory obtained by Augustus over Anthony and Cleopatra. It was given to Pope Boniface IV. by the Emperor Phocas in 609 A.D., and dedicated as a Christian church. It is esteemed the finest specimen of a circular building not surrounded by columns; the external diameter is 188 feet, the height, exclusive of the flat dome, is 102 feet, and the dome 36 feet, while the porch is 103 feet wide. The word Pantheon is derived from the Greek *pantheion*, meaning (a temple) of all gods.

Paper. " M. Varro writeth," says an old author, " that the first invention of making paper was derived upon the conquest of Ægypt, atchieved by Alexander the Great, at what time as he founded the citie Alexandria in Ægypt, where such paper was first made." The word " paper " is derived from " papyrus," an Egyptian reed whose stalks furnished the principal material for writing upon to the nations dwelling on the Mediterranean coasts. For many centuries papyrus, the stem of which was cut vertically into thin slices, was the only substance from which paper was made, and even now paper is principally manufactured from vegetable fibre, reduced to a pulp by boiling. It is stated that over 400 different materials have been suggested or used for paper manufacture, but rags and esparto grass are considered the best materials, though straw, wood and other fibres are used. The oldest manuscript written on paper which has been preserved to us in England is in the Bodleian collection in the British Museum, and bears the date of 1049, and there is a paper manuscript in the Library of Paris dated 1050. Up to the beginning of the 19th century all paper was made by hand, in moulds of various sizes, but machine-made paper is now manufactured in a continuous sheet, sometimes many miles long.

Paper-Money. The true standard of paper-money is often misunderstood. Its value depends upon whether it is a promise to pay coin or is merely a paper forced into currency by the law of the country in which it is issued. In the first case—that of paper-money such as Bank of England notes— the chance of loss to holders is guarded against by keeping up such a reserve of coin as experience has proved to be sufficient; but in the latter case the holder has no right to claim coin in exchange, as the paper has superseded the metal money. Of the disastrous effects of the forced currency of paper-money there have been abundant examples in recent times. France issued its " assignats " between 1789 and 1796, during which time they fluctuated in value from the equivalent in silver coin to a depreciation of 99—100 per cent., thus ultimately cancelling their value in exchange with other countries. Even England, when it partially restricted specie payments, from 1797 to 1821, found that its paper-money was depreciated by more than 25 per cent., and the financial history of all other countries, both in Europe and America, presents similar examples down to the present time.

Papier-Mâché. A French word, the literal meaning of which is masticated paper. The material is usually composed of paper as its principal ingredient, but common varieties are prepared from a mixture of any kind of fibrous substance, pulped into a homogeneous mass of doughy consistence. The pulp is rolled into thick sheets and cut into the required sizes; it is then subjected to heavy pressure between dies and afterwards dried. Its surface is then ready for gilding, painting and varnishing, and its toughness and lightness are remarkable.

Paradise. The word is used to denote a place of bliss, a region of felicity and delight; or, in theological terms, the place of the blessed dead awaiting the Last Judgment, and, sometimes, heaven. The

Hebrew *pardes*, from which our word is probably derived, is of Aryan origin, having special reference to the tree-studded parks around Persian palaces; and the Greek equivalent, *paradeisos*, is applied in the Septuagint to the Garden of Eden.

Paraphernalia. The various equipments, the bag and baggage which often go by this name, seem to have little to do with a bride, but, nevertheless, the word in its strict meaning denotes that which a bride brings to her husband over and above her dowry—her clothes, jewels, and ornaments of dress generally. For the word comes from the Greek *para*, beyond, and *phernē*, a dowry (from *pherein*, to bring).

Parasite. The word is derived from the Greek *para*, beside, and *sitos*, food, meaning one who feeds at another's expense. There is scarcely any animal, and very few plants, which does not support some parasites. The word " parasite " is used figuratively to describe a hanger-on, a mean and fawning flatterer, a sycophant.

Parchment. There seems to be no doubt that the word is derived from the name Pergamus, a city in Mysia, Asia Minor, the Pergamos mentioned in Rev. i. 11, and ii. 12. According to some authorities parchment was invented by Eumenes of Pergamus, the founder of the celebrated library of that city, about 190 B.C., whils others refer it to Crates of Pergamus, who, about 160 B.C., introduced it as a substitute for papyrus, on which an embargo was laid, by Ptolemy Epiphanes, as a means of restraining Eumenes in his endeavour to collect a library in emulation of the famous one in Alexandria. Parchment is made from the skins of very young calves, sheep, or goats; or, if desired to be extra fine and thin, from the skins of still-born lambs, kids, and calves; while coarse parchment for drum-heads, etc., is made from the skins of asses and he-goats.

Parhelion—Passenger 257

Parhelion. The word is formed from the Greek *para*, beside or near, and *helios*, the sun. It denotes a mock sun, a phenomenon common in the polar regions but very rare in Great Britain. Two such appearances were witnessed from Unst, the most northerly of the Shetland Isles, in August, 1858; and three brilliant suns, in the same horizontal line and of equal brightness, were observed from Strangford, County Down, Ireland, in 1871. The phenomenon probably arises from refraction and reflection produced by minute fragments of ice in the sky.

Parish. The word is derived from the Greek *paroikia* (*para*, beside, and *oikos*, a house). The origin of parishes is lost in antiquity; they may have been either civil or ecclesiastical—most probably the latter. Christianity established itself first in the towns, whence it put forth missionary efforts in every direction, and to the subordinate churches thus raised a district was assigned, which afterwards acquired financial endowment. Camden says that England was divided into parishes as early as A.D. 630, but Selden has shown that long after this the clergy lived in common. The parish is not merely an ecclesiastical division; it constitutes also an area for local government in civil matters, and is the smallest unit recognised for that purpose.

Parrot. The word is a contraction of the French *perroquet* (our Paroquet), which is derived from *Pierrot*, the diminutive of *Pierre*, otherwise Peter.

Parson. From the Latin *persona*, a person. "Parson" and "person" are thus the same word, the parson being so called (says Blackstone) "because by his *person* the Church, which is an invisible body, is represented."

Passenger. The word signifies one who makes a passage, and should properly be spelt "passager," the "n" being excrescent, as in "messenger," one who takes a message. "Passage" has its derivation in the Latin *passus*, a step, which comes from *passus*, the past participle of *pandere*, to stretch.

Patent. The word comes from the Latin *patens*, the present participle of *patere*, to lie open, and as an adjective is used figuratively to describe the quality of being open and evident to all. In that sense its pronunciation should be " pa'tent," but when used as a substantive, to denote Letters Patent from the Crown, it should be pronounced " pat'ent."

Patient. The root signification of this word, whether used as a substantive or an adjective, is seen in its derivation—the Latin *patiens*, present participle of *patior*, I suffer, endure. We are right, therefore, to speak of the " patience " of Job, considering all the suffering he had to endure, even if he did not bear it submissively. And the same idea of suffering and endurance—though in an extended form—is present in St. Paul's injunction to the Thessalonians (I. Thess. v. 14) to " be ' patient ' towards all men."

Patronage. The following account by Blackstone of the origin of Church Patronage is of interest :— " Whoever under the Roman Empire built a temple to a god had the right of nominating the officiating priests, and in the reign of Constantine, to induce wealthy men to found Christian churches the same privilege of patronage was transferred to them. In Britain, as well as elsewhere, the system prevailed, and when a gentleman built a church on his own estate, he was, as a rule, the patron."

Pauper. In ordinary language a pauper is one who has become chargeable to the parish, but in Law the term is applied to one who is allowed to have writs gratis, and counsel and attorney assigned to him without fee, and is excused the payment of costs, having first sworn that he is not worth £5.

Pawn-Broker—Pearls

Pawn-Broker. The following extract gives a succinct account of the origin of pawn-broking and the pawn-broker's sign :—" The Emperor Augustus Cæsar, B.C. 31, instituted a fund for lending to needy persons on pledge. The institutions, called ' Monti di Pieta,' arose at Perugia, in Italy, about A.D. 1462. The first pawn-brokers in England were Lombards, and the three balls still used as their insignia are said to have been derived from the arms of the Medici family, adopted, according to legend, in memory of Averardo de Medici, a commander under Charle-magne, who slew a giant and kept his mace or club, with three balls on the top, as a trophy."

Peak. As a component in place-names this is closely allied to the words " pike," " spike," " spit," and " beak." It is of Celtic origin and means a point, as in the Peak of Derbyshire, and the Pikes in Cumberland, while in Spithead we have an appro-priate name for the end of a long spit of sand.

Pearls. As jewels of rare beauty and high value, pearls must be of great antiquity. They are men-tioned in the book of Job (xxviii. 18)—one of the most ancient books of the Bible—and the pearl-fisheries of the Persian Gulf have been celebrated since the time of Pliny. Our Lord's parable of the man who sold all that he had in order that he might possess himself of " one pearl of great price " (Matt. xii. 46)—though, of course, the analogy must not be pressed too far—is an illustra-tion of the great esteem in which pearls were held by the Jews in Christ's time, for unless it had been considered possible to find a pearl of inestim-able value there would have been no point in the simile of the parable. The value of a pearl depends upon its size, shape, colour, and freedom from defects—a pearl five-eighths of an inch in diameter was sold in 1860 for £2,000. Pearls are found as a morbid growth in many shells, but the best are from the Oriental pearl-mussel.

Peats. " Turn the peats " is a north-country phrase equivalent to " change the subject." The allusion is to the square blocks of dried peat which are used for fuel, and which, when they become red-hot underneath, are turned over so as to allow the burning side give out its warmth and glow. The word " peat " is an example of the common interchange of " b " and " p "; " peat " was formerly " beat," from the Anglo-Saxon *betan*, to better (to mend the fire).

Pedagogue. The word is derived, through the Latin *pœdagogus*, from the Greek *paidos*, a boy, and *agō*, to lead. and was the name of the slave who led his master's children to school until they were old enough to take care of themselves. St. Paul, in his letter to the Galatians (iii. 24) refers to this office when he says that " the law was our schoolmaster to bring us unto Christ."

Pedigree. A table of pedigree is generally shown by connecting lines which radiate from the ancestor of the family to his descendants; these connecting lines commonly take the form of a bird's foot, and thus, according to Skeat, the French *pied-de-grue*, crane's foot, gave its name to the word " pedigree."

Pedlar. Even outlying villages and hamlets are now supplied with goods by the motor-van which comes from town, and the pedlar is dying out. Although he used to make his rounds on foot his name is not derived from the Latin *pedes*, a foot; for the older form of " pedlar " was " peddar " or " pedder," meaning one who carries a " ped," the provincial English for basket and probably the same as " pad." Spencer uses the word " ped " to denote a basket such as that in which a pedlar would carry his curious assortment of goods.

Peel. This is a Celtic word denoting a stronghold, found in many place-names along the Scottish border and in the name of the town of Peel in the

Isle of Man. Its frequency along the Scottish border is an evidence of the necessity laid upon every man in the times of the border warfare to make his house his castle in a literal sense.

Peers of the Realm. The derivation usually given for the word " peer " is the Latin *parem*, the accusative of *par*, equal, and, of course, the word is used in that sense. But the suggestion has been put forward that when the word denotes a peer of the realm it is far more likely to be derived from the Norman *pier* or *père*, father, and the wording of the old enactments, the literal translation of which is " by the common consent of the fathers and people of the realm," seems to support this opinion.

Pelican. The word is derived from the Greek *pelekus*, an axe. The common pelican is about the size of a swan, though its enormous bill and loose plumage make it look considerably larger. It sits during the night with its bill resting on its breast; and as the extremity of the bill is red, this may have given rise to the legend that the bird feeds its young with blood from its own breast. But it is possible that the legend has some foundation in fact, for in the Zoological Gardens, in 1869, it was observed that the flamingoes ejected into the mouth of the Cariamas a glutinous red fluid, which, on microscopical examination, was found to consist almost entirely of blood corpuscles. " Have we here," says Mr. Bartlett, " an explanation of the old story of the pelican feeding its young with its own blood? I think we have; for the flamingo was, and still is, found plentifully in the country alluded to, and it may be that, in the translation, the habit of the one bird has been transferred to the other."

Pen. A component in place-names. (*See* BEN.)

Pencil. This is a curious example of a double diminutive, for the word comes from the Latin *penecillus*, the diminutive of *peniculus*, itself a diminutive of *penis*, a tail. The literal meaning of " pencil " is, therefore, a very little tail !

Pendulum. It is believed that the ordinary pendulum was invented by Ebn Junis, of the University of Cordova, about 1100 A.D., while his companion, Gerbert, who was poisoned in 1102, is credited with the invention of the escapement. In 1581 Galileo recommended a pendulous weight as a true measurer, and in 1612 Sanitorius suggested the combination of the pendulum with wheel-work; while some thirty or forty years later Harris, and then Huyghens applied the idea to the making of clocks.

Penitentiary. The principal objects of a Penitentiary should be, says Blackstone, " to preserve and amend the health of the unhappy offenders, to enure them to habits of industry, to guard them from pernicious company." The first institution of the kind is said to have been established in 1786 by the Quakers.

Penny. The silver penny had an intrinsic value, as it contained silver to the amount of twenty-four grains Troy weight. But the penny of the workman's wage was only a token, a pledge which the master would redeem by paying its equivalent in corn or wool for food or clothing; for when the whole country was agricultural there were no shops except in the towns, often at a considerable distance. This is indicated by the fact that the oldest form of the word " penny " is " pending," meaning something pledged or pawned, and it has its equivalent in the Dutch *pand* and the German *pfand*, a pledge. All these words come from the Latin *pannus*, a rag, a piece of cloth—doubtless the earliest form of purse. It is easy to see that the phrase " to turn an honest penny " may have arisen from the practice of turning the wage-penny into goods, and hence the term gained its present meaning of " to trade."

Pentateuch. The word is formed from the Greek *pente*, five, and *teuchos*, a book, and is applied exclusively to the first five books of the Old Testament collectively. In Hebrew these books are called *Torah*, meaning the Law.

Perfect. The derivation of this word may be taken as an incentive to good work—it is the Latin *per-facio*, I do through, *i.e.*, I do throughly, thoroughly.

Peter's Pence. In Saxon times this was a t x of a penny on each house throughout England, which, beginning as an occasional voluntary contribution, was finally established as a legal tax under Canute, Edward the Confessor, and William the Conqueror. The name arose from its being collected on St. Peter's Day, and it was also called "Hearth Money" from being levied on every house. At first it was used for the support of an English college in Rome, then the Pope shared the gift with the college, and finally appropriated the whole. Edward III. repealed the tax, but it was soon restored, and it was not abolished until the reign of Henry VIII.

Petroleum. The word is formed from the Latin *petra*, a rock, and *oleum*, oil, and is a term applied to a variety of inflammable liquids found in many parts of the earth and formed by the gradual decomposition of vegetable matter beneath the surface. They are met with in most countries of Europe, but occur in abundance in the United States and in Canada. Paraffin is the commercial name for an oil obtained by distillation from Petroleum, and is also produced by the dry distillation of shale, etc. The word "paraffin" is formed from the Latin *parum*, little, and *affinis*, akin, denoting the inaptitude of the oil for combining with other bodies.

Pew. The church pew—with its arrogance or convenience, according to the different view of different persons—is familiar to all, and the origin of the word is curious. It comes from the Latin *podium*, which was the name given to the balcony next the arena, where the Emperor and other distinguished persons sat to witness the gladiatorial shows. The word *podium* is derived from the Greek *podion*, a little foot, and is cognate with the Italian *poggio*, a hillock, and the Spanish *poyo*, a stone bench near a door.

Pharaoh. This was the name and title of the king through a long-enduring line of monarchs in ancient Egypt. The word is derived from the Egyptian *Pra* or *Phra*, meaning the Sun.

Pharisee. The word is derived from the Hebrew *perushin*, the literal meaning of which is "those who are separate." The Pharisees were the most numerous of the three divisions of Judaism in the time of Christ, the other two being the Sadduces and the Essenes. They were so called because they kept aloof from Levitically impure food and separated themselves from those who neglected to keep the Mosaic law in its literal strictness.

Pharmacopœia. The word is formed from the Greek *pharmakon*, a drug, and *poiein*, to make. The official publication called the "British Pharmacopœia" is issued under the direction of the General Medical Council, and contains a list of medicines proper for use, with their characters, tests for determining their purity, and doses to be administered.

Pheasant. It is said that pheasants were present in great numbers near the mouth of the river Phasis, a stream which flows into the Black Sea, and the ultimate derivation of the word "pheasant" seems to be the Greek *Phasianos*, which means "pertaining to the Phasis." There is little doubt that the pheasant now naturalised in England had its original home in the East, and Martial says that it was brought from Colchis, the old name of the district in which the Phasis (the present Rion) flows.

Philomel. A name often applied in poetry to the nightingale, as, according to Greek mythology, Philomela, the daughter of Pandon, king of Athens, was changed by the gods into a nightingale. The Greek *philos* means loving.

Philosophy. The word is directly derived from the Greek *philosophia*, meaning love of wisdom, which term is said to have been suggested by Pythagoras, who lived about 570 to 500 B.C. The tradition is that, on being complimented on his wisdom, he said he was not wise but a lover of wisdom, the Deity alone being wise.

Phlegm. To be phlegmatic is to be cold and indifferent, lacking in ardour or passion. Yet the word "phlegm" is derived from the Greek *phleg-ein*, to burn! Dr. Arbuthnot endeavours to account for the discrepancy when he states that although "'phlegm' amongst the ancients signified a cold and viscous humour, contrary to the etymology of the word . . . there were two sorts of 'phlegm'—cold and hot."

Phœnix. In symbolical art and in heraldry the Phœnix is frequently depicted as an emblem of immortality, as, according to Greek mythology, the bird was supposed to live for five or six hundred years in the deserts of Arabia. As death approached she built for herself a funeral pyre of aromatic wood, which she set alight by the fanning of her wings, and so consumed herself; while from the ashes she arose again in youth and vigour.

Photography may be said to have sprung from the discovery made by alchemists, more than three hundred years ago, that fused silver chloride would darken on exposure to light. But it was not until 1802 that Thomas Wedgwood published his method of taking profiles upon surfaces treated with nitrate of silver, by exposing such surfaces to the light of the sun under the object to be represented; and for many years no method was known of fixing the picture.   In 1839, Henry Fox Talbot made known a process by which paper, with a surface of chloride of silver, was exposed in a camera-obscura, and the image developed by a solution of gallic acid.   In 1839, also, the Daguerreotype process was published—a process which is still used for making photographs where accurate measurements are required.   Further advances were made by the introduction of sensitive iodide and bromide of silver held in a film of collodion, by the adoption of the alkaline development for dry plates, and by the use of gelatine as a medium for holding the sensitive salts.

Phrase.   The ordinary talk of many persons is scarcely more than a string of phrases, and many who would scorn to wear ready-made garments do not object to clothe their speech in ready-made sentences.   The turf, the pulpit, the studio, the laboratory, every trade and every craft, has its own set of technical terms; but a phrase is more than this.   It is a saying that has become common property and is familiar to everyone.   It often embodies the concrete wisdom, the tried sagacity, of many generations, and is sometimes so old that its very origin is obscure.   And although we may have a veiled contempt for those who can only express themselves by a series of phrases, it must be admitted that phrases are a potent means of expression, and were they swept out of the language the greater part of the population would be silent.   Even the derivation of the word " phrase " points to the same conclusion, for " phrase " comes from the Greek *phrazein*, to speak.

Phylactery.   The word comes from the Greek *phulakter*, a watchman, a guard, and the article is used as an amulet against disease or danger.   The

Jewish name for phylacteries is the Hebrew *tephillin*, meaning prayer-fillets. They are small square boxes, generally made of parchment, in which are enclosed slips of vellum inscribed with passages from the Pentateuch, and to this day they are worn by the Jew on the head and left arm during daily morning prayer.

Physic. It is instructive to find, in tracing the derivation of this word, that its literal meaning may be rendered as that which is produced by nature, "physic," being derived from the Greek *phusikos*, natural, and *phuo*, I produce.

Pig in a Poke. There seems to be little doubt that it was a common custom to take little pigs to market in bags, and the Celtic and Irish word *poc* means a bag. Hence "to buy a pig in a poke" is equivalent to concluding a bargain without full knowledge of the result. Shakespeare says, "And then he drew a dial from his poke" ("As you Like it," ii. 7). The dial was a large timepiece, and the poke was the "pouch" of which "pocket" is the diminutive.

Pilot. The literal meaning of the word is "one who uses the sounding-lead," its derivation being the Old Dutch *pijlen*, to sound the water, and *loot*, lead.

Pink. There seems no reason to believe that the name of this flower has anything to do with its colour, which, indeed, is more often red or white, rather than pink. In all probability the flower takes its name from the cut or peaked edges of the petals, for the term "pink" is still used in needlework to describe the edge of a material cut out in scallops or evenly notched.

Pins. We are assured that until near the end of the 14th century, ladies were in the habit of using wooden skewers instead of pins, which latter were first brought from France in the year 1540. And we still use the word "pin" to denote a wooden skewer or stake, as in "tent-pin," and

s

"belaying-pin," while the signification of a pointed stick is implied in the derivation of the word "pin" in many languages, all such words being borrowed from the Latin *pinna*, a variant of *penna*, a pen.

Pity. "Pity's akin to love," wrote Thomas Southerne, some two hundred years ago, and St. Paul, in his letter to his Roman converts, tells them that "Love is the fulfilling of the Law," while it is plain that pity and piety are closely akin, as the derivation of the two words is the same—the Latin *pietas*.

Plague. The word comes from the Latin *plaga*, a blow, a stroke; implying that a plague is a blow divinely inflicted on account of sin. The malignant and contagious fever, which is believed to be almost identical with the worst kind of typhus, and which devasted London in the year 1665, was, and still is, known by the name of "The Plague." It is stated to have slain, in London alone, more than 68,000 persons—about one-third of the population. We can well believe that the Great Fire of London, which took place in the following year and was considered such a terrible disaster, was of the greatest benefit in cleansing the city and preventing a recurrence of the epidemic, by destroying the fever-haunted hovels with which the city then abounded. Our experience in India has shown us that though the plague is probably a "dirt disease" it is chiefly disseminated by rats, or, more exactly, by the fleas with which infected rats are infested. Infected rats are, from time to time, inadvertently brought to our poits in cargoes of grain from Odessa and elsewhere, and it is only by prompt and vigilant measures by the sanitary authorities that our country is preserved from plague infection.

Planets. The word "planet" is derived from the Greek *planetes*, meaning a wanderer, a name which was given by old-world observers to certain

heavenly bodies which seemed to wander about aim-
lessly in the sky, in marked contrast with the
orderly movement of the fixed stars. We now
know, of course, that planets are regular in their
revolution round the sun, and that their apparently
erratic course is due to the fact that both planets
and observers are in motion. The planets known
to the ancients were but five—Mercury, Venus.
Mars, Jupiter and Saturn—but we have brought
up the number to eight by the discovery of Uranus
and Neptune and by including the earth as a planet.
And in addition to these eight planets there is an
aggregation of minute planets called asteroids,
occupying—or, more correctly speaking, constantly
passing through in the course of their various
orbits—a position between Mars and Jupiter. The
first of these asteroids, of which several hundreds
are now known, was discovered through consideration of a remarkable empirical law, detected by
Professor Bode in the 18th century, as to the pro-
gressive distance between the other planets in relation to the sun, from which it was inferred that
there was a planet missing between Mars and
Jupiter. Patient examination of the heavens by
Piazzi and others, and intricate mathematical calculation by Gauss, a comparatively young man,
resulted in the discovery of the asteroid Ceres with
an orbit corresponding to the propounded theory;
and the hypothesis suggested is that these small
bodies are fragments of a planet rent asunder by
some powerful internal convulsion.

Plebeian. The word is generally used as synonymous
with low and vulgar, and its derivation is the Latin
plebs (genitive *plebis*), the people—the common
people as opposed to the nobles or patricians.
Some authorities are of opinion that the Roman
population consisted originally of patricians and
their dependants, and that a body of free plebeians
arose gradually under the elder Tarquin and Servius
Tullius. In B.C. 445 a law was enacted removing
the prohibition of marriage between patricians and

plebeians, and after nine years' controversy (B.C. 375-366) the Consulate was thrown open to the plebeians, and within fifty years thereafter they were admitted to the Censorship and the Priest-hood.

Plod. The word seems to have had its origin in the Gaelic *plod*, meaning a pool, and *plodan*, a little pool; the implied sense being to tramp through mire and wet, and hence to walk painfully and laboriously.

> " The Curfew tolls the knell of parting day,
> The lowing herds wind slowly o'er the lea,
> The ploughman homeward *plods* his weary way,
> And leaves the world to darkness and to me."
> (Gray's " Elegy.")

Plover. The word is apparently derived from the Latin *pluvia*, rain, and the bird is said to be called " plover " because it is mostly seen and caught in a rainy season.

Plunder. We do not find this word in the English vocabulary until about 1630-1640. According to Fuller it is of Dutch or German origin, and was first introduced into England by the soldiers who had fought under Gustavus Adolphus.

Poacher. The name certainly seems applicable to the man's act, for the word " poach " is synonymous with " pouch," which means a bag, what was formerly called a poke and is now styled a pocket. (*See* PIG IN A POKE.) A poacher " bags " the game and " pokes " it into his " pouch " or " pocket." A " poached" egg may have gained its description from being broken into a " pouch " (a bag of thin cotton) preparatory to boiling ; or perhaps because the yoke of the egg is enveloped in the white as in a " pouch."

Point-Blank. We use this term to express something which is plain, direct, explicit ; as a " point-blank " denial. Its literal meaning is a white spot, from the French *point blanc*, referring to the white spot in the centre of a target.

Portentous. Foreshadowing ill, from the Latin *pro*, forth, and *tendere*, to stretch. The under-lying idea is that of some huge object stretching forth a gloomy and dismaying shadow, admirably expressed in the line by Thomas Campbell : " And coming events cast their shadows before."

Posy.

> " I know the way she went
> Home with her maiden posy,
> For her feet have touch'd the meadows
> And left the daisies rosy."
> (Tennyson's " Maud.")

" Posy " now means a bunch of wild flowers, but formerly the word also meant a poetical motto or short verse *e.g.*, " the posy of a ring " (" Hamlet " iii, 2). It was the custom to send floral tributes with a motto, or poesy, attached, but as the flowers were selected to express their meaning in the language of flowers, they also were the poesy.

Gone to Pot. The phrase is but another way of saying that something has gone to ruin, is beyond repair, Doubtless the allusion is to the melting-pot, into which are thrown broken pieces and shavings of metal, especially gold and silver. When too small for use or damaged past mending they must " go to pot." The same idea underlies the phrase " potty rubbish."

Pot-Luck. In old days—and the practice is still in force in some few outlying villages—nothing came amiss to the great family cooking-pot suspended from the familiar pot-hook. Anything edible was thrown in, and to " keep the pot boiling " the fire was seldom, if ever, let out. When meal-time came, persons fished for themselves, and what they might happen to get was " pot-luck."

Pot-Pourri. A term we have borrowed from the French, the literal meaning of which is "rotten-pot." It is applied to a pot into which are thrown the petals of roses collected for the sake of the odour they give while decaying or rotting.

The Press. It would seem that as the idea of a thing is enlarged the significance of the word by which it is denoted is correspondingly extended. For instance, the word "navy" is derived from the Latin *navis*, which meant a single ship, but now embraces all a nation's ships-of-war, with their officers, men, and guns. And "the press," which originally meant the printing-machine by which the type was pressed upon the paper, has now come to signify the newspapers and literature of a country and all the art and business of printing and publishing.

Pretext. The word comes from the Latin *prætexere*, to weave before, and means, literally, something woven in front—an apt figure of some ostensible motive or reason put forward in order to conceal the real one, which is the present signification of the word. Moreover, the Roman *prætexta*—a purple-bordered garment, embroidered down the front, used by patricians and those in high office —may be taken as a figure of the aristocratic dress assumed by those who make their appearance a *pretext* for swindling.

Prepense. It may be that it is because "goodness prepense" is so rare that we never hear the expression, but "malice prepense" is a common term. It means evil premeditated, intentional, or —to follow the derivation of the word—weighed out beforehand. For "prepense" comes (though the French *pre-penser*) from the Latin *præ*, before, and *pensum*, weighed, and we retain the idea of weights and scales when we speak of weighing one's words or balancing the issues of a question.

Preposterous. There is a curious significance to be gained from the derivation of this word. It is the

Latin *præ*, before, and *posterus*, after, which may be rendered as esteeming that first which ought to be last.

Primeval. "This is the forest primeval," writes Longfellow in his poem "Evangeline"—a forest which owes not its existence to man's planting or to second growth after clearing, but which has been a forest from the earliest age. For the word "primeval" is derived from the Latin *primus*, first, and *ævum*, an age.

Primrose. The flower is often taken as deriving its name from the Latin *prima rosa*, the first rose, but the old name was "prime-rôle, which, by an error in popular etymology, was corrupted into prime-rose. or primrose." Of course, this sweet and dainty flower, the harbinger of Spring, is not a rose at all; it is —as its original name (prime-rôle) implies— the flower that holds the first place, the earliest, the most beautiful.

Prize. The word, as a noun, is derived from the French *pris*, taken, the past participle of *prendre* (in Latin *prehendre*), to take, to seize; and the winner of a race is still said to "take" a prize, although the custom is to present it to him afterwards. Prize-money is a share of the booty "taken" from the enemy, and in the hunting-field the "prize" is the note of the horn blown when the game is "taken."

Procrastination "is the thief of time," writes Young, in his "Night Thoughts"; and the proverb says: "Never put off till to-morrow what can be done to-day." The relation of the two phrases is to be found in the derivation of "procrastination"—the Latin *pro*, off, and *cras*, to-morrow. The term "crass,"—*e.g.* "a crass idiot"—comes from different source, from the Latin *crassus*, meaning thick, dense, gross.

Profile. Here, in a word, we have revealed to us the craft of the antique draughtsman by a method still

in use.   In drawing the side-face of a sitter a delicate plumb-line—a thread—is hung in front of the
face, touching the tip of the nose.   Against this
straight line the artist is able to calculate the angle
made by the forehead, nose, and chin.   The word
comes from the Latin *pro*, in front of, and *filum*, a
thread.

The Proprieties.   The expression has come to mean the
conventional customs of society—" What will Mrs.
Grundy say?"   Yet the word " propriety " did not
originally mean what the world would think of an
action, but how it affected oneself.   For the word
comes from the Latin *proprietas*, through *proprius*,
one's own; and to retain one's honour is to be a
" proper " man, just as to hold possessions is to be
a man of " property."

Prosperity.   " Much wants more," and the well-to-do
are not always the most " prosperous," in the
strict sense of the word.   But whether rich or poor,
as long as a man has any hope before him he may
be said to " prosper," for the word is derived from
the Latin *pro*, before, and *spes*, hope.

Punch.   (A drink.)   Both the word and the beverage
are so thoroughly British that few would look
abroad for a derivation.   Yet the name comes from
the East—from the Hindustani *panch*, and the
Sancrit *pancha*, both meaning five.   As the drink is
made of five ingredients—spirit, water, sugar,
lemon and spice—it is probable that the name, if
not the recipe, was brought to England by some
Indian nabob.

Punctual.   The punctual man is he who keeps an
ap-*point*-ment, and the word " punctual " is derived
from the Latin *punctum*, a point.   A similar reference to " point " may be found in the phrases " To
come up to the point," and " To look sharp," while
we hear of some persons that they " make a point of
being punctual," and from such one is likely to
have pointed remarks if one is unpunctual !

Purple. The famous Tyrian purple of the Phœnicians was probably a dull red colour, and was obtained from the murex, a Mediterranean bivalve; heaps of its broken shells, and the hollow places in the rocks in which they were pounded, as in a mortar, may yet be seen on the Tyrian coast. There is little doubt that the manufacture and sale of the dye was an important industry, and Lydia, the " seller of purple," to whom reference is made in Acts, xvi. 14 and 40, seems to have been a person of wealth and position. " Born to the purple " is a term denoting imperial or royal rank, from the colour of the royal robes, and was first applied, it is said, to the Byzantine Emperor, Constantine VII. (912-959). Purple was also the regal colour of the Romans (" They put on him a purple robe "—John xix. 2); it was afterwards assumed by the princes of the Roman Church and has now become the scarlet or " cardinal " colour, from the scarlet hat, stockings and cassock worn by Cardinals. The murex was called *purpura* in Latin, whence our word " purple "; and the Old Testament expression " red like crimson " (Is. 1. 18) is supposed to refer to the crimson-purple of the " purpura "—an indelible dye.

Purse. The purse of the serf was a rag (*see* PENNY), and the knot which contained the coin is represented, on a diminutive scale, in the seed-pod of the little flower called " Shepherd's-purse." But the article to which " purse " refers was of stronger material, for the purse of the rich was made of leather, as the word indicates, being derived from the Greek *byrsa*, a skin, a hide. From the same origin comes the French *bourse*, a word which is used to denote a purse and also the French Stock Exchange. We see the etymology in the word " disburse," which is equivalent to " dispurse," and in " bursar," meaning one who keeps the purse. Formerly a pitiful tale might be effectual " to loosen the purse-strings," but now most purses shut with a snap !

Puss. Children are taught the rhyme beginning " Pussy-cat, pussy-cat, where have you been?" they read about " Puss-in-boots " and play at " Puss-in-the-corner." We might suppose, therefore, that " puss " is merely a childish pet-name for the cat, as " bow-bow " is for the dog. But though it is, doubtless, an imitative word, probably derived from the sound made by a cat spitting, it is found in nearly identical form in Dutch, German, Swedish, Irish and Gaelic, and in all of these languages it has the same meaning—a cat.

To Purchase. We go to the stores, the lift carries us to the right department, we say what we require, and we make our purchase. Formerly it was a very different matter. There were no shop-windows with goods exhibited for sale (glass was almost unknown) but prentice-boys at the open booths shouted to the passer-by, " What do you lack? What do you lack?" People did not buy things because they were marked " Cheap "—they had *to hunt for* what they wanted. And the word " purchase " is derived from the French, *pourchasser*, to hunt for.

Quack. The word is undoubtedly an imitative one, from the sound made by the domesticated duck. Its application to a person who pretends to a knowledge of medicine, or who claims the discovery of some specific cure, has received more than one explanation. It has been thought to be a corruption of " quake," and to have reference to a supposed ability to charm away ague; but it is more likely to have arisen from the loud and boastful quacking of the duck, and the absurd and pompous waddle so characteristic of the bird.

Quadrille. The dance of this name seems to have been of Spanish origin, and is stated to have been introduced into England by the Duke of Devonshire, in 1813. The word comes from the Spanish *cuadrillo*, meaning a small square, appropriate to the dance in that it is executed by four sets of couples, each forming the side of a square.

Quadroon. The word is derived from the Latin *quartus*, fourth, and denotes a person who is one quarter negro and three-quarters white, the off-spring of a white and a mulatto. The mulatto is half-blooded, one parent being white and the other black.

Quagmire. The word is a corruption of "quake-mire," meaning soft, boggy, marshy ground, that yields and shakes ("quakes") under the foot.

Quail. To "quail" before a threatened blow or an impending disaster implies either the fear of injury or the expectation of acute sorrow, and the derivation of the word is the Anglo-Saxon *cwelan*, to die, and the German *qual*, agony. But the word "quail," when applied to the bird of that name (sometimes called "wet-my-lips" or "wet-my-feet," from a supposed similarity of sound in the male-bird's note), has its origin in the Old Dutch *quackel*, a quacker. There seems no doubt that the birds mentioned in the Old Testament (Exod. xvi. 13, etc.), the Hebrew *selav*, translated "quails," are the same which we know by that name. They are of migratory habit, and alight on the shores of the Red Sea to take rest before passing over the mountains, and they are also found by the Dead Sea. The flesh was, and still is, esteemed a delicacy, but to the Israelites, in their gluttonous lust in the wilderness, it brought dire disaster. (Num. xi. 31-33; Ps. lxxvii. 27-31.)

Quakers. A nick name for the "Society of Friends," originally applied by Justice Bennet, a Derby magistrate, in derision of George Fox, the founder of the Society, because he had admonished the magistrates to "quake at the word of the Lord." George Fox, an illiterate man, but of considerable natural ability, was born at Drayton, in Leicestershire, in 1624. He was apprenticed to a shoemaker, but as

the whole bent of his mind was towards
religion he soon began to preach, and by 1648 he
had gained many adherents.   He deemed it sinful
to take oaths or pay tithes, and thus encountered
vehement hostility from both civil and ecclesiastical
authorities, but he unflinchingly promulgated his
opinions, not only in England but also on the Continent and in America, until his death in 1691.
After the Revolution of 1688, the sect were
unmolested and were permitted to make affirmation
instead of oath, and they have rendered valuable
services in the cause of education and missionary
enterprise.   Their tenets may be summarised by
saying that they believe all forms of worship, even
the sacraments of Baptism and the Lord's Supper,
to be unnecessary, that the ministry should be
unpaid, that war and the taking of oaths are sinful,
and that the heathen names for the days of the
week and the observance of times and compliments
should be set aside.   Their style of dress, with
its plain shape and colour, which was once an
enforced observance among Quakers, has been
gradually discontinued.

Quandary.   It used to be accepted that the derivation of this word was a corruption of the French
Qu'en dirai-je?   What can or shall I say of it?
But according to Skeat, it comes from the Middle
English *wandreth*, which means evil plight, adversity, peril; being cognate with the Old Swedish
wandrade, difficulty, from *wand*, difficult.

Quarantine.   When a vessel arrives from an infected
port, or is suspected of having a contagious
disease on board, she is obliged to forbear
all intercourse with the shore, and is said
to be put in "quarantine."   The term
of isolation is of undetermined length, but
originally it was for forty days, and hence the application of the word "quarantine," which is
derived from the Latin *quadraginta*, forty.

Quarry—Queen

Quarry. There are two distinct words with this spelling—the " quarry " from which stone or marble is dug out, and the " quarry " of the chase. The first is derived from the Latin *quadrus*, square, and its literal meaning is a place where stone is squared. The derivation of the other "quarry " is not so certain. It may be that it comes from the term " carry," used in falconry when the hawk flew off with the prey it had struck; but the more generally accepted derivation is the Old French *cuirée*, denoting the intestines of an animal killed in the chase, those parts which were thrown to the dogs; whence, in course of time, the word " quarry " gained its present meaning of the object that is chased.

Quart. The literal meaning of the word is a fourth, being derived from the Latin *quartus*. It signifies, of course, the fourth part of a gallon, but while the old English measure for wines and spirits was considerably less than our standard quart, that for beer and ale was a little larger.

Quarters. Dr. Brewer tells us that when this word is used to denote a residence or place of abode, such as a soldier's quarters, or a bachelor's rooms, the word is derived from the French *ecarter*, to set apart. If this be correct (though most dictionaries refer the word to the Latin *quartus*, a fourth) it gives a corresponding interpretation to the words " quarter-deck " and " quarter-master," the former being the deck set apart in a man-of-war for the use of the officers, and the latter denoting the officer who superintends the issue of stores set apart for the soldiers, and who arranges that suitable lodgings are set apart for them.

Queen. The word comes to us from the Anglo-Saxon *cwen* (hard " c "), cognate with the Sanscrit *jani*, and is found in similar forms throughout the whole range of the Aryan languages. It has the same root as " genus," " kin," etc., and simply means a woman. The word " quean," though now restricted in English use to a woman of worthless character, has the same derivation, and in the 18th century in England was, and in Scotland still is, used for a young woman without any implication of disrespect or contempt.

Queen of Heaven. This title for a deity is very ancient; we find it among the Egyptians, the Greeks, and the Romans, and though the Jews were vowed to the worship of the one God, Jehovah, they could not refrain from paying honour to the Queen of Heaven. In Jeremiah, vii. 18, we read that " the children gather wood, and the fathers kindle the fire, and the women knead their dough, to make cakes to the Queen of Heaven." And in the forty-fourth chapter of the same book (verses 17 and 25) we find the prophet sternly rebuking the practice of burning incense and pouring out libations and making vows to such a deity. Even to the present day the craving for the worship of deified woman-hood still subsists, and with the Roman Catholics the Virgin Mary is the Queen of Heaven.

Queenhithe (London). This wharf is said to have been named after Queen Eleanor, the wife of Henry II., from it having formed part of her dowry. The word " hithe " (q.v.) is the Anglo-Saxon term for a landing-place, of which we have several examples —such as Rotherhithe, Greenhithe, Lambeth (formerly Loamhithe), etc.

Queer Street. The phrase " to be in queer street " is usually applied to one who is in debt, or, at any rate, is of doubtful solvency. It is supposed to have originated from the practise of tradesmen marking the sign " query " against the name of a customer of whose credit they were doubtful.

Quibble. A " quibble " is a prevarication, an evasion of the truth, and the word is a diminutive of " quib," which is a variant of " quip," itself derived from the Welsh *chwip*, meaning a sharp turn, a brisk move, indicative of the quick turn of thought and ready action of the mind in giving an evasive answer to a question.

Quick. The word comes from the Anglo-Saxon *cwic*, from the same root as the Latin *vivere*, and the Sanscrit *jiv*, to live, and though in the strict sense of " alive " or " living " it is obsolete, we find that meaning attached to it both in the Bible and in the Church of England creeds. Also we retain the signification of life in such words as " quickset " hedge, one set with living hawthorn instead of dead wood, such as hurdles or palings; in " quicksands," meaning sands which move and shift as if alive; and in " quicksilver," which runs about like a living thing.

Quinsy. The word has a curious origin. It is an abbreviation of the Old French *squinancie*, which is derived from the Greek *kynanche*, the literal meaning of which is " dog-throttling " (*kyon*, a dog, and *anche*, strangulation). The disease is, as we know, an abscess on the tonsil, attended with difficulty of breathing and swallowing.

Quintessence. The word is generally used as an extravagant superlative, and yet its literal meaning is simply " fifth essence." The explanation seems to be that the ancients admitted four elements only —earth, air, fire and water. To these the Pythagoreans (the disciples of Pythagoras, the great philosopher, born about 540 B.C.) added a fifth, an element so pure and subtle that it flew upwards at creation and formed the stars. It was called the fifth essence—" quint-essence."

Quit. The word is but an abbreviated form of " quiet," and in its sense of being released from some debt, obligation or penalty, it distinctly conveys the idea of peace and quiet.

Quiz. A word which, according to Dr. Brewer, originated from the manager of a theatre having laid a wager that he would introduce into the language, within twenty-four hours, a new word of no meaning. Accordingly, on every wall and on all places accessible, were chalked up the four letters QUIZ. Soon all the town was enquiring what they meant, and the word became current in the English language.

Quod (otherwise **Quad**). A contraction of the word " quadrangle " in the sense of the court attached to a college or a jail, and hence used as a slang term for a prison (*See* In Quad.)

Quota. This is really a Latin word, meaning a proportionate share, and is derived from *quotus*, how great, and *quot*, how many. The word " quote " has the same derivation, and means, literally, to say how many, though it is now used in the sense of repeating a passage from a book or the words of a speech, or as adducing an authority or naming a price.

Quoth. This is properly the past tense of the verb " queath," which is now only used in the compound " be-queath." It is generally employed in the first and third persons only, and precedes instead of following its nominative—as, " quoth I," " quoth he." It is derived from the Anglo-Saxon *cwedhan*, to speak.

Rabbi. A great man among the Jews, distinguished for age, rank, office, or skill. The modern Jewish Rabbi is not a priest in the sense of the Old Testament; he is a teacher of the young, delivers sermons, and assists at marriages and divorces. Different degrees are indicated by the several terminations. Thus " Rab " is used for any teacher or master; " Rabbi " means my master, and is a term often used in addressing Christ; while " Rabbon " means our teacher, our master, and is the highest degree.

Radium. The word has been formed from the Latin *radius*, a ray. The knowledge of radium is generally attributed to the discovery by Henri Becquerel, in 1896, of the uranium rays, but there are prior claims in those of Niepce de St. Victor, though prominent among all research on the subject are the names of M. and Mme. Curie. This lady, in her recent lectures, has stated that there is no proof of radio-activity being a general property of matter, although she admits that such an opinion would be reasonable and natural. She accepts the theory which would make helium a constituent of all radio-active atoms, and declares that the discovery of the production of helium by radium is one of the most important facts in the history of radio-activity. She asserts that the determining cause of radio-active phenomena is still unknown, and that none of the attempts to accelerate the destruction of radium—which is spontaneously reduced to one-half in about 2,000 years!—has yet given any positive result.

Rag-bushes. It is a custom with pilgrims visiting holy wells, in the hope of freeing themselves from some physical or moral evil, to hang rags on the bushes or trees near at hand, which have thus gained the name of " rag-bushes." The practice is common, in all recorded ages, in every quarter of the world, and is undoubtedly a relic of tree-worship.

Ragout. This word is used for highly seasoned meat-stews, and is appropriately derived from the French word *ragoûter*, the literal meaning of which is to bring back taste (appetite).

Railways. As early as 1602, nearly two centuries before the introduction of the locomotive steam-engine, the colliers laid railways for the purpose of making it easier to draw coals from the pits to the ships waiting for their cargo. But the rails they employed were made of wood, and it was not until 1767 that iron rails were used. On the modern railway the rails are generally of steel—the first steel rail was made in 1857—and the line is carried across country as nearly straight as possible; over valleys by embankments and

T

viaducts, over roads and rivers by bridges, through hills or elevated ground by tunnels or cuttings. The way or track of the railway is called the permanent way, and the distance between the two parallel rails on which the train runs is called the gauge. Until recently the motive power generally employed on railways has been steam, but that has now been superseded by electricity on the underground and suburban lines, and though it may be thought that the improvement in methods of railway transit has not been great since 1825, when the first railway was opened between Stockton and Darlington, there is now some prospect of decided advance. In the United States, where transit, particularly in regard to electric tramways, is in many ways better organised than in England, railways are called railroads.

Ransack. The word means, in its literal sense, to search thoroughly, and in most languages of Northern Europe we find similar words, all with the signification of searching. For instance, the Islandic *rannsaka* (from which the English " ransack " is derived) means to search a house, from *rann*, a house, and *sœkja*, to seek.

Rath. This is a word which is often found in Irish place-names, as in Rath-boyne, Rath-lin, and Rathmore. It is of Irish origin, and signifies a round earthen fort.

Raven. In the Anglo-Saxon the word is *hrefn* ("h" silent), and in Danish and German it is very similar—there seems no doubt that the name came from the cry of the bird. The raven plays an important part in mythology and folklore, and figures very early in Old Testament history as the bird first sent by Noah out of the ark after the Deluge (Gen. viii. 7); while it was by ravens that Elijah was fed (1 Kings xvii. 6) when he was hiding from the wrath of Ahab at the beginning of the three years' drought which the prophet had foretold. The raven was the bird of Odin, and in classic mythology was accounted of ill-omen, a character attributed to it by early English writers, and which it still bears, for there is a wide-spread belief in rural England that its appearance forebodes misfortune, a superstition which perhaps has arisen from the grave manner of the bird and its sable plumage.

Reaping-hook. The curved blade of steel, set in a short handle and used for reaping, is an instrument of great antiquity. In a harvest scene on a tomb at Thebes, dated B.C. 1490, a reaping hook is represented.

Receipt, Recipe. A "receipt" is a written or printed direction for compounding or mixing together certain ingredients, and is also a written discharge to a debtor for the payment of a debt. The word "recipe" is only properly used medically. It is the Latin for "take," and contracted into "R" it is used as a prefix to doctors' prescriptions.

Record Office. A large building in Fetter Lane, London, used for the preservation of public records, as its name indicates. The value and interest attached to some of these records is very great; among them is the original Domesday Book, the treaty of the Field of the Cloth of Gold, and the Papal Bull by which the title of Defender of the Faith was conferred on Henry VIII.

Recreant. This word is derived from the Low Latin, *recredere*, the literal meaning of which is to believe again. But it is more often used to denote one who is apostate and false; one who is cowardly and crying out for mercy. The "recreant knight" is familiar in many an old story.

Rector. The literal meaning of the word is one who rules, its derivation being the Latin *rectus*, the past participle of *regere*, to rule. In the Church of England the Rector is the clergyman of the parish where the tithes belong to him, as distinguished from the Vicar of the parish where the tithes are otherwise appropriated.

Reduce. This word which we now use in the sense of to bring into a lower state, to lessen, to impoverish, is an instance of a word changing its meaning in the course of time. Originally it meant to bring back, and this is the literal meaning, since the derivation is the Latin *re*, back, and *duco*, I lead. Bishop Taylor says, " A good man will go a little out of his road to ' reduce ' the wandering traveller."

Reply. We often use this word—which is derived from the Latin, *replicare*, to turn back—in the sense of answer. Its real meaning is something following an answer. Thus A. writes a letter ; B. answers it, asking some further question, and A. gives a reply.

Rhapsody. The original meaning of a rhapsody was the song of a Rhapsodist, one of a class of wandering minstrels in ancient Greece, who recited epics in public places. These recitations may be regarded as the forerunners of stage acting, and as forming, when combined with the Bacchic chorus, the complete Greek drama.

Rhe, Rhin. This is a root which is found in the names of many rivers. It is connected with the Gaelic *rea*, rapid, and with the Welsh *rhe*, swift, while it gains the signification of " running " from the Welsh *rhedu*, to run, and *rhin*, that which runs. Examples may be found in the Rhee, in Cambridgeshire, the Rhea, in Staffordshire, the Rea, in Salop and elsewhere, the Rye, in Yorkshire, the Rey and the Ray, in Wiltshire and Oxfordshire, and the Wrey, in Devonshire. Also we find this root in the Rhine and the Rhone, and in the Roden in Essex and the Ribble in Lancashire. Moreover, the same root appears in place-names, where it denotes a promontory, a point of land which

" runs " out to sea. Penrhyn, near Bangor, Penryn, in Cornwall, and Rinmore, in Devon, are all examples.

Rhetoric. The word comes from the Greek *rhetor*, an orator, and was originally confined to the art of speaking effectively in public, though now extended so as to include all eloquence, whether spoken or written. As early as the time of Aristotle (B.C. 384-322) there was a science of rhetoric, and his treatise on the subject is still valuable in its suggestions. Broadly speaking, the aim of rhetoric is to expound the rules of prose composition or speech, and it includes within its province accuracy of expression, the structure of periods, and figures of speech.

Rhubarb. This plant—the stalks of which make so familiar and acceptable an addition to our dietary in Spring, and the root of which is so valuable in medicine—gains its name from the Greek *rheon barbaron*, the literal meaning of which may be rendered as " the article which comes from the barbarous country of the river Rha," *Rha* being the old Greek name for the river Volga, on the banks of which rhubarb was indigenous. The word *Rha* means a flowing, a flux, and from *rheon*, its adjectival form, we get our words " rheum " (aches and pains) and " rheumatism."

Rhyme. The word comes to us from the Anglo-Saxon *rim*, meaning number, computation, and Skeat tells us that the spelling " rhyme " is not earlier than 1550. Rhyme consists of an identity in both vowel and consonant sounds, as in " try " and " cry," " light " and " sight," though difference in preceding consonants is permitted in such words as " way " and " lay," " find " and " mind." Words like " oar " and " o'er," " eye " and " I " are assonances, not true rhymes.

Rice. This grain must have been used for food from very early times in the world's history, and the similarity of the name in various languages is an indication of the fact. It is a marsh plant, and is believed to be a native of southern Asia, though it has been found, apparently growing wild, along some rivers of South America. It probably supports a larger number of the human race than any other cereal or any other plant.

Ricochet-Words.　Another name for words which are reduplicated as a means of intensifying their force, such as chit-chat, ding-dong, helter-skelter, hob-nob, riff-raff, see-saw, tittle-tattle, etc.　There are also words under this heading that are rhyming synonyms, such as musty-fusty, rosy-posy; wear and tear, high and mighty; while some have the Anglo-Saxon letter-rhyme, amongst which are safe and sound, jog-trot, etc.

Riddle.　Apparently this word would be more properly spelt with a final " s," as it comes from the Anglo-Saxon *rædelse* (plural *rædelsan*), from *rædan*, to read, to interpret.　Anything which man finds difficult to interpret he calls a riddle, but the greatest problem of all is man himself, who is (says Pope) :—
> " Great lord of all things, yet a prey to all;
> Sole judge of truth, in endless error hurled;
> The glory, jest, and riddle of the world ! "
> (" Essay on Man.")

Riff-Raff.　Skeat tells us that " rif and raf " was the Middle English for this term, derived from the Old French *rif et raf*, from *rifler*, to rifle, to ransack, and *rafler*, to snatch up.　Hence the words *rif* and *raf* came to denote particles of refuse and rubbish, and are applied to the scum and worthless characters of society.

Righteous.　The word—which used sometimes to be written " ryghtwys "—is formed of the two words " right " and " wise," and is derived from the Latin *rectus*, a past participle of *regere*, to direct to guide, to rule (as a straight line is ruled).　So that it may be truly said that the righteous man is he who is upright and wise, keeping to a rule he believes to be good, not swerving from the straight path in which he has set himself to walk. And the idea that straightness and wisdom are constituents of righteousness is indicated by the Psalmist, when he says :—" O that my ways were made so direct that I might keep thy statutes. Open my eyes that I may see the wondrous things of Thy law; give me understanding, and I shall keep Thy law; yea, I shall keep it with my whole heart." (Ps. cxix., 5, 18, 34. Prayer-book version.)

Rival. The word comes from the Latin *rivalis*, which is derived from *rivus*, a stream, a river. Trench tells us that the word " rivals ' is properly applicable to those who dwell on opposite banks of the same river, and that as such people are under strong temptation to quarrel about water privileges, it came to mean any who are in competition with each other and disposed to quarrel.

Roam. The etymology of the word is doubtful. Skeat suggests an Anglo-Saxon derivation, from the *ramian* (not hitherto found), meaning to stretch after, and hence to journey or rove about. But he adds, " it can hardly be doubted that the use of the word was largely influenced by the word ' Rome,' on account of the frequent pilgrimages thither."

Rob. It is curious to notice what an importance is given to clothing in old days, not only as an evidence of rank and position, but also by reason of its intrinsic value. We read, for instance, that the man who fell among thieves on his way from Jerusalem to Jericho was stripped of his raiment (Luke x. 30); and the pitiful clothing which was worn by Christ was eagerly divided and cast lots for by the Roman soldiers who had to carry out the sentence of crucifixion (John xix. 23, 24).

And this word " rob " is closely connected with clothing; it comes from the Old French *robbe* or *robe*, which means a robe, and its original sense was to despoil the slain in battle, to strip, to disrobe. In a similar manner the English " bereave " is formed from the Anglo-Saxon *reaf*, which means clothing.

Rococo. The term is employed to denote a bad taste in design and ornament generally, of a style which is lavish in its details, thrown together without propriety in effect or connection in idea. The word is derived from the French *rocaille*, which means rock-work.

Rontgen Rays. (*See* X-RAYS.)

Ros. This is a Gaelic syllable which frequently enters into place-names, where it signifies a prominent rock or headland. It must not be confused with the Welsh " rhos," which means a moor, and which is cognate with the Latin *rus*, indicating the country in its undrained moorland condition. Ross in Herefordshire, and in Northumberland, Rosneath by Loch Long, and Rosduy on Loch Lomond, are examples of the Gaelic " ros "—they are all on projecting points of land; while Penrhos, which occurs both in Wales and in Cornwall, and probably Melrose (if derived from the Celtic *maol ros*, the bare moor) indicate places situated on the moorland.

Rosetta-Stone. A slab of black basalt, found at Rosetta, in Egypt, in 1799, upon which was inscribed—first in hieroglyphics, secondly in the cursive writing of the period of the inscription, and thirdly in Greek—a decree of the priests of Egypt assembled in synod at Memphis, in honour of Ptolemy V. The inscription being thus repeated in three different characters, of which the Greek was known, became the means whereby the hieroglyphics of ancient Egypt were first deciphered. (*See* HIEROGLYPHICS.)

Rubicon. The phrase " to cross the Rubicon " means to take a decisive step in any enterprise, and arises from the legend that, at the breaking out of the Civil War with Pompey, Cæsar with his army crossed the stream called the Rubicon, exclaiming " The die is cast." For although the position of the Rubicon has not been exactly identified it is known to be one of three streams falling into the Adriatic and forming part of the northern boundary of Italy proper, and on that account the Roman generals were forbidden to pass it with an armed force, as to do so was considered equivalent to a declaration of war.

Rudge. As a component in place-names this word means a back or ridge, such, for instance, as that formed by the North and South Downs in Surrey and Sussex. Rudge, Rugeley and Reigate are examples.

Runes. It has been said that " the mystic Woden, or Odin, the inventor of runes, claims a higher place in the literature of Northern Europe than the Greek Cadmus." Runic characters are formed almost entirely of straight lines, and are supposed by Schlegel to have been derived from the Phœnicians, while another theory is that they are the original characters of the Indo-Germanic tribes, brought from the East. The knowledge of Runes was confined to a small class, and they were used for purposes of augury and as magical symbols. The word " rune " comes from the Anglo-Saxon *rūn*, meaning a mystery, a secret, and is cognate with the Middle English " roun " or " round," to whisper.

Ruth. The Book of Ruth is a beautiful and idyllic composition in pure Hebrew, written most probably shortly previous to, or during, the Exile. Its right to be included in the Old Testament seems never to have been questioned, perhaps because of the romantic marriage which the story relates as having taken place between Ruth and her aged kinsman Boaz, and by which Ruth ultimately became the great-grandmother of King David, and thus an ancestress of Jesus Christ. The word "Ruth," as used in the Hebrew text, is probably a contraction of *reuth*, signifying comely aspect, beauty.

S.P.Q.R. *Senātus Populus Que Romānus* (the Roman Senate and People). These words, which were inscribed on the standards of ancient Rome, have been satirised by the modern shopkeeper, who uses them to signify "Small Profits, Quick Returns."

Sabbath Day's Journey. With the Jews the allowable Sabbath day's journey was not to exceed the distance between the Ark and the extreme end of the camp—altogether 2,000 cubits, rather less than an English mile. The distance between the Mount of Olives and Jerusalem is given as a Sabbath Day's journey, in Acts i. 12.

Sack. (A bag.) When Joseph's brethren went down into Egypt, before they departed, "Joseph commanded to fill their ' sacks ' with corn." (Gen. xliii. 25). The Hebrew word is *saq*, and in a very similar form it may be found in Egyptian, Ethiopic, Greek, Latin, Scandinavian, and in most other languages. The ancients had no carts; everything had to be conveyed in sacks, often for long distances, by trains of camels and asses. The sacks would be suspended, by proper adjustment, on each side of the animal, and thus the word "sack" seems to have something to do with the equal distribution of weight or the right adjustment of a load, as in the verb to "sag," which means to sway with its own weight, to drop as with a burden (akin to Swedish *sacka*, to sink down; German *sacken*, to sink). And because when you lose a thing you stoop or sink down to look for it, the Scandinavian *sacka* meant also to seek; a meaning which is retained in the word "ran-sack," and in the phrase "to sack a city," sometimes interpreted as alluding to the sacks in which the soldiers carried off their booty. But to "sack" a city was to "seek" for treasure.

"To get the sack," "to give the sack," "I'll sack you," are all phrases indicative of a servant's dismissal, and are commonly said to arise from the master giving the servant his sack of belongings when he told him to quit. Yet the word had a wider meaning—the servant who left with his sack on his back had a place to "seek." "I'll 'sack' you" is equivalent to saying "I'll make you to 'seek' elsewhere."

There is a tradition that the word "sack" was the last uttered before the confounding of tongues, because, in the quaint wording of Dr. Johnson, "It is observable of this word that it is found in all languages, and it is therefore conceived to be antediluvian."

Sack. (Wine.) Some authorities believe the name to be derived from the French *sec*, dry. Others state that it was so called from having been brought down from the mountains in goat-skins, bags, or sacks.

Sacrament—from the Latin *sacramentum*. The oath of fidelity taken by soldiers on their enlistment into the Roman army. In the churches the word is used to signify a sacred token or pledge, or as the Church of England Catechism puts it: "An outward and visible sign of an inward and spiritual grace." The Roman Catholic Church acknowledges seven Sacraments—Baptism, Confirmation, the Eucharist, Penance, Orders, Matrimony, and Extreme Unction. The two sacraments of the Protestant Churches are Baptism and the Lord's Supper.

Sad. In early English this word seems to have been used in the sense of firm, settled, steady. The passage in the Bible "it was founded upon a rock" (Luke vi. 48) appears in Wickliffe's translation "it was foundid on a 'sad' stoon." Bread which is heavy or ill-made is still called "sad" bread.

Sadder and a Wiser Man. From the "Ancient
Mariner ":—

>"A sadder and a wiser man
>He rose the morrow morn."

>(Coleridge.)

Saddle. The saddle, like the yoke, was a grievance—
but one which must be borne. Hence, to be
"saddled" with anything is to have something
thrust upon you, and if you are blamed for some-
body else's fault you tell the accuser "to put the
saddle on the right horse." The saddle, like bit
and bridle, is of unknown antiquity, and it is not
wonderful, therefore, to find a great similarity in
the name in all Teutonic languages. Thus, for our
word "saddle" we have *sadel, zadel,* and *sattel,*
respectively, in Anglo-Saxon, Dutch and German;
while correspondingly, for our word "sad" (the
first syllable of "saddle") we get *sæd, zat,* and
satt; and it is certainly remarkable that the word
"sad" conveys an implication of that weariness
and tameness which the saddle has imposed on the
animal.

Safe. In barbarous times the man who was possessed
of any treasure had to find a secret place in which
he could hide it away; he would wrap it in a cloth
and bury it in a hole, like the slave who received
the one talent (Matt. xxv., 18)—as long as
he *alone* knew where it was he reckoned it was *safe.*
And our word "safe" is derived through the
Latin *salvus* and the Old French *sauf,* from the
Latin *solus,* alone.

To Sail close to the Wind. The phrase is an allusion
to the dangerous practice of sailing a boat so close
to the wind that it may at any moment heel over
and be swamped. In other words, it inculcates
that the upright position is the safe one, and that
"honesty is the best policy," even if the end in
view be not so quickly gained.

St. Andrew Undershaft. This church, standing at the
corner of Leadenhall Street and St. Mary's Avenue,

London, was so called because a shaft or maypole, much taller than the Church itself, was raised every year in its vicinity. Between one May-day and another, this Maypole was hung on hooks over the doors of a row of houses in *Shaft* Alley, near by. The last time the Maypole was set up was the May-day of 1517.

St. Paul's School. Dean Colet founded this school in 1509 for the free education of 153 poor scholars, the supposed number of the miraculous draft of fishes. (John xxi. 11.) The same number of scholars may still obtain a free education there, although others are now admitted for payment.

Sake. " For old sake's sake " is a phrase without parallel in the depth of its meaning, though, perhaps, the Scotch version " for auld lang syne " is not far from it. " For the sake of " means " because of," and " because of the cause " would be a fair rendering of " sake's sake." But no word can quite supply the place of " sake," for the Latin *causa* does not convey the sense of affectionate memory which clings to the Anglo-Saxon " sake "; and it is a pity that, while we retain the negative verb " to forsake " (to desert, not to stand by, a friend), the verb " to sake " is wanting. For the Anglo-Saxon *sacan*, to strive, and *sacu*, strife, from which we get " sake," recalled the striving together, side by side, against the common foe— the very word meant not only the fray but the memory of all that a comrade had been in many a perilous moment. No more fitting phrase, therefore, could be found to cherish the memory of old memories, by reason of the old reason, than " for old sake's sake."

Salary. The Romans made a daily allowance to their soldiers for salt which was called *salarium*, meaning " salt money." Hence came our word " salary." (*See* " Not Worth His Salt.")

Salt-cellar is a curiosity among words, its literal meaning being " salt-salt-holder," as " cellar " is a corruption of the French *salière*, a salt-holder. (*See* "Not Worth His Salt.")

Salute. From the Latin *salus*, health; to enquire after another's health in greeting. To discharge guns in a salute is to show that as no fear exists, no armament will be needed. A Royal Salute consists of firing twenty-one great guns. Various are the ways of salutation—to shake hands, to curtsey, to take off the hat, to present arms.

Salvo. The name which is given to the discharge of artillery in honour or welcome, a salute. The word comes from the Latin *Salve!* Hail! and *salvere*, to be well.

Sampler. In old days every little girl worked her sampler as a specimen of her skill in needlework. It was worked on fine canvas in cross-stitch, and was sometimes very elaborate. The alphabet, in various letterings, and the worker's name usually formed part of every sampler.

Sanscrit. The word denotes the ancient literary language of India, the most easterly of a range of languages reaching from Northern India, across Europe, to Iceland. We have no certain knowledge as to which is the older—Sanscrit at the one end or Icelandic at the other, but while Sanscrit is a dead language, Icelandic is still spoken. The whole range may be compared to a musical scale, the tones and semi-tones of which may be said to represent the various divisions of national tongues. Some strange tones occur which do not belong to this scale, such as those of the Basques in Spain, the Turks, the Magyars in Hungary, and the Finns; but with these exceptions all the people and tongues in this region are called Aryan. In the Chinese group of languages, words can only be piled together like stones, but in the Aryan languages they can be conjugated (yoked together, as the Latin *conjugatum* means), or made to fit; and the word " Sanscrit " is derived from the Sanscrit *sam*, together, and *krita*, perfected, fitted.

Sandwich. Originally meat between two pieces of bread, although now sandwiches have many forms. They were named, in the reign of George III., after the Earl of Sandwich, who was so great a gambler that he could not wait to eat his meals, but took his food in this form while he continued his play.

Santa Claus. (Sauk'ni Kolaus, *i.e.*, St. Nicolas), the patron Saint of children. St. Nicholas' Day is December 6th. In old days it was the custom for someone to dress up on December 5th to distribute toys among the good children. Nowadays, children are taught to expect the visit of Santa Claus late on Christmas Eve. A stocking is hung up and filled by parent or friend, and the little one only dreams of keeping awake to see the toy-laden Saint come down the chimney.

Sapper. A military term which has nothing to do with the sap of a plant or a tree, but which is applied to the Royal Engineers, who were originally organised as " Sappers and Miners." Their duties are many and various—erecting telegraphs and laying pontoons, preparing submarine mines and executing general survey work, acting in garrison as skilled mechanics, etc. The word " sap " comes from the Latin *sapa*, a pickaxe, and indicates the process of undermining. A weakening disease is said to " sap " the vital energies, or to " sap " the life-blood, while it is a common expression to say that a person's health has been " undermined."

Saracen. The sign of the " Saracen's Head " and the silk called " sarcenet " (from the Latin *Saracenicus-pannus*, Saracen-cloth) were introduced by the Crusaders who fought the Saracens, the Mahomedans who had possession of the Holy Sepulchre at Jerusalem. But familiar though the name " Saracen " was to the Crusaders, and in spite of the numerous Mahomedans now existing in various countries, there are now no people to whom the name " Saracen " is applied. This may be explained, perhaps, by the fact that the

Arabic name for the Mahomedans of the West (*i.e.*, the inhabitants of Morocco, whence the name " Moors ") was *Maghribe*, meaning the Western people, while those in Palestine and Asia were called *Sharkeyn*, the Eastern people, whence came the name " Saracen." Neither of the old Arabic names has survived; that for the Western people has become " Moors," from their country Morocco, while of that for the Eastern people—the Saracens—there is no trace among existing peoples.

Sarcasm.   A holding up to ridicule, a flaying with the tongue, a taunt.   From the Greek, *sarkayo*, to flay.

Sardonic.   In Sardinia there was said to be only one deadly herb, and that of such a character that those who ate of it died laughing.   From this reputed fact comes the word " sardonic," laughter in which evil lurks.   Homer makes the first use of the expression.

Sash Windows.   This form of window came into use after the Fire of London.   Formerly all windows were casements, opening out, instead of up or down.   The word " sash " comes from the French *chassis*, a variant of *chasse*, a shrine, which is derived from the Latin *capsa*, a boy, a case.

Satan.   A Hebrew word (*sātān*) meaning an enemy—the enemy of mankind; or, as Milton says in " Paradise Lost," " the adversary of God and Man."

Satin.   A silk material with such a glossy surface that it shines.   The literal meaning of the word " satin " is glossy like the hair, from the Latin *setinus*, glossy, an adjective derived from *seta*, the hair, To describe the beautiful gloss of chestnut hair, Tennyson takes the simile of the rich polish on the newly opened chestnut :—
> " The colour of the chestnut when the shell
> Divides three-fold and shows the fruit within."

Sauce—Scaramouch 299

And, indeed, the gloss of the chestnut when it first breaks would "take the shine out of" satin itself.

Sauce. The literal meaning of "sauce" is but "salted" (the Latin *salsus*, from *sal*, salt), and even the poor man can now easily get salt. But the real "poor man's sauce" is hunger, and "the best sauce is appetite."

Saucer. The word is now only used for the shallow dish which holds a teacup, but formerly it denoted a vessel in which ordinary cooked vegetables were served, then called "sauces," probably from the Latin *salsus*, salted, salt being a necessary accompaniment to vegetables. At that time "saucer" was spelt "sawser."

Scale. This is a Norse word denoting a shepherd's hut, and analogous to the Scotch word "shealing." It is found as a component in place-names, as, for instance, in Portin-scale, Scal-loway, and possibly in Shields, Galashields, and Sel-kirk.

Scamp. The very derivation of this word is an indication of the ignominy it conveys, for "scamp" comes from the Old French *escamper*, to flee, through the Latin *ex*, out of, and *campus*, the battle-field.

Scar. This is found as a component in place-names such as Scar-borough, the Skerries, and Skerry-vore. It is a Norse word meaning a cliff, the face of a rock, and is cognate with the Anglo-Saxon *sciran*, to divide. Hence, as pointed out by Isaac Taylor, we have "shire," a division of a country, the "shore" which divides the land from the sea, the plough-"share" and the "shears," instruments for dividing, and "share," a divided part. The primary meaning of "score" is to make notches on a stick or to divide (partially) by means of gashes, and a "scar" is the mark where the flesh has been divided.

Scaramouch. A term which is often used in a kind of friendly contempt for a slouching, untidy person,

U

and which is supposed to be derived from the name
Scaramuccia, a famous Italian buffoon, who acted
in England in 1673 and died in Paris in
1694. The Scaramouch was a character
in old Italian comedy who acted the part
of a boastful poltroon, and hence the word
has been used to denote a cowardly braggadocio.

Scarce. Gold and precious stones are of value because
they are scarce, and because they have to be carefully searched for and picked out from among tons
of refuse material. And the word " scarce " is
derived from the Low Latin *ex-carpsus*, picked out.
To get the " pick " of anything is to get the best,
and the best is always " scarce."

Scenery. People now travel all over the world for the
express purpose of seeing beautiful scenery, but
this, of course, was impossible in the days when
locomotion was so much more arduous, and the
very word " scenery " is of modern use in its present
application. For the primary meaning of " scene "
(from the Greek *skene*) was a covered place, whence
it came to mean a booth, a stage on which actors
perform, and thus the painted representation of a
scene on a stage was called " scenery. " But now
we have a much wider signification for the word,
so that Shakespeare's phrase " all the world's a
stage " bears a more literal interpretation than even
he anticipated.

Scent. As this word is derived from the Latin *sentire*,
to discern by the senses, the mute " c " which has
become incorporated in the spelling appears superfluous. In the word " sense," which is also derived
from *sentire*, it has found no place.

Schedule. The word comes from the Latin *scheda*, a
strip of papyrus, or, it may be, from the Greek
schede, anything formed by cleaving, a leaf. Both
these derivations are significant, for while the first
recalls the papyrus-strips which formed the
Egyptian overseer's day-book for registering the
work done by each workman under his control,
the second is reminiscent of the dried palm-leaves

on which were inscribed that most ancient literature—the sacred Vedas of India.

But the word " schedule " may also denote a blank form, and thus reminds us of the " new leaf " to which we all desire to " turn over "— a leaf which is fair and clean, ready to receive an account of deeds better than those hitherto recorded; while the phrase " to turn over a new leaf " brings to mind the kindred phrase " to take a leaf out of his book "—suggestive of taking the leaf and reading what another has accomplished, to follow his example.

School. The derivation of the word—the Greek *schole*—meant leisure, for the acquisition of true learning needs leisure; but while the scholar eats the fruit of the labourer's sowing, the labourer reaps the benefit of the knowledge which the scholar gathers. The word " school " is applied, like the word " church," to a building, but in each case the fuller meaning is that of a company of people. Thus a " school of learning " numbers all those who devote themselves to the same branch of study; a " school of fish " is a multitude of the same kind swimming together; while the " school of adversity " is the one universal school. Talking of schools, one recalls Tennyson's lines in " Merlin and Vivien " :—

" And smiling as a master smiles at one
Who is not of his school, nor any school,
. . . . . . he answered her."

Schooner. The word is said to have been coined in New England from the Provincial English " scoon," which is used to describe the throwing of a flat stone upon the water in such a way as to make it skip along the surface of the water. The schooner is a two-masted, sharp-built, swift-sailing vessel which rides lightly upon the waves.

Score. Our forefathers reckoned by scores—" the days of our age are three-score years and ten," says the Psalmist—and this system of keeping count propably represented the practice of counting by fingers and toes. But the word "score" comes from the Anglo-Saxon *scoren*, the past participle of *sceran*, to cut, and indicated a notch or incision made on a stick—a tally—(q.v.), for the purpose of keeping a reckoning. Shakespeare refers to the system :—" Our forefathers had no other books but the score and the tally." (1 Henry VI., iv. 7). Hence " to pay off old scores " is not only to pay off old debts, but to revenge grievances which have cut deep and left a lasting impression, for the number twenty was denoted on the tally by a cut longer and deeper than the others.

Scot and Lot. The word " scot " in this phrase comes from the Anglo-Saxon *sceot*, the literal meaning of which is that which is " shot " into a general fund, and it was applied to any tax or payment or con-tribution. Thus the term " scot-free " is equiva-lent to " tax-free." The word " lot " in this con-nection meant the proportionate payment allotted to and required from each person, and thus when persons were taxed, not to the same amount but according to the estimated ability allotted to them, they were said to pay " scot and lot."

Scotland Yard (London). So called because it was the site of a palace built for the use of the Kings of Scot-land when they visited England. The last of the Scottish Royal family to stay there was Margaret, Queen of James IV. Scotland Yard is now the headquarters of the Metropolitan Police.

Scoundrel. A low, mean fellow—one who should be " shunned." For the word " scoundrel " comes from the Anglo-Saxon *scunner*, *scunian*, to loathe, to shun, with the suffix " el," and the insertion of an extraneous " d," as in " thunder " and " tender."

Scratch-cradle, or Cat's Cradle. A corruption of Cratch-cradle, " cratch " being an old English name for a rack in which hay is put for cattle. And the first figure in the game, which is played with a piece of string stretched across two hands, is supposed to represent the manger-cradle of the Infant Christ.

Scrip. This word is not connected with " scrip " or " script," a writing, but is derived from the Icelandic *skreppa*, and means a bag, a wallet. The scrip for the journey referred to in Matt. x. 10, was doubtless a wallet or satchel in which food was carried.

Scruple. Before the general use of metals, when the balance was made of wood, a sharp-edged stone (Latin *scrupus*, a sharp stone) was used as a pivot on which to rest the balance-bar. The diminutive of this (the *scrupulus*), quite a little stone of 20 grains, was used as a weight. In weighing so small a quantity you would watch the quivering balance for some time, with scrupulous care, before deciding whether you had a grain too much or too little. To have a scruple is to be not quite sure if you are doing right—you weigh the matter in your mind and hesitate. The *scrupus* was anxiously watched by both buyer and seller, and thus the word meant not only a sharp stone, but also anxiety.

Search. While to seek is look anywhere, to search is to look for something known, or believed to lie within a certain radius. If we drop anything we walk round and round the spot looking for it. And the derivation of the word " search " is the Latin, *circāre*, to go about, *circus*, a circle. The French, by taking the first syllables, have abbreviated the two words to *chercher*, which we have contracted into " search."

Sea-Serpent. An animal of immense size, said to inhabit the ocean, but concerning which nothing definite is known. One of the first detailed accounts of modern times appeared in a book on natural history published in 1755, in which the sea-serpent is figured as raising itself from the water and spouting, but this figure has been matched with that of a squid. More recently several appearances of the sea-serpent have been recorded,—

notably by Captain M'quhae, of H.M.S. "Daeda-lus," in 1848; by the Master and the crew of the "Pauline," of London, in 1875; by Lieut. Haynes, of the Royal yacht "Osborne," in 1877; and by Major Senior, from the "City of Baltimore," in 1879. In all these cases the observers testify to having seen a monstrous animal of serpent-like form, and their good faith is beyond question. And although many sea-serpent stories have been satis-factorily explained away by the deceptive appear-ance which distance may lend to well-known natural objects, there still remains a residium sufficient to prevent modern Zoologists from deny-ing the possibility that some such creature as a sea-serpent may exist.

Second (of time). The Romans called the sixtieth part of an hour *scrupulum*. The sixtieth part of a " scrupulum " they called *scrupulum-secundum*, corresponding to our " second."

See. A bishop's " see " is really his " seat," the word being derived from the Latin, *sedes*, a seat; but generally it is used to denote the full extent of his jurisdiction.

Seedy. Weary, worn out, out of sorts, run to seed. Though generally supposed to be modern slang, this word dates, at least, from Goldsmith's time, as he writes :—" Little Flanigan here is a little seedy."

Sepoy. A corruption of the Indian word, *sipahi*, a soldier. " Sipahi" is derived from *sip*, a bow and arrow, the ancient equipment of an Indian warrior. A sepoy is now an Indian soldier in the British service.

Serene. " It's all serene." From the Spanish *sere'no*, all right !—the sentinel's countersign.

Set, Seter, Ster. Some variant of these words is a frequent suffix in place-names. They all signify a seat, a settlement, a dwelling, the first being of Anglo-Saxon and the two latter of Norse origin.

Such examples as Dorset and Somerset, on the one hand, and Ellan-seter and Ul-ster on the other, may be cited.

Settle. The settle, the chest, and the board (table) were the three requirements of the living-room in the old farm-house. A settle is a long, high-backed, oak bench, with arms at each end. Here on the settle, when the day's work was done, the farmer and his men settled themselves; and if he and his neighbour had any business to talk over they settled themselves on the settle and settled it. For the derivation of the word "settle," in whatever sense it may be used, is the Anglo-Saxon *setl*, a seat.

Seven. Seven removes was the limit of relationship, or family tie, among the Jews, and as kinship could stretch no farther, seven became a figure of extreme forbearance—"How oft shall my brother sin against me and I forgive him? Till seven times?" (Matt. xviii. 21). The wise men of old were infatuated with the number seven; they saw there were seven openings to the head—two eyes, typifying the sun and moon, and five entrances by the nostrils, ears and mouth, corresponding with the five planets, those mysterious wanderers in the heavens. This analogy, they said, had existed for all ages, and who was Copernicus that he should dare to upset it by pretending that the earth was another planet? Such a contention was almost blasphemous. Were there not seven days of the week, seven gifts of the Holy Ghost, seven Dolours of Our Lady, seven deadly sins, seven cardinal virtues, seven churches of Asia, seven sages, seven champions of Christendom, seven wonders of the world? So they consigned him to—well, *not* to the seventh heaven.

Sex. When this word appears as a suffix to the names of our counties it denotes the Saxon people, as in Es-sex, the kingdom of the East Saxons, Middle-sex, of the Central Saxons, Sussex, of the South Saxons, and the division formerly known as Wessex, of the West Saxons. These names are an indication of the state of our island at that time, not only divided between hostile peoples—Saxon, Celt and Dane—but the Saxons themselves at variance with each other. This suffix " sex " comes from the Anglo-Saxon *seax*, a word which is derived from the Old High German *sahs*, a short sword, and it was applied to the people we now call Saxons, because they carried such a weapon.

Sham and Shame. The derivation of the two words is probably identical, and is cognate with the Icelandic *skomm*, which means a wound. To be wounded, and thus vanquished, was to be put to shame; to pretend to be wounded was also a shame —a sham. And the shame of being wounded may be compared with the shame of wounded modesty, as to be exposed or wounded in one's self-esteem is to be put to shame. The phrase " speak the truth and shame the devil " implies that even the devil can be wounded, if not vanquished.

Shambles. The word originally meant benches—the benches on which meat was exposed for sale. It comes from the Anglo-Saxon *scamel*; and the Latin *scamellam*, a little bench. Our modern use of the word is to denote the building or yard where cattle are slaughtered.

Shawl. The word is of foreign origin—the Persian *shāl*. Cashmere shawls, and other expensive shawls of Eastern manufacture, were much in vogue in former years, but the old English outer garment, for both men and women, was the cloak. (" Now they have no cloke for their sin "—John xv. 22. " We should not dissemble nor cloke them (our sins) before the face of Almighty God " —Prayer-Book exhortation.) The merchant princes of London, and their ladies, wore long cloaks trimmed with furs; the watchman and the shepherd had each his cloak, and the farmer's wife stood in her cloak in the market town to sell her butter and eggs. But in 1562, Anthony Jenkinson, having voyaged to Lapland, and crossed Russia, reached Persia, bearing a letter on behalf of the Merchant Adventurers of London from Queen Elizabeth to the Shah, who presented him with a wondrous rich cloak of cloth of gold—a shawl.

Shilling. According to Skeat this word is derived from the verb *scylan*, to divide. The original shilling was marked with a deeply indented cross, and was divided up into halves or quarters.

Ship. The word ship is supposed to come from something " shaped," and a ship was originally nothing more than a tree trunk scooped out, shaped to float safely on the water.

Ship-shape. As neatly arranged as things on a ship, where, by reason of the confined space, great neatness is imperative.

Shire. The word originated in the Anglo-Saxon *scire*, from *sciran*, to divide. When the Saxon kings created an Earl, they gave him a Shire, or division of land; but at the Norman Conquest, Earls were, at first, called Counts, and the inference is that the Earldom thus became a County. An Earl's wife is still called a Countess.

Shoe at Weddings. The practice of throwing an old shoe after a bride is supposed to be for luck. But the custom originated from a Jewish formality, in which the bridegroom strikes the bride with his shoe to signify the obedience of the wife and the supremacy of the husband. The shoe played an important part in the symbolism of the Jews. We have an example in the Psalmist's phrase—" Over Edom will I cast out my shoe " (Ps. lx. 8), which is descriptive, in a figurative way, of the lordship assumed over Edom, and we know that, on the other hand, the removal of the shoe when entering any holy place was an expression of humility and unworthiness.

Shrew. The little animal of this name closely resembles the mouse in general form and appearance, with a long head and sharp-pointed muzzle. Its bite is sharp, and was supposed to be venomous, and hence the application of the word " shrew " to a woman with a long and sharp tongue. But withal, the creature was considered a clever little beast, and though it was an evil thing for a woman to get the name of a " shrew," it is by no means uncomplimentary to call a man " shrewd."

Sick. This word is used by the Americans in the sense that we use " ill." But their rendering is older than ours, and dates back to the Bible—" They that are whole need not a physician, but they that are sick " (Luke v. 31.)

Sight. The word is used in the United States in the sense of a large number, a meaning which is really old English, for it is used in this sense in " Morte d'Arthur."

Sidesman. According to Dr. Hook, this word is a corruption of "synod's-man." A sidesman's office is to assist the churchwardens in their duties, especially in collecting the alms in church.

Silk. The word is derived from the Greek adjective *serikos*, a name which is merely indicative of the country from which the material was brought, much as we call porcelain " china," or linen " holland." The Greeks knew there was a country from which came silk, brought to them by the Phœnician caravans over a long and difficult route, but of the land itself they knew nothing—it was bolted and barred against them by being impossible of access. So they called it *Seres*, the signification of which may best be interpreted by the Latin *sera*, a bolt, a door-bar, and through the Latin *sericum* came the Anglo-Saxon *seolc*, and our " Silk."

Silly. This word has completely changed in signification. It is derived from the German, *selig*, or the Anglo-Saxon *sælig*, meaning blessed. An early poet calls the infant Jesus " the harmless, silly babe," meaning the " blessed babe," or, a rather later interpretation of the word, the "innocent babe." From "innocent," the word has gradually come to mean "gullible," "foolish."

Skedaddle. To run away, to be scattered in rout. The Greek word *skedannumi* means to retire tumultously. In Scotland, "skedaddle" is used in the sense of spilling.

Slick off. To finish a thing "slick off," or "clean off" means to do a job quickly and thoroughly, there and then. Probably from the German, *schlicht*, sleek, polished, and Icelandic *slike*, sleek.

Slip. "There's many a slip 'twixt the cup and the lip." This phrase was used by a slave to Ancæos, the helmsman of the ship Argo. The slave had told his Master that he would never taste the wine of his vineyards, and so it fell out; for when a bottle of wine made from his own grapes was actually before him he was told that a wild boar was laying his vineyard waste. Ancæos put down the wine, untasted, went out to kill the boar, and was himself killed in the encounter.

Smack. The word is interesting by reason of its many meanings and derivations. A mother "smacks" her naughty child, something eaten or drunk "smacks" of an unusual flavour, and at the seaside we see a fleet of "smacks" starting for a fishing cruise. In each of these instances the word "smack," though spelt and pronounced the same, is a different word, distinct in meaning and derivation. In the first instance the word is clearly of imitative origin, the sound of the light, quick blow with the hand giving rise to word; in the second case the word comes from the Anglo-Saxon *smæc*, to taste; and in the last example the word should more properly be spelt "snack," being derived from the Anglo-Saxon *snacc* and the Danish *snakke*, a term applied by the Danes to their long, narrow boats, because of their snake-like movement on the water.

Snob. One who is not a gentleman, one who over estimates wealth or rank. In some colleges those who are not of noble birth are entered on the lists as *s. nob*, that is, *sine nobilitate*. This is supposed to be the source from which Thackeray is said to have invented the word to describe George IV.

Soap. Soap, so indispensable still, was undoubtedly used in ancient times. In Jeremiah ii. 22, we have : " For though thou wash thee with nitre, and take thee much sope, yet thine iniquity is marked before me." Our English rendering of the word is a form of *savon*, the French for soap.

Son. This word, when denoting a descendant, is used, in English, as a suffix, as in " Jameson," " Johnson," etc. In other languages, however, the equivalent word is more generally a prefix, as in the Norman *Fitz*, the Gaelic *Mac*, the Welsh *Ap*, the Irish *O'*, and the Hebrew *Ben*.

Spa. This general name for medical springs comes from Spa, in Germany, once the most fashionable watering place in Europe.

Spare the Rod and Spoil the Child. The first germ of this saying may come from Proverbs xiii. 24, where Solomon says " He that spareth his rod hateth his son "; but in Samuel Butler's " Hudibras," we find the present form :—

Love is a boy by poets styled ;
Then spare the rod and spoil the child."

Spouse. This word is generally thought to be the term for a married person, but it really means a person betrothed, promised in marriage; from the Latin, *spondeo*, I promise.

Squad. A small body of men assembled for drill—a contraction of the word " squadron." " The awkward Squad " is a term for raw recruits not sufficiently drilled to take their places in the regimental line.

Staple. We find this as a suffix in Anglo-Saxon place-names—Barn-staple and Dun-stable are examples—

where it denotes a market or, more exactly, a place where merchants would store their goods. We still use the word " staple " to denote the article which is the established industry of a place, but formerly it was applied to the place itself, rather than to the merchandise.

Stem the Tide. In a figurative sense the phrase means to check the on rush, the panic, tumult, or uproar; yet although the stem of a vessel " ploughs the wave," it can hardly be said to " check the tide." But the Anglo-Saxon word *stemn*, meant a staff, a stout cudgel; and we can imagine that one who found himself in danger of being swept down by the mob might resist the onslaught successfully with his *stemn*. There seems to be a similar allusion in the phrase to " stave " off disaster or misfortune.

Steward. In the old days, when much of the land was forest, the chief wealth of the Saxon consisted of pigs, as we may read in the opening of " Ivanhoe." At night the herd was brought home from the forest and the pigs were penned in their sties, but to guard them from robbers a man was appointed to keep watch and ward on the pigsties. He was called the *stig-weard*, from *stigo*, a sty, and *weard*, a ward; and hence the word " steward.'

Stock. The word is applied to many things—money in the public funds, capital subscribed, the goods contained in a shop, animals on a farm, thick broth stored for making soup, etc., etc. But the original meaning of the Anglo-Saxon *stocc* (in Dutch *stok*, in German *stock*) was a stick, or wood, and because wood had to be accumulated and stored up for winter use, it came about that anything collected together and reserved for a special purpose was called " stock."

Stoke, Stow. These are common suffixes in place-names, as in Basing-stoke, Alver-stoke, Tavi-stock, In-stow, and Bris-stow (now Bristol). The words are of Anglo-Saxon origin—a " stoke " or " stow " is a place stockaded, an inclosure surrounded with stocks or piles.

Stone Jug. This name for a prison, which sounds so like a slang term, is really very old, and is to be accounted for by the fact that the Greek word *kerāmos*, means either a stone jar or a prison. Homer, in the Illiad v. 387, and ix. 469, uses the word in both senses.

Strath. This is a Gaelic word found as a component in many Scottish place-names, as in Strath-blane, Strath-earne, and Strath-more. It means a broad valley.

Street. The high-ways of a city or a town are rightly called " streets," for they are paved, and the derivation of the word " street " is the Roman *strata via*, the paved way. And the reason why the name " street " or " streat " was applied to the old Roman roads which intersect the country is that, for many a mile, they were often paved—the then undrained marshy land through which they had to pass required it.

String. A piece of string is one of the common things of every-day life, used in a multitude of ways; but whether it be thick or thin, stout or fine, there is one quality which is essential to its usefulness—it must be strong enough for its purpose. And the derivation of the word " string " is the Anglo-Saxon *strang*, which means strong.

Stoker. The engine-driver no longer drives, and the stoker no longer stokes, for the one has no whip and the other no wood. In the old days when the smelting of iron was carried on in Sussex, the man who fed the furnace with logs of wood might rightly have been called a " stoker," for the word is derived from the Dutch *stoken*, to light a fire, and the Anglo-Saxon *stocc*, wood.

Storey. The first storey of a house cannot be the ground-floor, for the simple reason that the word "storey" means built up, being derived from the old French *estorer* and the Latin *instaurare*, to build up.

Story. The word is but an abbreviation of "history," which means an account of something known, being derived from the Greek *histor*, knowing, learned. Yet the child's exclamation "What a story!" has come to mean "what an untruth!"

Subtle. The word means not only crafty and acute, but fine and delicate, and its derivation seems to convey an implication of both these meanings. For "subtle" comes from the Latin *subtela*, under a web, and we are at once reminded of the cunning and crafty spider and its fine and delicate web.

Suburb. From the Latin *sub*, under, and *urbs*, a city; meaning under, or near, the city wall.

Succour. The good Samaritan succoured the man who fell among thieves. Unlike the Levite, who "passed by on the other side, . . he had compassion on him, and *went to him*" (Luke x. 32-34). And the derivation of the word "succour" is the Latin *succurrere*, to run up to.

Superstition. This word comes from the two Latin words, *super*, above, and *stare*, to stand. In old days those who escaped in battle were called *superstites*, meaning those outliving, surviving. Our meaning for superstition is religious credulity —the religion that lives on when real religion is dead.

Supplication. By supplication we mean earnest prayer or entreaty—literally the act of folding the knees, from the Latin *sub-plico*. But the Romans used the word for a thanksgiving after a victory.

Surgeon. The word was formerly spelt "chirurgeon," and is derived from the Greek *cheir*, the hand, and *ergon*, a work, implying the skilful work done by the hand in performing operations.

Surname. The word is formed from the French *sur* (equivalent to the Latin *super*), over and above and the English "name," on the analogy of the French *sur-nom*; and thus means the family name which the individual takes over and above his Christian or personal name.

Suttee. The word would seem to be a corruption of the Sanscrit *sati*, a virtuous wife, derived from *sat*, pure. Suttee is a form of funeral sacrifice—the sacrifice of the widow of the deceased—formerly common in Brahmanic India, in which the widow was burnt with her dead husband on the funeral pyre. Many went willingly to their fate, but others were driven to it by fear of disgrace or by priestly threats, or even by violence. The custom was abolished by law in British India in 1829, but for many years after it was continued in some of the native principalities. It is considered that although the comparatively modern ordinance of suttee is a corrupt departure from the early Brahmanic ritual, the practice is not a new invention by the Hindu priesthood, but a revival of an ancient Aryan rite, belonging to a period even earlier than the Veda—the oldest sacred volume of the Hindus.

Swan. So convinced were the ancients that the white plumage of the swan was its essential quality, that "a black swan" was a proverbial expression for something non-existent—or, at any rate, very rare. But the Black Swan—a very beautiful species—has been found in Australia, and was brought to Europe early in the seventeenth century.

Swindle. If we may take the Anglo-Saxon *swindan* as the derivation of "swindle," it would seem that the word has altered in signification. For *swindan* means to droop, and the original implication in "swindle" was apparently an assumed servility, an obsequious drooping to the ground.

Sycophant. The word comes from the Greek *sykon*, a fig, and *phainein*, to bring to light, to show. Though there is no doubt as to the etymology of the word, its exact history has been lost. It has

been said to have arisen from the practice of inform-
ing against persons who exported figs from Attica
and plundered the sacred fig trees, but more probably it was applied to one who brought figs to
light by shaking the tree—hence, one who makes
rich men yield up the fruit of their gain by
obsequious flattery and servility.

Symbol. The word comes from the Greek *syn-ballein*,
to put or cast together. Originally it meant the
corresponding part of a tally or coin, cut in two.
We use it to express a sign by which we know a
thing, an emblem. Also in theology as a creed or
typical religious rite, as baptism.

Taboo. The word comes to us from New Zealand and
the South Sea Islands, being the Maori *tapu* and
the Polynesian *tabu*, which means sacred. It was
essentially a religious ceremony, and could only
be imposed by the priests, but it was applied to
social and political affairs and to persons, places
or things. Its prohibitions were far-reaching, and
were strictly enforced under penalty of death;
they applied to almost everything offered in sacrifice to the gods, to seasons of preparation for a
festival and before going to war, to the degrees
of relationship permissible in marriage, and to
various customs in the preparation and eating of
food. For instance, a girl was not allowed to eat
that which had been cooked at her father's fire,
and a wife was forbidden to partake of what she
had cooked for her husband and sons. Though
the origin of many of the prohibitions under taboo
are intricate and obscure, there seems no reason
to believe that they were the result of mere
caprice, and on the whole their influence is considered to have been beneficial.

Tally. It is difficult to realise how small was the book-
learning among the working classes only some
two hundred years ago, but this word " tally "
(derived from the Latin *talen*, a slip of wood)

x

brings home the fact. The tally was a notched stick, employed as a means of keeping accounts, and for a long series of years tallies were issued by the English Government as certificates of its indebtedness, and were a recognised species of security. Adam Smith refers to them and states that in 1696 they were at a discount of 40 per cent. and upwards. The sticks used were generally of seasoned willow or hazel, and were notched at the edge to represent the amount of the debt, small notches signifying pence, larger shillings, and still larger pounds; while proportionately larger and wider notches meant 10, 100 or even 1,000 pounds. The stick was then split lengthwise, and one piece was given to the creditor, while the other was laid away as a record. The system of tallies was not abolished until nearly the end of the eighteenth century, and it was not until the reign of William IV. that the accumulated tallies in possession of the Government were ordered to be destroyed. They were then burnt in a stove in the House of Lords, but the stove, becoming overheated, set fire to the panelling of the room, and the Houses of Parliament were destroyed !

Tam. This word appears in the names of many of our rivers, as in the Thames (Tam-ese), the Tame in Bucks, Cornwall, Cheshire, and elsewhere, and perhaps in the Tay, the Taw and the Tavy. It means spreading, quiet, still.

Tandem. The word originated in University slang, being a play on the Latin adverb *tandem*, which means at length (after a certain interval of time). Hence, as a pun, it was applied to two horses harnessed at length—one behind the other.

Tavern. The word is derived from the Latin *taberna*, a hut, a booth, from the root *ta* or *tan*, to stretch, whence also we have " table " and " tabernacle." Taverns existed in England as early as the thirteenth century, and by an Act passed in 1284 they were compelled to be shut at the sound of the curfew. In the reign of Edward III. (1327-1377) only three were allowed in London—one in "Chepe," one in "Walbrok," and one in Lombard Street; but we find that during the reign of Edward VI. (1547-1553) the number permitted had been increased to forty. Taverns were first licensed in 1752.

Tariff. A very familiar word in these days in connection with "Tariff Reform." Yet it is really an Arabic word, *ta'rif*, meaning information, derived from *arafa*, to explain, to inform.

Tawdry. The word is said to be a corruption of St. Audry, otherwise St. Etheldrida, and to have been originally applied to the fair laces and gay toys sold at St. Audry's fair, which was held in the Isle of Ely on St. Audry's day, October 17th. Another version is that St. Audry, in her youth, was addicted to wearing gay clothing, and that hence her name was used to indicate any showy ornaments. It is certain that the word did not at first bear the signification it now has of paltry show and shabby splendour.

Tea. The word is a corruption of the Chinese equivalent, the common form of which is *tscha*. In English it was formerly pronounced "tay"; Pope uses it to rhyme with "obey," "stay," and "away," though later he makes it rhyme with "decree."

Teetotal. Apparently the word is a re-duplicated form of "total," originating, according to the generally accepted account, from the stuttering pronunciation of the word "total" by a lecturer advocating the temperance cause.

Telegraph. The literal meaning of the word is "I write at a distance," being formed of the Greek *tele*, afar off, and *grapho*, I write. In the same

way, " telescope " means " I see at a distance,"
from *tele*, and *skopeo*, I see.

Temper. To use this word only in the sense of evil
passion is incorrect; it means any passion or
feeling, and may rightly be applied to calmness
and moderation. The derivation of the word is
the Latin *temperare* (allied to *tempus*, time),
meaning to combine properly, a signification which
we retain in the word " temperament," and also
in " temper " when we use that word to indicate
the modifying of metals or the blending of
substances.

Tenterhooks. The phrase " on tenterhooks " is expressive of a state of worry and anxiety, and is in
allusion to the woven cloth which is stretched out
to dry on " tenter-hooks " passed through the
selvage. The word " tenter " is derived from
the Latin *tentus*, from *tendere*, to stretch.

Termagant. A term used (either as an adjective or a
substantive) to denote a person of quarrelsome
and violent temper. The word is interesting in
its origin; it is the name given by mediæval
romances to an idol which was represented as
being an object of worship by the Saracens, and
it was afterwards introduced into the old Morality
Plays as the name for a character of violent temper.
It seems, also, to have been applied to a ranting
actor overdoing his part (*see* " Hamlet " iii. 2).
The word came to us from the Old French
tervagant, which is derived from the Latin *ter*,
thrice, and *vagans*, wandering; and probably had
reference to the moon wandering in heaven, on
earth, and in the lower world, under its three
names of Luna, Diana, and Proserpine.

Terra-Cotta. A composition of pure clay and fine-
grained sand, dried in the air and baked in a kiln.
The literal meaning of the word is cooked earth,
from the Latin *terra*, earth, and *cocta*, the past
participle of *coquere*, to cook.

Testament. That which testifies, from the Latin *testari*, to be a witness. Hence applied to the written instrument by which a person declares his will as to the disposal of his property after his death, and to the two divisions of the Bible called the Old Testament and the New Testament.

Text. It is curious to find that the word "text," which we apply to anything written or quoted, comes from the Latin *textus*, meaning that which is woven, a fabric, the same derivation as that of our word "textile."

Thing. This is a Scandinavian word which may still be traced in some of our northern place-names. It is derived from the Old Norse *tinga*, to speak, and is allied to the English "think." The "Things" were judicial and legislative assemblies, and usually met on some island or promontory where they were secure from lawless disturbance. In the parish of Tingwall (for instance), in the Shetland Islands, there is a small lake in the midst of which is an island called Sawting, where such an assembly was doubtless held. On the island are four great stones as seats for the officers of the court, and access is obtained by stepping-stones in the shallow water. The names of these places—Ting-wall and Saw-ting—are memorials of these meetings, as are the names Ding-wall and Tain, in Ross-shire, Tin-wald Hill, near Dumfries, and Thing-wall in Cheshire, besides many place-names ending in "thing" or "ting" in the Shetland Islands.

Thrall. Trench has made the suggestion that this word is a variant of "thrill" (which is only another form of "drill,") arising from the practice of boring the ear of a slave in token of servitude, but more probably the derivation is the Anglo-Saxon *thrœgian*, to run; and thus the original meaning attached to a thrall would be a runner, a messenger—whence a servant, r slave.

Threshold. Literally, the thrash-wood, from the Anglo-Saxon *therscan*, to thrash, and *wald* or *weald*, a wood; meaning the piece of wood beaten by the feet of those who enter the house.

Thwaite. This, as a suffix to place-names, is distinctive of Norwegian settlements. Its meaning is nearly the same as the Anglo-Saxon *feld* (field), and it occurs more than forty times in Cumberland, but not once in Lincolnshire, where the Danish word " thorpe " (a village) is very common, thus indicating the different stock from which the two counties were populated.

Tide. " Time and tide wait for no man " is an old saying which the alliteration of the two words " time " and " tide " may have done much to preserve; but whether or not this be so, it is certain that " tide " is but another form of " time," being derived from the Anglo-Saxon *tid*, signifying time, hour. From the same source we get the words " tidy " and " tidings "; the first being equivalent to " timely," and the latter to " things that betide."

Tor. A Celtic word signifying a projecting, tower-like rock, found in the name Tor-bay and in the many Tors of Devon, Cornwall and Derbyshire. Its root may be seen in the Latin *tur-ris*, a tower, and it has many derivatives in place-names on the Continent.

Torment. Literally, a twisting, from the Latin *tortus*, the past participle of *torquere*, to twist, from which also we have " torture," " tortoise," " extort," etc. It may be that the word " torment " is directly derived from the Latin *tormentum* (from the same root—*torquēre*) which was an instrument for hurling stones.

Tory. The word comes from the Irish *tor* and the Gaelic *toir*, meaning a pursuer, and was originally given as an appellation to the Irish moss-troopers who, during the Civil Wars of the sixteenth century, plundered people under pretext of being in arms for the royal cause. It was afterwards applied, as a political term, to those who were supposed to be abettors of the Popish plot, and was eventually extended to the political party now called Conservatives, as opposed to the Whig or Liberal party.

Tramway (or Tram-road). Skeat, in his Etymological Dictionary, says :—" About the year 1800 Mr. Benjamin Outram made certain improvements in connection with railways for common vehicles, which gave rise to the silly fiction (ever since industriously circulated) that ' Tram-road ' is short for ' Outram-road,' in ignorance of the fact that the accent alone is sufficient to show that ' Outram,' if shortened to one syllable, must become ' out,' rather than ' ram ' or ' tram.' " The original meaning of the word " tram " was a beam or balk of timber. Stone tramways were introduced into London (in the Commercial Road) in 1830, but it was not till 1861 that an iron tramway was laid; it ran from the Marble Arch to Bayswater, and owing to popular clamour was taken up in 1862. Not until the Act of 1870 was any facility granted for another tramway.

Tre. A prefix in place-names widely distributed in England. It is of Welsh origin and is frequent in Brittany, but it does not occur in names derived from the Gaelic tongue. It is most frequent in Cornwall, where it occurs more than a thousand times if we include single homesteads. Consequently, it enters into a vast number of Cornish territorial surnames, as enunciated in the old adage :—

" By Tre, Pol, and Pen,
You may know the Cornish men."

But " tre " in this country is not confined to place-names in Cornwall, we find it in the counties of Devon, Somerset, Gloucester, Salop, Hereford,

Worcester, Lancashire, Yorkshire, Cumberland and Northumberland. Its meaning is simply a dwelling-place.

Trousers. The word comes to us from the French *trousser*, to truss, to girt in. Trousers, in their present form, were introduced into England about the end of the eighteenth century, but for many years after were not recognised as full dress. The Duke of Wellington was refused admission to Almack's in 1814 because he wore black trousers instead of breeches and silk stockings, but according to the frontispiece to Gronow's "Last Recollections," trousers were admitted to Almack's in 1815.

Trump. The word as applied in a game of cards is a corruption of "triumph," which is probably derived from the Greek *thriambos*, a hymn to Bacchus, sung in festal processions in his honour.

Tryst. The use of this word is mostly confined to poetry, and employed in the sense of a meeting by appointment, but it is simply a variant of "trust," and can be traced back to the Gothic *trausti*, a covenant.

U. and V. In the period of Middle English the letters "u" and "v" were used indifferently, and up to a comparatively recent date most English dictionaries combined the words beginning with "u" and "v." It appears that, according to modern spelling, no English word ends in "u," owing, says Ellis, in his "Early English Pronunciation," "to a rule made by no one knows whom, no one knows why, and no one knows when."

Uachter. A component in place-names. (*See* UCHEL.)

Ubiquity. The word is derived from the Latin *ubique*, everywhere, and ubiquity is one of the legal prerogatives of the king. Blackstone tells us that His Majesty, in the eye of the law, is always present in all his courts, though unable to distribute justice in person. The regal office is there, ready to undertake prosecutions or pronounce judgment for the protection of the subject; and for this reason the king does not appear by his attorney, as other men do, for in the mind of the law he is always present in his own person.

Uchel. This is distinctively a Welsh word and yet it is found in many place-names in Scotland, corrupted into " ochil," as in Ochil-tree, Ochil Hills, and in its original form in Uchel-tre in Galloway. The suffix in this case is undoubtedly the characteristic Welsh word " tre " (q.v.), and we are led to the conclusion that the Scottish lowlands were peopled by the Welsh branch of the Celtic stock. The word " uchel " means high, a height, and in the Gaelic becomes " uachter," as in Auchter-arder.

Ugly. There seems to have been some uncertainty as to the derivation of this word, and it has been suggested that it comes from the Anglo-Saxon *ouph-lic*, meaning like a goblin (an *ouph*); but probably the Icelandic *ugger*, fear, combined with *ligr* (which is equivalent to the Anglo-Saxon *lic*, like) is the true derivation. The old meaning of " ugly " was not merely something repulsive, but conveyed also the idea of ill-nature and evil temper, a signification which is still retained in the United States. In " The Lamplighter " we come across the sentence—" I'll not answer her back when she's ' ugly ' to me,"—and the expression " an ' ugly ' temper " is a common one with us. Darwin, in his " Descent of Man," has characterised " ugliness " as consisting in an approach to the lower animals, a definition which seems to convey both repulsion and fear.

Ulster. The original name for this Irish province is believed to have been Ulladh (pronounced Ulla), and it is to the Norsemen who settled in that part of Ireland that we owe the termination " ster " (or " stadr "), which means a settlement or dwelling.

Leinster and Munster have the same Scandinavian termination. Ulster king-at-arms is the title of the chief officer in heraldry for Ireland—an office created by Edward VI. in 1552. The long, loose overcoat called an ulster, so much in use a few years ago, was so named because it was usually made of Ulster frieze cloth.

Ultima Thule. An expression used to signify the final extremity in place or action. *Thul-e* is the Latin name given by the ancients to the most northern country known to them, and variously identified with Shetland, Iceland and Norway—thus *Ultima Thule* meant the farthest Thule, the end of the world. The etymology of the word "thule" is uncertain; it may be the Gothic *tiule*, meaning the most remote land, and connected with the Greek *telos*, the end; or possibly it may be the *Gezirat Thule* (the Isles of Darkness) of those adventurous traders—the Phœnicians.

Ultramarine. The literal meaning of the word is "beyond the sea," and as an adjective it is used in this sense. But as a substantive it denotes the beautiful blue pigment resembling the pure blue of the ocean, originally very rare and the most expensive of colours. It was obtained by grinding and burning lapis-lazuli, and was much prized by artists both for its beauty and permanence. It is now prepared artificially by the fusion of kaolin, glauber salt, carbonate of soda and charcoal, producing a green substance which is changed to blue by the addition of sulphur.

Ultramontane. Literally, that which is beyond the mountains, a term originally applied by the French to the Italians, as being on the other side of the Alps. The term has since been used to designate those who look upon the Pope as the fountain of all power in the Church, as opposed to the French school of thought which maintains the right of self-government in national Churches, and has come to be employed to denote the ultra-popish party—the " high-church " party—in the Roman Catholic Church.

Umber. A well-known colour much used by artists in depicting shadows. Hence its name, which is an abbreviation and corruption of the Italian *terra d'ombra*, the literal meaning of which is earth of shadow, *i.e.*, earth used for shadowing (shading). It consists of an ochreous earth, occurring naturally in veins, or prepared artificially from admixture. The best is that brought from Cyprus under the name of Turkish umber.

Umbrage. The general meaning of the phrase " to take umbrage " is to be offended, to be jealous of another as standing in one's light, the feeling of being overshadowed. And the derivation of the word implies this—it is the Latin *umbra*, shade, shadow.

Umbrella. No such book as this would be considered complete without some reference to the umbrella, but there is really little to be said that is not generally known. Its ancient use was as a sunshade, and in the British Museum there is a bas-relief from Nineveh representing a slave holding an umbrella over the head of a king. The introduction of the umbrella into our country, as a protection from rain, is generally accredited to Jonas Hanway, who was born in 1712 and died in 1786, and there is no doubt that his use of it created a disturbance among the sedan-chairmen and hackney-coachmen, who deemed it their monopoly to protect from rain. But it must have been in fairly common use before his time, as we find Swift writing, in 1710 :—

> " The tucked-up sempstress walks with hasty strides,
> While streams run down her oiled umbrella's sides."

And in 1711 the poet Gay writes :—
> " Or underneath th' umbrella's oily shed
> Safe thro' the wet on clinking pattens tread."

And again :—
> " Let Persian maids th' umbrella's ribs dis-
>   play . . .
> Britain in winter only knows its aid
> To guard from chilly showers the walking
>   maid."

Umpire. The word is properly " numpire," from the Old French *nompair*, not paired, odd, derived from the Latin *non*, not, and *par*, equal. Hence the true meaning of the word is an odd, or third, person called in to decide between two disputants.

Una. The poet Spenser (1533-1599), in his " Faerie Queene," has used this word as a proper name to personify truth :—
> " . . . Her angels face,
> As the great eye of heaven, shyned bright,
> And made a sunshine in the shady place."

The word " Una " is the feminine singular of the Latin *unus*, one.

Unclean. Not only in Judaism, but probably in every religious faith which has existed, there has been a distinction between what is ceremonially clean and unclean. To this day, food cooked by a Sudra or an outcast is unclean to the Brahmin, and it is at the peril of his caste if he eat it.

Uncle Sam. This nickname for the United States Government—used in the same way as John Bull for England—is supposed to be a jocular interpretation of the initials U.S. which appear on the property of the United States Government.

Uncial. The Latin *uncia* was the twelfth part of anything, and denoted an ounce (as the twelfth of a pound), or an inch (as the twelfth of a foot). Thus the term " uncial," as applied to ancient writing, is said to signify that the letters were an inch in size, but such a derivation is doubtful. The word is used to denote Greek and Latin writing of large size as distinguished from that entirely in small characters, and uncials differ from the older large-sized letters in being composed of curved instead of straight lines, giving a rounded appearance to the characters and allowing of their being written with greater rapidity.

Uncouth. The proverb " uncouth, unkist,"—signifying that what is unknown is uncouth—is ascribed to the poet Chaucer, and is an apt illustration of the derivation of the word "uncouth," which comes from the Anglo-Saxon *uncudh*, meaning strange, unknown. But long before Chaucer's time St. Paul enunciated the same idea :—" If I know not the meaning of the voice, I shall be unto him that speaketh a barbarian, and he that speaketh shall be a barbarian unto me." (I. Cor. xiv. 11.)

Underwriter. The term is generally applied to a member of the Society called " Lloyd's," whose business consists in granting marine and other insurances. Such a person writes his name at the foot of the insurance policy, usually in conjunction with others, when each person is said to " take a line." The practice of signing—writing under—the conditions of the insurance has given rise to the term " underwriter."

Unicorn. Though there is no doubt that this is a fabulous animal, its existence is frequently mentioned by Greek and Latin authors. Aristotle, the Greek philosopher, calls it the Indian Ass, and Ctesias (about 400 B.C.) describes it as being about the size of a horse, with a white body, red head, and blue eyes, having a horn on the forehead a cubit long, which is entirely white at the base, black in the middle, and red at the end. In heraldry two unicorns were borne as supporters of the Scottish royal arms for about a century before the union of the English and Scottish crowns in 1603, after which the unicorn was used as one of the supporters of the royal arms in the place of the red dragon of Wales.

Union Jack. Technically, the name of the British national flag is the " Union." The Jack is a small flag, a diminutive of the " Union," flown from the bowsprit or forepart of a ship; in the Royal Navy plain, in the Merchant Service with a white border. When flown from the mast with a white border it is the signal for a pilot, and is called the Pilot Jack.

University. The word is derived from the Latin *universitas*, the whole of anything, and it is commonly thought that it is applied to the Universities because they embody several subordinate colleges. But such is not necessarily the case, as some universities, such as Dublin, consist of one college only, and when the term was first applied to seminaries of learning it meant the whole body of teachers and scholars. In this sense it is used at the beginning of the thirteenth century, and is applied to Oxford in a document belonging to the year 1301. Later, the Latin term *universitas* acquired a technical meaning, and came to be used much in the same sense as the present word " University."

Until. This is a substituted form of " unto," by the use of " till " for " to." Till (*til*) is of Scandinavian origin, and in Scotland and some parts of England and Ireland it is still commonly used in the sense of the Anglo-Saxon word " to."

Upas-Tree. The name is applied, in a figurative sense, to anything baneful or of evil influence, the tradition being that a pestilent vapour rises from the tree, killing everything which it touches. The origin of this fable is to be found in an account published in 1783 by Foersch, a Dutch physician, who states that in the vicinity of the upas " not a tree nor a blade of grass is to be found, not a beast or bird, reptile or living thing " can exist in the surrounding valley. It is now known that the desolation attributed to the upas-tree was really the result of the escape of carbon dioxide from vents in a valley enclosed by volcanoes, and the tree has been seen growing with others in forests, while in 1844 it was introduced into Kew Gardens with no deleterious effects. But the juice of the tree is a virulent poison, owing to the presence of strychnine, and the smallest wound by an arrow tipped with this poison is fatal.

Urim and Thummim. These are two Hebrew words meaning respectively Light and Perfection, but in what way they were to be " put in the breastplate of judgment " which the High Priest was to wear " when he goeth in before the Lord," as enjoined in Ex. xxviii. 30, still remains very obscure. Dr. Brewer tells us that " Urim and Thummim " were three stones deposited in the double lining of the High Priest's breastplate, one representing " No," one " Yes," and one " No Answer," and that when a question was to be decided by " Urim " the priest drew out one of the stones as an answer. This is one of many conjectures as to the nature of " Urim and Thummim," but authorities are not agreed upon the question.

Usher. The literal meaning of the word is a door-keeper. It comes to us through the Old French *ussier*, which is derived from the Latin *ostiarius*, a door-keeper, from *ostium*, a door, from *os*, a mouth. We retain the original signification of the word in the verb " to usher," when we speak, for instance, of being " ushered " into a presence.

Usquebagh. However deleterious alcohol may now be considered, there can be no doubt that, formerly, it was held in high estimation, as shown by the meaning of the names it has received. The Irish and Gaelic word for whiskey was *uisgebeatha* (the modern " usquebagh "), which means water of life, and we have the same meaning in the Latin *aqua vitæ*, and in the French *eau de vie*, while among

the Jews of old, wine was extolled as that which
" maketh glad the heart of man." (Ps. civ. 15.)

Utopia. The generally accepted derivation of this
word is the Greek *ou*, not, and *topos*, a place;
hence it may be taken to signify nowhere. We
have equivalents in the Scotch *kennaquhair*, and
the German *weissnichtwo*, and it seems to be used
in this sense by Sir Thomas More as the name for
the imaginary island where everything is perfect.
On the other hand another derivation has been
suggested in the Greek *eu*, happy, blessed, in conjunction with *topos*.

Utter. As a verb, this word is most frequently used to
denote the act of speaking, pronouncing; but, as
its derivation (the Anglo-Saxon *utian*, to put out,
to eject) shows, its fuller meaning is to put forth,
either by word or otherwise. This signification is
retained in the expression " to utter base coin,"
which indicates the act of putting bad money into
circulation. As an adverb the word has a similar
implication; it is derived from the Anglo-Saxon
uttor, the comparative of *ut*, out, and thus means
outer, so that " utter " and " outer " are doublets.

Vagrant. The ultimate derivation of the word (the
" r " is an intrusion) is the Latin *vagari*, to
wander, but in law the term is much more com-
prehensive, and the idea of wandering is almost
lost. Vagrants may be divided into three
grades :—Beggars and idle persons able to maintain themselves and families but neglecting to do
so; persons who have been found guilty as rogues
and vagabonds and have repeated the offence;
and such as are styled " incorrigible," having
been found guilty of more than one repetition of the
offence. The punishment varies in severity in
accordance with the grade.

Vain. The derivation of the word is suggestive—it is,
most probably, the Latin *vacuus*, empty.

Valance. It would seem that in former times the hangings and drapery of beds were both costly and elaborate, and the old four-post bedstead, enclosed in curtains and tester, was but a survival of greater magnificence, of which the valance is all that remains to us. All this is recalled by the word "valance," which is derived from the name Valence, a place in France, near Lyons, formerly famous, as it still is, for the silk made there.

Valentine. According to Dr. Brewer this word is a corruption of "galantin," meaning a lover, a gallant, and St. Valentine's Day was selected for sending valentines because of the similarity of name. But the more accepted explanation is that the date was chosen because birds generally begin to mate about the time of St. Valentine's Day, which is the 14th February; on which day, so far as legend may be trusted, the saint was beheaded at Rome, under the Emperor Claudius.

Valerian. The root of this plant (which is sometimes called cats'-herb, from the attraction which its smell has to cats) is a valuable medicine in hysteria and epilepsy, and as a tonic. From its use in pharmacy it gains its name, for the word "valerian" is derived from the Latin *valere*, to be strong.

Valet. The word "valet" is the same as "varlet," the original form of which was "vaslet," an abbreviation of "vassalet," itself a diminutive of "vassal."

Vampire. A nocturnal demon, supposed to suck out the blood, and even the souls, of its victims. Yet we learn from Tylor—no mean authority on primitive beliefs—that "vampires are not mere creations of groundless fancy, but causes conceived in spiritual form to account for specific facts of wasting disease." The superstition is found in Polynesia and in the Malay Peninsula, but it is in Slavonia and Hungary that it has its special

v

home, and it is from these countries that the name " vampire " is derived. But the vampire-bat is a real animal, a native of Southern America, and it is often the cause of much trouble by attacking horses. Darwin has related that when he was in Chili he bivouacked one night near Coquimbo, and his servant, noticing that one of the horses was very restive, went to see what was the matter. Thinking he could detect something, he suddenly put his hand upon the horse's withers, and secured one of these vampire-bats.

Van. The vehicle which we call by this name—the huge covered waggon used by railway companies and other carriers—is familiar to all who know London, and in this connection it is curious to find that the word " van " is an abbreviation of " caravan "—the Arabic *qairawan*—which we associate with a long line of camels crossing the sandy desert.

Vandals. The name comes from the Latin *vandali*, the literal meaning of which is wanderers, and is cognate with the English " wander." The Vandals were a Teutonic race, originally inhabiting the southern shores of the Baltic, and they began to be troublesome to the Roman Empire about 160 A.D. In the year 410 they mastered Spain, and before many years had elapsed they had crossed into Africa. Thence they spread into Italy, and, in 455, plundered Rome, but thereafter their power declined.

Vegetate. It is not uncommon to use this word in describing, or complaining of, a dull, secluded life in the country, where, as there is nothing to enliven or animate, one is said to " vegetate." And yet the literal meaning of the word is exactly opposed to this signification, for it is derived from the Latin *vegetatus*, the past participle of *vegetare*, to enliven, to quicken. In the same way the word " vegetable " is derived from the

Latin *vegetabilis*, which means animating, full of life.

Vehement. When we speak of a man with a " vehement " spirit, or characterise an action as " vehement," we do not usually imply any taint of insanity; and yet the literal meaning of " vehement " is to be carried out of one's mind, from the Latin *vehere*, to carry away, and *mens*, the mind.

Venison. When Jacob called for his first-born son, Esau (Gen. xxvii. 1—4) and said—as our translation has it—" take thy weapons, thy quiver and thy bow, and go out to the field and take me some venison, and make me savoury meat such as I love, that I may eat; that my soul may bless thee," the word " venison " is correctly used, even if it was not the flesh of the deer that Jacob longed for. Any game hunted and killed is " venison," for the word specifically means " hunted," being derived from the Latin *venari*, to hunt.

Ventriloquism. The name has its origin in an erroneous supposition that ventriloquial sounds were produced from the belly (Latin *venter*, the belly, and *loqui*, to speak). In reality they are formed in the same manner as in ordinary speech, except that the lips are moved as little as possible, so as to convey the illusion that the performer is not speaking. The art of ventriloquism was known, in all probability, from very ancient times —certainly both to the Greeks and the Romans.

Venus. The Latin name for the goddess of love and beauty, the Greek *Aphrodite* and the Phœnician *Astarte*; generally supposed to be of eastern origin. The word " Venus " is from the same root as " venerate," and is allied to the Sanscrit *van*, to love, and the English " win." Among the famous statues of the goddess are the Venus of Milo (or Melos), discovered in 1820 by Admiral

Dumont in Melos, one of the Greek islands; and the Venus of Cnidus, the undraped statue by Praxiteles, which, it is said, the people of Cnidus refused to part with even at the price of their national debt. It is asserted that in the best days of art the goddess was always represented as draped, and that the nude statues are of later and decadent times.

Verdict. The responsibility that rests with the jury in giving their verdict is implied in the very word " verdict "; it comes from the Latin *vere dictum,* a true saying.

Verger. The literal meaning of the word is one who bears a rod or wand of office; it is derived through the French *verge* from the Latin *virga,* a twig. a switch, a rod, one of the small rods in the *fasces* of the lictors with which criminals were scourged. The officer who bears the staff of office before a bishop or other cathedral dignitary is rightly called a " verger," and the name has descended to the official who attends to and takes care of the interior of a church.

Vermicelli. An Italian word, the literal meaning of which is " little worms " and so named from the wormlike appearance of its slender tubes or threads. It is a mixture, prepared in perfection at Naples, of cheese, yolks of eggs, sugar, and saffron, and differs only from macaroni in being made in smaller tubes.

Vesta. The wax match which goes by this name is, presumably, so called after the Roman Goddess Vesta, whose sacred fire was kept continually burning and who was worshipped, together with the Penates, at every meal at which the family assembled round the hearth in the middle of the room.

Vex. This is one of those words in which the derivation is very suggestive. We all know how a series of small annoyances will vex and irritate us, much as if we were carrying about a jolting and uneven burden. And the word "vex" comes from the Latin *vexare*, to shake or jolt in carrying, being an intensive form of *vehere* (past tense *vexi*), to carry, from which we get the word "vehicle."

Viking. The literal meaning of the word is a creek-dweller, from the Norse *vik*, a creek or inlet, and the Anglo-Saxon suffix *ing*, signifying son of or belonging to. The Vikings were the Scandinavian warriors who harried the British Isles during the ninth and tenth centuries, and afterwards the word "viking" came to be used for any robber—in a Norse Biblical paraphrase the giant Goliath is called a "viking." From a misapprehension of the etymology, the word is often pronounced "vi-king," being confounded with sea-king, with which it is wholly unconnected. "A sea-king was a man of royal blood, and entitled to the name of king when in command even of a single ship; the sea-kings were often vik-kings but not every viking was a sea-king." (Cassell's Ency. Dict.)

Violet. The similarity of the name of this flower in many languages seems worthy of note; in French it is *violet*, in Latin *viola*, in Greek *vion*, in Spanish and Portuguese *violeta*, in Italian *violetta*. The colour of the violet is said to indicate love of truth and the truth of love, and the flower itself to be emblematical of innocence. "I would give you some violets, but they withered all when my father died," says poor Ophelia (Hamlet iv., 5); implying (it would seem) that, despite the truth of her love, her love of truth precludes her from bestowing the flower of innocence on a blood-stained family.

Viper. The only poisonous English reptile, otherwise called an adder; there are two or three varieties slightly differing in colour. The word is derived from the Latin *vipera*, a contraction of *vivipara*, the literal meaning of which is " she that produces live young." (*Vivus*, alive, and *parere*, to bring forth.)

Vixen. This word is the feminine of " vox," the name used in Southern England for " fox," and is the only instance which has survived of the Old English mode of forming the feminine gender by adding the suffix " en " to the masculine word.

Viz. A familiar sign, often used to express " namely." It is a contraction of the Latin *vide-licet*, itself a contraction of *videre*, to see, and *licet*, it is allowed. In the days when all books were written by hand, and generally in Latin, the abbreviation for the Latin *et* at the close of a word was very similar to the letter " z," and hence the contraction '' viz " came to be used in the place of *viet*, which was the abbreviated form of *vide-licet*. (*See* Oz.)

Volume. The word comes from the Latin *volumen*, a roll—the " scroll " of the Bible—from the same root as *volutus*, the past participle of *volere*, to roll. It came to be applied to a book because the ancients wrote their books on rolls, which were wound round a stick. The roll was placed in a wrapper, and in many cases was anointed with cedar-wood oil, in order to protect it from the ravages of insects.

Vote and Vow. The two words are doublets; they are both derived from the 'Latin *votum*, the neuter past participle of *vovere*, to vow. We have now given a separate signification to the two words, but it might be well, in view of the responsibility incurred by a vote, to bear in mind how closely " vote " and " vow " are allied.

Voyage. The signification of this word is now restricted to a journey by water, but the derivation of the word is the Latin *viaticum*, denoting the provisions and requisites for any journey—the root being *via*, a way. Perhaps one of the most remarkable voyages of antiquity is that referred to in the chronicles of the kings of Israel (ii. Chron. x. 21). Solomon and Hiram apparently fitted out a well-found navy, which, from the productions it brought in from year to year, would seem to have reached India, for the names used to designate apes, peacocks, etc., are Malabar words, suggesting that South-Western India was visited.

Vulgate. The application of this term in connection with the Holy Scriptures may not always be understood and is seldom explained. The word means general, common, being derived from the Latin *vulgatus*, and is applied to a celebrated and widely diffused version of the Bible in the Latin language. It is believed to have been made by St. Jerome, who was born in Dalmatia A.D. 329, and died at Bethlehem A.D. 420. At the urgent request of Pope Damasus (about 383) he undertook to revise the Latin version of the New Testament by the Greek original, and was able to correct many false readings, interpolations, and corruptions. He next revised the Latin version of the Old Testament by means of the Greek Septuagint, and finally, having acquired a knowledge of Hebrew, he translated the Old Testament from the original language. The entire version was a great advance upon its predecessors, but gradually the text was corrupted, and after the invention of printing there were several revisions. Wickliffe's Bible was made from the Vulgate, which has thus largely affected the English Authorised Version, as well as those published in many other languages.

Vulture. The literal meaning of this name is appropriate for such a bird of prey; it signifies a plucker, a tearer, being derived from the Latin *vellere*, to pluck, to tear. The vulture is a bird of repulsive habits, but extremely useful in performing the

office of scavenger in the hot climates it inhabits.
It feeds on the ground, walking with comparative
ease, and does not carry food to its nestlings
but supplies them with food from its own crop.
It has long been a question whether it discovers
its prey by sight or smell, but it is now generally
accepted that it chiefly finds its food by sight.

Wait. The word " wait " apparently comes to us
from the old French *waiter* (now *guetter*), and can
be traced back to the Anglo-Saxon *wacian*, both of
which mean to watch, to wake; hence we get the
signification of the term " Waits " as applied to
the band of persons who promenade the streets
performing music at Christmas-time.   In former
times the name " Waits " was applied to a body
of minstrels, attached to the households of great
persons, who paraded and watched during the
night and sounded the hours, and until recently the
Waits of the City of Westminster were regularly
sworn before the court of Burgesses.   Many
English towns had licensed Waits—Exeter, among
others, having a regular company—and the instruments used were a kind of hautboy, called shawms.

Walnut. The literal meaning of the word is " foreign
nut," being derived from the Anglo-Saxon *wealh*,
foreign, and *hnut*, a nut.   The tree is a native of
Persia, and was cultivated by the Romans as early
as the first century, A.D.   There seems to be no
record of the date of its introduction into Britain,
but it was certainly common in mediæval times,
and its wood was held to be the best known until
the importation of mahogany.

Walrus. The name is of Scandinavian origin and is
apparently an inverted form of the Icelandic *hross-
hvalr*, a horse-whale; it has been suggested that
the name was given because the animal sometimes
makes a noise like the neigh of a horse.   The
adult walrus, of both sexes, develops immense
tusks, often two feet long and weighing ten pounds
and upwards, which it uses for digging out shell-

fish and for raising its body out of the water by thrusting them into the ice-floes. These tusks also form terrible weapons of offence; by a quick turn of the neck the animal can strike upwards, downwards, or sideways, with equal dexterity.

Wanton. The literal and original meaning of the word is unreclaimed, uneducated, not taken in hand by a master. It is derived from the Anglo-Saxon *wan*, wanting, and *towen* (or *togen*), the past participle of *teon*, to draw, to educate, to bring up.

War. An English word; it appears in the English language as early as the Laws of Canute (1017-1035). It is cognate with the old French *werre* (now *guerre*), from the Old High German *werra*, which means vexation, strife, confusion.

Water-Spout. This remarkable phenomenon is usually formed in the following manner :—A dense cloud projects from its centre a body of vapour, in shape like a sugar loaf with the point downward. This cone gradually assumes a spiral form, and dips more and more towards the sea, where a second cone is formed, having its point upwards. Suddenly the descending and ascending cones meet in mid-air and become one united pillar, moving onward with more or less velocity. It continues in this form for a short time only, and then bursts, often with terrific violence. In November, 1855, five ships lying in the harbour of Tunis were thus destroyed in a moment. The cause of these phenomena are probably two-fold—electricity and vortical motion, of which vortical motion has been proved to be an important factor, artificial waterspouts having been produced by a tourniquet rotating over water at the rate of 1,500 to 2,000 revolutions per minute.

Weald. The vast tract in Kent and Sussex now called the weald (from the German *wald*, a wood) is the remains of an ancient forest which stretched (says Isaac Taylor) for 120 miles, with a breadth of 30 miles, along the northern frontier of the kingdom of the South Saxons. The old Roman road which ran through this district was called Well Street (the wood-road), and almost every local name for miles around terminates in "den," "field," "hurst" or "ley," indicating the former existence of this great forest. (*See* LEY.)

Weary. According to Skeat this word is connected with the Anglo-Saxon *worian*, to wander, to travel, from *wor*, a moor or swampy place. Hence the original meaning would imply the tramping over wet and swampy places, such as would be most likely to cause fatigue.

Wedlock. The second syllable of the word has no reference to an indissoluble union contracted in marriage, but to the gift it was customary for the husband to bestow upon the bride, the word being derived from the Anglo-Saxon *wed*, a pledge, and *lac*, a gift. To "wed" is to pledge oneself, and comes from the same root as the "wages" paid, the "wager" laid, and the "gage" thrown down in challenge.

Week. The space of time—seven days—which we call a week is of very ancient origin; probably it arose as a convenient division of the natural (the lunar) month. But when America was discovered it was not found among the aborigines there, nor did it exist among the Polynesians, the Japanese, or, in all probability, in ancient China. But in India it is almost universal, and so it has been, from unknown antiquity, in Scandinavia, the names of the several days being identified under the same planets in the two regions, so that could an inhabitant of Sweden be transported in a moment to India he would find he had arrived there on the same day of the week as that on which he left. During the early period of their histories the Greeks and the Romans had no institution of weeks, and Cassius, writing in the second century, A.D., considered that the week and the planetary names for days had been recently introduced into Rome from Egypt.

Whale. "Very like a whale" is a phrase expressing improbability and disbelief, and is used by Shakespeare—"Hamlet" iii. 2—but scarcely in that sense.

Wheat. Notwithstanding the antiquity of wheat there seems to be little doubt that white bread was generally esteemed a luxury. This is indicated by the word "wheat," which, in all Scandinavian languages, signifies white, to distinguish it from rye, and from the black oats and black barley of Northern Asia.

Whiskey. Literally, water; from the Gaelic *wisge* (or *uisge*), a contraction of *uisge-beatha*, water-of-life. (*See* USQUEBAGH.)

Whisper—Whistle. Both words are of imitative origin, probably suggested by the wind—"that grand old harper."

Wick. This is a suffix which is found in many place-names of both Anglo-Saxon and Norse origin, but—as pointed out by Isaac Taylor—there is a difference in its application. The primary meaning seems to have been a station, but with the Anglo-Saxons it was a station or dwelling place on land, while with the Norsemen it was a station for ships. Hence the inland "wick" usually denotes a house or a village, while the "wick" on the coast is indicative of a station established by pirates, rather than a settlement by colonists. Even in inland places, however, such names as Droitwich, Nantwich, and Northwich are probably derived indirectly from the Norse *wic*, a creek, a bay, as they are all places noted for the production of salt, which was formerly obtained by the evaporation of sea-water in shallow bays, a method to which the word "bay-salt" testifies. Hence any place for making salt came to be called a "wych-house," and places where rock salt was found took their names from the wych-houses built for its preparation. We learn from the Doomsday-book that a tax was imposed on the production of salt, and the name Droitwich ("droit" meaning a right, a due) seems to contain an allusion to this.

Window. In the days before glass was in common use the window was rather for ventilation than for light, as the word itself indicates, being derived from the Icelandic *vindauga*, the literal meaning of which is wind-eye (*vindr*, the wind, and *auga*, an eye).

Witch. The Anglo-Saxon word was *wicce*, the feminine of *wicca*, a wizard. *Wicca* is a corruption of *witga*, and originally meant a seer, from *witan*, to see, to know.

World. The cognate forms of this word which run through all the Scandinavian tongues clearly show that the word is a composite one. Thus we have for its derivation the Icelandic *verr*, the Old High German *wer*, the Anglo-Saxon *wer*, and the Gothic *wair*, all cognate with the Latin *vir*, and all meaning a man; while as a terminal we have the Icelandic *old*, the Anglo-Saxon *yldo*, and the Middle English *elde*, all implying age, or old age. Thus, as Skeat has shown, the right sense of " world " is age of man, or course of life.

Worse. The word comes to us from the Anglo-Saxon *wyrs*, and is from the same root as " war." The " s " being part of the derivation, " worser " would be the more proper form, and was in actual use in the sixteenth century as a grammatical word, though it is now considered incorrect. Similarly, " worst " is a contraction of " worsest."

Worth. This is a suffix which appears in many English place-names, where its meaning is nearly the same as that of " ton " or " garth." It denotes a place warded or protected, and was probably an inclosed homestead for the churls, subordinate to the " tun." We find the word in such names as Kenil-worth, Tam-worth, Worthing, Wands-worth and Wal-worth.

Wretch. The literal meaning of the word is "one driven out," from the Anglo-Saxon *wrecan*, to drive out, and is cognate with "wreak," in the sense of wreaking vengeance.

Write. The derivation of this word carries us back to the time when writing was an art so difficult and important that it was generally executed in the most imperishable material, such as stone. For the original sense was to cut, to score, to engrave, as shown in the Anglo-Saxon *writan* and in many cognate words of Scandinavian origin.

X. As the initial letter in a word, " X " only occurs in words of Greek origin, or in those formed from the Greek, most of which are of a scientific nature. As a numeral " X " indicates ten, and, as such, was originally composed of two "Vs" ("V" signifying five) placed one above the other, the lower one being inverted. In ordinary writing "X" is frequently used as an abbreviation for Christ, and is then not the same as the English " X," but represents the Greek "X", which is equivalent to "Ch"—X'mas for Christmas, is a familiar example. The use of an "X" on beer-barrels is said to have arisen as a method of indicating that the beer they contained had paid the ten shillings duty, while the "XX" and "XXX" would seem to be mere trade-marks, intended to convey an impression that such beer was twice or thrice as strong as that which had paid ten shillings duty.

X-Rays. (Otherwise called Rontgen Rays, the " o " being pronounced as the "e" in "camel"). Their discovery was made by Professor W. C. Rontgen, in November, 1895, while he was experimenting with Crookes' tubes. He found that these rays passed freely through substances impervious to light, even human flesh, and he obtained pictures showing the bones of living persons. Although these rays were known to differ from light-rays there remained some uncertainty as to their character, and on that account Professor Rontgen gave them the name of "X-rays," signifying that there was something yet to be discovered, as "X" represents the unknown quantity in algebra. In surgery and medicine the X-rays have proved of inestimable value, as shadow pictures are readily obtainable of bullets and other foreign substances in the human body, or of calculi and badly set limbs which could not otherwise be correctly diagnosed. The apparatus is now considered necessary for the proper equipment of every hospital, and was of great service in the South African war. It is also employed to detect imitation gems, as the real stones allow the rays to pass through, while the dense lead-glass of the imitation gems gives a shadow picture, like bone in the human body.

Xantippe. The name has come into proverbial use for a scolding and nagging wife, and is frequently used in that way by classical writers, as in Shakespeare, in the "Taming of the Shrew" (i., 2). Xantippe was the wife of Socrates, the great philosopher of the Athenians, of whom it has been said that "he brought down philosophy from the heavens to earth."

Xeres. An alternative name for the wine called sherry, from the fact that sherry (formerly called "sherris") was brought from Xeres, a town near Cadiz, in Spain.

Xylonite. A word formed from the Greek *xulon*, which means wood, denoting an article of commerce now generally called "celluloid." It is made by a process of immersing paper in sulphuric and nitric acids and, having an appearance like ivory, it is manufactured into many articles for which ivory and bone were formerly used. It is highly inflammable.

Yacht. The vessel gains its name as indicative of its speed, for the word "yacht" is derived from the old Dutch *jachtin*, to speed, to hunt.

Yahoos. The term is sometimes used, figuratively, to denote persons of low and despicable character, as it was a name given by Swift, in "Gulliver's Travels," to a fictitious class of animals, having the forms of men but with the understanding and passions of the lowest brutes. In this satirical tale horses are the ruling race, to whom the men are completely subject.

Yankee. There are several explanations of the origin of this word, but perhaps the most probable is that given in Bartlett's Dictionary of Americanisms, in which it is stated that the word was an effort of the American Indians to imitate the sound of "English," which they pronounced "Yengees." Skeat, however, compares the Lowland Scotch *yankie*, a term denoting a sharp, clever woman, and also *yanker*, which is applied to an agile girl, an incessant talker; the fundamental idea of these words being that of quick motion— very applicable to the alert action and quick wit of the typical American.

Yankee-Doodle. The name given to what is now regarded as the National Air of the United States. There are various accounts of its origin, but in all probability the tune is English, and not more than about one hundred and fifty years old, as the first mention of it in print seems to be that in the Boston "Journal of the Times," for September, 1768. In Dr. Groves' Dictionary of Music we find it stated that the air " as a melody . . has little beyond simplicity in its favour, but there is a quaint, direct and incisive character about it which redeems it from vulgarity."

Year. In Anglo-Saxon usage this word was unaltered in the plural, in the same way as " sheep " and " deer." This use seems to have been maintained up to Shakespeare's time, for in " Much Ado about Nothing " the watchman talks of one who " has been a vile thief for this seven-year." We have a survival of the old style in the modern phrase, "a two-year old colt," etc.

Yeoman. The origin of this word appears to be uncertain, but Skeat is of the opinion that it probably comes from the Anglo-Saxon *ga*, a district or village, with the suffix, "man."

Yew. The word comes to us from the Anglo-Saxon *iuu*, and seems to be connected with the Gaelic *iubhar*, which means a bow, as well as a yew-tree, showing how intimately the tree was associated with bow-making. The value of the wood for making bows is one of the reasons generally assigned for the tree being found in so many English churchyards, but it has been suggested, with much evidence of probability, that the tree was considered sacred long before the introduction of Christianity into these islands, and that the church has been built on the site hallowed by the yew, rather than the yew planted in proximity of the church. Certainly, many of the yew-trees found in our churchyards—some of them of enormous size (such as that at Fortingale, at the entrance to Glen Lyon, the trunk of which was originally fifty-six and a half feet in circumference) —must have existed before the erection of the church.

Yoke. The word has become associated with the thought of servitude and submission, or with the idea of a weight to be carried and a burden to be borne, perhaps from the well-known text :—" Take my yoke upon you, and learn of me . . . for my yoke is easy, and my burden is light " (Matt. xi. 29-30). But the original meaning of the word was that of coupling or joining together, as it has its origin in the Sanscrit *yuga*, a yoke, a pair, a couple, from the same root as the Latin *jungere*, to join. The old ox-yoke—which may still be seen on some farms in Sussex—is a wooden bar, hollowed, and made into a curve near each end, and fastened on the necks of a pair of oxen, by which means the two are coupled together for drawing the plough.

Yokel. There seems to be some doubt as to the origin of the word, but Skeat suggests that it represents an unrecorded Anglo-Saxon word, viz. :—*geacol*, meaning cuckoo-like, foolish, from *geac*, a cuckoo. The Lowland Scotch *gowk* is used to denote both a cuckoo and a fool.

Yule. Yule-tide is, of course, Christmas-time, but why the term " yule " should be applied to Christmas it is not easy to determine. Of the solutions given, Skeat prefers that which makes " yule " to signify noise or outcry, especially the sound of revelry and rejoicing. In Anglo-Saxon we have *gylan*, to make merry, to keep festival, and in German there is *jolen*, to sing in a high-pitched voice, from which latter we get (through the French) our word " jolly."

Zany. This name (otherwise *Zanni*) used to be applied to the buffoon who took a subordinate part to the professional clown, mimicking the clown's tricks and playing the fool in general. The word " zany " comes from the Italian *Zanni*, which is equivalent to *Giovanni* (John), the most common of all Christian names, and thus used as a name for anybody, and ultimately for a fool or simpleton.

Zeal. " It is good to be zealously affected, always in a good thing," writes St. Paul to the Galatians (Gal. iv. 18); but zeal, with its burning, passionate enthusiasm, may be manifested either in a good or a bad cause. The word " zeal " means, literally, boiling heat, being derived from the Greek *zeo*, to boil. The name " Zealots " has been given to a fanatical Jewish sect, which, shortly after the time of Christ, struggled desperately against the Roman Empire until the fall of Jerusalem was accomplished.

" For modes of faith let graceless zealots fight;
His can't be wrong whose life is in the right."
(Pope.)

z

Zebra. The name is a native one, generally accepted as of Ethiopian origin. The external characteristics of the animal are those of the Ass rather than of the Horse; the tail is almost bare except at the extremity, where it has long hairs, the mane is short and stiff, and the legs have no warts. It is rapidly vanishing before the progress of cultivated land, and will probably become extinct before long. It has been tamed to man's use, but its vicious temper renders it of little value as a domestic animal.

Zenith. The zenith is that point in the heavens which is highest to a spectator at any place on the earth's surface. If the earth were a perfect—instead of an oblate—sphere, and a straight pole were placed in an absolutely perpendicular position on any part of the earth's surface, that pole would point in one direction to the centre of the earth and, in the other, to the zenith. The word "zenith" comes to us from the Spanish *zenit*, but it is not surprising to find that it is traced back to the Arabic *samt*, which means a path, a trail, for the Arabians had no small knowledge of astronomy and were well acquainted with the movements of the heavenly bodies, so far as they could be detected without the aid of the telescope.

Zephyr. The word is derived from the Greek *zophos*, which means the west, and also darkness and gloom, because the west is the quarter of the heavens in which the sun sinks " and leaves the world to darkness." Yet, poetically, any soft, mild and gentle breeze is a "zephyr," which was personified as the gentlest of all the sylvan deities.

Zest. The word comes to us through the French *zeste*, from the Latin *schistus*, divided, its literal meaning being a piece of lemon-peel. Hence it is used to denote that quality which gives a pleasant taste or relish.

Zinc. A metallic element found in abundance in many parts of Great Britain, and extracted from the ore by mixing it with charcoal and coke and subjecting the mixture to a full red heat in an earthen retort. Zinc is an important factor in the manufacture of galvanised iron, and preparations of it are widely employed in medicine. By means of the spectroscope it has been ascertained that zinc is present in the sun.

Zingari. The Italian name for a gipsy (q.v.), and often introduced into English songs in describing Romany dances, etc.

Zodiac. The word comes from the Greek *zodiakos*, meaning that which pertains to animals. It is applied to a particular zone in the heavens through which the sun passes in the course of the year, because this zone contains the twelve constellations which, from the most ancient times, have borne the names of the Ram, the Bull, the Twins, the Crab, the Lion, the Virgin, the Balance, the Scorpion, the Archer, the Goat, the Water-bearer, and the Fishes.

Zone. The literal meaning of the word is a belt, a girdle, (from the Greek *zonē*), and it is applied to any particular region of the earth or the heavens. (*See* ZODIAC.) Geographically it is used to denote the five imaginary belts surrounding the earth, viz., the North Frigid Zone, between the North Pole, and the Arctic Circle; the North Temperate Zone, between the Arctic Circle and the Tropic of Cancer; the Torrid Zone, between the Tropic of Cancer and the Tropic of Capricorn; the South Temperate Zone, between the Tropic of Capricorn and the Antarctic Circle; and the South Frigid Zone, between the Antarctic Circle and the South Pole.

Zoological Gardens. The word " zoological " signifies that which pertains to zoology, the science of animals, from the Greek *zoon*, a living creature. The London Zoological Gardens, which are pro◄

bably the finest in the world, were formed by the Zoological Society of London and opened in 1828. The Society was founded in 1826 " for the ad'vancement of Zoology and Animal Physiology, and for the introduction of new and curious subjects of the Animal Kingdom," and in 1829 it acquired its Charter of Incorporation.

Zoroaster. A name identified with the Parsee religious belief, and a term which is sometimes understood to mean a series of religious teachers rather than a single person. The first Zoroaster, if there was more than one, is believed to have lived as early as Moses, but he was the reformer, rather than the originator, of the faith called after his name. The creed, which is that professed by the old Persians and their successors the modern Parsees (sometimes called Fire-worshippers), teaches that there has always existed a certain Entity, whose name may be translated " Time without Bounds," who has brought into existence two powerful beings in perpetual conflict—the Good and the Evil. With this another creed—that of fire-worship— has become commingled, possibly through the Magi, and both these beliefs go to constitute the modern Parsee faith. There appears to be little doubt that the teaching of the primitive Zoroaster was much purer than the system of doctrine which has long passed current in his name.

Zounds. An exclamation of the nature of an oath, being a contraction of the expression " God's Wounds," referring to the traditional wounds inflicted on the Christ at His crucifixion. (*See* ODDS.)

Zymotic. The word is formed from the Greek *zumotikos*, and means that which produces fermentation. It is applied to those diseases which are communicable by a fermenting virus, such as Measles. Scarlet-fever, and Small-pox

A LIST OF WORDS AND PHRASES
USED IN THE GREAT WAR

A LIST OF WORDS AND PHRASES USED IN THE GREAT WAR

Ac dum. At once; be quick. Hindustani.

Adam and Eve on a raft. Poached eggs on toast.

Addressed to. Aimed at (of a shell).

Afters. A second dinner-course, as rice or stewed figs, following " skilly."

Ak Emma. Air Mechanic. Derived from the old signalling aiphabet in which A became Ak and M Emma, in order to avoid confusion with other letters.

Alleyman. German (Hun).

All Old Crocks; Angels of Christ. A.O.C.

All over himself (he is). Full of beans.

All smart. Everything's all right.

All spruced (or togged) up and nowhere to go. Said of a soldier who has smartened himself up a little more than usual.

All the way. To the bitter end; to any limit.

Ally! " Go away "; " clear out." " Ally toot sweet " (*Allez tout de suite*).

Ally Sloper's Cavalry; Fred Karno's. A.S.C.

Ammo. Also **Ammu.** Ammunition.

Angel's whisper. Defaulter's bugle-call.

Angrēji. English. This is an old corruption.

Antika. Any antique.

" Any complaints ? " The invitation given at every meal by the orderly officer for the men to criticize the *menu* (and woe betide those who responded to it !) became a stock phrase, used in all manner of ways.

Any more for any more ? An intimation, shouted by an orderly in charge of serving meals, that more was to be had if any wished for it.

Anzac picket (to be on). To be " dodging the column " at the Anzac Hostel, Kantara, E.

Apple-and-pears. Stairs—an old army expression.

Apree ler gare finee. Expression used commonly in France (*après la guerre finie*).

Apron. A type of wire fence.

Archie. Anti-aircraft shells of all descriptions.

353

ARMISTICK (ARMITIST). Armistice.

ARMY-DODGER. A man who sought to evade military service.

ASIATIC ANNIE. A Turkish gun (or guns) which fired across the Dardanelles.

ATEK. Attack. ATEKAI. Attacks.

AUNT MARY ANN. Variation on "Sanfaryan" (*cela ne fait rien*).

AUSSIE. Also AUSSIE-LAND. Australia, as well as an Australian soldier.

BABES (THE). Something very good.

BAG. Sufficiency. "A bag of beer." Bags=plenty.

BAGS OF ROOM. Heaps of room.

BAKE. Head.

BALL O' LEAD. One's head.

BAND-STAND. Cruet. (Barrack-room.)

BANTAMS. Short soldiers.

BARBED WIRE (ON THE). Present location unknown; not necessarily indicative of a casualty.

BARISHNYA. Strictly an unmarried lady. To Tommy, any "bird."

BARKERS. Sausages.

BAR-POO (TO GO). Lose one's nerve. Pile up one's bus.

BASE-WALLAH. Soldier mostly at the base.

BAT-OUT-OF-HELL. Speed.

BATTER (TO GO ON THE). To indulge in a drinking bout.

BATTER. Slope in wall of trench or parapet.

BATTLE BOWLER. Steel helmet.

BEAN-O. From "bean-feast." A spree.

BEETLE OFF (TO). Go away, run away—like a beetle.

BEGGAR ONE'S CONTRACT. Spoil anything, make it not worth while.

BEGNET. Jocks' word for "bayonet"; also called "knife" and "sword."

BELGIQUE (BELGIES). Belgians.

BELL-BELLUM. Any kind of river boat.

BELLUM (Arabic). A canoe-shaped boat.

BELLYBANDS. Cholera belts issued to British troops.

BERGOO (BURGO). Porridge. Spelling various.

BERM. Ledge in parapet.

BIG BERTHA. The German long-range gun which fired on Paris.

BIG NOISE. For any important personage.

BILJAM. Belgium.

BILL JIM. An Australian.

BILLY-CAN. Mess-tin.

BINGE. Social gathering. As verb—to imbibe alcohol.

BINTING (GO). To go on leave to Cairo to seek female society. (*Bint*, a girl, Arabic.)

BĪRAI. Beer. The singer says that the beers of France (Phrānsī kā bīrai) cooled their bodies!

BIRDCAGE. Wire creations of various kinds.

BIRD-LIME. Time. " What's the bird-lime ? "

BISCUITS. Small, square, very hard mattresses, 2 ft. 6 in. square, three to one bed.

BĪSĪ. V.C. (Kulbīr Thāpā le pāyōni bīsī ghaile liāundā mān: Kulbīr Thāpā won the V.C. by bringing in wounded.)

BIVY (BIVVY). Make-do shelter; bivouac.

BLACK MARIA. Heavy high-explosive German shell—so called on account of thick black smoke emitted when bursting.

BLANKETY-BLANK. Captain's language. (Trenches.)

BLIGHTY. England, home and hospital; anywhere this side of the Channel. From Hindustani, *belati.*

BLIGHTY-ONE. A wound severe enough to cause a man to be sent to England for treatment.

BLIMP. The name given to the small dirigible airships employed chiefly for coast defence. The origin of the term is not known, but it was curiously descriptive, in view of the smug, corpulent appearance of these craft.

BLINDAGE. Sandbag erection to hide from view.

BLIND HALF HUNDRED. Anti-aircraft batteries.

BLIND-O. Very drunk.

BLINK. Stump of a cigarette.

BLOB. A glass of beer.

BLOKE (MY). Batman's designation of his officer.

BLOODS. Third-class shots (Old Army).

BLOTTO. Drink; also drunk.

BLOW A REED (TO). To have a lot to say.

BLOW OFF THE LINE (TO). To lose.

BLOW THE GAFF. Give away secrets.

BLUE (IN THE). Said when an attack has gone forward and has lost touch.

BLUE-DEVILS. French chasseurs.

BOBBING DRILL. Practice-aiming at targets. (Musketry training.)

BOBERJE (BOBADJI, BOMMAJEE). From Hindustani *Bawarchi,* a cook.

BOCHE. German.

BOGEY (MAKE A). Make a mistake.

BOLO HOUSE (THE BOLO). Air Ministry.

BOMBARDIER FRITZ. *Pommes de terre frites*—a favourite estaminet dish (see *Punch* some time in 1916).

BOMB-DODGER. A person who removed from his usual place of residence in London or the eastern counties in order to be out of the air raid zone. Many went to " Jerusalem-on-Sea "—i.e., Brighton—or up the Thames valley.

BONDHOOK (BONDOCK). Rifle. " The soldier's best friend." From Hindustani (cf. Swahili *Bunduki*).

BONZA (BONZER). Good, excellent. Colonial word.

BOOKA. Hungry. (India.)

BOOKED (TO BE). To be done for.

BOOKS (THE). Playing-cards.

BOOZER. An estaminet.

BOOZILIER. Fusilier.

BOSKY. Tipsy.

BOUNCE (ON THE). At an opportune moment.

BOWLER. " To be given your bowler." To be demobilized—returned to civilian life—and therefore to resume your bowler hat. Coined, I believe, first in the Egyptian campaign and Palestine—chiefly used for officers—equivalent to *dégommé*, though the latter expression really means to lose your appointment.

BOX OPEN AND BOX SHUT. Offer of cigarette; offer closed.

BRASS HAT. Senior Staff Officer.

BREEZER (GI'S A). Give me a rest.

BREEZY. Also "to have the breeze up." Windy.

BRIEF. A soldier's discharge from the service.

BRITISH WARM. A short overcoat much worn by officers of all ranks, but not a uniform garment.

BROKE (TO BE). To lose one's stripes (Old Army).

BROODY. Lethargic. *Sergeant* (r e p r o v i n g l y): " Are you going broody ? "

BUBBLY. A tout, or one who keeps guard when illegal games are played.

BUCKSHEE. Extras; a gift; something for nothing. (Corruption of *baksheesh*.)

BUFF STICK. Orderly man. (Barrack room.)

BUKRA. To-morrow. Arabic.

B——R-ALL (THERE IS). There is nothing.

BULL-RING (THE). Training camps at Etaples and elsewhere.

BULLY THE TROOPS. Hardly slang. A more expressive form is " To be b-ggered about," to be given unnecessary drill or manœuvres.

BUNCE. Something for nothing.

BUNG IN IT (PUT A). Shut the door. (The Army huts at Winchester.)

BUN-STRANGLER. Teetotaller (Old Army).

BUNTY. Nickname for a short man.

BUS. Pilots and observers generally referred to their own machines as "buses," but later in the war this term came to be regarded as rather bad form for some reason or other.

BUSHEL AN' PECK. One's neck.

BUSS. Alone, only. " He had his coat on buss"—he had only his coat on.

BUZZER. Signalling instrument. Signallers.

CAIN AN' ABEL. Table.

CALABOOSE. Prison. Arabic.

CALM LAYLAS. Egyptian Labour Corps—from their song " Kam Layla, Kam

Yom ? " (How many nights, how many days?)

CAMEL-WALLAH. See remarks against Base-wallah.

CAMOUFLAGE. Innumerable variants of this word were current. A certain M.G.C. Sergeant-Major always called it " camel flower."

CAN (A). A simpleton.

CANARIES. Instructors at central training schools in France, from yellow armbands worn.

CANNED. Intoxicated.

CANTEEN MEDALS. Drippings of beer on tunic.

CANTEEN-STINKERS. Cheap cigarettes.

CANUCK. Canadian.

CAP-BADGE. A bone. After distributing the meat ration the orderly might say, " Does anyone want a cap-badge ? "

CAPE OF GOOD HOPE. Soap.

CARRY ON. Continue.

CATCH A COLD (TO). To get " wind up."

CATEGORY MEN. Men whose physical condition denied them the pleasures of the front.

CAT-STABBER. Clasp-knife. (Trenches, because of splicing attachment.)

CAT-WALK. Pathway paved with bricks (one brick, or 9 in., wide) between fields on a Belgian farm.

CEILING (AN AEROPLANE'S). The highest point to which it will climb.

CHALK-FARM. One's arm.

CHANCE ONE'S ARM. Get into

trouble (whereby a N.C.O. might lose a stripe).

CHANCING HIS MIT. To try.

CHAR. Cha, tea.

CHARLIE. Infantryman's pack.

CHAT. A louse.

CHATTY. Lousy.

CHAT-UP. A spell of killing vermin.

CHEQUE. Discharge.

CHERRY-NOBS. Military police.

CHEWED UP (TO BE). To be " told off," reprimanded.

CHEWING THE FAT. Fault-finding.

CHEWING THE RAG (OR THE FAT). "Grousing," grumbling.

CHIN-CHIN. Here's to you ! A form of toast.

CHINESE ROLLS-ROYCE. A Ford car (R.A.S.C.).

CHINKS. The Chinese Labour Corps.

CHIPERNE. Shut up.

CHIT. Voucher for rations, clothing, etc.

CHOKED OFF. Reprimanded ; successfully retorted upon.

CHOW-UP. Controversy.

CHRISTMAS-TREE ORDER (IN). Said of a man with his full equipment and all his possessions on him.

CHUCK. Bread, food.

CHUCK IT. To stop talking.

CHUCK UP (GIVE HIM A). Give him a salute.

CIRCLE ROUND. Search for.

CIRCUS. The Circus was the name always given to the band of multi-coloured and very fast small scouting machines led by Richthofen, the leading German airman, from the beginning of 1917 until his death in 1918. The machines, which generally made their appearance fifteen or twenty at a time, were painted with all the colours of the rainbow, red, blue, green, in stripes, stars, and Futuristic effects, and the picture they presented as they appeared from behind a cloud on a fine summer's day, while terrifying to the last degree, was certainly striking enough to justify the name of the " Circus."

CIVVY. A civilian.

CIVVY KIP. A feather-bed. *Tommy* (looking for a comfortable billet) : "Madame, avez-vous un civvy-kip ? "

CLEAR OFF AT THE TOUTE (SUITE). Get away quickly.

CLICK WITH A GIRL. Make her acquaintance without formal introduction.

CLICKED. Caught; also said to mean lucky; in receipt of something.

CLINK. Guard-room, detention.

CLOB LOUT. Heavy on feet.

CLOBBER. Clothing or equipment lying about in an untidy state.

CLODS. Money (usually copper coins).

CLUTCHING HAND. Quartermaster.

COAL-BOX. German heavy shell; name given from thick black smoke emitted on bursting.

COB. To stud, frost or nail the shoes of horses to prevent slipping.

COBBA. Friend.

COCKPIT. The observer's compartment in an aeroplane, with its machine-gun, ammunition, Very light, pistol, and other fighting paraphernalia, was called the cockpit.

COFFEE AVEC. Coffee with a drop of rum, cognac, or any spirit.

COFFIN-NAILS. Woodbines.

COGGIDGE. Paper — either newspaper or writing-paper.

COLD (IT'S) ENOUGH TO MAKE A JEW DROP HIS BUNDLE. It's very cold.

COLD (YOU LEAVE ME). You annoy me.

COLD FEET. Term for fright.

COLD-MEAT TICKET. A soldier's identity disc.

COLOUR. Colour-sergeant.

COLUMN (TO DODGE THE). To shirk a duty; dodge the front line; to be absent from parade.

COME ON TALLY PLONK (TALLER CANDLE) ? How are you getting on ? (*Comment allez-vous?*)

COMIC BUSINESS. Flying.

COMIC CUTS. Divisional orders.

COMMO. Communication, e.g., " Commo trench."

COMPRI ? Do you understand ?

CONCHIE (CONSCIE). A conscientious objector.

CONK OUT (TO). To give out, to fail. An aeroplane

engine never failed, it always " conked out."

CONTOUR CHASING. Flying very low.

COOTY. Lousy; dirty.

COSH. Stick used by night patrols.

COTTON ON (TO). To understand.

COUGH AND SNEEZE. Cheese.

COUGH IT UP. Speak out.

COW-JUICE. Milk.

CRABS. Lice.

CRACKERS. Going mad.

CRAWLING, CREEPING, SQUARING. Buying favours.

CRICKET BALL. Hand-grenade fired with match-head. Used between the " jamtins " and the Mills.

CROWN AND ANCHOR. One of the most popular gambling games in the Army. Played clandestinely in estaminets, billets, and out-of-the-way places by the troops, with the aid of dice and a coloured cloth bearing the four aces and two signs—a crown and an anchor.

CRUMBY. Verminous.

CRUMP. H.E. shell—from the sound of the burst.

CRUSH. A body of men; company platoon, etc. " What crush do you belong to ? "

CULLY. Pal, chum.

CUM-SAH or U-JAH. Used instead of " what's-itsname." From comme ça.

CUP AND WAD. Cup of tea and bun in the canteen.

CUP YOU AND ME. Tea.

CUSHY. Khushi, properly adj., pleasant. The noun " pleasure " is khush, whence " cushy," something pleasant, a soft job.

CUSHY ONE IN THE BAKE. Sarcastic description of a bad head-wound.

CUT. Intoxicated.

CUT THAT OUT. Stop acting the fool. (Canadians.)

CUTHBERT. A stay-at-home, especially in Government offices.

DAG UP. Clean up. (Barrack-room.)

DAMFUL. To deceive.

DAMPER (HAVE A). Have a drink.

DARKEY. Nickname for Smith.

DATE (TO HAVE A). To have an appointment.

DEAD-NUTS. A certainty.

DEATH WARMED UP (TO FEEL LIKE). To feel ill.

DECK (OFF THE). Leaving the ground.

DEEP END (TO GO OFF THE). To get excited or angry.

DÉGOMMÉ. Reduced in rank —no disgrace attached— applied to brigadiers, etc., who became colonels after the Armistice, when establishments were reduced.

DEKKO. From the Hindustani verb Dekhna, to see. Dekho is the imperative, look or see ! Similarly Dekker.

DELIBLE. A N.C.O. (?= washout).

DERAKS. Playing cards.

DERBY. Lord Derby's " Overseas men."

DERSIE. A tailor.

DIAL. A clock; also one's face.

DICKY DIRT. One's shirt.

DIED OF WOUNDS. Answer for absent man on his name being called.

DIE-HARDS. Nickname given to the Middlesex Regiments.

DIGGER. Soldier of the Australian or New Zealand Expeditionary Force.

DIG IN THE GRAVE. Shave.

DIG ONESELF IN (TO). To insinuate or work oneself into a soft or safe job and hold tight.

DIG OUT. To tidy up generally. (Army billets in France.)

DINKUM. Truly, honestly.

DIRTY LITTLE IMPS. Durham Light Infantry.

DIRTY ONE (A). A bad wound; a misfortune.

DISHAMBAR. December.

DISHAMBAR MAINĀ. Month of December.

DIXY. From Hindustani *Degchi*, a cooking pot.

DOBRA AND NIET DOBRA. Russian for "good" and "no good."

DOCK. Hospital.

DOG-END. Stump of cigarette.

DOG-FIGHT. A quick fight.

DOGS. "Hot dogs." A name given to Frankfurter sausage.

DOINGS (THE). Thing that is wanted.

DOING THE TAP. Winning game of cards.

DO ME DAGS. Fags, cigarettes.

DONKEYS. Transport mules.

DONKS. Mules.

DOOLY. Milk.

DO ONE FOR THE KING. To do a twenty-four hours armed guard.

DOPE. Anæsthetic.

DOPEY. Fool; inefficient soldier.

DORK (also DOORSTEP). A thick slice of bread.

DO SVIDANYA! Good-bye! The Russian expression meaning *Au revoir!*

DOSS. Sleep.

DOT HIM ONE. Hit a man with one's fists.

DOUGH. Money.

DOUGHBOY. An American soldier.

DOWN (TO HAVE A) ON A MAN. To have a grudge or spite against him.

DROP HIM A STICK OF BLACK-ING. Hit a man with one's fists.

DRUM-UP. "I've some sugar. If you get tea and hot water we'll have a 'drum-up.'"

D.S.O. Dirty shirt on.

DUB-DUB. A complete failure.

DUCKBOARD. A board laid down to facilitate getting about in mud, only wide enough for single file.

DUCKBOARD HARRIER. A battalion runner, or anyone employed as a messenger in the trenches.

DUCK DISEASE. Short legs. The appearance of a soldier with short legs was rendered more ludicrous, since he was bound to wind round them puttees of the ordinary length.

DUD. A shell which has failed to explode.

DUFF. Pudding.

DUGGIE. Earl (Douglas) Haig.

DUG-OUT KING. An officer who always kept in his dug-out.

DUG-OUT. One who has seen his best days. A white-haired Colonel would invariably receive this distinction.

DULL THUD (A). A bad wound. A misfortune.

DULLMAJOR. Name given by prisoners of war to an interpreter (from the German *Dolmetscher*=interpreter).

DUMP. Where soil or rock from excavations, garbage, etc., is unloaded.

DUNNAGE-BAG. Canvas bag to carry clothing.

DURATION (FOR THE). For the duration of the war.

EARHOLE. Wanting to borrow.

EDGE. Adjutant.

EDIFICATION. Sergeant's word for education.

EGGS A-COOK. Hard-boiled Egyptian eggs.

ELEPHANT. A hut having the sides and top made of rounded sheets of iron.

EMBUSS (TO). To put troops on a motor-bus.

EMMA GEE. Machine-gun, from the initial letters M.G. as pronounced by the signallers.

ERB. Substitute used when a man's Christian name is unknown.

ERFS. Eggs.

ESMA. Listen. Arabic.

EVERY CREDIT. An expression always used by the men: no one knows the meaning.

EYEWASH. Camouflage. "Blarney" is rather inadequate. "Eyewash parade" is a G.O.C.'s inspection or similar affair. To clean a dirty camp with whitewash (*à la* Guards).

FADE AWAY. Make oneself scarce.

FAG. Cigarette.

FAGGOT, YOU! (YOU OLD). You silly old woman.

FAIR COP. Fairly caught.

FAIR DOOS. A proper share.

FASHY. Angry.

FAT. Good luck.

FED-UP. Satiated.

FILLY. Young girl.

FINI. It's finished! All gone!

FINISH. To finish; end; be done for.

FIRESIDERS. Men who did not join up.

FIREWORK DISPLAY. A heavy bombardment, usually accompanied by red, white, green, and blue lights.

FIVE-MILE SNIPER. Gunner in heavy artillery.

FIX (ON THE WORD). Punctually. "I was there on the word, Fix."

FIZZA. Parade (Barrack-room.)

FLAG-WAGGER. Signaller.

FLAMING ONIONS. An anti-aircraft device of the Germans, the precise nature of which, or its means of propulsion, seems never to have been clearly established. Its object was clearly to set fire to the machine. Seen from close quarters this projectile appeared to take the form of a sequence of green flaming spheres; by the manner in which they followed each other up and then fell after reaching the top of their trajectory many pilots and observers thought that they were joined together, and some indeed claimed to have seen the string or wire. In any case, they must have been very disappointing to the Germans, for there was never an authenticated instance of a machine having been brought down by them.

FLEA-BAG. Described as an officer's valise, is surely the Army sleeping-bag.

FLIP. A flight (or, to fly).

FLOG IT (TO). To sell or to walk it.

FLY (TO BE). To be smart.

FLYING KITE. Aeroplane.

FLYING PIG. Large type of trench mortar. Inter-trench torpedo shell. It has fin-like projections, and in flight its shape suggests a pig.

FOOTBALL. A circular-shaped trench-mortar missile used by British—about the size of a football.

FOOTSLOGGING. Marching.

FOR THE JUMPS. To go for trial for any offence.

FOUR BY TWO. Army biscuits, or pull-through for rifle.

FOUR-FLUSHER. A cheat or " swanker."

FRAY BENTOS. Tinned corned beef.

FREEMANS. Anything free.

FRITZ. A German.

FROG AND TOAD. On the road.

FROGGIES. French soldiers.

FUJILIERS. Fusiliers.

FUNK-HOLE. Dug-out or shelter.

FUSILIER (YOU'RE A). Term of reproach from one rifleman to another.

GADGET. Almost any instrument or device on an aeroplane was, and probably still is, a gadget.

GAFF. A concert. (France.)

GASPER. A cheap cigarette.

GAS-PIPE CAVALRY. Army Cyclist Corps—so called because of the bicycles.

GASSED AT MONS. Answer when a man's name is called who is absent.

GERMAN BANDS. Hands.

GERMAN SAUSAGE. German observation balloon. (Trenches.)

GERRY. German.

GET AWAY WITH IT. To be " crimed " and found not guilty.

GET DOWN TO IT (TO). To sleep. "Well, I'll go and get down to it."

GET THE NEEDLE. Annoyed.

GETTING THE WIND UP. Alarmed.

GIPPA. Gravy.

GLASSHOUSE. Military prison.

GONE DIS. (A contraction of "disconnected"—a term used by the R.E. signals.) Generally employed to indicate vacuity of mind.

GONE PHUT. An expression denoting an unsatisfactory condition of affairs.

GONG. A medal.

GOODS (THE). The Gordons.

GOOSEBERRIES. A wire entanglement the shape of a gooseberry. (Trenches.)

GORBLIMEY. The first soft caps issued in 1914 without a wire. These had no waterproof lining, but had a broad cloth chin-strap attachment (to cover the ears and back of the neck), which folded over the crown of the cap when not in use. The name was well deserved. Later applied to any soft cap with no wire.

GORBLING. A soft cap with pushed-in front greatly affected by young subalterns until caught by the A.P.M.

GO WEST. Killed.

GRAFT. Work (Old Army).

GRANDMOTHER. Heavy howitzer.

GRANNY. A 9·2 gun.

GRASSHOPPER. Policeman—derived from "Copper."

GREASE (TO). To get away.

GREASE. Butter.

GREEN UN. Green envelope.

GREYBACK. Army shirt.

GRIFFEN (TO GIVE THE). To give a secret warning, or "to give the wire."

GROG. Rum.

GROUND-WALLAHS. The term by which those officers of the corps whose duties, either technical or administrative, did not take them into the air, were known. In the words of a leading light of the Royal Flying Corps, "They loop not, neither do they spin."

GUBBINS. Stuff, personal belongings, stores, etc.

GUFAR (Ar.). A river tub.

GUNFIRE. Tea.

GUP. Information picked up by troops when off duty.

GUTSER. A "knock out." Also used figuratively.

GUY. American for "Tommy."

GYPO. An Egyptian.

"HALF-CROWN BRIGADE." A "second-sixth" (2/6) battalion.

HAMMER (THAT'S THE). Idea.

HAND-CART CAVALRY. Stokes trench mortar brigade.

HARD JACK. Bully and biscuit.

HARD SKIN. Rough kind of man.

HARNESS. Equipment.

HARRY TATE. R.E.8 aeroplane.

HATE (MORNING AND EVEN-
ING). Terms applied to
the daily bombardment of
our line, generally for the
purpose of registering distances, by the German
artillery early in the war.
HEAR FROM YOU (LET'S). Get
a move on.
HECTIC SHOW. Dangerous
flying.
HEINIE. German (American
word).
HENCORE. Encore.
HISSY. " Ici."
HOB (TO BE ON). Teetotaller.
HOOCH. Whisky.
HOOK (A). A successful
practitioner of the art of
" dodging the column."
HOOKEM (THAT'S THE).
Rather, " That's the
order," " That's the regulation," From Hindus-
tani, *Hukam*, an order.
HOOKS. Spurs. Chiefly to
recruits. " You've for-
gotten your hooks,
lad ! "
HOT AIR. Very frequently
heard in the corps in
reference to the reports of
those pilots or observers
who were inclined to
report rather more impor-
tant enemy movements on
the ground than they had
actually observed.
HOT-CROSS BUN. Red Cross
ambulance.
HOUSÉ (ÉE). A game.
HOW. Howitzer.
HUMP. To carry a load.
HUMP YOUR PACK (TO). To
march on foot carrying
all your gear.

HUN. Applied to the enemy,
of course, but more usually
understood in the Royal
Flying Corps to apply to
an officer undergoing a
course of instruction as a
pilot.
HUSH-HUSH. A caterpillar
tank.

IN DOCK. In hospital.
IGGRI. Quickly. Arabic.
(Cf. " Iggri corner," near
Bullecourt, so named by
the Australian troops.)
I-I. How are you ? (Pass-
word on line of march.)
IMSHI (Ar.). Go; get out.
INDIA-RUBBER GUN. German
high-velocity gun.
INVALID FIRE. Enfilade fire.
IRON RATIONS. (Properly,
tinned tea and sugar,
tinned corned beef, etc.,
which every soldier carried
with him for emergencies
only.) Shells. " Gerry is
sending us plenty of
iron rations to-night."
"Gerry's iron rations "
were the shells of our
artillery.
ISSUE. Anything supplied
by the army ; e.g., a ration
cigarette is " an issue."
ITIS. (Pronounced " eye-
ties."). Italians.
ITTY-UMPTY. Usual spelling,
" iddy-umpty." It repre-
sents the sounds made by
signalling flag when sending Morse signals.

JACK JOHNSON. German
heavy high-explosive shell ;
so called from the thick,

black smoke emitted on bursting.

JACKY. A Turk (used in Gallipoli as well as " Johnny ").

JAM. Good.

JAM JAR. German missile of the "toffee-apple" description.

JAM ON IT. Similar to "cushy job"; something nice and easy.

JAM TIN. The early type of bomb made in a discarded jam tin.

JANKERS or PADDY DOYLE. C.B. or "time."

JAPAN. Bread. (Doopang.)

JERK (PUT A). Put a move on.

JERKS. Physical drill.

JERRY. A German.

JERRY OVER. Lights out.

JIGGER. Bicycle. (France.)

JILDY. Quick, smart. "Look jildy"—be quick.

JIMMY. Form of salutation to any English soldier.

JOANNER. Piano.

JOCKS. The Scotch troops.

JOHNNY. A Turk.

JOYBAG. A sandbag containing souvenirs, rations or "winnings," carried over and above one's regulation equipment.

JOY-RIDE. A flight undertaken for purposes of pleasure or sight-seeing.

JOY-STICK. In simple language, the lever which was pulled back if the machine were required to go up, and pushed forward if it were required to go down.

JUDY. A Palestine Jew. (*Yahudi*: Arabic.)

JUGGED. Imprisoned.

JUICE. Petrol (R.A.S.C.).

JUMP. Get a free ride on (e.g., jump a lorry).

KAMERAD. Spoken as a sign of submission—in imitation of the German prisoners.

KELLEK (Ar.). A large skin raft.

KIBOSH. To put a stop to.

KID (TO). Deceive, defraud; "get round" a person.

KING'S HARD BARGAIN. A man who was not worth his pay.

KIP. Bed.

KISS ME SERGEANT. Answer to orderly sergeant's "good-night" after he has read orders for following day.

KISSWOSH. Thingummybob.

KITCH. A man who enlisted in Lord Kitchener's new Army.

KNEE DRILL. Church parade.

KNIFE-REST. Portable wire structure to put in front of trench.

KNOCK ALONG. Move on.

KNOCK OFF. Acquire by artifice; steal. "I knocked it off from a rookie in 'C' Coy."

KNOCK THE END IN. Spoil the whole thing.

KNOCKED UP A CATCHER (TO BE.) To be found out.

KNOCKER. Non-payer.

KUNTRACHI (F. and Turki). A contractor.

KWAYESS. Good, all right. Arabic.

LACKERY. Wood; a wood-collector was known as a "lackery-wallah." Hindustani.

LAD OF THE VILLAGE. Cheery companion.

LANCE-JACK. A lance-corporal.

LANDOWNER (TO BE A). To be killed—thus occupying a small piece of land.

LANDSLIP. A caterpillar tank.

LAVATORY LANCERS. Westmorland and Cumberland Yeomanry.

LEADSWINGER. A malingerer.

LEAN ON YOUR CHIN STRAPS. Phrase used on the march.

LEAVE NOTHING LOOSE. Loyal North Lancs.

LEGS ELEVEN. Nickname for an officer with exceptionally thin legs.

LEMONADE-WALLAH. Teetotaller (Old Army).

LICK INTO SHAPE. Make a soldier.

LID. Steel helmet.

LIMPET. A man who had a good job behind the line, or in a Government office at home and clung tightly to it.

LINE (UP THE). The front, as referred to by troops in the rear.

LINSEED LANCERS. Royal Army Medical Corps.

LIZZIE. Heavy naval gun run forward by railway.

LOAF O' BREAD. One's head.

LOB (TO). To throw a hand-grenade. "Lobbing one over."

LOFTY. Popular term for a tall man.

LONGNOSED CHUM. Horse.

LOOPY. Daft; silly; mentally deficient.

LOOT. A subaltern. "One-pip loot," a second-lieutenant (from single star on shoulder). "Two pip loot."

LORRY HOP (LORRY JUMP). To get a lift on the road by jumping (on to) a lorry.

LOT'S WIFE. Salt.

LOUD ONE (A). A bad wound, a misfortune.

LOUSE (TO). To clean or wash. Usually to take a bath in difficulties and half a mess-tinful of water.

LOZENGES. Revolver ammunition. Probable origin: when it had coughed a bit give it some more lozenges.

MACONOCHIE. Meat and vegetable ration in tins. From name on one maker's tins, but applied to any make.

MAHAILA (Ar.). A large river sailing boat.

MAHNGEE. Anything to eat (manger).

MAIDEN'S PRAYER. Observation balloon.

MAJOR. Sergeant-major (commonly used).

MAKKI. Machine-gun.

MAKOO. None; not to be had; out of stock.

MALEESH. It doesn't matter. (Arabic.)

M. AND D. Medicine and duty. Disgusted was the

malingerer when marked " M. and D." by the Medical Officer.

MANGLE. An affectionate (or otherwise) nickname for a machine-gun.

MARCHA. March.

MARCHA KA MAINA. The month of March.

MARIONETTE. The minaret of a mosque.

MARK TIME ON. Retain; hang on to.

MARSAL. Marseilles.

MARSINGAN. Machine-gun.

MAT (ON THE). Said of an officer or soldier who was in trouble and appeared before his superior officer for admonition or correction.

MATE (MATEY). The most frequent term of address used among the troops.

MEAT-SKEWER. Bayonet.

MESOPOLONICA. Any unknown destination in the East. In phrase " Drafted to Mesopolonica."

MIKE (TO). To slack.

MINGLE. Officer's hospital slang. Used of occasions when nurses and patients met socially on equal terms under official approbation (and supervision).

MINNIE. A shell from a Minenwerfer.

MITTS. Hands.

MOANER. Equal to " pessimist " in civil life.

MOBILE (A). The Egyptian Expeditionary Force term for a march in the Sinai Desert.

MONKEY (TO). To fool about

with; touch. " Don't monkey with that magneto."

MONKEY MOTIONS. Physical drill.

MOOSH. Guard-room or detention barracks.

MOPPING UP. Clearing dugouts and trenches after having captured them.

MOURNFUL MARIA. Syren at Dunkirk used to signal approach of long-range shell.

MUCK IN (TO). To share; used especially of sharing of a section's rations.

MUCKIN. Old Army for butter. Hindustani, *Makhan*.

MUD-CRUSHER. An infantry soldier.

MUD-LARK. Anyone singing in the trenches. (Trenches, 1914.)

MUMP (TO). To cadge.

MUNGAREE. Bread or food. A word used by the Egyptians (who evidently thought it was English) and adopted by our troops. " Give it mungaree "— give me some food.

MURPHY. Potato.

MUTTON CHOPS. R. W. Surreys (from emblem of lamb and flag).

MUTTON-FISTED. Heavy on controls of plane.

MUTTON LANCERS. Another name for the Queen's R. W. Surreys (who, I believe, are " Kirke's Lambs " of Charles II's time).

MYRRH. Rum.

NA-POO'D. Done for; put out of action; killed. (In use from at least 1917.)

NECK (GET IT IN THE). Receive a stiff punishment Also be killed; " knocked out."

NECK (YOU'VE GOT A) ON YOU. You've got cheek.

NICK. Guard-room or detention barracks.

NIGHT OPPS. Night operations.

NITCHIVO. Russian equivalent to " Napoo." Used by Tommy in every way. " Nothing doing "; " I haven't got it."

NIX. Nothing; no. " Nix on that "—nothing doing. " Nix beer." (German: *nicht* or *nichts; nix*— Army of the Rhine).

NOBBY. Nickname for Clarke (Old Army).

NO BON! No good (for supposed French *non bon,* i.e., *pas bon*).

NO. 9. An aperient pill.

NON-STOP. A shell that passed overhead.

NOT HALF! Expression of agreement or disagreement.

NOTHING TO WRITE HOME ABOUT. Nothing exciting.

NOTTS AND DOTTS. Notts and Derby Regiments.

NUMBER ON (GOT YOUR). A bullet or shell intended for you.

O.C. SOCKS. A man detailed for a one-man job such as collecting the platoon's socks would be " Officer Commanding Socks."

ODDS AND SODS. Details attached to Battalion Headquarters, e.g., sanitary men.

OFFICE. The pilot's seat. With its many instruments, writing-pad, speaking-tube, etc., the name was an apt one.

OIL (ON THE). A drinking bout.

OLD BILL. Any soldier with a drooping moustache.

OLD CHINA. A friend or pal.

OLD MAN (THE). The Company Commander or Commanding Officer; Colonel.

OLD SWEAT. A pre-war timeserving soldier.

ONE OF OURS. Said of shell dropping near the frontline trenches. " It's all right; it's one of ours."

ONE OF THE BOYS. Cheery companion.

ONE UP (TO HAVE). Said of second-lieutenant with one star on his sleeve, or of lance-corporal with one stripe.

ON THE NOD. Free; gratis.

ON THE PEGS. Under arrest.

ON THE WIRE. When a man is wanted and cannot be found.

OO-JAR-YA-PIV (OO-JAR-CAPIVEE). Used when at a loss for a word. " Thingummy-bob " (cf. gadget). Any old thing.

OOJIBOO. The hardest worked word. Signified anything, its nearest equivalent being " gadget." Once I heard this dialogue :—*Lorry driver* : " Sorry, Flight, but in the fog a fellow passed me on the wrong side and carried away my oojiboo." *Flight Sergeant* : " That's the second side-lamp you've done in this week."

Oo-la-la ! Exclamation of pleased surprise.

Organ (to want the). To wish to borrow money.

Ours or theirs ? Expression frequently heard in the trenches when a shell came over.

Outfit. Squadron.

Over the bags. Equivalent to " over the top."

Over the top. Taking a position at the point of the bayonet. Used of ascending from the trenches to no-man's-land. Over the top and the best o' luck !

Packed up. Killed.

Packet. A wound. " So-and-so has caught a packet."

Padre. The battalion chaplain.

Paltan. Battalion (pre-war).

Pancake landing (to). To lose flying speed and drop vertically. (*Vide inf.* : Pile up one's bus.)

Pane of glass. Monocle.

Parapet Joe. A soldier always on the parapet.

Parky. Cold. (Trenches.)

Pass out (to). To die.

Patrolai. Patrols.

Pawnee. Water. Hindustani.

P.B.I. Poor Bloody Infantry.

P.B.I.'s. Permanent Blooming Infantry.

Peas in the pot. Very hot.

Pea-shooter. Rifle.

Peechy. Presently, shortly. " I'll be there peechy."

Peg (on the). Having had one's number and name taken and reported to the C.O. as charged with some trivial military offence.

Peg out (to). To die.

Perishin'. Used as an intensive, e.g., " Perishin' thirsty weather."

Phaira. (Gun)fire. Topai ko phaira. Fire of the guns.

Pharst Tard. First-Third, i.e., First Battalion of the Third Gurkhas (pre-war).

Phizog. Photograph. (Trenches.)

Phrānsī. France, French. This is new: the time-honoured corruption is Farangī, Feringhee.

Physical jerks. Physical drill; Swedish drill.

Pianny. Drunk.

Piassa. A cleaning rod used for cleaning 4-in. Stokes mortars.

Pickled monkey. A species of animal served by the Germans to prisoners of war as food. Its identity was never determined by the recipients.

Pig's ear. Beer.

Pig-sticker. Bayonet.

Pile up one's bus (to). To crash.

Pill-box. A miniature fort

constructed chiefly of concrete, sometimes upon a steel foundation and immensely strong.

PINEAPPLE. A trench mortar explosive used by Germans. So called because its side and external surface is similar to a pineapple.

PIP. Star worn on shoulder and sleeve of an officer.

PIPPED. Wounded.

PIP-SQUEAK. Rifle-grenade; also German shell.

PLATES. Feet.

PLINKITY-PLONK. Vin blanc.

PLUM-PUDDING. Heavy trench-mortar shell.

POILU. French infantryman.

POM-POM. French 75 mm. cannon.

POND (THE). The English Channel.

PONGELOW. Beer (Old Army).

POOP (POUP). Off. Used of artillery firing.

PORK AND BEANS. Portuguese troops.

POSHED UP. Dressed up for a special occasion.

POT AND PAN. The " old man."

POTATO-MASHER. A German bomb which is stuck on the end of a stick—like a hammer.

POT-HOLE. Shell-hole.

POULTICE SWALLOWERS, LINSEED. R.A.M.C.

POZHÁLYSTA. Please.

POZZEE. Jam. Hindustani.

POZZEE-WALLAH. A man who is fond of jam. Hindustani.

PROG. Food.

PRUSSIAN GUARD. A flea.

PUDDING-BASIN. A steel helmet.

PUKKA. Real; proper. Hindustani.

PULL-THROUGH. A tall thin soldier.

PUNG (TO). Signaller's word, meaning to go to sleep while on duty at the telephone.

PUSH THE BOAT OUT (TO). Stand treat.

PUSHER. A young woman.

PUSHING UP DAISIES. Dead and buried.

PUT A JERK IN IT. Smarten your actions.

PUT DOTS ON ONE. To bore or tire.

PUT YOUR SKATES ON. Get clear, to evade duty.

QUARTER BLOKE. The Quartermaster Sergeant.

QUARTERMASTER'S ERASMIC. Soap issued for Tommy's toilet, but really intended for floor-scrubbing.

QUARTER TO TEN. 9·45 in. trench mortar.

QUARTERS. Quartermaster Sergeant.

QUEER FELLA. Anyone in command.

QUIDS IN. Said when everything appears to be to one's advantage.

QUIFF. A tuft of hair brushed up on the forehead.

QUIRK. The name given to the B.E. type of machine, which, while stable, was a very slow and stately sort of craft.

QUITE IN ORDER. Not unusual, no surprise need be expressed.

RACE-CARD. Morning Sick Report. (Kitchener's Army.)

RATTLED. Nervous, scared; also angry. "The S.M. got rattled when I asked for an extra blanket."

REAR UP. To get angry.

RED CAPS. Military Police. At the Base these wore hats having the crowns covered with a red material.

RED EYE. Rum.

RED HAT. Staff Officer.

RED HERRINGS. Staff Officers wearing red hat-band and tabs—on home service.

RED HUSSAR. A brand of ration cigarette. Any cigarette.

RED INK. Vin rouge.

RED LAMPS. Banned estaminets.

RED WINGS. Staff officers (Anzac).

REST CAMP. Cemetery.

RIGHTO (RIGHTHO). All right.

RISE AND SHINE. Get up.

ROB-ALL-MY-COMRADES. Royal Army Medical Corps, the initials being the cause of this honourable nickname. The derivation of this nickname for the Royal Army Medical Corps was scarcely "honourable." It originated in 1915 after a large number of officers' kits had been rifled in hospital trains taking wounded and sick from the front to the various bases. The matter became a scandal, and it was not till a number of examples had been made of R.A.M.C. orderlies that the practice ceased.

ROB EVERY POOR SOLDIER. R.E. (Postal Services).

ROGER. A gas cylinder. The word was used as a code word to denote gas cylinders in an operation just prior to July 1st, 1915, and hence came into current speech.

ROLL (TO). To turn the machine completely over sideways. A side-loop.

ROOKIE (ROOKEE). Recruit.

ROOTI. *Roti*, bread.

ROTTEN IRISH RAGTIMERS. Royal Irish Rifles.

ROYAL STANDBACKS. A legendary unit that suffered from "cold feet" —"the Royal Standbacks, last into the field and first out."

RUBBER GUN. Long-range gun.

RUBBER HEELS. Long-range gun shells.

RUB OUT (TO). To die.

RUMBLE. Disturb, annoy, upset.

RUMBLED (TO BE). To be found out; usually in connection with malingering or shirking duty.

RUM JAR. Trench-mortar bomb.

RUN. Charged with a

military offence, however trivial.

RUPERT. A kite balloon.

RUSH A BREW. Make tea.

SAIDA! Good day! Arabic.

SALLY-FAIRY-ANN. Variant for "san-fairy-ann."

SAMMY. An American soldier.

SANDBAG MARY ANN. That's all right, chum.

SANDSTORM. A soup consisting of ground maize or analogous grain boiled in water. The ground grain would sink and, with the added resemblance of colour, would appear like a patch of sand (and tasted like it!).

SAN-FAIRY-ANN. It doesn't matter (*cela ne fait rien*).

SARGA. Sergeant. Arabic.

SATARONBIL, TERUMBIL. An automobile; motor.

SAUSAGE. Observation balloon.

SAUSAGE HILL. Prison camp in Germany. To "go to Sausage Hill" meant to be taken prisoner.

SCOACH. Rum.

SCOFF. A very old Army term for "eating."

SCROUNGE. To get hold of anything but in the recog nized way.

SCROUNGER. Cadger.

SEKSIN. Section of a company (pre-war).

SEND IT DOWN, DAVY, LAD! The soldier's prayer for rain and the "No Parade" call. Used "sarcastic" during wet weather.

SERGEANT-MAJOR'S TEA. Army tea was usually lamentably devoid of sugar or milk when issued to privates; if, however, the tea *ever* happened to be served sweetened it was termed "Sergeant-Major's tea" owing to the not erroneous impression that N.C.O.'s of this rank did not deprive themselves of good things in this respect.

SHACKLES. Stew of doubtful quality.

SHAMUN DAFAR (F.). A railway.

SHEMOZZLE. A row, quarrel. Possibly a corruption of Przemysl.

SHERBET. Anything intoxicating.

SHINER. Nickname for Black.

SHINY SEVENTH. 7th London R.F.

SHOOTING GALLERY. The war zone; the front line.

SHOOTING-IRON. A rifle.

SHOOT UP. To fire rapidly in going into a town or village; "to shoot up the village."

SHOT AT DAWN. Expression for general idea of punishment.

SHOT UP THE BACK. Put *hors de combat* by some sally. Found out.

SHOW A LEG. Get up.

SHUN! Word of command; attention!

SHUT YOUR FACE. Shut up; hold your tongue.

SICK (TO GO). To parade for medical treatment.

SIKIN TARD. Second-Third Gurkhas (pre-war).

SILENT SERVICE (THE). The Royal Navy, with a shade of jocular ironic meaning when used by soldiers.

SKATES. Wire shoes issued to the infantry in Sinai and speedily condemned as worse than useless.

SKEIN. A glass of beer.

SKILLY. Stew.

SKINT. Without money.

SKIPPER. Used for "Captain," as in the Navy.

SKIVE. To shirk a duty.

SKOFF. Food. Also to eat.

SKOLKURING. Definition: the illegal trading of Army food and material to civilians.

SLACKS. Trousers.

SLIP (OR PUT) IT ACROSS HIM. Hit a man with one's fists.

SLIPPERY SAM. A gambling card-game.

SLOPE HIPE!! Slope Arms!!

SLUM (TO). To shirk.

SMOKE (THE). London.

SNACK UP. Have a meal.

SNAFFLED. Caught.

SNAKE-CHARMERS. Buglers. (Route march.)

SNIP. The regimental tailor.

SNIP. Easy.

SNOB. Army shoemaker.

SNUFF IT (TO). To die.

SOCK IN IT (PUT A). Form of request to make less noise. If a comrade was singing or had too much to say, a polite way of bidding him "Shut up."

SOFT NUMBER. Easy job.

SOLDIER'S FAREWELL (A). Good-bye and go to the devil.

SOLDIER'S FRIEND. Rifle.

SO-LONG! *Au revoir.*

SONNY. Substitute for a man's name.

S.O.S. Rockets.

SOUVENIERED. "Won" by finding or otherwise.

SPARE (TO LOOK). To have nothing to do. (Old Army.)

SPARE FILE. Military term for odd man in ranks: used to designate anybody loitering, doing nothing.

SPARE GENERAL. Derisive reference to conceited N.C.O.

SPARKY. Nickname for wireless operator.

SPASSIBA. Thanks.

SPIT AND POLISH PARADE. General inspection.

SPOT OF BOTHER. A little trouble.

SPRUCE. To deceive.

SPRUNG. A degree of intoxication: half-sprung; sprung; well sprung.

SPUD. Potato.

SQUARE DINKUM. On the straight.

SQUAREHEAD. A German.

SQUARE PIECE. A perfectly correct young woman allotted by custom or consent to a particular soldier.

SQUARE-PUSHING. To walk out with a girl. (Cf. phrase "square-pushing boots.")

SQUATTI. A private.

SQUIFFY. Half drunk.

STAGGER-JUICE. Any intoxicating drink.

STALL (TO). To keep the nose pointing upwards until the machine automatically loses flying speed and falls out of control. Often done unintentionally with disastrous consequences.

STAND BY (TO). Not to be absent. " Stand by your kits, lads ! " intimated the approach of a suspicious person.

STAND-TO. On the alert; the period just before dawn when a surprise attack might be expected.

STARIE CHELEVEK. An old man. A term applied to the C.O., or any other person in authority.

STEELER. A steel helmet.

STEP (THE). A ledge in the trench enabling troops to stand in necessary position for firing.

STICK IT. Persevere (in some dangerous or uncongenial task).

STIFFS. Dead.

STOCKING-SOLES GUN. A gun firing a high velocity shell.

STOP ONE (TO). To be hit by a bullet.

STOUT FELLOW. A brave man.

STRAAFE. A bombardment.

STRIKE A LIGHT ! I am surprised. (Exclamation on hearing bad news. Trenches.)

STRING AND GLITTER BOYS. Men detailed for guard. The " string " is the lanyard, generally confined to service on ceremonial occasions.

STRIPES. Any N. C. O., usually a sergeant.

STUCK INTO (TO GET). To attack.

STUNG. Caught financially; swindled.

STUNT. A raid or small attack.

STUNTING. Elaborate flying.

SUDS. Government ale.

SUICIDE CLUB. The Machine Gun Corps. Also applied to other units at different times.

SWADDY. A soldier (Old Army).

SWAGGER-STICK. Cane for walking out.

SWEATING. Nearly got it.

SWEATING ON LEAVE. Next on list for leave.

SWEATING ON THE TOP LINE. A phrase from the game of " House."

SWINGING IT. Malingering; swinging the lead.

SWINGING ON THE EAR. Frequent request for a loan.

SWINGING THE HAMMER. Malingering; swinging the lead.

TAILS UP (THEY'VE GOT THEIR). They are in good spirits.

TANKS. The tanks got their name from the belief when they were being manufactured that they were water-carriers for the troops in Egypt.

TAPED OFF. Take the measure of a man.

TATER-MASHER. A German hand-grenade.

TAXI-DRIVER. Pilot.

TELLING THE TALE. A defaulter trying to explain his sins of omission and commission.

TERRIERS. Territorial troops.

"THAT'S THE STUFF TO GIVE 'EM!" Plenty of rations.

THROW HIS WEIGHT ABOUT (TO). To be officious.

TICKET. Certificate of disability from the Army.

TICKLERS. Improvised bombs made in "Tickler's" jam tins.

TICK OFF. Reprimand; find fault with. "A ticking off."

TIC-TOCS. Army Signal Corps.

TIN HAT. Steel helmet.

TIN HAT ON IT (JUST ABOUT PUT THE). Nearly spoilt everything. (Trenches.)

TIN LIZZIE. A Ford car (R.A.S.C.).

TIN-OPENER. Bayonet.

TOBY. A shrapnel helmet.

TOFFEE-APPLES. Trench mortars. A circular-shaped trench-mortar missile used by British—about the size of a football (cf. Football).

TOFFEE-NOSED. Stuck up. (Trenches.)

TOKE. Bread.

TOLD OFF. To be reprimanded.

TOOTER THE SWEETER. The sooner the better.

TOOTHPICK, PERSUADER, TOASTING-FORK. Bayonet.

TOTTIES. Potatoes (spuds).

TOUTE-SUITER. Long-range gun. (Canadian equivalent of English "rubber gun.")

TRES BEANS. *Très bien.*

TUBE TRAIN. A shell producing a noise similar to that of a tube train.

TUG. Nickname for Wilson (Old Army).

TURN IT IN. To die.

TWIST (TO). To defraud.

TWO DOTS AND A DASH. Fried eggs and bacon.

TYPEWRITER. Machine-gun.

UMPTEEN. Large but indefinite number.

UNCLE CHARLIE. Marching order. (Route march.)

UNCLE NED. Bed.

UNSTUCK (TO COME). To be found out.

VAN BLANC ANGLAYS. Whisky.

VAN ROUGE. Vin Rouge.

VELVET (TO BE ON). An easy job.

VERTICAL BREEZE. Equivalent to "wind up."

VIOLETS. Onions.

WADS. Small cakes.

WALLAH. A servant; a slacker or one who has an easy job. Roottee-wallah—the orderly who doled out bread. Hindustani.

WAR BABY. The youngest member of a platoon.

WASBIRD. An elderly man—say forty or more—who wanted to enlist.

WASH-OUT. A complete failure.

WET ONE'S STRIPES (TO). Stand a treat—of a newly made N.C.O.

WHAT ABOUT IT? When are
you going to "get a move
on"? (On continual halts
on march up to trenches.)
"WHERE DID THAT ONE GO
TO?" On hearing shell
burst.

WHIZZ-BANG. A very high
velocity shell. A German
light shell, the whizz and
the explosion occurring
a l m o s t simultaneously.
Also a small motor travel-
ling truck running on
light or heavy railway
and carrying two or three
people.

WIN (TO). To acquire; to
steal.

WINDY. Nervous, fright-
ened.

WINKLE-PIN. Bayonet.

WIPERS. Yprés.

WIRE AT LOOS (ON THE).
Answer given for an
absent man on roll call.

WIREPULLERS. R.E.

WONKY. Having lost one's
nerve.

WOOLLY BEAR. High explo-
sive timed to burst in the
air. Named from its black
smoke.

WULLA. *Voilà.*

XAROSHIE. (Pronounce "x"
as Scottish "ch.") An
expression of satisfaction.
Equivalent to *Très bien*
and as much mutilated in
pronunciation.

YAH NE PANEMJYU. "I don't
understand." An expres-
sion most frequently used
by Tommy in making
love to his barishnya.

YANKS, SAMMIES. Troops of
the U.S.

YELLOW PERIL. Cheap cigarettes.

ZDRÁSTVITYE! Contracted
very often into "Zdrást!"
The Russian form of
greeting meaning "Be
healthy!" Adopted by the
troops it became the
general form of greeting
among themselves.

ZERO. The exact time of
attack.

ZIG-A-ZAG (ZIGZAG). Drunk
(understood by French
soldiers and civilians).

ZOOM. To pull the nose of
aeroplane up sharply so
that it has appearance of
leaping upwards.